M000158362

The Cambridge Introduction to
British Fiction, 1900–1950

Examining the work of more than a hundred writers, in a wide variety
of genres including detective, spy, gothic, fantasy, comic, and science
fiction, this book is an unusually comprehensive introduction to
the novels and short stories of the period. Providing fresh readings
of famous modernist figures (Joseph Conrad, Ford Madox Ford,
James Joyce, Virginia Woolf, E. M. Forster, D. H. Lawrence, and
others), Robert L. Caserio also brings new attention to lesser-known
writers who merit increased study. He provides readers with an
overview of modernist fiction's intellectual milieu, and addresses its
contextualization by history and politics – feminism, global war, and the
emergence of the welfare state after World War II. An ideal introduction
for the student, this book offers a thought-provoking reexamination
of literary history, and an exploration of the unique value of fiction's
portrayals of the world.

Robert L. Caserio is Emeritus Professor of English, Comparative
Literature, and Women's, Gender, and Sexuality Studies at The
Pennsylvania State University, University Park. He is the editor, with
Clement Hawes, of *The Cambridge History of the English Novel* (2012),
and the editor of *The Cambridge Companion to the Twentieth Century
English Novel* (2009). His many publications include *Plot, Story, and the
Novel: From Dickens and Poe to the Modern Period* (1979) and the
Perkins Prize–winning *The Novel in England, 1900–1950: History and
Theory* (1999).

The Cambridge Introduction to
British Fiction, 1900–1950

ROBERT L. CASERIO

The Pennsylvania State University, University Park

PR881.C367 2019
Caserio, Robert L., 1944-
author.
The Cambridge introduction
to British fiction,
1900-1950
Cambridge : Cambridge

CAMBRIDGE
UNIVERSITY PRESS

CAMBRIDGE
UNIVERSITY PRESS

University Printing House, Cambridge CB2 8BS, United Kingdom

One Liberty Plaza, 20th Floor, New York, NY 10006, USA

477 Williamstown Road, Port Melbourne, VIC 3207, Australia

314–321, 3rd Floor, Plot 3, Splendor Forum, Jasola District Centre, New Delhi – 110025, India

79 Anson Road, #06–04/06, Singapore 079906

Cambridge University Press is part of the University of Cambridge.

It furthers the University's mission by disseminating knowledge in the pursuit of education, learning, and research at the highest international levels of excellence.

www.cambridge.org
Information on this title: www.cambridge.org/9781107029286
DOI: 10.1017/9781139248907

© Robert L. Caserio 2019

This publication is in copyright. Subject to statutory exception
and to the provisions of relevant collective licensing agreements,
no reproduction of any part may take place without the written
permission of Cambridge University Press.

First published 2019

Printed in the United Kingdom by TJ International Ltd, Padstow Cornwall

A catalogue record for this publication is available from the British Library.

Library of Congress Cataloging-in-Publication Data
Names: Caserio, Robert L., 1944– author.
Title: The Cambridge introduction to British fiction, 1900-1950 / Robert Caserio.
Description: Cambridge ; New York : Cambridge University Press, 2018. |
    Series: Cambridge introductions to literature
Identifiers: LCCN 2018035159 | ISBN 9781107029286 (hardback) |
    ISBN 9781107674127 (paperback)
Subjects: LCSH: English fiction–20th century–History and criticism.
Classification: LCC PR881 .C367 2018 | DDC 823/.91209–dc23
    LC record available at https://lccn.loc.gov/2018035159

ISBN 978-1-107-02928-6 Hardback
ISBN 978-1-107-67412-7 Paperback

Cambridge University Press has no responsibility for the persistence or accuracy
of URLs for external or third-party internet websites referred to in this publication
and does not guarantee that any content on such websites is, or will remain,
accurate or appropriate.

To Kristoffer O. Jacobson, beloved spouse; Julio C. H. Caserio, beloved son; Letitia C. Archard, beloved sister

Contents

Preface

The present volume is different from other introductions to the same period. Volumes with like titles assume that a highly selective approach is the suitable starting point. A straitened selectivity, however, has drawbacks. To focus the beginner's attention on relatively few novelists is to suggest that those not "introduced" are of secondary or marginal interest. It also obscures the links among diverse fictions of a given era, depriving the reader of an overall view. Books that introduce British fiction 1900–1950 through the lens of "Edwardian" or "Georgian" or "high modernist" or "late modernist" or "interwar modernist," or through the lens of "themes" or "subgenres" or "contexts" – the various specializations of scholarship – run the risk of being motivated primarily by fashion or market forces, and often do a disservice to a broader exploration of the subject. This book aspires to an alternative possibility: it seeks to present an unusually comprehensive range of British narrative fiction combined with extensive and intensive analyses.

This book also differentiates itself from other introductions by presenting an overall view that examines seriously, and asks its readers to examine seriously, the nature of fiction itself, theorized or acknowledged as a distinct discourse, with an autonomy of its own. The producers of British fiction 1900–1950 are leading theorists of fiction's special and autonomous nature, as Chapter 2 attests. Scholarly commentary has oftentimes obscured and superseded fiction writers' own ideas of fiction, and blunted their force. I always have valued scholarly commentary, and I encourage readers to pursue the texts listed in this volume's "Further Reading." Nevertheless, this book attempts to return the novelists' own ideas about fiction, and their fictions themselves, to primacy.

This book attempts one more thing: to resist the tendency in scholarship of the last five decades to characterize the novel form in the period under review as a distorted reflection or symptom of real history and real "politics," or as an illustration of more truthful intellectual discourses – for example, sociology, psychology, anthropology, philosophy, or history. To be sure, not all scholarship has made such characterizations. The scholars of the International

Society for the Study of Narrative have recently attempted to formulate a definition of "fictionality." Rita Felski's work poses a challenge to the notion of "critique." All of those efforts are valuable, but they, and similar efforts, remain minority ones, and they were anticipated by ideas expressed by the majority of writers of fiction surveyed in Chapter 2. I align myself, first and foremost, with this modernist majority. To do this I have frequently foregrounded the place of romance, the opposite of reality and realism, in the modernist period. I read romance's persistent prominence there as a marker of fiction's autonomy.

In Chapter 6 and the Coda, I address historical, political, and economic context in a way that I hope will satisfy readers' desires for connection with a real, or a differently real, documentary world. Prior to that, however, I turn in Chapter 4 and Interchapter 4 to nonfictional discourse from the period to show how fiction both engages and borrows from nonfictional discourse (and from the world at large), but nonetheless – by maintaining its special nature – provides a different, but equally valid, vision of the world, rather than merely a subordinate one.

Fiction's power to transform historical reality by expressing it newly, or by evading or escaping history altogether, is traced in Chapters 3 and 5. Chapter 3 addresses the work of, among others, Dorothy Richardson and Henry Green, who enlist fiction to overturn conventions of thought and expression that ordinarily frame feminist, working-class, and anti-imperialist struggles for liberty (topics also discussed in Chapter 1). H. G. Wells paradoxically shares Richardson's and Green's insistence, even though he is the arch-critic of "the novel" in his era. Wells occupies what I call a modernist anti-modernist position, not least because his scientific romances make him depend on fiction's force, even as he wants to depress its role in the fight for a new world order. Romance plays an irrepressible role in fiction's most entertaining modes, as Chapter 5 expounds them; modernism is equally irrepressible there. Modernism becomes a conscious topic or object of representation in detective and spy fiction, in comic fiction, and in fantasy fiction. Moreover, it uses them self-consciously to defend its detachment, and fiction's detachment, from immediate worldly relevance.

I intend these pages to be pedagogically as well as speculatively useful. Chapter 1 looks at two points easily ignored in our classrooms: (1) a general reluctance to deliberate the trustworthiness of periodization in literary history and (2) a lack of student preparation for reading narrative fictions *as fictions* rather than as sociological, psychological, historical, or political reports and documents. Regarding the matter of periodization, Chapter 1 proposes a hypothetical period, covering fewer than fifty years, to test periodizing impulses – to test, above all, *modernism.* Regarding the lack of student awareness of the protocols for reading narrative fiction, Chapter 1 considers fiction, without an immersion in narratology, as a *treatment* of topics or themes, whereby a novelist or a storyteller shapes what is told, and presents ways of seeing it, rather than as something identical with those same topics and themes.

A practicable syllabus for a course in the period attuned to today's undergraduates can be constructed on the basis of the interchapters and the Coda. For a course that lasts a standard fifteen weeks (as is typical in US universities), an instructor might assign the texts discussed in the interchapters (but choosing only two from Interchapter 4's comparisons of historians' ideas of history and narrative fiction's ideas of it). Such a syllabus would give undergraduates a manageable reading task of nine full-length texts, supplemented with sample stories by Kipling, Mansfield, Bowen, and Wilson. Then, by using the analyses in the interchapters as take-off points for discussion, and by reading the chapters as contexts for the interchapter selections, students and teachers can gain enlarged exposure to relevant texts. The exposition of the difficult thought of non-novelists in Chapter 4 and the initial survey of political–economic contentions in Chapter 6 will inform students, especially those outside of the United Kingdom, about thinkers and ideologies of which they are unlikely to have any experience or any reading knowledge.

Graduate students of this period of British fiction, which is rightly or wrongly identified with modernist aesthetics, will also find this book useful. It provides them, in one volume, with a coordinated view of the period's primary texts, not only including a variety of fictional modes – realism, romance, short story, adventure tale, detective story, spy story, comic fiction, science fiction, and fantasy – but also encompassing texts from the realm of nonfictional discourse. It should ease students' difficulty in setting examination lists, and might open alternatives to conventional choices they might make, to the benefit of their future research.

Lastly, the eponymous term *British* is problematic. I know it is. Much has been written about this problem in the past; much will be written about it in years to come. For the purposes of this book, I have for the most part bracketed the problem. It is true that the authors I survey include those who were English, Welsh, Scottish, Irish, South African, New Zealander, West Indian, and Indian – in other words, some authors who were not solely or even in some cases primarily "British." These various identities, and others, should claim our attention. But so should the identity of fiction itself. I believe that the writers examined in this book – *as a group* – help us know what fiction is. Their shared quests for archetypes of the welfare state and their imaginative pursuits of commonalities relate to their practice of fiction. They relate to their ideas of what fiction is. As does their shared, almost ubiquitous detachment from such things. I believe the knowledge we glean from these writers is necessary and foundational, for both our understanding of fiction and for our current and future understandings of the term *British*.

Acknowledgments

Susan Welch, Dean of the College of the Liberal Arts at Penn State, University Park, and Mark S. Morrisson, Head of English, generously allowed me release time from teaching so that I could advance the writing of this book. Ray Ryan at Cambridge University Press patiently supported its long progress. Maria Di Battista and Daniel O'Hara magnanimously read an earlier, much more expansive version, and offered encouraging, welcome advice about revision. Scott Black, Jonathan Eburne, Aleksandra Hernandez, and Richard Kaye kindly commented on portions of the manuscript. Penn State's Institute for the Arts and Humanities and Penn State's Rock Ethics Institute contributed their resources. Penn State research interns Jon R. Kautz and Jeffrey Romano helped. I am grateful to Sarah Lambert at Cambridge University Press, and to Elavazhagen Divyabarathi at SPi Global, for supervising the production process; to Jill Hobbs, for her acute, patient copy-editing; and to Tanya Izzard, for her comprehensive, exceptionally user-friendly index.

A special thank you is also due, as always, to S., P., L., and R.

During the time of the book's composition I was directly or indirectly motivated to keep on with it by Brunella Antomarini, Mieke Bal, Leo Bersani, Michael Bérubé, Hester Blum, the Brothers Quay, Luca Caddia, Pia Candinas, Christopher Castiglia, Patrick Cheney, Tim Dean, David Denby, Jeffrey R. Di Leo, Richard M. Doyle, Robert R. Edwards, Grant Farred, Allan Hepburn, T. Scott Herring, Timothy Hyman, Elizabeth Jenkins, Julia Spicher Kasdorf, Charles Lock, Marina MacKay, Peter Lancelot Mallios, Mark E. Merin, Carla Mulford, Camille Paglia, Christopher Reed, Marie Secor, Alan Singer, Roy Skodnick, David Squires, Henry Staten, Steven Watson, and my co-editors at *jml: Journal of Modern Literature*, Paula Marantz Cohen, Rachel Blau DuPlessis, Janet Lyon, Daniel O'Hara, and Jean-Michel Rabaté. What there might be of value in the following pages owes itself to the intellectual standards and achievements of those I have named. The shortcomings are mine.

I can't but fall short in expressing my gratitude to my spouse, Kristoffer O. Jacobson, one of the dedicatees of this book. In our conjoined life, he is the essential inspiring source of well-being and mind.

Chapter 1

British Narrative Fiction in Terms of "Period" and "Treatments"

Exploring "Periodization"

An exploration of the grounds for studying 1900–1950 as a definable literary era claims our initial attention. Although this book takes those years as its boundaries, neither history nor literary history starts or stops on a dime. Suppose, then, for argument's sake, as a test case for the larger span of years, that we hypothesize 1895–1916 as a literary historical period.

Topical subject matter given to fiction by history is one basis of any periodization. We have good reason to claim that women's real-life struggle for social and sexual freedom is a prominent issue throughout the years under consideration. Multiple novels reproduce the struggle. Grant Allen's *The Woman Who Did* (1895), for example, tells the story of a clergyman's daughter, Herminia, who sees marriage as an artificial construction of gendered differences whereby the husband owns his wife. So, when Herminia falls in love, with enormous self-possession she rejects marriage with her lover, and bears out of wedlock the child she has conceived by choice.

Herminia and her creator Grant Allen, it can be argued, open a "period" divide between their modern selves and "the Victorians" (even though Allen is a "Victorian") when Herminia asserts that the early nineteenth-century novelist Mary Shelley and the Victorian novelist George Eliot were not forthright in their novels about the sexual freedom by which they lived. In a later novel, Elinor Glyn's *Three Weeks* (1907), the beauty and ecstasy of sexual relations out of wedlock are expressed by the heroine (a Slavic princess), who seduces a willing young English aristocrat. The princess is another of George Eliot's critics: "your George Eliot," she tells her lover, "must be classed as immoral because, having chosen her mate [G. H. Lewes] without the law's blessing, she yet wrote the highest sentiments of British respectability!"[1]

A widespread alliance of male and female novelists on behalf of women and in opposition to "respectability" is evidence of the trustworthiness of the hypothetical periodization. The heroine of H. G. Wells's *Ann Veronica* (1909) breaks off a conventional engagement to give herself to a biologist who is her university professor, who has had previous affairs, and who has yet to leave his wife or to declare his love. No matter: she tells the biologist flatly that she wants him, and they go off together on an Alpine holiday. In E. M. Forster's *Howards End* (1910), Helen Schlegel, one of the novel's two sister heroines, is a single mother, proudly refusing marriage to her child's father. The heroine of D. H. Lawrence's *The Rainbow* (1915), Ursula Brangwen, benefits from the spontaneous abortion of a child whose father is an English soldier she has loved, but whom she does not want to marry. Evasion of marriage and motherhood becomes a virtual ideal as well as a common topic in the years we are considering. *Ann Veronica* was considered outrageous. *The Rainbow* was prosecuted for obscenity. But censorship was foredoomed by the array of novels and novelists against it. As Ann Veronica's biologist says, "Rules are for established things. ... Men and women are not established things; they're experiments, all of them."[2]

The topic of women's freedom inspires associated topics, each of which illustrates rebellion and inspires novels to become experiments in liberty from regulation. Adultery, in the fiction at the turn of the twentieth century, is treated as a matter to be faced with intelligence, and to be justified or not justified in terms of the individuals committing it. Henry James's *The Golden Bowl* (1904) depicts the struggle of a young wife to regain her husband: he is having an affair with her stepmother, who also is her best friend. The wife's aim to win her husband back is not presented in terms of what is moral or immoral, but rather in terms of the possibilities of her employing her intelligence to realize her desire. The only morality, James's narrative attests, is the application of mindfulness to the difficulties and possibilities of life's givens.

The ways in which common topics are seen, more than the topics themselves, offer another basis for periodization. The long history of fiction repeatedly presents transgressive women or adultery as topics of interest. Topics in themselves, therefore, might be unreliable period markers. In the "period" 1895–1916 there are other leading topics besides women's liberty: class conflict; new industrial and media technologies; the moral authority of religion; the politics and economics of the British Empire. The perspectives in the light of which those topics and their meanings are presented, especially if those perspectives are uniformly shared, might amount to a more solid basis for determining a literary-historical era.

Solidity is a relative matter, however. Informal parlance about fiction makes *topic* and *theme* interchangeable. But a topic, or a subject of "topical" interest, is merely a noun or a noun phrase – *women*, or *sex*, or *marriage*, or *liberty*; a theme is a statement about a topic. Statements, when denominated as themes, imply a unifying aspect of a fictional narrative, an idea or "message" that sums up a story or a novel. A reader might claim that the unifying idea of *The Woman Who Did* is that marriage all but enslaves women. But such a statement is just one of the "messages" in Allen's text. Topics other than marriage jostle with a putative single theme, as do characters and events. Herminia hopes that her bastard daughter will become a feminist leader. Yet the daughter rejects her mother's principles, and her mother, too. Instead of only proclaiming a vision of progressive development, *The Woman Who Did* suggests the vulnerability of revolutionary advances to decisive reversal.

At the very least, then, there is in Allen's novel more than one "theme": programmatic assertion of liberating progress; uncontrollable baffling of the same. We could draw on the novel to formulate additional "themes." Their multiplicity indicates the difficulty of basing a "period" on widely shared perspectives about topics alone. Allen's novel illustrates what might be a constitutive lack of unified perspective in any narrative fiction, let alone in an entire "period." Other kinds of discourse are less likely than fiction to resist unified meaning.

The resistance opens a distance between a fiction's historical referents – its borrowing from history or its mirroring of fact – and itself. The very fact that a writer chooses fiction rather than another mode of expression indicates the writer's desire to be detached from a real environment, even if seeming to engage it. This distance helps to immerse us in the world of the fiction, at the real world's expense: we must be careful of hastily making direct or easy connections between a novel and what it is "about" outside of the fiction. The topical and thematic interest gives way to ideas and imaginations that might be valuable because they are more compelling – at least during the time we are reading – than the real history in which they originate.

Violet Hunt's *White Rose of Weary Leaf* (1908) presents in its heroine, Amy Steevens, a variant of Herminia; in fact, the second half of Hunt's novel has for its epigraph a poem "written" by Grant Allen's character (the real writer is Allen). Amy works as a secretary, and then as a housekeeper, for two aristocratic families, the heads of which successively fall in love with her. She refuses to reciprocate, not because she condemns adultery – she has the same view of it as Henry James – and not because she thinks marriage ("the absurd bond that Society exacts," she calls it[3]) is sacred. Rather, her motive for resistance is her refusal to think that love, or sexual passion, or sexual liberty, should be an all-determining influence. Her second employer attracts her, nevertheless, and at a critical moment, he deceitfully manipulates her into sexual relations with him. Once undeceived, Amy feels no outrage: "Why should she have made difficulties, ... who had chosen to maintain that the sexual relation was a mere matter of detail?" Magnification of the detail was merely unacceptable "abstract morality" (275). What is not a matter of detail for Amy is her sense that "poor human life, without truce or power of appeal" is guided by "some Superior Power" that is identical with "Caprice" (275). She stands up to Caprice: she insists that there will be no continuing sexual intimacy between herself and her employer. He will have to keep his emotions to himself, as Amy will keep them to herself. She keeps them so, even when she discovers that she is pregnant, and must move to London to face single motherhood.

A victim of Caprice's superior power after all, Amy dies in childbirth. She has not mastered fate, even though she has achieved liberation from the moralities and conventions regulating sex. Herminia's poem – Hunt's epigraph! – prays to Caprice that Herminia can be numbered among those who have suffered mischance rather than have caused suffering. The poem is aptly adapted to the story, but the story seems ill adapted to the topic and the history of women's liberation. If Hunt's fiction is mirroring history, is it not, especially in the light of Amy's death, voicing – thematizing – its opposition to women's freedom, and to the contemporary struggle for it?

An adequate answer to the question cannot be affirmative, because it would ignore the fact that Amy's feminist, anti-patriarchal ideas are never withdrawn by her or by Hunt's narrator. What would be ignored, simultaneously, is that the other characters as well as Amy move beyond our convictions – and the facts – concerning progress in the real social practice of women's liberation. It is as if the novel were referring to reality so as to substitute its story and ideas for the accepted public associations and commitments that the story includes. It is those historical commitments, in the light of the narrative fiction, that might appear limited. There is more to Hunt's invented history of Amy – more uncertainty, even more resistance to narrative shaping – than can be comprehended by actual liberties.

White Rose of Weary Leaf is not unique – not even among stories written by allies of women's suffrage – in its simultaneous appeal to topical interest and its suggestion of the inadequacy of that appeal. Elizabeth von Arnim's *The Pastor's Wife* (1914), published more than twenty years after Grant Allen's novel, values a woman "who did *not*." Von Arnim's heroine, Ingeborg, is the repressed victim of her ghastly family, headed by an Anglican bishop, and of her ghastly husband, a German pastor. She is tempted by an English painter to run away with him, but she resists the adulterous occasion.

The effect of von Arnim's narrative is to enlist the reader's anger against male egoism's obliteration of any such female life as the heroine's. At the same time, the narrative implies a superficialness, even a cheapness, in infidelity or adultery or promiscuity as alternatives to matrimonial duty. In relation to the values historically associated with progressivism, of which the women's movement and Grant Allen are part, the implication is dissonant. Why should not Ingeborg throw in her lot with the painter? Duty, as the novel dramatizes it, is nothing but a mask for patriarchal sadism. But just as von Arnim's narrator makes the reader feel rebellious against marriage and Duty, so it also makes the reader feel that Ingeborg rightly rejects her opportunity for passion. The seized opportunity would betray an "awful candour of soul"[4] that the painter recognizes in Ingeborg, and that dwarfs desire. Moreover, the specificity of the character of Ingeborg as von Arnim invents it requires complex description. Ingeborg is a "curious admixture ... of childishness and spasmodic maturity ... at one moment ... entirely impulsive and irresponsible, and a moment before ... quite intelligent and reasonable, and a moment afterwards ... splendid in courage and recklessness" (308). The complexity becomes more the object of the narrative than the story's comparatively simplifying historical references to gender inequity.

What fiction gives to historical "themes" with one hand, it takes away with the other. The latter gesture is hard for readers to come to terms with when real lives and real misery are historically at stake. Appearing side by side with fiction's pictures of women's oppressed state are novels and stories about the deprivation that informs the reality of working-class life. There is good reason to argue that the suffering of labor is a "theme" that contributes to, perhaps even determines, the periodization we are considering. Indeed, Thomas Hardy's *Jude the Obscure* (1895) and George Gissing's novels (from the 1880s to 1905) feature hopeless entrapments that oppress the working class.

This grimness undoubtedly strikes a reader as insupportable: something must be done (or ought to have been done!) to change the history that the fiction evokes. That, however, will be difficult to judge by the "message" of such fictional representations as Arthur Morrison's *Tales of Mean Streets* (1894), about the poor in London's East End. Morrison pictures the brutal intensification of patriarchy – hence, labor's self-betrayal – in society's lower depths. Apparently a lower-class unemployed man can, with impunity, exemplify the sadism of marital Duty: in "Lizerunt," an alcoholic assaults his mother and his pregnant wife for not bringing in money (or for saving it), and forces his wife into prostitution. In "Without Visible Means," striking London dock workers set off on foot to northern ports, hoping to find employment there. One of the least of them, suffering from tuberculosis, is robbed and abandoned by his fellows. In Morrison's fiction the working class's ruthless exploitation of its own members replicates the exploitation from above. There is no escape upward. Neddy in "Three Rounds," unable to find a job, competes in boxing matches to little profit. When he wins one, the pain of being beaten makes him forget victory; and the victory simply moves him on to the next beating.

If Morrison's fiction transcribes historical reality more than it cultivates invention, the prospects for any social change – let alone revolutionary change – seem nil. Nevertheless, fiction's ability to exploit its own inventiveness by the way it treats topics introduces constructive freedom into a world whose hard facts argue for freedom's absence. Morrison's later fiction about the East End calls attention to the importance of his fiction's way of seeing its objects, even more than its interest as real history. In *The Hole in the Wall* (1902), a working-class artist, commissioned to construct a pictorial sign-board for "The Hole in the Wall" (the dive after which the novel is named), takes his time with his depiction because artistic representation, he says, is "simple enough" only when "'you're thinkin' o' subjick instead o' treatment.'"[5] In the art of fiction, treatment takes precedence over "subjick" even when the subject is life.

Treatment suggests a basis for periodization other than topic or theme. If we find, in 1895–1916 and beyond, either a uniform way of seeing and forming the objects of narrative fiction or a common emphasis on the overall importance of "treatment," then we might more surely justify the period hypothesis we have been pursuing.

The working-class novel that most forcibly "treats" the working class's historical betrayal (by capitalism, and by itself) and, simultaneously, its utopian socialist possibility is Robert Tressell's *The Ragged Trousered Philanthropists* (1914). Almost a day-by-day account of a construction crew's building of a manufacturer's luxury home, the novel concerns a laborer, Owen, who is a sign-painter, a socialist, and an artist. His artistic ability is shown in his design for the home's drawing room, which the manufacturer commissions him (on the cheap) to make. That work epitomizes for Owen the beauty of labor – good work for its own sake rather than for profit's sake. Unfortunately, the question of profit is always crowding in.

The workers are Tressell's "subjick." His invention of Owen's task is his "treatment" of his subject, so that Owen's beautiful design can be seen as an epitome of socialist and artistic values that are not exchangeable for exploitative capitalist ones. Readers working through the text are made to view the "subjick" anew, but Owen's fellows cannot grasp an alternative perspective about themselves. Owen and another worker, Barrington, are mocked for urging conversion to socialism. Owen, fatally tubercular, goes to his grave overwhelmed by perplexity. His fellow workers do not want to oppose the economic causes of their poverty even when they know them. Nevertheless, on his deathbed, Owen still hopes.

His ally in hope is Barrington. In the novel's last pages, Barrington, an unshakable socialist, discloses that he has been a down-and-outer only by disguise: in fact a rich man's son, he has pretended to belong to the working class so that he can find out how it lives. Owen accepts the disclosure without comment, curiously blank in the face of Barrington's fiction. Does Tressell "treat" his narrative's status as fiction by shrugging off, Owen-like, the part that disguises reality? Does he want readers to attend to the fiction as nothing but a convenient cover for a socialist textbook? Affirmative answers are creditable, but they would be wrongly limiting. Barrington has been constrained to approach the reality of class by way of a fictional detour; that detour was his road to truth. Without immersion in fiction, Barrington would not have arrived at his goal.

"Treatment" might also be called "form" or "craft" or "technique." The narrative artist is a technologist of sorts when it comes to handling subject matter. The claim of fiction to represent an alternative reality – indeed to be an alternative reality, one on which an alternative knowledge of fact and history might even depend (as Barrington depends on a fictive identity) – takes a compelling turn in novels and stories about technology in our "period." Rudyard Kipling's treatments of subjects such as trains, ships, and airplanes; global communications; civil engineering; and radio exemplify fiction itself as a technology, an ally of ever-advancing revolutions in economics and labor. In Kipling's "The Ship That Found Herself" (1895), the protagonist is a new cargo-steamer, "the outcome of forty years of experiments and improvements in framework and machinery."[6] Its maiden voyage tests the improvements. Once the ship is launched, there are no people in the story. Instead, the components of the ship talk to each other when in response to a powerful storm they try to live up to their functions. They must balance their separate rigidities with "give." The rivets are especially shaken. Other mechanical voices exhort them to share the strain of the seas, because only collective effort will get the ship past its virgin test. Once it does, the ship has found herself: an integrated identity has emerged. Technology achieves in its nonhuman constituents the solidarity that Owen despairs of.

Of course, the materialist-oriented realism of Kipling's story about a solidary collective labor is all fantasy. The parts of a machine do not discuss their will to cohere or to respond to strain, unless we allow a fictive projection to persuade us of that. The projection is not a match with material fact, but rather an ideal of integration. Real engineers who design real machines might be motivated by such an ideal – a perfect mechanical fusion of stability and flexibility, of self-containment and responsiveness to everything outside. But the ideal, even if it inspires industry, escapes history. A fiction, in contrast, can be the vehicle of the ideal, and embody it. Indeed, in "The Ship That Found Herself," Kipling seems to treat the ship as a metaphor for his story. The story has become the subject. A narrative fiction's words are its machines and rivets, disseminated and structured as events, characters, and ways of seeing. To discover what the fiction is "about," we must attend to the writer's handling of its component structures, each of which is a voice, and each of which speaks to, and rivets, other parts of the text. In various phases of rigidity and "give," the separate elements can come together into a unity only at the end.

Yet the integrity of the text is also the sign of a division. The unifying of elements takes place at best only inside the text, under the guiding craft of the writer. The unity between fictional vehicle and nonfictional meaning, and between fiction and historical material fact, is more apparent than real. Moreover, inasmuch as the story loans itself to extended simile – the ship is treated as a person, even though it is inanimate; the ship is treated as a likeness of a fiction's inward construction – the narrative is divided between its immediate "message" and its separable meaning (the meaning is an interior cargo!). The ship in Kipling's story finds itself, but the reader finds that the ship's meanings are not self-identical, and instead solicit translation into other terms, including those of the form of the story.

To get out of history and into the fictional transport promises an alternative view of life, a creative detachment. A great body of fiction has for centuries "treated" its subjects in a mode called "realism." This mode invites analysis of fiction as if it were both a match for history and inseparably attached to it. An equally great body of fiction has, for even more centuries, treated its subjects in a mode known as "romance." Romance is detached from everything ordinary, limited, and limiting. Its characters verge on or are ideals – of evil as well as good. Such fiction includes supernatural agents, magic and magical powers, animals and inanimate things that talk, sites without location on any real map, interplanetary travel, and entire alternative worlds. Horror stories and gothic tales are spin-offs of romance. Which moral or ethical standards regulate or judge those alternative worlds is up to the writer of the romance to invent. Almost invariably romance fiction makes central to its interest a quest story: a protagonist's search, through thick and thin, for a wondrous object or person.

Despite the differences in the realist and romance modes of treatment, it might be argued that, in many writers' practice between 1895 and 1916, the contrast between the modes breaks down. Undermining realism by subverting the divide between it and romance, these writers emphasize fiction's ability to forge its representations rebelliously in regard to previous artistic convention.

As a result, fiction's power to form or reform historical topics and themes becomes itself a conscious, newly prominent topical interest of novelists. The terms "form" and "treatment," as I have been using them are intended to be synonymous. Despite the diversity of the fictions by Hunt, von Arnim, Morrison, Tressell, and Kipling, we have noted in them an emphasis on treatment that amounts to an underlying convergence.

The convergence suggests the aptness of applying a period term to it. "Modernism" is the now customary name for an era of artistic expression that enhances the profile of treatment, and that is accompanied by nontraditional experiments with the form of fiction, with uses of language, or with both. In the years we are considering, the revelation of realism as no less an invention than romance becomes a "modernist" keynote. It is one example, and one result – only one – of a generalized new consciousness about the nature of fiction and, as it were, the technology of making it. The period label signifies an investment by writers in laying bare and making explicit in their work the "machinery" whereby novels and stories only apparently represent the real world.

To be sure, the novelty of "modernism" in verbal art is complemented by real historical changes – the women's movement, the socialist movement – that also reject the past. The word *modernism* was earlier used in Thomas Hardy's *A Laodicean* (1881) to characterize the novel's economically and emotionally liberated heroine, its world's advanced technologies (telegraphy; photography, including a rudimentary photo shop), its innovative architecture, and its new neutrality in regard to moral values – in short, for novelty as a historical fact, no less than as an aesthetic mode. In Victorian usage, the term also means a revolt against religious authority. (That revolt prominently appears in novels discussed in this chapter's next section.) As we move into and past the 1890s, modernism accretes associations with additional rebellions. By 1929, its place as a recognizable and secure period marker is exemplified in Laura Riding and Robert Graves's *A Survey of Modernist Poetry*, a retrospect of innovative verse in previous decades.

The present pages establish the marker again, and underwrite it. In doing so, they suggest history as fiction's mainspring. Nevertheless, the twinning of factual and fictional innovation does not conclusively assure a cause-and-effect relation between what happens historically and what results in fiction. Modernist fiction is not automatically motivated or determined by facts outside of it. We might be wary of mechanical explanations – such as determinism – because science in the very period we are considering undermines causal thinking. The era's discovery of radio waves disrupted our reliance on intelligible causation. Radio made matter seem disembodied, liberated from our usual ways of manipulating things. A new mystery, conjuring sounds or words out of the air, seemed now to govern the sources of events. In "Wireless," a Kipling story from 1905, an amateur experiment with radio signals is jammed by an unexpected transmission: John Keats, the poet who died in 1821, is broadcasting from an eternity of Herzian waves one of his famous odes. Dissolving differences between past and present, between far and near, between death and life, the crossed wires of the technological experiment imply that prior modes of thought cannot explain modern – or modernist – physics. Moreover, old technologies of communication (poetry, writing, history) are not the recognizable entities we thought them.

Inasmuch as new science frees the world from causal determinism, science and fiction suggest that they are a match. History, too, in the light of a liberty from the limits of determinism, can be seen as another romance, rather than as a matter of fixed facts. Consequently, it would seem, fiction cannot claim a radical freedom of invention as its own special nature. Nevertheless, that fiction's inventiveness can be at one with the new reality of the world is not a problem but a hope. The time- and fact-transcending dimension of "Wireless" portends the actuality of the impossible. It is a portent that comprehends utopia. H. G. Wells's *A Modern Utopia,* also from 1905, communicates with a double of the world we know, but one where gender, class, and race struggles are resolved. The resolution is here and now, even as it is distant, thanks to fiction's uncanny wavelengths.

Still and all, the "awful candor" of fiction keeps it at a distance from history even when the latter, or science, seems to be going fiction's way. Wells's *The Island of Doctor Moreau* (1896) represents a scientist who believes that evolution can be manipulated by surgical technology. Making use of dismemberments and grafts, Dr. Moreau splices together individuals of different nonhuman animal species in the service of producing novel humanoids. If he can make the spliced beasts into near-humans, then an accelerated evolution for human animals – toward enlarged rationality, and freedom from subjection to pleasure and pain – can be realized by the next phase of research. The narrator of the story, who has by chance landed on Dr. Moreau's island, is appalled by what he discovers: the spliced creatures are living botches. Yet when the narrator returns to life in London, he is convinced that his fellows are no different from the creatures of Dr. Moreau's mangling. Humanity seems the product of a mad inventor who experiments blindly for experiment's sake, despite the cost in pain and terror for his subjects. Reality and romance are horribly one. An experimenter who splices unlike things to invent a new life form or a new reality in this way might be seen to exemplify God – or a writer of fiction, especially a modernist one.

In that case, the modernist is also a mad inventor. This grimly critical picture suggests what might lie at the root of our period, but its power derives, once again, from fiction's distance from reality. It is able to invent a critical difference, and to take up a critical position, in regard to an actual world that fiction only apparently duplicates.

The Modernism of Samuel Butler, George Moore, and George Meredith

Literary history must be cautious in regard to periodization, inasmuch as historical topics or experiments in fictional treatment in one era might not be so distinctly unlike those in another era. Fiction's version of women's struggle for liberty belongs originally, at the very least, to the eighteenth century. Representations of the working class by novels at the turn of the nineteenth century are preceded by similar representations – and treatments – in the 1840s and 1850s (for example, Charles Dickens's *Hard Times* [1854]). Formal play with realism and romance in the years examined here points to the origin of modern fiction all the way back to Cervantes's *Don Quixote* (1605). Its nearer epitome is the work of Walter Scott, whose first novel was published in 1814. Literary history has fewer unique turning points than the history of historians.

And yet. . . . A trio of novels, published in the twentieth century's first two decades, affords a closer look (for now!) at the centrality given to formal treatment – to the very art and artifice of fiction – by novelists in 1895–1916. The fictions are undoubtedly experimental ones, in a sense that supports the epithet *modernist.*

At first sight, Samuel Butler's *The Way of All Flesh* (1903) does not promise any alternative to fiction's realistic imitation of history. The narrative begins as if it were a straightforward unfolding ("When I was a small boy at the beginning of the [nineteenth] century I remember. . ."[7]). But the promise of sequential autobiography is withdrawn: instead of developing his own history, the narrator, Edward Overton, chronicles the male line of three generations of the Pontifex family. The characterization of the second-generation Pontifex, Theobald, yields, if only temporarily in chapter VIII, to letters exchanged by Theobald and his father, whereby the characters represent themselves, over-leaping minimal treatment (possibly subjectively distorted) by the narrator. The source of the letters is Theobald's son Ernest, the narrator notes.

The casual introduction of Ernest Pontifex belies what the reader will not discover until 100 pages into the novel, when Ernest is born. *The Way of All*

Flesh is primarily about Ernest, the male of the third generation. Overton is his godfather, and will become something of a fairy one. Butler courts the reader's assumption that the novel is about Theobold because he wants Overton to represent Ernest's family heritage as an example of how history, even at the familial or individual level, can causally determine its effects. Theobald's life is determined when his father forces him to become a clergyman. Theobald, in turn, will force Ernest to undertake the same vocation.

The narrator's objective, "realistic" telling and endorsement of this causal sequence is belied by the experiment in narrative form that is under way. Even before Overton reveals that the story is Ernest's, Overton several times breaks the frame of objective reporting. He suddenly protests against "the unhappy relations which commonly even now exist between parents and children" (43). Soon after he exclaims that morality is "an utter swindle" (51). Apropos of morality, he adds a little later that pleasure is a "safer guide [of conduct] than either right or duty" (117), and that virtue and vice need not be disentangled. He then intrudes into his narration the testimony of the adult Ernest (who has only just been born in the narrative) on the unhappy relations between parents and children. The modern family is an evolutionary blunder, Ernest claims. It is "incompatible," he tells his godfather,

> with high development. . . . Certainly there is no inherent love for the family system on the part of nature herself. . . . The fishes know it not. . . . The ants and the bees . . . sting their fathers to death as a matter of course, and are given to the atrocious mutilation of the offspring committed to their charge, yet where shall we find communities more universally respected?" (140–1)

Such intrusions lead to another surprise: amid his practice of an historian's impassivity, Overton says, without having told us anything about his own life, that "whether I like it or no I am portraying myself more surely than I am portraying any of the characters whom I set before the reader" (85).

Butler here reminds us that every narrator, even an "omniscient" one, is to be read as a character. What is the purpose of the uncontrollable self-portrait in *The Way of All Flesh*? In the light of Overton's and Ernest's comments, it begins to seem that its purpose is primarily Overton's polemical argument against "the family system" and only secondarily a story.

The criticism of family fits the modernism we are considering, inasmuch as it is aimed at the patriarchal system that Ernest's father and grandfather exemplify, and that, as other fictions demonstrate, crush women. The system also crushes men. The chronicle of the Pontifex family is thus an argument against a system that for both genders ought to be terminated. Certainly,

Ernest's history enacts such an ending. His undergraduate career includes his seduction of Ellen, a family maid, who is driven away when Theobald discovers the fact. Forced thereafter into the priesthood, Ernest attempts to honor church doctrine and ecclesiastical conduct. But he grows bewildered by doctrinal controversies; he is bilked of his money by a fellow cleric; and, overwhelmed by sexual desire, he importunes a woman whom he mistakenly believes to be a prostitute. He is arrested for sexual assault and jailed. When he is released from prison, he rediscovers Ellen, marries her, sets up a laundry business, and fathers a family. But Ellen is faithless. Only after Ernest separates himself from her, places his children with a foster family, and flees England does he begin to have a life. The radical separation from "family" is the beginning of Ernest's career as a famous essayist.

His essays attack "the marriage system." Quotations from them are part of the novel's conclusion. The essays also question the historical foundations of the Church; or, rather, because those foundations had been sapped anew in the nineteenth century (and their evidence further subverted by Darwin), Ernest's writing counsels readers to be no more than indifferent when it comes to religion. For Overton and Ernest, the involvement of Christianity and history is founded on a romance fable: Christ, questing for our redemption, achieves His goal by slaying the dragon of this world and death itself. The problem with this fable is that it provokes violence. One of Overton's earliest memories, resulting from Theobald's repeated readings of an episode in Numbers wherein a man is stoned to death for gathering firewood on the Sabbath, involves his distaste for religion's cruelty. If it had not been for Theobald's priesthood, Theobald and his wife might not be the spitefully angry parents they are. The clergyman and Numbers lead Overton to his own likening of Christian families to insects. He sees them as bees maddened by representations of flowers, because they are unable to arrive at the flowers themselves. They will never arrive, he realizes, because the god they are seeking, and wanting to feed on, is nothing but an eternal absence.

We might think that Overton's tale of the Pontifexes, by opposing the illusions of the religious narrative, shows us Butler moving his novel toward real history, and treating fiction as the trustworthy alternative to romance. Yet history, too, Overton implies (and Butler behind him), is no more a touchstone of reality than any other mode of accounting. Historical records must be understood for what they are: inventions that should not be taken seriously. "Who but a prig," Ernest asks, echoing Overton, "would set himself high aims, or make high resolves at all?" (490). He implies that historical actors and their historians do. But to take them seriously is to be like the insects, erroneously trusting in representations. What Overton trusts instead is encapsulated in his employment. He is a writer, above all of stage comedies, especially of the kind he calls "burlesques": hybrids of satire and parody. His "best piece," he says in an aside (while reporting a meeting with an insufferable patriarchal school-master of his godson's), was "a treatment of English history during the Reformation" (154). The treatment makes Henry the Eighth, one of his wives, and his allies and enemies come together to "dance a breakdown": a rollicking country jig. So Overton reduces a great historical turning point to musical comedy. Overton does the same with the famous English allegorical romance, Bunyan's *The Pilgrim's Progress*, in which the hero Pilgrim quests for sal-vation. The pilgrimage in Overton's version is a Christmas pantomime in which some of the characters, pious in Bunyan's tale, are drunkards and tricksters. Moreover, in the pantomime, tempting censorship, Christiana is scantily clad.

Because romance narrative is affiliated with religious narrative, comic drama is the alternative better suited to Overton's perspective. It suits Ernest equally. In his undergraduate days he writes an essay about the Greek comic dramatist Aristophanes in which he contends that the Greek tragedians were merely dull sermonizers. They are as unworthy of interest, Ernest writes, as the equally dull Psalms of David.

By shaping his novel so that its ultimate perspectives are divided between a comic dramatist and an essayist, Butler initiates a characteristic modern rebellion against the literary convention that is narrative form itself. After all, according to this novel, narrative has been the unreliable vehicle of a religious story and a consequent historical story, both of which merit a breakdown, for the sake of liberation – from insect madness.

George Moore's *The Brook Kerith* (1916) extends the modernist undermin-ing of narrative and Scripture in *The Way of All Flesh* by experimentally treating the story of Jesus. Besides intensifying previous interminglings of reality and romance, Moore introduces a powerful novelty in narration. *The Brook Kerith* goes against the grain of any expectation that the teller of a narrative, whether external to the story or a character in it, will maintain a unity of perspective; it is such an expectation that leads to unreliable thematizing.

Moore's protagonist is Joseph of Arimathea, who in the Gospels recovers Jesus's dead body from the cross and ensures its burial in a sepulcher. Joseph has been on a lifelong quest for spiritual elevation. Pursuing his philosophical and theological studies, Joseph encounters the monastic Jewish sect of the Essenes, and from them he hears of the Essene shepherd Jesus of Nazareth. For half the novel Joseph pursues Jesus, as the latter becomes increasingly inspired, works miracles, and declares that he is the Messiah. Joseph does not become one of the apostles, but his enduring attraction to Jesus brings him to the foot of the cross as a suppliant for the Messiah's body.

The Gospels in *The Brook Kerith* take on the role of the historical fact to which Moore's fiction seems subordinated, and to which it refers for its meaning. Hence *The Brook Kerith* exemplifies fictional realism. But Moore's narrative also parts company with the Gospels. Joseph learns that a few hours on the cross are not enough to kill a crucified man. On the off chance that Jesus might remain alive, Joseph bribes the Roman in charge of the crucifixion not to spear the victim, nor to break any of its bones. The off chance comes to pass. Having laid Jesus's body in the sepulcher, Joseph realizes that he is still alive. He secretly restores Jesus to health. The restoration sequence turns Moore's tale into something of a thriller: will Jesus and Joseph be found out? How will discovery impact the sightings of the resurrected Jesus reported by the Apostles and other persons beyond Joseph's walled garden, from which Jesus, who never died, has not strayed? The temporary suspense ends when Jesus returns to the Essenes. They do not recognize him as the Jesus who, after leaving them some years previously, announced himself as the Christ, and was crucified.

Jesus's return to the sect is conjoined by Moore with his innovative, modernist–experimental treatment of narration. For two-thirds of the narrative (300 pages), Joseph is the central focalizer of the story. The external narrator tells and sees things primarily in the way that Joseph sees and tells things to himself. The reader shares that inwardness, and trusts to its continuity. But when Jesus parts company with Joseph in the twenty-fourth of forty chapters, Joseph is lost to the narration. Three chapters later, his death at the hands of robbers is perfunctorily reported, with no inward account of his final days or hours. The effect on the reader is like that of being taken out of one novel and thrust into another. The novel now is being focalized by Jesus. He is no longer the self-same being who proclaimed himself the Messiah. His religious career shames him: it was egoism and fanaticism. Brooding in secret on his past, he does not disbelieve in God, but disbelieves in "gather[ing] the universal will into an image and call[ing] it God."[8] He allowed himself to do that, and the result was "violent words and cruel deeds." Part of the violence was the condemnation of sin. He wonders if "God were not ... the last uncleanness of the mind" (366).

Moore's treatment of the narrative as a form of dislocation, whereby Joseph's mind is severed from the reader's, and Jesus's thoughts are severed from Joseph's, reinforces the representation of discontinuous identity in Jesus. Not only is he not what he was as the Messiah, but even as an Essene he is not what he was in his previous years in the monastery. The splitting of his identity is intensified by the split in focalization that the narrative undergoes – a split intensified by yet another deviation. The romance story of Jesus's resurrection is abroad in the world of the novel, even as the novel contradicts it. *The Brook Kerith* sets utterly divergent narratives, those espoused by the Gospels and by Moore, against each other. As a final intensification of their divergence, Moore makes the Apostle Paul turn up at Jesus's monastery, where, based on the story that the novel has identified as the false one, Paul preaches the resurrection. Moore's Jesus, who has kept the secret of his rescue by Joseph, can no longer suffer the untruth. He tells the true story of his crucifixion, and his change of beliefs, to the Essenes and to Paul. The result is Paul's disbelief. He insists that *this* Jesus is, if not a malicious impersonator, a madman. And Moore, in the final pages of the novel, gives his experiment in narration another turn of the screw: he drops Jesus as the focalizer, and puts Paul in his place – and the reader's way of seeing is made to become Paul's.

Although the final events of the narrative are those recorded in the Acts of the Apostles, Moore's last sentence declares that "The rest of [Paul's] story is unknown." The effect of the entire novel is to disturb what in any story can be known – or to question whether any story can lead us to knowledge. "He is rapt," Moore's Jesus says to himself about Paul, "in the Jesus of his imagination" (477). Given what *The Brook Kerith* has represented, the reader takes Jesus's comment as authoritative, in touch with the real, as Paul is not. Yet Moore's novel, and its readers, are also rapt in a romance Jesus of their imaginations, whom Moore has invented, in contrast to the Jesus of the Gospels. If we believe that Moore's Jesus is the more real one – the more likely and plausible one – our belief has no basis but in its author's imagination. Which story is real and which is romance: the one according to the Gospels, or the one that the Churches take for true history, or the modernist one that Moore has invented as a realistic tale? Even while raising these questions, *The Brook Kerith* keeps the answers in suspense. The suspense is intensified by Moore's shifting focalization, emphasizing the gaps among the different ways of seeing. All told, *The Brook Kerith* illustrates modernism both in its religious sense and in its period sense, inasmuch as the latter argues for a dominant emphasis on experimental treatment in narrative fiction.

The suspense of resolution in Moore will dishearten readers who want fiction to convey a clear knowledge of something, or a thematizing "message" or moral, applicable to problems of living. But recall that Tressell's Barrington adopted a fictive existence as his preparation for changing the real world. Provided that readers can be patient of indirection, applications of fiction – even of its epitome, romance – to personal life and to collective political and historical realities are as possible as they are debatable.

No historical fact in our hypothetical period is more important than the globe's domination by the British Empire. In the late 1890s, with the onset of the Boer War in South Africa, the Empire begins to falter. But the faltering is not yet very apparent, and the Empire seems unshakable in relation to its nearest colonial subjects: the Irish, the Cymri (the Welsh), and the Scots. The Irish clamor for liberty from the English, for "Home Rule," is of a piece with the contemporary feminist and working-class demands for change. In *Celt and Saxon* (1910), the last, unfinished novel by George Meredith, the Irish anti-imperialist cause is treated in terms of romance. There is reason to claim the novel as a modernist one.

By the time of his death in 1910, Meredith had been celebrated as a master of experiment in fiction for fifty years. Because he therefore is classifiable as a Victorian novelist, Meredith's work unsettles "periodizing" – unless he is seen, from the tautological perspective of hindsight, as a proto-modernist. Our hypothesis sees him that way. His last novel situates at the center of his romance another princess (like Elinor Glyn's) of an unnamed Middle European or Middle Eastern state, to whose throne her husband aspires. But the princess is the offspring of Anglo-Welsh parents, and her landed inheritance, according to her Welsh grandmother's will, is Welsh. Thus the Princess Nikolas (née Adiante Adister) belongs on the Celtic side of Meredith's title, in which the copula *and* is misleading. The narrative's Irish characters repeatedly express the desire of the Celtic and Cymric peoples to uncouple from their conquerors, the Saxon-descended English. Central as the princess is, it is paradoxical to describe her so: she makes no appearance in the 300 finished pages of the novel. Yet she is a magnetizing, polarizing force. The leading Irish protagonist – Patrick O'Donnell – falls in love with her portrait (such things happen in romance) and hopes to aid her political machinations, which include a plot to assassinate the monarch who is in her husband's way. What is a Welsh female aristocrat displaced into a fantasy kingdom doing in a novel that is about current real Irish–English antagonisms?

The antagonisms are fiercely voiced, in excoriations of the English by the Irish, page after page. Patrick begins the sequence by describing England – to the princess's echt English father, who is an earl – as "a bundle squatting fat on a pile of possessions and vowing she won't budge"[9]; what the earl calls the "one nation" of England and Ireland Patrick describes as "one family where the dog [Ireland] is pulled by the collar" (44). When the earl rhapsodizes about lost English opportunities to ruthlessly colonize South America, Patrick thinks of how strange it is to hear "victorious lawlessness appealing solemnly to God the law" (84) – especially when Irish "rebels" are the so-called lawless ones. Patrick's anti-Saxon declarations are only starters. No English male character is given approval: the external narrator says that one of them, a journalist "entirely deficient in sympathy with the oppressed, a fanatical advocate of force," is "in great need of a drubbing" (168). The attacks culminate in the narrator's dedicating an entire chapter (VIII) to an essay on the moral and political failures of John Bull, the personification of Anglo-Saxon's squat on the world. Abetted by journalism's inflationary construction of him, John Bull is a death-dealing character in a jingo romance. Unfortunately for Celt and Saxon alike, the narrative's essay chapter claims, the romance is mistaken for reality.

Yet Meredith fights fire with fire, false romance with true. Meredith's narrator, scarcely distinguishable from Meredith, apologizes for chapter VIII's "interlude, or rather inter-drone" (242). The interlude must be written nevertheless, he says, because "the theme [English imperialism and the John Bull fantasy that undergirds it] must be treated . . . realistically" (243). And then "realistically" is redefined by the interlude: not by "Bull's notion of the realism of the butcher's shop" – a realism that is faithful only to material circumstance – "but with the realism of brain and heart conjoined" (243–4). In opposition to the romance of jingo imperialism, there is an alternative, a possible "ideal of country, of Great Britain . . . conceivable to the taste of Celt and Saxon in common" (242). The earl, typically Bull-inspired, would call this fusion "fiddle-faddle verbiage," in contrast to his own "undecorated plain speech" (24). But undecorated plain speech is a bully's way of talking. The alternative, a decorated speech, eloquently pervades Meredith's narration. It is a complex eloquence, because, like Meredith's treatment of his entire narrative, it is articulated in realist mode (history-referring) and romantic mode simultaneously: their mutual inter-drone. The narrator (and Meredith) self-consciously projects a confirmation of the simultaneity of modes in the description of Patrick writing a letter intended to convey conflicting news items, each upsetting to the opposed interests of two different readers. He must treat the items so that their difference is obscured and their upsetting aspects finessed. He succeeds by "conjoin[ing] . . . two entirely heterogeneous pieces of intelligence [and] adroitly interfus[ing] them" (140). Patrick's achievement is likened to the magic of Prospero's wand in Shakespeare's romance comedy *The Tempest*. The wand exerts the magic of rhetorical treatment: specifically, the magic of "the skillful Irish development of the rhetorical figure anastrophe, or a turning about and about" (140).

The narrative of *Celt and Saxon* takes divisive historical perspectives, and contrastive treatments of narrative, and turns them about and about, as a narrative experiment. *Anastrophe* denotes an unusual order of words or clauses. The presence of the missing Princess Adiante is perhaps anastrophic. She comes before the story, and she is projected as coming into it only afterward. Perhaps a hypothesis of her function in the narrative can now be posited. The novel begins with Patrick's passage from Ireland to England, and his first thoughts of the princess. Those thoughts, says the narrator, take him out of a "tangle" of perplexities "into the happy open spaces where the romantic things of life are . . . natural" (21). In those spaces reality is doubled, yet with a difference. Thanks to the spaces, Patrick can keep intellectual hold of the real princess and yet duplicate her according to his own desirous reinvention of her. Such doubling (mirrored in Patrick's letter-writing) requires a place of its own, in which the imaginative replication of reality can occur. It is formulated by the narrator as "a reserved place" (54) within the self. But fiction materializes that place outwardly, in the open. In the reserved place of materialized fiction, comparisons arise between what is and what should be or might be.

Perhaps Meredith wanted to make Patrick's vision of the princess replicate how it is that the English see the Irish: as renegades from a united national family, as violent plotters against a legitimate ruler. If so, Patrick in pursuing the princess will undergo an indirect engagement with his own rebellious homeland. Reality will be doubled for him, and he will have another opportunity to take up a distance from that reality – a saving distance, it would seem, because he will see himself and his original point of conflict anew, and therefore see them both with a difference. Novelty has a tough time entering history, even in 1895–1916; not so, however, in the romance dimension of modernist narrative fiction. The birth of innovation in any experimental fictional treatment (of which romance is a sign) does not mean fiction's weakness or irrelevance. What is produced in fiction, however obliquely and at whatever price of alienation from the immediate present, might yet undo the real imperialist Bull.

The following interchapter is an analysis of the seminal work of another Irish writer, who for a century has functioned in literary history as the cynosure of modernism. It is offered as a summary instance of what the present chapter has proposed: that narrative fiction's treatment of topics and themes, its way of forming and re-forming them, deserves a central place in how we read novels; that in the historical years covered by this chapter and this book, the central place of treatment and form, in the production and the reception of narrative fiction, justifies (albeit with due caution) a modernist periodization.

James Joyce's *A Portrait of the Artist as a Young Man* (1916)

James Joyce's first novel exemplifies the modernist impulse. Its young artist, Stephen Dedalus, like Butler's Ernest and Moore's Jesus, struggles with religious belief and rejects his faith. One root of his struggle is sexual desire, which, on behalf of women as well as men, he wants to liberate from "the family system" and moral restriction. Stephen amalgamates his rejection of Catholicism with a rebellion against two national communities. One community is the Ireland ruled by imperialist England; the other is the nascent Ireland that is the hope of a nationalist independence movement. Neither Celt nor Saxon matters to Stephen, inasmuch as both conform life to limited, boundary-drawing identities. Joyce's protagonist introduces an anti-nationalist as well as an anti-imperialist impulse into characteristics that are denoted by modernism.

Beyond the identities that Stephen rejects, one glimpses another romance. Joyce's novel is a realist one, given its reference to contemporary history, yet Stephen's surname belongs to fantasy. In Greek mythology, Daedalus is a heroic inventor who devised a maze in which to imprison a man-eating monster, the Minotaur, half-human and half-bull. Stephen wants to restrain the bullying forces of history that feed on him. Critics customarily predict Stephen's rebellions will fail, just as Icarus, the son of Daedalus, fell when he abused the ability to fly that his father invented for him. Whether or not the prediction is warranted, it treats Stephen as an Icarus who belongs to myth and romance, even as he lives in quotidian reality. Criticism follows Joyce in doing so. Like Meredith's Patrick, Joyce writes simultaneously in contrastive modes.

Joyce's next book, *Ulysses* (1922), refers to quotidian historical reality and simultaneously to Homer's *The Odyssey*, the romance version of Homeric epic. True both to modernism and to the liberties of fiction, *Ulysses* pulverizes narrative even as it seems to be one. Each of its chapters is a self-contained experimental "treatment." It turns such discontinuities of narration and focalization as appear in *The Brook Kerith* into a full-blown formal method.

It is an equivalent in fiction, for better or worse, of Dr. Moreau's splicings. *A Portrait of the Artist as a Young Man* serves as rehearsal for *Ulysses.*

Joyce's modernist experiment with treatment is under way in *Portrait* from its opening sentences, which begin with a variant of a fairy tale's "Once upon a time," and simultaneously reduce fantasy to a realistic mimicry of Stephen's infant mind. The experiment is operative when the narrative appears to become a theological discourse. The midmost of the novel's five chapters consists largely of sermons delivered to the boys of a Roman Catholic school. Readers are likely to be as moved as Stephen is by the sermons' stunning pictures of the dire results of trespass against God's love. Nevertheless, even thematizing readers who seek to derive a "message" – a kind of sermon – from any novel might wonder at the extensive length Joyce grants to the homilies. Is the author using Stephen's story to convert us? The priest emphasizes "the last things": "death, judgment, hell and heaven."[1] Oddly, the last things take up the middle of the novel's narrative. It is as if Joyce wants to subvert narrative sequence, and to playfully make his reader aware of that. The sermons themselves are not narrative: they are Joyce's exercises in essayistic rhetoric, a tour de force of inventive meditation. But, even as Joyce arrests the narrative element, the character who delivers the sermons, Father Arnall, emphasizes the extended temporal sequence on which stories depend. For him and for his listeners, salvation – like narrative – depends upon time's protraction. Satan fell, the sermonizer claims, because, surrendering to "the single thought of one instant," he disregarded the involvement of instants with first and middle and last things. "He who remembers the last things will act and think with them always before his eyes," according to Father Arnall (97). With last things set before his eyes, Stephen rededicates himself to the Church. In the very next chapter, however, having those things before his eyes wearies Stephen, and he refuses a priestly vocation. His turn in chapter III to salvation (and its narrative structure) shrinks to an instant in his life history.

It is a powerful instant. Contrastive ones precede and succeed it. In Joyce's first chapter, a very young Stephen, unjustly beaten by a priest for appearing to slough off classwork, makes an instant decision to march into the office of his school's chief administrator, where he receives exoneration. His protestant action successfully challenges the school's ecclesiastical hierarchy. In the second chapter, Stephen, now age sixteen, is precociously (out of step with expected sequence) frequenting Dublin's brothels. His desire values immediate carnal pleasure rather than the eternity of body and spirit that is God's. He chooses finally to live according to present instants rather than in a progress to eternity. In chapter IV, he imagines a personal freedom in which, liberated from Church, family, imperialism, and anti-imperialist nationalism, he can make himself anew. He conceives his liberty (winged by his association with Daedalian namesakes) as only "an instant of wild flight" (148), but the very instantaneousness of it confirms his aim. In the novel's last chapter, when he tells a friend that, a rebel to church and state alike, "I will not serve" (211), he repeats an assertion that Father Arnall in his sermons assigned to Satan's "sinful thought of one instant" whereby Satan fell.

The word "instant" studs Joyce's text. Its frequency is a symptom of his modernist anti-narrative tendency. The tendency shows again when the last chapter presents a virtual essay (another sermon, or a Meredithian "inter-drone") by Stephen about the nature of drama, which is a non-narrative genre. Above all, the narrative is spliced by Joyce onto the contrastive form of lyric. Stephen's way of seeing things seeks utterance in non-narrative verse. His gradual construction of a lyric poem becomes the novel's finale, absorbing the extension in time of the story elements. The lyricization of narrative emphasizes the momentaneousness that Stephen embraces. Underwriting Stephen's association of "an instant" with freedom, Joyce ends the text by canceling the difference between what an external narrator tells and what Stephen thinks and feels. The novel's final pages become Stephen's first-person notation of passing instants: his diary entries as he prepares to leave Ireland for the sake of self-fashioning, and to practice the art of lyric poetry, abroad.

"The lyrical form," Stephen asserts, is "the form wherein the artist presents his image in immediate relation to himself" (188). The form suits him, because he prefers it to immediate personal relations or to mediated relations to nation or church. What can replace those relations remains unknown. But the unknown, even if undefinable, is the aim. Chapter V unfolds Stephen's construction of his lyric poem, in a form called a *villanelle*. His poem's lines, repeating and echoing themselves, seem to subordinate definite meaning to an undefinable music. Thus they exemplify a quest "to fly by" (to avoid) not only the personal and institutional meanings that mediate Stephen's world, but to escape even his world's linguistic "nets" (179). When Stephen transforms a phrase from a theological tract into a description of "A day of dappled seaborne clouds" (146), the metamorphosis makes him hear a "nebulous music" that inspires his flight from his origins. Joyce is already realizing Stephen's flight. "He turned his mind to unknown arts" is a motto Joyce selected from Ovid's Latin poem *Metamorphoses* as the epigraph for *A Portrait*. The unknown arts might include the modernist lyrical novel. Even if such an experimental hybrid is a monster, Joyce does the mythical Daedalus one better: his experiment is the equivalent of the Minotaur that Daedalus's maze was intended to baffle, and simultaneously is the equivalent of the inventor's a-mazing, monster-containing artifice.

The nebulous music is motivated above all by Stephen's effort to escape the nets of national and religious orthodoxies. Even in their anti-imperialist form, they provoke the lethal divisions that Joyce presents in chapter I, which portrays a decidedly unpeaceful, ill-willed family Christmas dinner. The Church has recently condemned the adultery of Charles Stuart Parnell, the leader of the Home Rule movement. In doing so, the Church used the pulpit to torpedo the hero of the fight for independence. One dinner guest violently approves of the Church's interference, while Stephen's father and his friend Mr. Casey proclaim the need to divorce Ireland from the Church – and from God.

Irreconcilably deadlocked, the outward divisions seed self-division in Stephen. Because the death of Parnell, announced in chapter I, is immediately succeeded by an episode of sexual scandal among Stephen's schoolmates, and then is succeeded in chapter II by Stephen's sexual initiation, the narrative implies that Stephen's character is guided by an eroticizing introjection of Parnell. Stephen's sexual life enacts a version of Parnell's "sin." His "sinful" desire becomes a virtual sanctuary for the dead leader. Stephen's escape from the Church is a further rescue of Parnell from the censure of Catholic sexual morality.

Stephen's escape from nationality as well as from the Church makes sexual liberty an interface of politics and religion. The Irish nation, even in its anti-British aspect, endorses a sexual morality that is no different from the Church's. Underneath the endorsement, Stephen sees, is women's desire to contradict it, as well as men's. Stephen's Irish nationalist friend Davin confesses to Stephen an experience in which he was tempted by a young Irish wife to spend the night with her. Davin rejected the opportunity for adultery. He did not want to compromise his sexual purity or to adulterate his nationalism, which he saw the woman as symbolizing. In effect, he insists on the separation between eros and the state, as a way of chastening eros, and of securing the state. He reiterates, Stephen realizes, the condemnation of Parnell. In contrast, Stephen wants sexual desire to be a reserve space (as Meredith would call it) for a freedom that exceeds what religion, or marriage, or the nation, or the state allows. Will he make his lyricism another of freedom's reserved spaces?

Politics and religion involve their partisans in unshakable narratives about themselves and their worlds. Wanting to make lyric instants of wild flight the reserve space, Stephen thinks of "a batlike soul waking to the consciousness of itself in darkness and secrecy and loneliness" (160, 194, 210). The as-yet-unrealized soul is evoked three times in the text, which assigns it variously to

Irish women, to the entire Irish "race" (i.e., nation), and to Stephen. The likeness does not attractively express the high-flying associations of Stephen's surname, nor the lyric songsters – nightingale, skylark – of Stephen's hero-poets Keats and Shelley. But the escape Joyce imagines for Stephen, and the escape from narrative that Joyce imagines for his "portrait," are motivated by the hazards of capitulating to convention. The narrative component of *A Portrait* is, according to its content and Joyce's treatment, interlocked with those hazards. They are historical, real, and material. The lyric aspect of the novel promises a freedom of invention whereby to counter them.

One might contend that Joyce's and Stephen's escape from politics is political after all, and most valuably so because it seeks to re-envision public order alongside its metamorphosis of narrative art. True enough. But politics might not be the last word in life. Fiction's inventive powers might fly above it, without engendering a fall. If such a flight is scoffed at, as only a romance and not a reality, then the rebellions that characterize modernism will likely be dismissed. Dismissal would face a wall of opponents. They, and the debates about narrative fiction in which they are absorbed, are represented in the following chapter.

Chapter 2

The Artist as Critic

Ideas of Fiction, 1889–1938

In the first half of the twentieth century, British writers produce essays and books about the ideas that shape their imaginative discourse. The prominence they give their reflections, which are a leading historical context of their work, is a mark of their era. Simultaneously, modernist artist-critics employ their ideas to philosophize about the nature of fiction, without regard to the latter's location in delimited time or place. Perhaps "modernism" happens not as a period, but periodically, whenever or wherever there is a revolt against what fiction writers think of as moribund convention in art as well as in life. Modernism might designate any renewed authorial self-consciousness about the nature of fiction. In the light of this reflexive tendency, critical attention to modernism inevitably moves where the writers take it: into speculation about what fiction is, and what it should be.

A characteristic "period" bias, therefore, turns its exemplars, and our objects of study, away from external references. It turns away because it theorizes the autonomy of fiction – its independence – from responsibility to anything but its own ends. Art's autonomy includes its freedom from an obligation to represent the world. Moreover, novels and stories are not required, as we will see modernists argue, to serve the cause of other kinds of thought, as exemplified by morality, politics, and religion. And whatever the subject matter of fiction, even if it purports to be a verisimilar one, a "modernist" art must not compromise the novelist's commitment to the precedence of "treatment" over subject.

The fate of fiction's claims to autonomy – in effect, its claims to being a discourse of a special kind – unfolds throughout the half-century we review in this chapter. This chapter's three sections first survey leading modernist proponents of autonomy. They include Ford Madox Ford, whose "impressionist" idea of fiction subverts history for the truth of romance; Virginia Woolf, who thinks novels must free themselves from narrative; and Rebecca West, who claims that art's independent integrity is a biological necessity. Such modernist assertions provoked resistant, opposing ideas from those authors' contemporaries. The chapter's middle segment collects attempts to establish anti-modernist positions, including Wyndham Lewis's criticism of modernist fiction's avoidance of truth and personhood; H. G. Wells's arraignment of modernist fiction because of its distance from politics; and G. K. Chesterton's hostility to it because of its flight from religious orthodoxy. Nevertheless, these types of resistance have a tendency to become what I will call "anti-modernist modernisms." The final segment is a recapitulation: a third generation of modernists recycles the contest of ideas about the nature of fiction already sounded in two previous generations.

Each of the divisions of the present chapter includes reversals or contradictions that texture the aesthetics of modernists and anti-modernists alike. Ford's defense of Henry James's ideas of fiction contends that James is politically inspiring because his fiction is detached from politics. A like paradox, or dialectic, affects ideas of impressionist "treatments." They replicate a passive registration of experience, yet they require an author to be actively directive in rendering passivity. More than a few leading antagonists of modernism can be fairly categorized as anti-modernist modernists. Chesterton's opposition in the name of Christian orthodoxy comes to look like, or veritably be, a double for the ethos and the art he criticizes. As creative writers theorize their work, an unruly logic can overtake them. Perhaps the nature of fiction, a net they cannot fly by, is the reason.

Autonomies of Fiction

Oscar Wilde lays out his modernist ideas about autonomy in "The Decay of Lying" (1889) and "The Critic as Artist" (1890). In the former, Wilde's spokesman "Vivian" declares that "no great artist ever sees things as they really are."[1] "The modern novelist presents us with dull facts under the guise of fiction" (972) because he thinks his vocation is "truth-telling." Such truth-telling depends on an idea of representation that intends to reproduce the world as it is. But an artist's vocation, if understood in reproductive terms, can only be "fatal to the imagination" (973). If a fiction is dependent on outside invention, it is not autonomous. Lying, in contrast, sees things as they are not. "Art is really a form of exaggeration," Vivian says; inasmuch as it selects elements of recognizable reality to work on, it "over-emphasises" them. The medium of exaggeration is "style," and style is the only Truth, with a capital "T" – it is not the comparatively minor truth of sociology, or of "scientific historians," or of "compilers of statistics" (981). On the basis of style, fictions habitually pursue new modes of treatment. Fictions make life correspond to art, not the other way around. Formulating the autonomy of fiction, Vivian contends that "art never expresses anything but itself"; thus, it never "expresses the temper of its age, the spirit of its time, the moral and social conditions that surround it" (987).

If no great artist ever sees things as they really are, then neither does a great critic. According to "The Critic as Artist," criticism, too, is "independent" of its objects, "no more to be judged by any low standard of imitation or resemblance than the work of poet or sculptor" (1027). "The highest criticism" is "the record of one's soul" (1027). The self-involvement is contemplative, indifferent to practical active life. "The aim of art is simply to create a mood. ... The sure way of knowing nothing about life is to try to make oneself useful" (1042). When the critic interprets or analyzes works of art, he is expressing his moods – "beautiful sterile emotions" (1039) – and impressions in response to them

Whereas Wilde declared the importance of the artist-critic seeing things as they are not, Conrad in his 1897 preface to the novella *The Nigger of the "Narcissus"* declared the modernist artist's vocation as "above all, to make you *see*."[2] It is to see things as they are, apparently, because Conrad begins his statement with an assertion that the artist "bring[s] to light the truth, manifold and one, underlying ... every aspect" of "the visible universe" (5). But then follows a distinction between art's way of bringing truth to light, and other ways. Conrad says that philosophers and scientists, who inhabit the realms of idea and fact, care for "our" minds and bodies, and are dedicated to "the perfection of the means ... of our precious aims" (5). "It is otherwise with the artist" (6), he says. What is left for the artist to do, if his function is not to further the achievement of our aims? According to Conrad, the content of art does not even involve the rhetoric of "persuasion" (6). All these negations come close to something like Wilde's association of art with contemplative emotion, withdrawn from action, and linked to the creation of mood.

Conrad's mood – not an idea, not even a fact – is one of "solidarity," "which binds together all humanity" (5). The subject of the mood is not Wilde's individual, but rather "the disregarded multitude ... the voiceless" (5). Those who are socially and historically invisible, then, are what the novelist will make us see and hear – although he will present them by making fiction autonomous from philosophy and science. It is a perplexing presence, because words are all the novelist has to evoke it. And words slip and slide. The prose art work requires, Conrad says, "complete, unswerving devotion to the perfect blending of form and substance" (6–7). That devotion, according to Conrad's preface, is comparable to lifting stones, digging ditches, and uprooting tree stumps. The subject of *The Nigger of the "Narcissus"* is the wearying labor of the ordinary seamen on sailing ships before the days of steam. Conrad projects his current work – writing fiction – onto the working class employed by a bygone industrial technology.

His renewal of the dignity and values of the working class's superannuated industry, for all its exertion, is already humbled by its mortality. For Conrad, the aim of art "is not [to be found] in the clear logic of a triumphant conclusion" (8). No ultimate meaning, no inspiration for reform, is available in it. Both art and life are ends in themselves – not means for gainful use. In this sense, each has an autonomy of its own. Art offers its audience only "a moment of vision, a sigh, a smile" (9): "all the truth of life is there." Conrad's preface forecasts Stephen Dedalus's focus on the "instant." Nonfictions, trying to make more of life's momentariness, distort and obscure the truth. What there is to see, and what fiction's autonomy makes us see, is the fleeting instability we have in common.

Wilde's picture of fiction's autonomy constitutes a version of romance: a liberty of art from all limits. Conrad's picture constitutes a version of realism, inasmuch as it asserts limitations even while it frees life and fiction from deceptive alternative perspectives. Henry James's ideas of fiction, expounded in 1907–1909, in his retrospective prefaces to his collected novels and stories (the so-called New York Edition), makes modernist claims for fiction's autonomy by oscillating between the realism and the romance.

How a fictional character sees what happens in the narrative in which he or she is embedded is an ancient component of storytelling. James gives the "seeing" component of narrative a new "period" salience. He employs a kind of external narrator who, instead of narrating the tale on the basis of superior knowledge, or in a manner that makes the narrator more interesting than the story, is only just abreast of the protagonist's unfolding experience. This aspect of James's art was summed up in 1921 in an influential redaction of his prefaces by another novelist, Percy Lubbock, in Lubbock's *The Craft of Fiction* (Lubbock's novel, his only one, is *Roman Pictures* [1923]). Lubbock emphasizes the advantage of combining a character's limited sight with the advancement of a story. Narration appears to cease: "the impression enact[s] itself," Lubbock says.[3] The point has everything to do with realistic mimicry: in reality, there is no external narrator telling each of us our stories.

Yet it is not long before James tilts the balance between an aim to reproduce life and an aim to reinvent it in favor of autonomous treatment. "Art . . . plucks its material . . . in the garden of life," James writes in the preface to his novel *The Ambassadors* (1903), "but it has no sooner done this than it has to take account of . . . the process, that of expression . . . with which the . . . luck of mere finding has little to do."[4] The expressive treatment of a subject results from what James calls "the compositional problem" (319). The working out of the problem is the novelist's adventure, separable from, yet analogous to, a fictional protagonist's adventures in working out his or her life. In their liberty from outward reference, the compositional aspects of fiction evoke the freedom from responsibilities to the "real" that characterizes romance.

James treats one particular topic in terms that argue his defense of romance, simultaneous with his defense of art's autonomy. That topic is fiction, and those who write it. In stories about writers collected in *The Lesson of the Master* (Volume XV of his New York Edition), James dramatizes the dedication to storytelling that he issues in his preface. The idea that generates the entire set of James's imaginary authors is "the artist enamoured of perfection" (221) – of perfection in the fusion of subject with treatment. It is another version of Conrad's "perfect blending." Such fusion can occur in fiction, but rarely or never emerges in other discourses or in life.

Having fabricated such perfect writers and writing for his tales, however, James found himself rebuked by critics who asked that the real-life bases of his invention be identified – or that James confess his betrayal of realism and reality, for the sake of his mere fantasy. Responding to the challenge, James's preface becomes a critic-artist's manifesto. James sees his fiction as a "campaign" on behalf of "the something better" – in the world of writing – "that blessedly ... *might* be"; "the possible other case ... where the actuality is pretentious and vain" (222). If Anglo-American culture produces no writers enamored of perfection, and no writings of high caliber, then "there's a kind of rude intellectual honour to which we must, in the interest of civilization, at least pretend" (222). James pretends by "*creating*" (222, James's emphasis) – that is, by inventing "the record" of the artistic honor and perfection he assigns to some of his protagonists and their books. The invention itself, he says, is a sign that "a high aesthetic temper needn't, after all, helplessly and ignobly perish" (223). Indeed, the fiction writer must "exhibit," alongside all the real "futilities and vulgarities and miseries of life" "some fine example of ... the opposition or the escape" (223). James's appeal to "escape" allies his picture of artistic perfectness with an "ironic" (222) relation to history, and with the liberty and autonomy of romance. Of course, irony – like romance – situates itself at a distance from what is. So does artistic treatment; so does fiction. The distance between fiction and reality is to be respected because, for James, it gives readers an opportunity to turn to valuable account even the life they miss.

Ford Madox Ford's critical study *Henry James* (1913) begins with the thesis that James is "the greatest of living writers and in consequence, for me, the greatest of living men,"[5] because his work is a political achievement as much as a literary one. How can the Jamesian autonomy of fiction, with its romance underside, support Ford's opening claim, which emphasizes James's realism? Ford asserts that James's greatness "is that of the historian" of three civilizations (United States, England, France), and claims that his work has "set down" not what James "wants to invent but what Destiny" has dictated (122). Consequently, James does not use his record of history in novel form to advocate for the alteration of "divorce laws or marriage laws or prison laws or social laws" (28). When it comes to morality, war, the lower classes, and religion, Ford says, "all these things are so much in the melting-pot of conflicting theories that for anyone to dogmatise" (120) about them is to participate in illusions. "The normal novelist" dogmatises illusively when he presents readers with simplifying stories about "the oppressor and the oppressed" (82). In contrast, James impassively registers a fallen civilization – a social and historical reality between 1870 and 1913 productive of "despair" and "disillusionment" (144, 145). The result of such a disciplining of invention, Ford says, is James's disclosure that "We stand to-day, in the matter of political theories, naked to the wind and blind to the sunlight" (47). That is why James "deserves so well of the Republic" (49) and has a "claim to be the greatest servant of the State now living" (65). By rendering a truth that impresses itself upon him – impersonally, as it were – James's service is achieved by his choice to step away from partisan politics, for the sake of an autonomy of vision as "severely withdrawn" "as any religious" (109).

What makes this paradoxical movement possible is James's participation in what Ford calls "the supreme discovery in the literary art of our day": "Impressionism" (152). Impressionism in prose fiction is not a simple phenomenon. The term suggests passive receptivity: we receive impressions from our experience, rather than the other way around. But, Ford says, "the supreme function of Impressionism is selection": an active, directive treatment. It is a deliberate method for the artist, who can give us, Ford says, "the impression" of "vibrating reality" (153), in the process of a mind's "passing . . . perpetually backwards and forwards between the apparent aspect of things and the essentials of life" (153). The result of such passages is impersonal disclosure of what is essentially, and hence objectively, true. James's Impressionist-disciplined impersonality registers in "unbiased" mode the world that dogmatizations obscure. That is the "directive" significance of James's preface to *The Lesson of the Master*. James, Ford concludes, "had tried to find his Great Good Place – his earthly Utopia – in England, in France, in English literary life. He had failed" (146). But the failure of discovery serves the future Great Good Place. As he unfolds James, Ford makes clear that the realist novelist and Impressionism are inseparable from the romance of Utopia, as well as from the romance of compositional method that is the essence of fiction.

Ford's celebration of James recalls Conrad's differentiation of fiction from dogmatism. Conrad and Ford collaborated in writing what Wells would have called a "scientific romance," *The Inheritors* (1901), and a novel, *Romance* (1903). *Romance* is a historical novel, but its very title entangles realism with its antithesis. Ford intertwined them again, shortly after Conrad's death, in *Joseph Conrad: A Personal Remembrance* (1924). What is undoubtedly surprising, however, is the new turn the reality–romance dyad, and the artist–critic dyad, is given in *Joseph Conrad*. Ford calls his "remembrance" "a novel."[6] "This . . . is a novel, not a monograph; a portrait, not a narration: for what it shall prove to be worth, a work of art, not a compilation" (vi). With this assertion, Ford's memoir further innovates modernist experimentalism. The history – a biography, or autobiography, of the Conrad–Ford relationship – becomes a novel that is also a critic's manifesto: a theory of fiction.

Ford's reiterations that the memoir is a novel – "this is a novel" (136), this book is written "in the form of the novel" (191) – imply that our lives are at once fact and fiction. Does this mean that there is no truth in them? If so, why would Ford go on to say that "this novel" about Conrad and Ford "is the rendering of an affair intended first of all to make you see the subject in his scenery" (vi)? The deliberate echo of Conrad's 1897 preface advances in 1924 a truth claim: the novel will, above all, make you see Conrad truly. Apparently, to think in terms of "reality," on the one hand, and fiction, on the other hand, gets in the way of getting at the truth. The truth, Ford declares, is to be found, as we've seen in James's case, in impressions and Impressionism. A novel objectivity!

In the segment "It Is Above All to Make You See," Ford turns the memoir into an anatomy of fiction's new mode of treating truth. A novel "must not be a narration," because life is "complexity, tantalization, shimmering, haze" (204) – it is not a story. To give the objective sense of those uncertain things, the novelist must direct the constituents of our impressions accordingly. For example, characters must not speak to each other, but must speak past each other. Such "interrupted method of handling interviews" (204) suggests a like method of handling time. Time past, time present, and time future are equally implicated in an atemporal haze. The problem with novels as traditionally constructed is that they go directly forward from one chronological episode to another.

What about things that might be less hazy than life – morality, philosophy, politics? "It was the basis of all Conrad's work not to have the moral tacked on to the end" (178), Ford writes. As for "philosophy," "the one thing you cannot do is to propagandise, as author, for any cause. . . . Your business with the world is rendering, not alteration" (223). Ford repeats here what he claimed about James's impersonal, objective witness of civilization. But Conrad, unlike James, "was avid of political subjects to treat" (141); indeed, he was "a politician. He loved the contemplation of humanity pulling away at the tangled skeins of parties or of alliances" (57). Nevertheless, he was "a student of politics" impersonally: "without prescription, without dogma, and, . . . with a profound disbelief in the perfectibility of human institutions" (57). Conrad's ability to keep his novels detached from dogma perhaps derived from his having held contradictory personal political views. Ford notes the contradictions as *Romance* illustrates them. Its protagonist, an English loyalist, is caught up involuntarily in eighteenth-century colonial rebellions against Great Britain and Spain. He is wrongly accused of being a revolutionary. Ford equates Conrad with the loyalist. Yet the lure of the novel for Conrad was not unperplexed loyalty. "For, if Conrad were the eternal Loyalist, nevertheless the cruel stupidity of Crown and Government officials was an essential part of his creed. He was a politician – but a politician of the *impasse*" (44). His fiction repeatedly, objectively, and impressionistically pictures the impasse.

Yet even as Ford evokes Conrad and exemplifies Impressionism, he seems to represent life as the impasse: a deadlock between realism and romance. In the memoir/novel's penultimate segment, "That, Too, Was Romance," Ford revisits the miserable final weeks in which the collaborators worked on their novel. True to the Impressionist theory of dialogue, the writers talked past each other, to the point of mutual exasperation. Nevertheless, Ford's "novel" about Conrad ends with its protagonist Ford looking back and averring that his real history, too, has been a romance. Appropriately, he begins the final pages of *Joseph Conrad*, "The End," by quoting *Romance*'s last paragraph. Fiction thereby takes over the fact of Ford's history, and Ford's remembrance of Conrad becomes a novel that, wonderfully enough, is also true. It is a kind of truth, romance and reality at one and the same time, that history cannot equal.

A modernist thronging around the idea of autonomy inspires E. M. Forster to join it. Although Forster's novels conform to historical realism (albeit alongside a rebellious modernist ethos), his critical study *Aspects of the Novel* (1927) announces that it will analyze fiction ahistorically. "History develops, Art stands still,"[7] Forster proposes. Art's standing still makes it, paradoxically, difficult to grasp. A historical handle is convenient for getting at novels. A form- or treatment-centered handle is also convenient. But Forster is shy of definitive grasp in both directions. He emphasizes "aspects" of fiction, because that tactic "leaves us the maximum of freedom" (49) for speculating about it.

Forster's freely expressed judgments include his version of modernist impatience with storytelling. Time rules daily life, and all narratives, but Forster thinks that there is a life beyond time: "the life by values" (36). There is danger in narrative's solicitation of values. When stories are thought of as explanations of the world, as objects of partisanship and fixed belief, they incite a primitive allegiance to them. Consequently, "Intolerance is the atmosphere stories generate" (48). It might be best for novels to communicate "values" via mysticism, Forster says, because mysticism could short-circuit narrative.

Fiction's characters matter to Forster more than its stories. On the basis of character, *Aspects of the Novel* distinguishes between fiction and real life. Once again, the nature of fiction's freedom from reality bears on Forster's argument. Character in life is difficult to know, Forster points out. We do not remember our births, what we remember about our lives is not always reliable, and we will have no consciousness of our death. Our knowledge of others is yet more limited. The difference between "Homo Sapiens and Homo Fictus" (63) is that "In the novel we can know people perfectly, and . . . we can find . . . a compensation for their dimness in life. In this dimension fiction is truer than history, because" – and here we find Forster catching up with Ford's memoir – fiction "goes beyond the evidence" (70). It is to be trusted for that reason. Unfortunately, Forster thinks, character in fiction is as constrained by plot as much as storytelling is constrained by time. Plot exemplifies the element of planning and eventfulness in fiction – in both content and form. Forster wonders if plot as well as story can be done away with. Character should be interesting for what it is, not for what it does. What it does is external; it is the historian's province. Fiction is the hope of holding out against "the great tedious onrush known as history" (173).

Setting fiction free from the tedious element, Forster dedicates his final chapters to "fantasy" and "prophecy." Identifying those as leading aspects of the novel, he categorizes *Ulysses* as fantasy, and he situates Joyce, D. H. Lawrence, and Virginia Woolf on what he calls "the fantastic–prophetical axis of fiction" (113), another site of autonomy. Prophecy provides Forster's "life values" their consummation – and resistance again to definition. What prophecy is in terms of content doesn't matter, Forster says. Prophecy is an "accent of voice," a "song" (139) that "lies outside words" (142), so this aspect of fiction is especially lyric (the experiment of *A Portrait of the Artist* is being confirmed). It transcends any and every definite form or treatment. Hence, in his last chapter, "Pattern and Rhythm," Forster opposes James, because he argues that James's fiction subserves plot, making the latter a rigidly unifying pattern. "Rhythm" is the prophecy-related alternative to "pattern." "The only living novelist in whom the song predominates, who has the rapt bardic quality, and whom it is idle to criticize" is Lawrence. "What is valuable about him cannot be put into words" (147).

Given Forster's inability, we can turn to Lawrence himself. Freedom from "character," as both life and fiction have constructed the latter, is the essence of Lawrence's "song." In a famous letter of 1914, Lawrence announces that for him the interest of character, in or out of fiction, is a relatively inhuman element in it – "more interesting . . . than the old-fashioned human element – which causes one to conceive a character in a certain moral scheme and make him consistent." His letter describes character as beyond the reach of identifiable outline. Accordingly, "You mustn't look in my novel for the old stable ego – of the character," Lawrence says. There is another ego" – precisely where is not clear – "according to whose action the individual is unrecognizable, and passes through . . . allotropic states, . . . of the same single radically unchanged element." The unchanged element defies development – defies a story line. Innovative characterization requires "some other rhythmic form."[8] In the posthumously published "Why the Novel Matters," Lawrence elaborates. "I shall never know my me," he writes. "[M]y ego . . . only means that I have made up an idea of myself, and that I am trying to cut myself out to pattern."[9]

The novel genre, he envisions, will repair itself once it puts definite characters, messages, clichéd emotions, and recognized moralities behind it. And yet, for all Lawrence's uniqueness, a typically modernist rebellion guides his ideas. In "Morality and the Novel" (1925), Lawrence argues that if a novelist tries to tell something that makes one meaning or emotion dominate an interrelated multiplicity of meanings and emotions, then he is himself "immoral." "True relatedness" cannot be reduced to a rule or an absolute of conduct or thought. Rules and absolutes betray "life," by which "we mean something that gleams, that has the fourth dimensional quality" (529). "The novel is the one bright book of life"; in prose fiction's capacity for vital "tremulation" (535) lies its superiority to other discourses.

Whereas other modernists posit differences between fiction's form of relatedness and life's, Lawrence does not. For Lawrence, life is already an avant-garde; it wants, and is, the freedom that novels can model. For the novel to be "realistic" in the pre-modernist way would put it, and its writer, in the position of unbalancing the relational complexities of the world by substituting simplifying verbal pictures or "representations" for their referents, and by trusting the substitutes. Even as Lawrence's stories appear superficially to be representational, his treatment of them undermines the appearance. Autonomous art and autonomous life resist surfaces.

When Lawrence the artist turns critic, his desire for liberty causes him to read the surface of texts as a symptom or screen for life going on independently, and unconsciously, below. Thomas Hardy, Lawrence says, expresses an explicit metaphysical absolute in his novels, but his stories and characters contradict it. Likewise, American literature on its surface represents American democratic ideals, but underneath are "the first hints and revelations of IT." IT is that other hard-to-locate ego – a "powerful disintegrative influence upon the white psyche"[10] – that Lawrence adumbrates in his letter about character.

Lawrence's practice of criticism as a symptomatizing protocol, and as perhaps an aspect of prophetic song, is a political one, especially because it pivots on a racial or ethnic category: white European consciousness, which is being made equal (at last?) to races and ethnicities it has dominated. But politics is a social phenomenon, and Lawrence's usage of "relatedness" is paradoxically antisocial: "society" and "politics" belong to the already-formulated, already-experienced conceptual containers of what life and fiction together have constructed. It is liberty from the containers that is needed, because they have become gross abstractions, out of relation to what they name. Genuine relatedness for Lawrence pertains not to society but to the cosmos, and to quivering uncertainty. They are the novel's home.

Forster's female exemplar of fiction's fantastic–prophetical axis, Virginia Woolf, reviewed *Aspects of the Novel*. She lamented Forster's informal approach, finding it indifferent not only to history but also to the novelist's very medium: words. Woolf also found Forster (and, no doubt, Lawrence) overly dependent on life: "[W]hat is this 'life' that keep[s] cropping up so mysteriously in books about fiction? Why is it absent in a pattern . . . ? Surely the definition of life is too arbitrary and requires to be expanded?"[11] Woolf concedes, however, that Forster speculates valuably by forecasting a future for fiction that would require new forms for it.

Woolf's polemics on behalf of women's personal and economic liberation – *A Room of One's Own* (1929) and *Three Guineas* (1938) – and her fantasy fiction *Orlando* (1928), the story of a 400-year-old protagonist, whose gender changes from male to female in the middle of the novel, are inseparable from her hopes for the novel genre's metamorphosis. The 1929 text originated in an invitation from the women's colleges at Cambridge University to speak about women and fiction. To speak about this topic, Woolf found it necessary to reprise fiction's determination by male-dominated history – by fiction's lack of autonomy, in other words. But when women began increasingly to write novels, in the eighteenth century and after, they initiated their economic independence. Now, Woolf concludes, the women whom novels helped to free can free fiction from its imprisonment by conventional topics and forms. Woolf imagines a novelist, Mary Carmichael, whose first novel, *Life's Adventure*, is not about the usual male–female romance, and not constrained by the usual male perspectives. A modernist, Carmichael has broken up the temporal dimension of storytelling, and. concomitantly, makes it impossible for Woolf "to feel the usual things in the usual places, about love, about death"[12] – about life.

The confounding of assumptions about the usual topics of fiction includes the confounding of gender distinctions. *A Room of One's Own* is a feminist tract, but it also is to be understood as an anti-feminist tract. "It is fatal to be a man or woman pure and simple," Woolf declares, and "it is fatal for anyone who writes to think of their sex [i.e., gender]" (136). Obsession with gender pervades the history of characterization in novels. Accordingly, experiments with character are as essential to Woolf's hope for the future of fiction as they are to Lawrence's.

In "Modern Fiction" (1919) Woolf expresses discontent with ideas of character that substitute artificial constructs for what Woolf calls "a luminous halo" of impressions that "surround[s] us from the beginning of consciousness to the end."[13] H. G. Wells, Arnold Bennett, and John Galsworthy betray that halo, according to her judgment of them in "Mr. Bennett and Mrs. Brown" and "Character in Fiction" (1923–1924). In both essays, Woolf seeks to free fictional character from identification with history's determining context. That identification, she charges, is Wells's, Bennett's, and Galsworthy's method. Accepting such a method as trustworthily "realistic," readers swallow the illusion that fiction is not a discourse of its own, is dependent on what it is not. The writers Woolf criticizes also have a habit of giving fictions a social message. For a reader to complete one of their novels, Woolf says, "it seems necessary [for the reader] to do something, to join a society, or . . . to write a cheque."[14] If "doing something" in the name of a cause – the cause of women's economic independence – is the purpose (or a leading purpose) of *A Room of One's Own*, even that purpose is a net Woolf wants to evade.

Woolf's "Mrs. Brown" is a woman whom Woolf imagines as a potential character, not as a realized one. If she exists in life, both she and life are beyond the confines of representational, referential realism. What is beyond opens the prospect of a transformation of the novel genre altogether. In 1927, "The Narrow Bridge of Art" – the first of a series of essays by Woolf culminating in "Phases of Fiction" (1929) – predicts that the future novel "will have little kinship with the sociological novel or the novel of environment," and will not "limit psychology to the psychology of personal intercourse." It will provide a picture of "more impersonal" relationships, giving "the outline rather than the detail" of them. It will "stand further back from life" than conventional representations do.[15] "Poetry" is Woolf's term for the new "standing back."

Pursuing its autonomy, fiction will be free not to be its traditional self. Poring over centuries of novel-writing's phases, Woolf settles on Laurence Sterne's extraordinary experiment in fiction in the eighteenth century, *Tristram Shandy*, as the foremost prophet of fantastic new liberty for the novel. A proto-modernist, Sterne leads Woolf to novelists who are "the poets." They include Emily Brontë as well as Melville, Tolstoy, and Proust. Each of them presents a double vision of their subject matter: one side is turned to the light of ordinary day, one side to a shadowy non-narrative, impersonal "beyond" "that . . . can be described only in a moment of faith and vision by the use of metaphor" (139). "It was some such function as this that poetry discharged in the past" (145).

Woolf's and other modernists' insistence on fiction's special character as a discourse independent of others might strike us as, however intriguing, a baseless speculation – on a fantasy axis indeed. But Rebecca West's *The Strange Necessity* (1928), a major speculation about *Ulysses*, gives the idea of the autonomy of fictional discourse a grounding in biology – in material, embodied "life." (We shall have to overlook the possibility that if art is based in biology, it is not unqualifiedly autonomous.)

West's argument begins with an anecdote bearing on Joyce's investment in the lyric genre. Reading his collection *Pomes Penyeach,* West finds it to be "as blank as the back of a spoon" and of "gross sentimentality."[16] She speculates that Joyce has been so convinced of his "revolutionary quality" that he has overlooked his "reactionary" sentiment (20). That leads him in his fiction to manipulate his readers by simultaneously titillating their prurient interests and soliciting sentimental pity for his characters. The prurience and the pity are extraneous. Art does not allow extraneous elements, West contends. The literary artist must be guided by an integrity and coherence implicit in his topic and treatment, and by a working through of his material for the material's sake alone.

West faults Joyce's Stephen Dedalus, who reappears in *Ulysses* as one of its two male leads, as an example of the extraneous treatment to which Joyce inclines. "There is working [in Joyce's characterization of Stephen] a narcissism, a compulsion to make a self-image . . . with an eye to the approval of others" (22). The result is not revolutionary at the level of form, any more than it is at the level of (sentimental) content. Because the artist's "confounded freedom of choice" is all the more possible in his election of "treatment," if a writer "goes wrong in dealing with the content of his work, in the emotional values, where the psychic necessity which made him write the book is working to make him say what he means, he is far more likely to go wrong in dealing with its form" (23). Joyce goes very wrong, West maintains, in his so-called stream of consciousness and his imitation of experience in terms of sentence fragments (West calls them "verbal sneezes" [35]). The verbal streams and sneezes must all be turned back into sentences to be understood. Only the form of a complete sentence, West insists, provides the syntax that makes thought and expression possible.

Yet West can praise, and celebrate, even where she blames. Joyce's other male protagonist Leopold Bloom is a character that West assesses as "one of the greatest creations of all time," and through which "something true is said about man" (43). It is the function of fiction, West believes, to say "something true," and to say it in a way that no other discourse can. We want to know humanity, and we want to know the world, she reminds us, in ways that only verbal art affords. Strangely, then, fiction, more than science or any other discourse, is necessary to life. West comes to her belief precisely as a result of having questioned Joyce's weaknesses and strengths. The weakness has robbed her of something she requires. The strength, illustrated by the invention of Bloom, makes her freshly feel that Joyce's achievement matters to her life in a way that is like nothing else, whether pleasurable or painful, material or social, mental or historical.

How or why can this be so, for West and for others? She notes preliminarily that we all experiment with our lives: we "work out [our] fantasies in the sphere of conduct to a certain extent; ... compelling them into forms and patterns which are concentrated arguments concerning reality and [our] opinion of it" (63). The arts work the same form-giving and patterning effect on our fantasies, but do so on the basis of "less actual but more permanent" materials (67).

Fictions express what West calls "an investigatory reflex" (75). Turning to the behavioral and cognitive science of her era, she derives her phrase from the Soviet scientist Leonid Pavlov. His *Conditioned Reflexes* expounds the development in the brain cortex of investigatory reflexes in response to "excitatory complexes" (126). Excitatory complexes are external stimuli. The brain cortex is aroused by excitatory complexes, which are the brain's determining conditions. But the brain cortex's investigatory reflex also "apprais[es] and control[s] all the determining conditions" (126). Art works in the same directive way as the brain's investigative cortical reflex. Both share a "like effort to select out of the whole complexity of the [excitatory, determining] universe . . . units which are of significance to the organism, and to integrate those units into what excites to further living" (127). Here West echoes the dialectical character of James's, Conrad's, and Ford's Impressionism: the impact of external conditions on consciousness becomes transformed by selective or directive reshaping.

What an individual investigatory reflex does in response to an excitatory complex, art does for a collective response to external excitements. It develops a prosthetic trans-individual organ, an autonomous biological and cognitive one – a "super-cortex" (128) that is art. Art the super-cortex synthesizes "all the more complicated forms of experience" (129). It embodies an ever-growing repertory and repository of complexes and reflexes. Vast as it is, however, the super-cortex is not a single universal phenomenon. If art is a super-cortex, it is a collective experience. Among the various excitatory experiences, the collective one is indispensable. According to West, when an artist cuts loose from that context, which is invariably national – when a Joyce or a George Moore escapes the net of his Irish community – the extraneous seeps in. Exiles attempt to discover alone, entirely as individuals, what only a cultural as well as artistic super-cortex can supply them. They can succeed at this, West admits (George Moore especially, she notes), but all the odds are against such success.

West's turn in *The Strange Necessity* away from what seems a biological necessity without specific cultural determination and toward a national super-cortex that complements art is surprising. An excitatory complex called "Great Britain" might mean – and justify – the imposition of that cultural "cortex" upon others – upon Scotland, upon Wales, upon Ireland, upon all the countries of the Empire. Yet West's national super-cortex cuts both ways. It implies an anti-imperialist logic. The autonomous cortex that is a community's cultural tradition must not undergo alienation – not by internal exile, not by external takeover. After all, art as West sees it helps one to live; it does not oppress one's life, or estrange it. Fiction makes West feel "transcendent joy" because its assured biological and cognitive contribution to "the value of life" makes life "different from what it appears, . . . not lamentable, [but] grandiose" (198).

West's equation of art with a national super-cortex seems the antithesis of Joyce's and Stephen Dedalus's flight from Ireland in the name of art's independence from nationality. Nevertheless, beneath the surface opposition, one glimpses the possibility of converging perspectives. Perhaps the "strange necessity" itself expresses a reflex conditioning: by ideas about autonomy in West's environment. Hypothesizing art to be a more primary contributor to personal well-being than the nation is, on the basis of Joyce's and Pavlov's work, West construes the figure of Bloom as, in effect, a variant of Forster's *Homo Fictus* (character as we know it in art, rather than in life). Our humanity as she projects it in Bloom's light is a super-cortex version of *Homo Fictus*.

To be sure, West's projection might be fantastic in the worst sense: a symptom of foundational self-contradictions in modernist art's pursuit of autonomy. It is self-contradictory, we might argue, for a James to prefer the romance of "treatment" to the realism he also practices, or for a Ford to write biography and yet to claim for his work a truth that "the great tedious rush of history" (as Forster puts it) cannot equal, or for a Woolf to desire novelists to not be novelists but "the poets" instead. Moreover, we might argue that it makes little sense for Forster to celebrate unreal *Homo Fictus* and yet to designate red-blooded Lawrence as the best of writers. Lawrence, after all, is so much the enemy of "character," and so much the prophet of "life"! Even so, and *pace* Forster, why must "the bright book of life" – fiction – be for Lawrence a necessary supplement ? For all his passion for vital immediacy, Lawrence depends on artifice (only somewhat less than Wilde or James) for the expression of his vision. Moreover, a "vision" belongs, as Forster also notes, to a romance world or to the future rather than to "life." If these aspects of autonomous art are more incoherent than they are complex, resistance to modernism requires a hearing. The next section hears it, in plural forms; and also remarks that the resistance has contradictions of its own.

Resistances; or, Anti-Modernist Modernisms

Resistance in the Name of Art. Vernon Lee, a "Victorian" novelist-critic productive into the 1920s, writes fiction that can be included on the axis of modernist fantasy. Her *Louis Norbert* (1914), a variant of H. G. Wells's *The Time Machine* (1899), is about a pair of researchers who virtually travel into the past when they become the doubles of the archival figures they are investigating. Despite her conformity to the post-Victorian "period," Lee, surveying modernist thought in *Gospels of Anarchy* (1909), judges it to be anarchical because of its "modern formula of skepticism and revolt."[17] Adversely forecasting Lawrence, Lee insists that "the modern formula" corrodes ego, self, and will. The anarchistic faction, she says, seems to want to undo those things once and for all, but self and will, she protests, require rehabilitation of them as trustworthy constructive faculties. Impressionism would seem to be another misstep. "Reality is valuable to us only as the raw material for something very different; the artistic sense alters [reality] into patterns" (235). Although those patterns are not the equal of immediate life, they provide us with invented characters with whom we can sympathize precisely because they are not misty modernist filaments of relatedness.

Like Lee, the artist-novelist-critic Wyndham Lewis believes in self and will. Against modernist impersonality and liberty from stable egos, Lewis, laying out his argument in *Time and Western Man* (1927), insists on everyone's "formally fixed 'self.'"[18] He trusts "ME" (132) – not IT! – to do his thinking and willing – and knowing. Lewis asks, is it not "socially of capital importance that [a person] should regard himself as *one person* . . . ? It is only in that way that you can hope to ground in him a responsibility to all 'his' acts" (341). The relativism of "relatedness" – as Lawrence defines it – means the end of science and knowledge as "hard and visible truth," a relegation of truth to "a fluid and malleable" state that can be pursued only "symbolically and indirectly" (295).

Lewis, despite cofounding the avant-garde modernist journal *Blast* (1914), includes Joyce, Woolf, and Lawrence on a roster of doubtful artistic achievements. He respects Joyce – as a "genial and comic writer" (74) – and yet diminishes Joyce's originality: his characters and Irish content, Lewis finds, verge on clichés, and his stylistic innovations are a pastiche of Charles Dickens, Gertrude Stein, and Lewis's drama *The Enemy of the Stars* (1914). According to Lewis's diagnosis, most importantly Joyce's experiments are Impressionist derived. The inward instant, illustrated for Lewis in *A Portrait of the Artist as a Young Man*, is only the other side of the coin of a generalized modernist belief in a ceaselessly metamorphic flux of time and experience that dissolves the externality of the world.

Lewis's criticism is economically and politically based. Because Impressionism in art (and complementary modernist philosophies such as that espoused by Henri Bergson) is rooted in indefiniteness, it inspires, and flatters, a social order that, increasingly resistant to reasoned truth, becomes infantilized. Childhood, Lewis points out, is the stage of life in which identity is evanescent, emotion and sensation prevail, responsibility is absent, and fantasy is indeed autonomous. Inasmuch as writers have pursued autonomy for themselves in artistic modes that retreat from personhood and objective intellectual rigor, they deliver themselves into the hands of interests that are only superficially friendly to independent thought and creativity. Mass infantilization is a profitable enterprise. It gives global capitalism an opportunity to promote childhood's characteristics as templates for communication media, entertainment, and art. Technological progress – in the form of "a gigantic plague of numberless mechanical toys" (295) – can also be newly directed at an escape of persons from responsible maturation. Democracy, as a front for an oligarchy that is hand in glove with the industries that erase the line between adulthood and extended childhood, has no interest in counter-weighting the dissolution. Ironically, the modernist pursuit of autonomy in art celebrates, in its content and form, the end of a practical personal autonomy ever more lamentably missing in reality.

Lewis believes that art can and must recover the solid externality that the subjectivity of Impressionism erodes. Clearly, he rejects any claims Impressionism makes to objectivity. That does not mean that he wants to exchange the stable subjective ME for its objective opposite, nor that he believes things are either internal or external. Lewis argues that the human eye's physiology and operative power cancel the antithesis between subject and object, illusory appearance and outward reality. The cancellation is exemplified in the prose of his fiction, which turns words into instruments that baffle attempts to sort perspectives into impressions. His aim, above all, is to make the reader think more than feel. Not that feeling is dismissed. But, according to Lewis, by thinking in the light of a recovered externality, the reader will take up a certain distance from ordinary humanity, especially in terms of the sensational or emotional mode that Impressionism promotes.

Here we get the first inkling that the anti-modernist can be a modernist, too. Lewis assigns art his own version of autonomy: an independent distance from the world. Satire (instead of, say, romance) is now the term for the distance. Lewis gives the term a new slant, by uncoupling previous identifications of satire with moral judgments. That is, satire newly stands for an intellectual awareness of curiously inhuman elements in human life. Those elements are our animal essence and our technological reinvention of our biological selves. The reinvention has made us identical with machines, even as we remain animal beings. Art makes it possible – should make it possible, Lewis thinks – for us to see the absurdity of the conjunction and the disjunction. In seeing the absurdity, we can laugh at our strangely mechanical-animal out-of-joint condition. Self-conscious, self-critical laughter is where our autonomy, and art's, resides. Rebecca West, one notes, does not bear in mind the possibly comic mechanical aspect of her art-cortex.

In *Men without Art* (1934), Lewis describes his satiric distantiation as something "ascetic, in the interests of other-worldliness" (183).[19] The artwork itself, directed by "the entire human capacity – for sensation, reflection, imagination and will" (12), serves as material evidence of the alternative world. Life and art together are "a game – a game in the sense that no value can attach to it for itself, but only as it is well-played or badly-played" (234). Life, "a very bad business," can be countered if *homo animal ridens* – humanity, the laughing animal – can call on its "dangerous, philosophic, 'god-like' prerogative." Its prerogative is a "wild nihilism that is a function of reason and of which ... laughter is the characteristic expression" (232). Interestingly, Lewis attaches to his sentence about wild nihilism an illustration from Joyce. The creation of Leopold Bloom, he says, expresses what Lewis means by the prerogative art can accord to reason's wild nihilism.

Although Impressionism is the enemy within for Lewis, his art found a greater enemy without: politics. The hollowness of Western democracy moved Lewis to consider the appreciable possibilities of alternative political forms, including communism and fascism. Yet he maintained his satirical–critical (i.e., autonomous) detachment from them, to the outrage of their partisans among his fellow writers. It struck Lewis that intolerant political ideologies had become replacements for religious ones. To maintain art's need to be free from political controversies and censure, Lewis felt constrained to write book after book about them. Immersed in politics, his anti-political polemics on behalf of art thus intensify his creative self-splitting: he becomes an anti-modernist modernist.

The same epithet fits Laura Riding, an American who established herself as an important force in England during her collaboration with the poet-novelist Robert Graves. In *Anarchism Is Not Enough* (1928), a counter-manifesto to Lewis and a criticism of Woolf, Riding's anti-modernist modernism makes the terms "real" and "unreal" take on new meanings. Apparently unconvinced by Lewis's claim that truth (and our eyes) cancels the split between subjectivity and objectivity, Riding hypothesizes that Lewis depends on treating society and history, which are external to his individual perspective, as an objective, collective reality: "the collective-real," Riding calls it, in contrast with the "individual-real."[20] But both realities are phantoms, Riding argues, and she sees Woolf caught up in the same antitheses. Woolf's *To the Lighthouse* (1927) presents the individual-real as "physically self, real because as physical it shares the simple reality of nature" (47).

The individual-real in Lewis and Woolf is for Riding a form of anarchism: an intellectual and artistic disorder. Accordingly, the holds on us exerted by both individual and collective realities, Riding believes, must be broken. To break them, she formulates paradoxical alternatives: "the unreal" and "individual-unreal." The way to the unreal is through the "social disappearance" (75) of "intrinsic self " (78), through "unbecoming" on both the individual and the collective fronts.

If fiction could move into Riding's version of unbecoming, it would present "an incentive not to response but to [the reader's] initiative" (114). Response would underwrite the individual-real. What kind of stories can stimulate a reader's initiative to transcend response, and hence to venture into the

individual-unreal? *Anarchism Is Not Enough* answers with experimental narratives. One of them is "An Anonymous Book." That narrative is simultaneously an essay and something of a review of the eponymous nameless book,
which contains a collection of tales, with titles such as "The Flying Attic" and
"The Woman Who Was Bewitched by a Parallel." The reviewer-essayist-
narrator explains that some of the stories group themselves in order to project
a figure identifiable as "the Queen." The Queen and her world illustrate the
unreal in which Riding locates poetry and fiction:

> Nothing in her queendom contradicted anything else [note the contrast
> with Lewis's volumes of combative contradiction!]; . . . everything was
> so, everything was statistical, everything was falsification, everything
> was conversation, and she was an anonymous particularity conversing
> with herself about her own nothingness, so was outside the chaotic
> conversation of events, she was Queen.   (177)

Riding's critical essay-stories unfold again in her *Progress of Stories* (1935),
where "truth" becomes the pivotal term. Stories can lead to truth if they break
readers of the habit of understanding fictional characters and events as
models of "realities." But stories cannot be the truth, or declare a common
agreement as to what the truth is. "Until we are quite sure that we are not
telling one another lies – not being exactly sure who we are – we prefer to tell
one another stories which are only nearly true."[21]

Riding's aims for writing are antisocial, inasmuch as what is "social"
("collective-real"), verbally and in fact or in eventfulness, is for her an illusion,
an untruth, despite its being commonly believed in. Criticizing T. S. Eliot and
Aspects of the Novel as well as Lewis and Woolf, Riding insists that "the
purpose of poetry is to destroy all that prose formally represents. [Poetry] is
an exclusive medium, and its merit depends on the economy with which it
can remove the social rhythmic clutter of communicative language" (*Anarchism*, 116). Is this not another formulation of autonomy? Riding seems to
consummate the very tendencies that she criticizes: her stories, opaquely
experimental in diction and treatment, complement every idea of fiction we
have surveyed, inasmuch as they pressure the clutter of communicative
language that upholds social convention as well as novelistic convention.

Resistance in the Name of Politics. The clutter of communicative language
seems the only possible medium for other modernists, or for anti-modernists,
who see the social world as a state of intolerable political injustice and economic disorder. For those others, to speak about that world, and to seek to
change it, means to work within terms more immediately intelligible than
Riding's, more ordinary than experimental.

H. G. Wells was the first champion of *A Portrait of the Artist As a Young Man*; nevertheless, in the service of politics Wells's ideas about fiction make him an anti-novelist modernist novelist, despite his prodigious production of fictions. His *Boon* (1915) dramatizes Wells's commitment to political, economic, and historical priorities rather than to art. Indeed, the art of the novel, Wells bitingly proposes, especially as James and Conrad exemplify it, is reactionary, and deserves to be doomed.

Wells's protagonist is a deceased author, whose incomplete works, edited and annotated by Boon's literary executor, constitute Wells's volume. Boon's commitment is exactly Wells's: to forge "the mind of the race," motivated by a need for "something that should bring together all [the modern state's] various activities, which go on now in a sort of deliberate ignorance of one another, which would synthesize research, education, philosophical discussion, moral training, public policy."[22] Only in light of such a synthesis, Boon feels sure, can humanity take charge of its future.

Boon's incomplete text, "The Mind of the Race," was to have outlined the synthesis by representing a world conference on the subject. The imaginary conference would include a literary wing, with James and George Moore in attendance. But the conference organizer will "be very impatient about art" (102), especially as James's ideas illustrate it. James's ideas, the organizer (through Boon) charges, center on the "the novel [as] a work of art aiming at pictorial unities" (107). The result is a self-enclosure – one might put the word "autonomous" into Boon/Wells's mouth – that Boon judges to be an "evisceration" (108) of persons and life. "All art, too acutely self-centred, comes to this sort of thing" (107–108), the sort of thing that is independent of other discourses and practical use. To supplement his judgment Boon develops a satirical version of a James story. Thereafter, Conrad and Ford are derided in the service of Boon's anti-elitist desire to see the death of "Literary Greatnesses" (161) and therefore of "authors."

Wells continued to write novels and simultaneously to attack them. In "Digression about Novels," a segment of Wells's *Experiment in Autobiography* (1934), Wells opposes the notion that a novel's principal interest should aim, as he believed Victorian fiction did, at illustrating "established values," even if revealing "some little-known abuse."[23] Neither Victorian fiction nor James's novels (about whom Wells continues to complain) had any "idea of the possible use of the novel as a help to conduct" (411). The Wellsian novel, in contrast, is not centered on mirroring established values, or unity of composition, or anything except future-directed experiments with values as yet not established. Indeed, Wells's idea of fiction is not so much an expansion of the novel but a "getting right out of it" – into what Wells calls "experiments and essays in statement" (418), for the sake of shaping the reader's practical exertions on behalf of a prospective new world order.

Nevertheless, Wells's constant attachment to iconoclastic experiment betrays his alliance with modernism. Even in his politics Wells is motivated by an avant-garde rejection of "Victorian" "period" values. He despises nineteenth-century imperialism and jingoism. Moreover, although he variously approves of socialism, communism, and fascism for their governmental potential, he early on – before the Great War – dissociated himself from ideologies of class conflict, which he identifies with "the class-war cant, of fifty years ago" (686), meaning the 1880s. Marxism is dated; it is not modernist!

Perhaps nothing symptomizes Wells's implicit fellow-traveling with the likes of autonomy-inspired writers more than his thoughts about "character." It is one of the conventional aspects of "the novel" that Wells also dismisses. Indeed, he dismisses it in relation to himself. Describing his autobiography as a dissection "of my former self," he confesses that he is unsure about his present "persona," virtually repeating Lawrence's "I shall never know my me." His "sustaining idea" – "the planned reconstruction of human relationships in the form of the world-state" – is facilitated by "the modern escape to impersonality" (707).

Wells's career is applauded by a left-wing writer, the young novelist Ralph Fox, in his review of *Experiment in Autobiography* in *Left Review*, a leading Marxist journal between 1934 and 1938. Not that the communist Fox agrees with Wells's idea of a classless "open conspiracy" (as Wells called it) on behalf of realizations of utopia. Nor does he agree with Wells's low assessment of fiction. In response to a claim by Wells that "the novel will give way to biography," Fox defends fiction as the agent of a "full truth" that biographical materials will always fall short of revealing.[24]

The implication of Fox's sentence is that a Marxist can accept, as much as any apolitical modernist can, a trustworthy veracity in fiction. Fox unfolds the possibility of novelistic truth in *The Novel and the People* (1937), published shortly before he died while fighting on the side of the Spanish republican government in the Spanish Civil War. In Fox's pages the novel becomes another version of Lawrence's bright book of life. But in his version the novelist bears "a special responsibility to the present and the past of his country"[25] – albeit not in any merely conventional way. Similarly, in no simple, one-sided sense, the leftist novelist is to use the novel to advance a "materialist" philosophy and "socialist realism" (12). For Marxism, the material – that is, economic – base of historical conflict and progress is an indispensable touchstone. But, Fox says, so is imagination. Materialism and "Art," imagination's product, are, and must be, allies in the production of fiction and revolution. Sometimes those allies may be in conflict, but that conflict itself is creative, conducive to changing reality.

Present-day fiction, Fox finds, falls far short of its responsibility to effect change, because English novelists have forgotten that the novel is an epic genre, and that epics integrate philosophical thought, the creativity of human action, and the importance of character, especially of heroic character. Joyce, Lawrence, and Aldous Huxley's novels have diminished "man in action, . . . able to become the lord of his own destiny" (101). Surprisingly, Fox designates the work of Kipling – no leftist! – as a vehicle of "real vitality" because "Kipling soaked himself in the folk speech of England and America, nor was he ever afraid to seize on its . . . manifestations in the new popular mythology growing [from] the development of power machinery" [139].)

Cut loose from epic ambitions, novels have disintegrated into specialized modes. Fox estimates Forster as "our only considerable contemporary novelist" (61), but his "approach [in *Aspects of the Novel*] is a reflection of this [disintegration], with its division into novels of 'story,' novels of 'fantasy,' novels of 'prophecy'" (68). "Socialist realism," Fox contends, will return novels to their epic origins. Such realism "does not at all correspond with . . . little more than a scarcely disguised political tract" (109). "It is completely foreign to the spirit of Marxism to neglect the formal side of art" (134). Epic characters in leftist-inspired novels, emerging from the complex conditions their authors imagine for them, should speak in the light of multiple treatments in the same text – but not according to the separated subgeneric modes of expression into which fiction has fallen. Apparently *Ulysses*, despite its multiplicity of treatments, illustrates the disintegration that Fox laments: he would reintegrate them.

Among the treatments that Fox prescribes for fiction is a formal element of world-historical importance. Fox reminds his readers that capitalism has created a global framework of existence, canceling the difference between "'backward' and 'advanced' peoples." It has thereby created "the conditions for a world art, a world literature" (44). "Today . . . the true national interest . . . is in supporting the . . . great movements for democracy and national liberty which are re-vitalising the Arabian, African and Indian peoples" (154). Without a component derived originally from them, Fox asserts, the "modern and revolutionary imagination . . . essential to the revival of the novel" cannot be achieved.

The essential component is "the element of colour, fantasy and ironical vision which we have almost lost since the Renaissance." "It came then from the East" – and passed into the work of Cervantes and Shakespeare. "This reinforcement of imagination must come to us again now that Asia is awaking from her long sleep" (160). Because Fox makes it possible for us to deduce the nature of fantasy from Cervantes and Shakespeare, we can gather that he means it to be synonymous with romance. Just as the anti-modernist, anti-novelist Wells cannot evade casting many of his experiments in statement in the form of narrative fiction, so Fox cannot separate the autonomous elements of fiction – fantasy and romance – from realism. For him to resist or protest modernism in the name of political responsibility is not to engage, it seems, in any merely stark opposition.

The East–West contact Fox advocated was inherent in the Commonwealth countries that produced writers shaped by British traditions – and in revolt against them. Among the foremost colonial writers in the 1930s is the Trinidadian leftist C. L. R. James, who arrived in London in 1932, where he published fiction (*Minty Alley*, 1936), drama, political journalism, and a polemic on behalf of West Indian independence. Like Fox, James honors the co-equal authority of imagination and Marxist materialism. In 1950, he began a study of Melville, whose picture of Ahab in *Moby Dick* James saw as a forecast of all modern dictatorships. James solicits Melville, because he thinks modernist works – he names *Ulysses* and Woolf's *Mrs. Dalloway* – lose sight of the interests and needs of the people's collective life. Likewise, criticism, he argues, has lost touch with the collective.

Nevertheless, in exploring the question "What is art?" in an autobiography of 1963, on behalf of the collective, James brings together the sport of cricket with the verbal and visual arts to argue their mutual likeness at the level of form. The formal aspects of fictional treatments, James says, are models of the "style" that distinguishes superlative sportsmen; their sports are analogues of fiction, whose authors' styles are the equivalent of the players.' Both sport and art, he says, minister to a vital political and democratic necessity: "expanded personality" and "a more complete existence" for all.[26] The claim unites James with modernist writers who, unlike him, believe in "the novel" even if they see it as withdrawn from immediate political relevance. The claim, along with Fox's like ideas, also (unwittingly) turns the tables on Wells: it suggests that his aggressions against art are what is dated, and that the "Victorian" Marxists are the avant-garde.

Resistance in the Name of Religion and Philosophy. Modernism's contest with pre-modernist religious authority persists during our "period" because it coincides with fiction by avowedly Christian novelists, including G. K. Chesterton, Charles Williams, and C. S. Lewis. In *Orthodoxy* (1908), Chesterton associates modernism with "the ordinary aesthetic anarchist who sets out to feel everything freely."[27] But "it is always easy to be a modernist" (101),

Chesterton asserts, because freedom from limits evades conflict and results in a slack single-mindedness, usually pessimistic in attitude. It is far more bracing to be a Christian, because Christianity exacts of its adherent a paradox-laden demand: a Christian must be limited by the Church's theology, yet energetically test his freedom both on behalf of that theology and against it. Every Christian life exemplifies a "duplex passion" (93).

The collision of opposing passions provokes the person (and the soul) to action, to adventurous contest, and hence to engage what Chesterton calls "the romance of orthodoxy." One example of the adventure is the gospel assertion that "He that will lose his life, the same shall save it." "This paradox is the whole principle of courage," Chesterton comments (93), and he uses a soldier's life to exemplify it. "A soldier surrounded by enemies, if he is to cut his way out, needs to combine a strong desire for living with a strange carelessness about dying" (93). The soldier's paradoxical dilemma epitomizes the orthodox believer's challenge. Chesterton piles up additional epitomes, until he can declare that "the more I found that while [Christianity] had established a rule and order, the chief aim of that order was to give room for good things to run wild" (95). They run wild because in all "moral problems," such as those involving "pride, ... protest, and ... compassion," the virtues brought to bear on one situation will be counteracted, and made relatively not good, by the same virtues brought to bear on another situation. Church doctrine is the stabilizing measure – and the inciting cause – of the wildness. "By defining its main doctrine, the Church not only kept seemingly inconsistent things side by side, but ... allowed them to break out in a sort of artistic violence otherwise possible only to anarchists" (96).

It is clear from the last sentence that Chesterton's deployment of paradox aims to construct his anti-modernism in an effort to outdo the modernists at their own anarchic game. If modernism is to live up to its rebellious purpose, if it is to be vital, one gathers, it should bear the signs and the conduct of its supposed opposite. The ultimate anarchist rebel, according to Chesterton, is Jesus. On the cross he voiced despair, and thus became a "god who has himself been in revolt," and who "seemed for an instant to be an atheist" (138).

Chesterton's study *Robert Louis Stevenson* (1928), about an author who had long been a byword for romance, is at odds with the cultural moment of its appearance. What had anarchic modernism to do with adventure stories by Stevenson for boys, and for boys whose manhood might mistake British imperialism for swashbuckling? Those questions would have dominated the critical attitude toward Stevenson in the late 1920s. According to Chesterton, during that era the modernist novelists Aldous Huxley and Dorothy Richardson were proving (unintentionally) "that free life and free love are really worse than any ascetic had ever represented them."[28] Stevenson was antithetical to that ascesis; he also signified little to modernist psychology, which dissolves individual identities and wills into "nameless universal forces streaming through the sub-consciousness" (172). "Modern philosophy," in Chesterton's summary view of it in *Orthodoxy*, "does not really believe there is any meaning in the universe" (157). Therefore "it cannot hope to find any romance; its romances will have no plots. A man cannot expect adventures in the land of anarchy" (*Orthodoxy*, 157), which is a result of a modernist "fallacy of internalism" (*Stevenson*, 143).

If the best fiction is romance, Chesterton argues, then despite the historical costumes Stevenson's figures wear, history is not the theater of his narratives, which cannot be judged at the bar of reality. Stevenson's playing space is purely fictive, a puppet show, Chesterton says, in which characters enact a search for happiness that conforms to the quests inscribed in Christianity – the good things running wild, and the seeking of courage. The roots of the latter and of fiction lie in a happiness that (for Chesterton) is realized in childhood, and that modernism is unable to supply (*pace* Lewis).

But Stevenson did not ally himself with entertainment genres such as the boy's adventure story because he assigned supreme value to young audiences. Instead, his alliance was an experiment in style, a treatment fusing low, middle, and high cultures. Chesterton does not note that the same amalgam of demotic romance and high culture shapes Conrad's work, and *Ulysses*'s pastiche of modes. He also does not note that Stevenson is one of the proponents of artistic autonomy, yet his chapter on "Experiment and Range" in *Stevenson* seems to bear witness to it. Each of Stevenson's works, one might argue on the basis of Chesterton's hints, is an exercise in genre or in another writer's style (the other writers include Walter Scott and George Meredith). Emphasizing treatment as inseparable from content, Chesterton virtually claims that in 1928 the Victorian is au courant, yet also avant garde. Fiction will return to storytelling and romance in the post-modernist future, Chesterton predicts. In effect, as in *Orthodoxy*, Chesterton's argument reverses what is not modernist into what is. It thereby underwrites the tendency within debates about modernism to become theorizings about the decontextualizing thrust of fiction. And yet, despite (or perhaps because of) Stevenson's cultivation of fiction in the mode of puppet theater and autonomous romance, Stevenson became detached enough from worldliness to deliver anathemas against imperialism in his nonfictions, *A Footnote to History* (1892) and *In the South Seas* (1896).

Another novelist whom the makers of modernist canons neglect is the popular fiction and short-story writer W. Somerset Maugham. Maugham acknowledges his lack of modernist prestige – and his downright opposition to it – in *The Summing Up* (1938), his meditation on his fictions and his life-study of philosophy. The reasons he assigns for being devalued are familiar: "It has been my misfortune that for some time now a story has been despised by the intelligent."[29] Maugham resists his contemporaries' focus on treatment rather than content. He recognizes the interest of that: "the novelties [techniques] presented gave a sort of freshness to well-worn material and were a fruitful matter of discussion" (620). But Maugham also punctures the claims to innovation. The Jamesian method that Lubbock promulgated was "only a slight variation from the autobiographical form ... ; to speak of it as ... a great aesthetic discovery is somewhat absurd" (621). As for modernist exploitation of "stream of thought," stimulated as it was by psychoanalysis and by a novelist's ordinary working relation to his own "subconscious," "it was a clever and amusing trick, but nothing more" (621). The technical innovations, Maugham predicts, will be commonplace in the future of fiction, where less fuss will be made about them: "The artist is absorbed by his technique only when his theme is of no pressing interest to him" (621). After the modernist goes out of fashion, content will resume its centrality alongside storytelling,

As he emphasizes his despised commitment to storytelling, however, Maugham quietly and unintentionally advances aspects of his record that suit "the intelligent" of his "period." The impulse for his book is his need to "get some kind of coherence" (481) into his thoughts about his work and life. Nevertheless, he alludes to his life rather than presents it, because he has only "a partial self" (528). Existing in his writing, and searching for facets of his personality there, he can render his life only impersonally. As for his interest in plain narrative, its plainness masks its role in his history. Maugham turned to it as a rebellion against his success as a playwright. Drama dictated conventional realist or naturalist treatment, whereas the novel offered Maugham a freedom of invention, and hence the possibility of achieving what novels and short stories "sometimes achieved": "perfection" (582–583). Not that he thinks he achieved it! Nevertheless, Maugham did gain an increased creative liberty, especially in regard to moral values. Fiction makes it possible for the writer to transcend the nets of "ordinary standards. [The artist] creates his own values ... [W]hat [men] call virtue and what they call vice are ... indifferent elements in the scheme of things out of which he constructs his own freedom" (603).

But fiction's aesthetic domain, Maugham believes, cannot be the ultimate depository of urgent questions about God, life, death, and meaning. Thus, in the last segment of his book, Maugham subordinates the survey of his writing career to retrospection of another quest he undertook: to discover adequate answers to life's perplexities. At first, he remembers, his acquaintance with Immanuel Kant suggested a supreme marriage of philosophy and fiction. Hadn't Kant demonstrated that humanity could only know "the construction of [its] mind," with the result that all the rest of its knowledge was "fiction"? Unfortunately, Kant's "perfect theory" had one drawback: it was "unbelievable" (649). Thereafter Maugham recounts his testing of one thinker after another, from St. Ignatius, Spinoza, and Schopenhauer, to Heisenberg, Einstein, and Bertrand Russell. He emerges from this long, wide-ranging test as an agnostic, not only about religion but about truth.

Falling back in effect on a neo-Kantian position, Maughan proposes that humanity "lives not by truth but by make-believe, and idealism ... is merely [an] effort to attach the prestige of truth to the fictions [humanity] has invented" (673). In the end, he finds, only "goodness" is the one thing to trust, the final answer. But "goodness" is hard to define. On his last page Maugham defines goodness as "right action" (682). "Who can tell," he adds, "in this meaningless world what right action is?" The answer is, again, modest. It is action "in conformity with [one's] nature and [one's] business." All one needs, Maugham concludes, is to know what those are. In the light of such a conclusion, although *The Summing Up* consciously resists the aesthetics of modernism, its ultimate doubt accords with the frame of mind out of which modernist ideas of fiction develop.

Generational Recapitulations

When the journal *transition* in 1929 solicited critics' responses to Joyce's fiction-in-progress *Finnegans Wake* (1924–1939), Samuel Beckett, Joyce's young secretary and one of the respondents, lambasted West's *The Strange Necessity*. The quarrel between Beckett and West, 23 and 37 years of age, respectively, is curious, because they are of different generations, but on the same modernist side: they have Joyce in common. Equally modernist, they devote themselves to formulating what fiction is, no matter its determination by time and place. For Beckett, fiction is distinguished, unlike any other discourse, by its fusion of treatment (he calls it "form") and content. That is essential to its autonomy. A fair reading of *The Strange Necessity* might claim that for West the same holds true; after all, she argues that Joyce fails inasmuch as he separates the form from the content. But Beckett charges that West's analysis confirms the separation. As he sees it, Joyce's form for West "can fulfill no higher function than that of stimulus for a tertiary or quartary conditioned reflex of dribbling comprehension."[30] Are the two modernist novelist-critics talking past each other? Is this in effect a modernist generational squabble?

The possibility of a settled answer is inseparable from *Finnegans Wake*'s modernist defiance of ordinary comprehension. A typical sentence from it, bursting with rebellion against convention, including sense itself, is the vehicle of Beckett's discussion: "The efferfreshpainted livy in beautific repose upon the silence of the dead from Pharoph the next first down to ramescheckles the last bust thing" (2). This is not nonsense, Beckett exclaims, nor does it need translation: "Here is direct expression" (11) of what above all there is to see and to listen to in the writing, which amounts for Beckett to a new directness of sense. Any contrary claim of nonsense derives from assumptions that form "is so strictly divorced from content [or from abstractable sense] that you can comprehend the one almost without bothering to read the other" (13). In *Work in Progress* (as *Finnegans Wake* was called in 1929), language is rescued from being "abstracted to death" (15). A hardened habit of intellectual and linguistic abstraction, Beckett argues, has enchained readers to false distinctions: between topic and treatment, content and form, words and their meanings, stories and discourses. Joyce's writing is "not *about something; it is that something itself*" (14, Beckett's italics). The modernist language of *Finnegans Wake* is intended to show how it is we, not it, who are abstracted, habitually estranged, in all we feel and think.

Beckett adduces the Enlightenment Italian philosopher Giambattista Vico and Dante's *Divine Comedy* as aids to reading Joyce. In *The Strange Necessity*, West had appealed to Manichean religion as a way of comprehending *Ulysses*. Might Beckett's illustrative procedure, countering West the modernist elder, appeal to *his* reader's dribbling comprehension? Only superficially, it appears. As Beckett explains, Vico's ideas about humanity's historical cycles prefigure Joyce's resistance to abstractions. They are adapted by Joyce "as a structural convenience – or inconvenience. His position is in no way a philosophical one" (7). Moreover, Beckett evokes Dante to point out a modestly useful measure for our comprehension of Joyce's impact on the genre of "the novel." Dante relied on an idea of purgatory as a sign of his drive to meaning's "culmination" (21). Those who want a final meaning, for whom such finality is heaven or hell in life or in fiction or both, will undergo *Finnegans Wake* as a purge. The novel's modernist vocation, as Joyce exemplifies it, is to maintain "a continuous purgatorial process": "no more than this; neither prize nor penalty; simply a series of stimulants to enable the kitten to catch its tail" (22).

Beckett's figure of speech seems hardly honorific, given our colloquial sense of tail-chasing as a useless effort. Is the art of fiction primarily, even exclusively, a going around and around without issue? Beckett appears to say so.

A stranger necessity than West's! And within modernism, whose growing span of decades had produced generations of adherents, is there a going around and around without definitive issue, as the West–Beckett contention might suggest? That its issue should be less self-contained became increasingly urgent in the 1930s because of global political turbulence. If modernism were to endure, should it be less autonomous, taking West's relatively heteronomous direction (with its qualified criticism of Joyce) in preference to Beckett's freshly intransigent example of autonomy?

E. M. Forster was writing novels no longer, but he and his work were seen – by a younger generation – as the way forward. Rose Macaulay (of the older generation) suggests so in her *The Writings of E. M. Forster*, which treats the sequence of Forster's novels as a progress from scenes of personal life to scenes – above all in *A Passage to India* (1924) – of "concern with politics."[31] Referring to Forster's address to the International Congress of Writers in Paris in June 1935, she describes "Mr. Forster mak[ing] a rout about liberty; an increasing rout as liberty suffers increasingly in this sinister age" (283). In the fight against fascism, according to Macaulay, Forster accepts that writing must sacrifice its less partisan aims. Forster "minds too much about the poor to cling whole-heartedly to our ramshackle democracy" (289). Writing must attach itself to communism if the latter "does evil that good may come" (288). To sure, there is something old-fashioned about Forster, Macaulay concludes. His modernism belongs – in 1938! – to an "older culture" (297). But "the older culture has the advantage that it accepts the newer more often than the new the older. Such acceptance narrows the gulf across which writers of one decade talk to writers of another" (297).

Forster appears as a touchstone of value in another commentary of 1938, Cyril Connolly's *Enemies of Promise*. This book assesses the endurance, or the demise, of modernism. Although Connolly includes the works we consider modernist under the heading of "the modern movement 1900–1922,"[32] (27), the two-decade periodization is for him the extreme limit of longevity. He is not sure that the fictions of 1900–1922 have maintained their vitality. And what kind of novel published in 1938, Connolly asks, might survive for another ten years – especially in light of the potential for a cataclysmic war that inhibits forecasts? The 35-year-old Connolly, having published a novel (*The Rock Pool*, 1935) about dead-end bohemian lives in an out-of-the-way corner of the Riviera, was looking for a way forward for his own fiction.

He sees a promise of fiction's future in Forster's work. Forster is "gaining ground among intelligent readers," his "pollen fertilizes a new generation" (27). The reason is significant: Forster was never available for enlistment as a poster boy for modernism. Most writers who emerged in 1900–1922, had, Connolly proposes, a single faith: "whether realists, intellectuals or imaginative writers, . . . they believed . . . in the sanctity of the artist and in his sense of vocation. They were all inmates of the Ivory Tower" (29). They withdrew from the world, abandoning it for the realm of artistic autonomy. Forster escaped with his life (perhaps at the cost of his productivity) because he did not practice the sort of "style" – "a relation between form and content" (17) – that the ballyhooed modernists did. The same escape, Connolly implies, was made by Maugham, whose *The Summing Up* he quotes honorifically.

Connolly includes Virginia Woolf among the Ivory Tower cohort, not least because of her anti-narrative, anti-realist lyricism. The cohort is for Connolly a "Mandarin" one, because its extremities of style are distant from colloquial usage and communicable meaning. The distance was "of value," Connolly concedes, because "After the postwar disillusion [those writers] offered a religion of beauty, a cult of words, of meanings understood only by the initiated at a time when people were craving such initiation" (55). But the offering now is passé, Connolly declares. In addition, he notes that the Ivory Tower began to be undone by its own inmates – by Lawrence and Wyndham Lewis, he thinks. The current mark of the undoing, Connolly argues, is a resurgence, against Mandarinism, of the vernacular. Its best practitioners are the young George Orwell and Christopher Isherwood. Their plainness of statement and treatment, which makes their intelligence available to all readers, is their great innovation. To be sure, their accessibility is also dangerously readable (74): it risks banality. Still, their work, Connolly thinks, might endure the ten years of survival that for Connolly is the new measure of value – and of a literary period. The young will take from the Mandarins what is best: "the striving for perfection, the horror of clichés" (80). At the same time, the democratic, readable character of the new writers' work will avoid the Mandarins' "wooly profundities" (80).

The battle between the newer and the older styles, presumably with Connolly on the new side, will shape the future. But wryly, almost comically, Connolly ends the first third of *Enemies of Promise* with a withdrawal from an ultimate partisanship. "It is the privilege of living in the twentieth-century that one can take both sides in such controversies" (82). It is a modernist privilege! The very form of his book demonstrates his taking both sides. He devotes the last third of his text to a retrospective account of his childhood and adolescence. The portrait of the artist-critic as a young man discloses the personal origin of the critic's divided feelings about modern – and modernist – writing, and about the need to go beyond it. Just as fiction's attempts to honor its past and find a future for itself remain in suspense, the growth of the critic's mind remains in suspense as it tries to honor the past, yet surpass it.

In thus appending to his criticism the personal genesis of its bias, Connolly surprisingly reinvents literary analysis and history by cross-pollinating it with memoir. The resulting hybrid strikes the note – again – of modernist experiment. Ford Madox Ford's memoir of Conrad might well be a predecessor. If it is considered so, it narrows the chronological and generational gap between 1924 and 1938 – and qualifies any view of *Enemies of Promise* as a form of the future. In the novelist on whom Connolly pins his hopes for the next decade, Christopher Isherwood, there is also a considerable backward tie – consciously to Forster, unconsciously to Ford – in *Lions and Shadows*, another book of 1938.

Isherwood's previous work, representing life in England and Germany after the Great War, attests to Connolly's description of a post-modernist renewal of accessible writing. The colloquial narrator of *Lions and Shadows* is Isherwood in his own person. The book is a memoir. At the same time, the author declares that he has taken such license with the reality of his friends and acquaintances that – shades of Ford – his text must be "read as a novel."[33] The kind of "novel" Isherwood is writing derives from Forster, who placed "less emphasis . . . on the big scenes than on the unimportant ones: that's what's so utterly terrific. It's the completely new kind of accentuation" (174) – the kind Connolly applauds.

But there is another kind of accentuation, Isherwood tells us, derived from Forster's "exciting" (168) notice in *Aspects of the Novel* of the French novelist Andre Gide's experimental fiction *The Counterfeiters*. Gide uses his text to make dizzying leaps from fiction to reality and back again. It is surely a Mandarin mode. Going against the grain of what Connolly applauds, Isherwood adapts Gide's technique for *Lions and Shadows*. He constructs his text as a complex hall of mirrors, in which his real life and his fiction are now differentiated, now fused. *Lions and Shadows* was originally Isherwood's title for an autobiographical novel that Isherwood describes, even generously quotes from, in 1938. The novel was discarded, and so never published. Now Isherwood publishes it, yet does not publish it, in this new version, which dizzyingly reproduces and interleaves narratives from the first *Lions and Shadows* as well as from a story cycle about Mortmere, a romance realm that Isherwood and his friend Chalmers (the novelist Edward Upward) invent as alternative histories to the ones they are living. Both men hate their studies, their peers at Cambridge, and their own middle- to upper-class origins. Yet when disputes between the government and the Trades Union Council over wages in the coal industry erupt in the General Strike of 1926, Isherwood remains a neutral bystander – all the while hating himself "for being neutral" (179). He "tried to get on with my novel" (179) – the one that was to become his first, *All the Conspirators* (1928).

"I thought of the novel," Isherwood tells his reader, speaking of the genre and not just of *All the Conspirators*, "essentially in terms of technique … a game with [the] reader; … with tricks … I imagined the novel as a contraption … whose action depends upon the exactly co-ordinated working of all its interrelated parts" (259) Although the statement might be a retrospective view, it also describes the continuing gambits played with identity and reality in *Lions and Shadows*. Isherwood's text exemplifies a compromise between accessible style and Mandarin artifice – and might well lean in the direction of the latter.

What idea of fiction is most at stake in Isherwood's version of Connolly's anti-modernist modernism? Isherwood's first four novels are all realist works rooted in reference to historical events that are not the product of a novelist's imagination. The Great War and its aftermath shape the lives of Isherwood's characters, just as a homeless World War I veteran whom Isherwood meets by chance shapes Isherwood's life in *Lions and Shadows*. The soldier, Lester, "had no world" after the war. "I came to regard Lester as a ghost – the ghost of the War" (257). The encounter with the ghost, to Isherwood's surprise, inspires his novel's completion. Inasmuch as *All the Conspirators* and its successors are derived from the Great War, they are historical novels; yet they are also ghost stories, a fictional mode that is not "realist." The realism of Isherwood's fictions hides their attachment to an opposite genre. By involving his personal history with the shade of the previous version of *Lions and Shadows*, with the Mortmere fantasies, with imaginations of Isherwood's novels to come, and with the living ghost Lester, Isherwood foregrounds the fictional character, rather than the realist character, of his work. After all, *Lions and Shadows* appears to say, Isherwood's life can best express itself as a departure from the reality of history. His pursuit of living is underwritten by an independent pursuit of shadows. Whatever kind of contraption a novel is, Isherwood suggests, it does not betray its freedom from history, even when it is being historical.

If we think of Wilde and James as a first generation of modernists, and Joyce, Woolf, and West as a second generation, then Beckett, Connolly, and Isherwood are modernism's grandchildren. For all the generational differences or the generational efforts to distinguish one age from another, an experiment such as *Lions and Shadows* shows the continuity of ideas that framed an era for a half century, and it continues the period's intensive exploration of the nature of fiction.

Joseph Conrad, Ford Madox Ford, and Virginia Woolf

Joseph Conrad, *The Nigger of the "Narcissus"* (1897)

The racist epithet in the title of Conrad's novel might immediately alienate readers from Conrad's text, let alone from the idea of fiction in his preface. Weighed in the balance with British and other populations' prejudice against blacks, fiction that stresses momentary impressions will seem frivolous – all the more if Conrad's narrative, taking racism as its subject matter, treats the prejudice dispassionately. Indeed, the narrative presents without criticism the crew of the *Narcissus* and its stereotyping, scapegoating response to a tubercular fellow seaman, the West Indian black James Wait. Between the preface's claim that the solidarity of mankind inspires the novelist's work and the novel itself, there is a potential discord. Where is the solidarity to be located, or respected, if the distinction between Waite and his fellows is harped upon, and in opprobrious terms? Moreover, one of the sailors, Donkin, combines a repulsive character with a continual advocacy, in Wait's name, of the rights of man. It is as if Conrad wants to discredit the democratic ideology that is the only promise, for blacks or for the working classes typified by the crew, of liberty from prejudice and exploitation. Surely Conrad's idea of fiction should take a stand against racism, or take a stand against the exploitation of the seaborne proletariat!

If one focuses on Conrad's treatment of his subject, however, political indignation might become a less relevant response. The novelist deliberately names his story's vehicle – the ship *Narcissus* – to suggest what the very title announces, almost explicitly: racist epithets are a property of narcissism, they belong to it. They do so because narcissism is self-regard, stimulated by defensiveness against the ultimate enemy of self-love. That enemy is death, not skin color or caste.

The racism in Conrad's novel blindly projects the racist's fear and hatred of his mortality onto the racist object. James Wait is dying; he is a disabled sailor, a living personification of vulnerability. He prefigures the mortal disabling that all his fellow workers must undergo. We might say, enlisting the preface's language, that we are indeed being "made to see": to see that the distinctions of social life are organized to protect us against the fact of our common demise. The distinction the crew makes between itself and the ill black man is its attempt to guarantee its superiority to strange others and to the grimmest of strangers, the final reaper. But the crew's fear of mortality is narcissistic vanity. Wait's name is introduced into the text as an explicit pun. It is not much of a stretch to consider it as available to pronunciation, especially in Cockney utterance, as "white." Consider how the diphthong *ai* moves toward the long *i* sound in such words as "*Aye*," often repeated in the text as a term of consent. Donkin pronounces *magistrate* as "magistryte."[1] In the very sound of things, the vaunted difference between black Waite and whites collapses. The ship is burdened with multiple narcissistic souls. Nevertheless, when the crew begins to ally itself with "Jimmy," it enacts (even if it cannot articulate) the knowledge that racism is an irrelevantly diverting discrimination. Conrad's narrator announces in the first chapter that from the start the narrative is the story of an ending: "they" – all the crew – "are gone now – and it does not matter . . . a truth, a faith, a generation of men goes – and is forgotten, and it does not matter!" (25).

To be sure, it matters to the few who remain; the narrator of the novel, one of the crew, has loved his mates and his work. Although he scarcely appears as an "I," he is one of the five men who rescue Wait from death when the *Narcissus* all but capsizes, submerging the cabin that is Wait's sick bay. Wait must be dug out, or rather torn out, from the portion of deck that remains above the water line. The agony of his delivery, for himself and for the men, in bitter cold, and with the sailors lashed to the ship against the force of the hurricane wind, is a kind of Caesarean section. The dying man is born again. But the ship, as well as its 26-member crew, is moribund. They are a doomed industrial form, a technology being superseded by steam power. The ship survives the overwhelming storm, but the city in which she comes to rest is compared to "a vision of disaster" (122), a fitting terminal. Her arrival is again an ending: "*The Narcissus* came gently into her berth; . . . She had ceased to live" (123).

The labor on board is presented by Conrad as a struggle to rescue life from impairment. To paraphrase the never-say-die cook (who is also an evangelical Christian), "as long as [the *Narcissus*] swims" (64) an absolute commitment to survival is in order. If death shoulders the sailors with a burden, they must take it on, and make it productive. In contrast to the community of labor, dying is solitary work. The work of Wait's delivery is not solitary but it is not solid. Labor builds achievements to make a life-and-death difference in the world. Racism perversely echoes labor in making black-and-white distinctions.

But work is at best an idealization or an ever-unrealized hope of creative effect. The hope unfortunately falls back into invidious discriminations.

Conrad's preface forecasts the novel's drama about the fragility of labor, the sense that all constructive doing verges on undoing. It imagines the reader watching "the motions of a labourer in a distant field" (8). Those motions imply a straining effort, but that effort is seen to fail. "In a brotherly frame of mind, we may bring ourselves to forgive his failure," Conrad comments about the distant toil. "We forgive, go on our way – and forget" (8). Conrad's sentence forecasts what the novel's narrator will say of the crew's work. Lest we think that in this image of labor Conrad is condescendingly distant from the workers whom time – another ocean – will drown, the preface likens the artist's labor, and the artist's attempt to stave off mortality, to the crew's: "And so it is with the workman of art. . . . Success is very far off. . . . And thus, . . . we talk a little about . . . the aim of art, which, like life itself, is . . . obscured by mists" (8).

Given Conrad's involvement of work and writing with narcissism and death, his narrative's relation to the rights of man requires attention. Donkin's complaints about the unjust exploitation of workers begin as soon as he steps on board. His coddling of Jimmy exhibits his intuition, obviously confirmed by the narrative, that race and class categories intersect. After the ship survives the storm, and as Wait's death is momentarily expected, Donkin tries to foment a mutiny; in the dark of night he pitches a belaying pin at his captain's head. The captain faces down the assault, rightly betting that Donkin does not have the courage, or the influence on his fellows, to sustain revolt. Donkin's rebelliousness is tainted. That his complaints are opportunistic and hypocritical is proved by his taunts of Jimmy as the man dies, and by his theft of the dead man's property.

If a reader makes an analysis of the novel turn on Donkin as if Conrad's portrait of him signals Conrad's contempt for human rights, the analysis will overly simplify the text. That Donkin is a liar does not mean that human rights are lies. The narrator identifies "the rage and fear of [Donkin's] disregarded right to live" (76). Although Donkin's emotions dishearten his co-workers, the events of the novel argue that a right to live cannot be disregarded. Wait has a right to live even on his deathbed, and his fellow workers risk their own lives to secure it. Yet the narrative also suggests that this right is not identical with, and not to be measured by, political rights.

Death's proximity to life suggests that life is a chance and momentary phenomenon. If that is so – the possibility is plausible – any political order, even the best political order, cannot govern, let alone reach, elemental aspects of experience. The crew's work during nature's onslaught on their *polis* – the boat – is as good a demonstration as any of human rights at their best as well as at their limits. Wait's liberty, and the crew's, is inextricable from bonds of labor and support that simultaneously inhibit liberty. As the men rescue Wait, they are tied down to the ship's sides and to one another. The officers are not free, either. The captain recognizes his need to submit to Donkin's rage and fear, rather than punish Donkin for them. Conrad suggests – again via a play with orthography and sound – that the officers are death's subjects, too, as vulnerable as are Donkin and Wait. The chief mate is continually clearing his throat with an "Ough!" sound, as if he were participating Wait's tubercular cough.

In his later novel *Nostromo* (1904), Conrad might be said to revisit his picture of human rights in *The Nigger of the "Narcissus."* *Nostromo*'s vast canvas portrays an imaginary South American republic. Its republican order is dominated by global investment capital, and its leading capitalists in effect (but not in legal form) enslave the working-class hero, Nostromo. Instead of maintaining a solidarity with his fellow have-nots, Nostromo accepts being bought and sold by capitalism in exchange for the pursuit of what he takes to be his individual rights. Personal narcissism facilitates his acceptance. The result is shown by the novel to be disastrous for him and his democratic heritage. Equally disastrous in *Nostromo* is global capitalism. Its corrosive power is exhibited as an effect of the highest form of humanity's self-love. But no more than the crew of the *Narcissus* or Nostromo can capitalism surmount the "difficult and evanescent" human condition. Capitalism, too, is, and will be, a passing episode in history. Accordingly, the writer's task, as the preface says, is "to arrest, for the space of a breath, the hands busy about the work of the earth." The writer's hands, however busy in recording impressions of others' handiwork as well as his own, can reveal them only in terms of "a moment of vision, a smile, a sigh – and the return to an eternal rest," because "all the truth of life is there" (9).

Ford Madox Ford, *A Man Could Stand Up* – (1926)

Ford's Impressionist method is given a tour de force demonstration in his tetralogy of novels, *Parade's End* (1924–1928). *A Man Could Stand Up* –, the climactic novel in whose very title the dash signals an interruption, is about the Great War's interruption of an incipient love affair. The lovers are Christopher Tietjens, the younger son of an ancient English landholding family, and Valentine Wannop, the daughter of a female novelist who was dear to Tietjens's late father. The war is not the only disruptive force. Tietjens is miserably married to an adulterous wife. Because she is a Roman Catholic (he is not), she will not divorce her husband despite her adulteries. Tietjens, in contrast, does not commit adultery (the first novel of the tetralogy is *Some Do Not . . .*). Although he is a figure of rectitude, Tietjens has a knack for getting into situations that make him look the opposite. One of those situations is his love of Valentine, who in far-flung gossip is taken to be his mistress. He has not communicated with her for the two years he has been at the front, but both lovers continue to long for each other.

Life, like longing, is complemented by Impressionism's "indirect, inter-rupted method."[2] Not until slap in the middle of Ford's novel does one arrive at a sentence that in pre-modernist fiction would have constituted a first page: "In the complete tranquility and inaction of an April morning with a slight westerly breeze, Tietjens realized that he was experiencing . . . the emotions of an army practically in flight."[3] The April morning is chronologically the earliest day in this volume of the tetralogy. But Ford's idea of fiction means that the novel cannot begin in April 1918, because life in time is always – for Ford – a whirligig of phenomena that are as much out of time as in it.

Ellipsis marks are a constant on Ford's pages, conveying typographically the prevalence of interruption. The interruptive method motivates Ford's decision to initiate the first part of *A Man Could Stand Up* – on November 11, 1918, the end of the war, but then to set the middle of the novel in the previous April, before returning in the novel's last part to Armistice Day. Nevertheless, with almost maddening treatment, at the same time that the middle of *A Man Could Stand Up* – is an interruption of the narrative's forward progress, the middle is also strictly sequential. It begins 32 minutes before a German counterattack on the trenches in which Tietjens is the acting commanding officer. So exact is Ford's representation of the sequence that the reader moves through the countdown minute by minute, without interrup-tion. The continuity takes almost 50 pages to cover.

The forward motion of the clock is counterpointed by the freely associated thoughts in Tietjens's head. They flow in and around outward circumstance. The narration rarely has the external objectivity of view that produces "In the complete tranquility and inaction of an April morning" and its kin. In a typical moment – the middle of a telephone call (with frequent interruption of transmission) to Valentine on November 11 – Valentine's thought is reported by the narrator in a way that fuses the narrator's externality, temporal suspension, and Valentine's talking to herself:

> But perhaps you were not always with yourself spiritually; you went
> on explaining how to breathe without thinking of how the life you

were leading was influencing your . . . What? Immortal soul? Aura?
Personality? . . . Something!

   Well, for two years . . . Oh, *call* it two years, for goodness' sake,
and get it over! . . . she must have been in . . . well, call *that* a "state
of suspended animation" and get that over too! A sort of what they
called inhibition. She had been inhibiting – *pro*hibiting – herself
from thinking about herself. Well, hadn't she been right? What had
a b—y Pro-German to think about in an embattled, engrossed,
clamouring nation, especially when she had not much liked her
brother-Pro's! A solitary state, only to be dissolved by . . . maroons!
In suspension!   (519)

In modernist narration such as this, questions, surmises, musings, unsettled
thoughts, and feelings overtake telling. To reproduce "the haze of life" is the
Impressionist-inspired motive.

   At the front the men under Tietjens's command – men whose class origins
are below his – admire his ability to create order, think of him as an insider
(whereas his class equals consider him an outsider), and tell him admiringly,
"You're a law hunto yourself!" (571). They mean that he stands apart from the
law and the lawlessness the war exemplifies. As Ford describes it, it is a chaos
that devours whole peoples for aims that, behind a democratic mask, are
purely power-mongering. One's nation is no less an enemy than the enemy.
"The people at home" (612) exert harassing demands on the soldiers. Tietjens,
who has experienced it without letup, desires an opportunity to resist the
chaos. When the strafe begins, he feels encouraged "to realize that he was a fit
person to take responsibility" (561).

   The previous novels justify his realization. But history and social order as
Ford portrays them sap the individual and collective virtue needed for their
redemption. Even by such efforts as that made by Tietjens, the collective
condition cannot be managed any longer by individual rectitude. Tietjens is
haunted by an earlier episode in the preceding novel (*No More Parades*
[1925]). In that incident he refused to grant leave to a cuckolded soldier,
because the soldier was likely to be killed by his wife's lover. The almost
immediate outcome of the refusal – the irony of responsibility – was the
soldier's being killed by the Germans. When Tietjens takes command in April
1918, he experiences such an irony again. As soon as the strafe begins, the
trench in which Tietjens is standing is blown up. He escapes injury but must
rescue a young subaltern, Aranjuez, from the mud in which the explosion has
buried the latter. The rescue is a success. As Tietjens carries Aranjuez in his
arms away from the site, however, a sniper's bullets hit Aranjuez in the face
and blind him.

How is it possible responsibly to escape the blinding force of history? A symptom of the internecine war at home is that almost as soon as the strafe ends, Tietjens is relieved of his command: exactly the communal responsibility he wants. His own godfather, a top-ranking general motivated by professional and erotic jealousy, has betrayed him. The road to a renewed collective, beyond the accountability of lovers and immediate friends to each other, is blocked.

The long-frustrated desire of the lovers is resolved when they meet in London in the novel's last third. Their coupling, however, must also break with the past, including the public and historical traditions that have nurtured them. The intelligence, learning, and courtesy that characterize Tietjens and Valentine are their inheritances: his, from the feudal loyalty and duty to retainers that mark his family heritage; hers, from the enlightened scholarship and imaginative writing that are exemplified by her Victorian parents' vocational pursuits. Both Tietjens and Valentine must become persons of the present. In 1918, the past, despite its noble endowment of present remnants, can function only as an impulse to depart from it.

The formal interruptions that constitute Ford's method of narrative treatment match Tietjens's desire that he and Valentine interrupt – permanently – their attachment to the social order. For Tietjens to accept his inheritance would mean harnessing himself to growing "richer and richer and richer" (635) – to a profit-driven end that is an economic face of perpetual war. Committing himself to a life in decent poverty, he will put his learned good taste to work in an antique furniture business. Moreover, whereas his estate would require a "Quality" (635) woman to be his wife, Tietjens's future modest living space will be shared by Valentine only. His feudal manners are displaced onto the camaraderie, freed of class bias, that marks the company sharing the reunion night. A motley crew of Tietjens's soldiers, including the blinded young man, drop into Tietjens's London quarters. In effect, they celebrate the end of older orders of authority. The event reaches a climax when Tietjens must stand up to Valentine's mother, because Mrs. Wannop, true to Victorian disapproval of "irregular unions" (661) – meaning sexual relations out of wedlock – pleads with him not to set up house with her daughter until he is divorced. Tietjens's anti-Victorian, modernist struggle with Mrs. Wannop takes place during the course of a phone call, an event that parallels the interruptive telephone in the narrative's first chapter. Tietjens leaves the phone, resolved to sleep with Valentine that night.

The resolution means that Tietjens ends by doing what "some [including himself] do not" do in the tetralogy's first installment. Yet the new likeness between him and others is also a difference. Tietjens's distaste for adultery – for its surrender to fleshly self-indulgence – has not waned. He desires

Valentine for her "exact intellect" and for being "someone to talk to" (607). In her, the raw force of eros, sexily diffused, is refined into spirit. The refinement exemplifies Ford's way of showing a departure from the past that is also an opportunity for reinventing it. If adultery is an aristocratic tradition, and a fictional tradition, Ford's portrayal of Tietjens's and Valentine's break with them is nevertheless a new version of romance. The lovers are the most intelligent and the most romantic couple in English modernism.

The modernist novelist extricates social custom and literary form from their previous anchors in historical practice. The present world order fore-closes a return to what was. But the interruptive, hazy, and shimmering method in Ford's practice takes an inheritance and makes it new. If past values are to be exercised again, they have to be redirected toward as yet untried modes of experiment. Tietjens and Valentine, however romantically, figure for Ford the advance guard of discovery.

Virginia Woolf, *The Waves* (1931)

The Waves exemplifies Woolf's attempt (on the prophetic axis) to materialize the future of fiction. The future will be relatively story-less. "What are stories?" asks Bernard, one of the six protagonists of the novel, who might be construed as a surrogate for his author. "I begin to doubt if there are stories," he continues. "There are facts ... but beyond it all is darkness and conjecture."[4] As an alternative to identifying facts of life with narrative, *The Waves* provides an ensemble of lyric utterances. In the long wake of *A Portrait of the Artist as a Young Man*, the prose lyric in Woolf's work facilitates a discourse attuned more than narrative to darkness and conjecture. The latter are presented as the essence of consciousness. The waves of Woolf's title are those of the ocean, but they also are thought-waves, forming and breaking on the shores (and limits) of self. "The streamers of my consciousness," as one of the characters describes it, "waver out and are perpetually torn and distressed by their disorder" (93). Despite the disorder, the characters establish a meditative as well as a lyric discourse in response to life and death. Is *The Waves* finally a novel, or a poem, or a sequence of essays? It wonderfully takes shape, building the future of fiction, as a modernist hybrid of generic expectations.

The Waves reduces to a minimum events that ordinarily structure stories. The sun's diurnal passage, the ebb and flow of ocean, two reunion dinners over the course of 20 years, Percival's death, Bernard's marriage and father-hood, Neville's recovery from the loss of his beloved Percival, Rhoda's affair with Louis, Rhoda's suicide: those phrases name "what happens." But to say so magnifies things that the text mentions rather than represents. The text unfolds as a waiting for events. If there is history in *The Waves*, it is pared to bare sequences of light and sound, and to a banal compulsion suffered by the characters. Their history or story is that they merely must go on. The knocking together of "railway trucks in a siding" is offered as a figure for their progress: "Knock, knock, knock. Must, must, must. Must go, must sleep, must wake, must get up" (234). Bernard blesses the compulsion, because without its requirement of consecutive forward movement "we should be undone" (234). The compulsory sequence belongs to fiction's prior modes of consequential storytelling and of historically realist characterization. In the novelists whom Woolf scolded – Bennett and Galsworthy – we have seen characters stand in for their historical environments. *The Waves* is not a historical novel.

By deflating history Woolf achieves the alternative characterization she hoped for. There are six characters in search of a life in *The Waves*, but their delineation as characters, like the delineation of life, is evanescent. The characters are not sure of who or what they are. "Myself," Bernard thinks, comes and goes, definitely indefinite; "what I call 'my life' is not one life that I look back upon; I am not one person; I am many people; I do not altogether know who I am – Jinny, Susan, Neville, Rhoda, or Louis [the novel's other protagonists]; or how to distinguish my life from theirs" (276). The collective identity is also conjectural, because its components are shaky, or repudiated by some of its separable owners. Neville asks Bernard, "Who am I?" (83); Rhoda cannot feel herself to be either an individuated self or a collective one; Susan and Louis define themselves as outsiders, and undergo spasms of self-hatred as a result; Jinny exists more as an impulsive body ("[M]y imagination is the body's," she says [220]) than as a psyche. A seventh character, Percival, is not a protagonist but rather a screen on which the others project a fantasy of selfhood as an achieved entity. Percival's fantastic status is corroborated by his inability to survive: posted to India as a colonial administrator, he is accidentally killed soon after he lands on imperial soil. Given Percival's romance-derived name, his death means that quest narratives, or their echoes, are moribund designs for living. His demise also suggests that the characters have no trustworthy national or imperial ground to stand on, any more than they have selves to trust.

The verbal means whereby Woolf liberates characterization from the conventions of historical realism in fiction is remarkable. The characters speak to themselves, and hence indirectly to the reader, about what they think and feel about the "events" and about each other. Except for two minor moments in which the characters appear to converse (Neville presents a poem to Bernard, Rhoda and Louis confer), there is no dialogue. Moreover, although we might expect a novel called *The Waves* to give a "stream of consciousness" that is relatively formless or anti-formal, Woolf's work does not. Despite being described as torn and distressed, the characters typically use distinct modes of expression. They treat their topics – "life," selfhood, and meaning – in articulate periods, studded with elaborate noncolloquial metaphor or simile.

A random excerpt from one of Bernard's monologues typifies Woolf's texture:

> We have been walking for hours it seems. But where? I cannot remember. I am like a log slipping smoothly over some waterfall. I am not a judge. I am not called upon to give my opinion. Houses and trees are all the same in this grey twilight. Is that a post? Is that a woman walking? Here is the station, and if the train were to cut me in two, I should come together on the further side, being one, being indivisible. But what is odd is that I still clasp the return half of my ticket to Waterloo firmly between the fingers of my right hand, even now, even sleeping.   (235)

Bernard's well-formed sentences, and his sententiousness, do not constitute a vulgate. He speaks an artificial discourse, as do the five others. Moreover, as the prose assigned Bernard meditates on concrete things – a post, a person – it (through him) does not situate them concretely ("But where?" "Is that a post?"). Perhaps the grey twilight, by submerging distinctions, is the equivalent of a stream of consciousness. But the final sentence, while evoking a firm fingerhold, tends toward abstracted disembodiment. The narrating "I" is asleep, but outside of his body inasmuch as he can still report his condition. The novel does not give us the haze or shimmering that life is, even as it tempts us to think it does. Prophetic of a mode of post-impressionist visual art, Woolf moves the treatment of her characters' utterances toward a uniform abstract expressionism.

Despite the abstract uniformity of Woolf's prose, the six characters are distinguished by what their monologues emphasize: Bernard's ever-failing attempts at storytelling interwoven with his unfailing sociability, Jinny's addiction to flirtation, Susan's commitment to motherhood and rural life, Louis's ashamed harping on his Australian origins, Neville's yearning solitude, Rhoda's bottomless insecurity. When all the voices but Bernard's cease in the last segment of *The Waves*, another result of Woolf's experimentation is effected: the reader feels shocked, made to miss the voices that, in their mode of expression at least, are the same as Bernard's, and hence are not missing.

Does Bernard speak for all of them, in a way justified by the uniformity? If a voice that lives on speaks for voices that are gone, are survival and extinction an intertwined process?

Intertwined though they be, Woolf's novel keeps in front of its readers the gap between its own formal artifice and the wavering phenomena of life and death. As the ocean evoked at the start of each chapter surges against the lyric and essayistic conjectures it inspires, Woolf offers her idiosyncratic reinvention of fiction as a defense against dissolution. Louis figures the defense as "a steel ring of clear poetry" (128). Visual art is another shield. Bernard, learning about Percival's death at the same time as his son is born, is reminded of the "knocking on" of life's progress. He suddenly finds insupportable "one thing [leading] to another – the usual order" (155). Hoping to "submit myself to the influence of minds like mine outside the sequence" (155), he enters an art museum. He is unsure if consoling ocular impressions can be derived from the paintings, but he thinks there might be something "unvisual beneath" (156). And there is. "Something is added," he feels in the presence of the pictures. "Something lies deeply buried. For one moment I thought to grasp it. But bury it, bury it; let it breed, hidden in the depths of my mind some day to fructify" (157). Bernard steps out of the museum, back into "the machine" of compulsions, but Woolf's fiction insistently values his instant of escape. Rhoda, too, while considering the death of Percival, is oppressed by her involvement with mortality: "I . . . shall sink with no one to save me" (160). Yet she is saved by a vision equivalent to Bernard's. In the depths of the waves of appearance she glimpses "the thing that lies beneath semblance[s]. . . . The structure is now visible; what is inchoate is here stated" (163).

To refer experience to art, and to find consolation in art's visible and invisible structures, Rhoda concludes, amounts to making a "dwelling-place" (164) for freedom from "must, must, must." Her idea (and Woolf's) of a unity of structure and statement, of form and content, is a version of modernism's commitment to fiction's autonomy.

Chapter 3

Seeing Modernism Through

Seeing Periodization Through

"Periodization" is most justifiable, I've proposed, when and where it bases itself on innovations of artistic "treatment." Despite H. G. Wells's antagonism to his fellow modernists, he, too, is swept up in formal experiments that deliberately break the mold of practice. His Great War novel, *Mr. Britling Sees It Through* (1916), rejects conventional narrative unity. It starts out as a comic self-portrait (Wells as Britling), but ends in painful sadness. Britling has always neglected his son, until – to his subsequent shame and grief – the young man, in his letters home from the trenches, reveals himself as an extraordinary person. On the one hand, by making the son become a major character only just before he dies at the front, Wells violates James's or Lubbock's ideas about how to construct fiction artfully. On the other hand, Wells' violation in effect agrees with his antagonists' modernist aims: to propel "treatment" emphatically against the grain of expectations.

Britling, once he is bereft, strives in a parallel way. He swears he will see the war through to the end by doing or writing something so radically striking that it will prevent future holocausts. He wants to do so in order to "set up the peace of the World Republic amidst these ruins. Let it be our religion, our calling."[1] Yet he cannot find or devise an adequate form or utterance for what he wants, so that he becomes exasperated by his "tinpot style," "his incomplete control of . . . rebel words and phrases that came trailing each its own associations and suggestions to hamper his purpose" (428). His writing falls apart into non-narrative fragments. But he maintains his will to move beyond the strangled meanings that result from stereotyped thought and emotion.

To expand the resources of expression is one motive of the experiments in fiction that we continue to survey. Their modes of treatment promise an answerable style – the right words and the right forms at last – for our ultimate concerns, in the same way that the hope of adequate expression compels Britling to go on writing. The present chapter unfolds further the interest in the relation of topical subject matter – derived from history – to the modernist era's fictive inventions. To begin with, a striking reminder of the grounds for "periodizing" is afforded us by a comparative sampling of a modernist specimen – an excerpt from Wyndham Lewis's story collection, *The Wild Body* (1922–1927) – with a Victorian fictional text, George Gissing's *The Nether World* (1889). "In the troubled twilight of a March evening ten years ago," Gissing begins,

> an old man, whose equipment and bearing suggested that he was fresh from travel, walked slowly across Clerkenwell Green, and by the graveyard of St. James's Church stood for a moment looking about him. His age could not be far from seventy, but, despite the stoop of his shoulders, he gave little sign of failing under the burden of years; his sober step indicated a gravity of character rather than bodily feebleness, and his grasp of a stout stick was not such as bespeaks need of support. His attire was neither that of a man of leisure, nor of the kind usually worn by English mechanics. Instead of coat and waistcoat, he wore a garment something like a fisherman's guernsey, and over this a coarse short cloak, picturesque in appearance as it was buffeted by the wind. His trousers were of moleskin; his boots reached almost to his knees; for head-covering he had the cheapest kind of undyed felt, its form exactly that of the old petasus. To say that his aspect was venerable would serve to present him in a measure, yet would not be wholly accurate, for there was too much of past struggle and present anxiety in his countenance to permit full expression of the natural dignity of his features. It was a fine face and might have been distinctly noble, but circumstance had marred the purpose of Nature; you perceived that his cares had too often been of the kind which are created by ignoble necessities, such as leave to most men of his standing a bare humanity of visage.[2]

Gissing's paragraph epitomizes Victorian realism, and hence is tied to an historicizing model of representation. "Ten years ago" signals a dependence on a temporal reality that for this narrative will be primary; the focus on the old man's age reinforces the framework. The descriptions of his clothing, highlighting class-related components, refer to the groupings that the nineteenth century understood to be sociohistorical fact, reflected by fiction; the man's very face, with its conflicts and continuities between past and present, is the flesh of history. Inasmuch as the old man "looks about him," he seems to be seeking direction; he doubles the reader's looking about to find out where the story is, where it is going, and how the old man fits it. The discovery of fit, the paragraph implies, will be a matter of further historical explanation. Nevertheless, if the story discovers the old man as a person who escapes defining conditions, another possibility of "fit" shows itself. "Nature" makes it possible, or will make it possible, for both "you" the reader and the precisely objective narrator to discover in the man a dignified "bare humanity of visage." Gissing's opening implies that narrative fiction is a journey to either historical or natural truth.

At the opening of Lewis's "Bestre," the narrator, walking along a quayside in Brittany, notices "an athletic Frenchwoman, of the bourgeois class"[3] behind him. The following paragraphs describe her and the narrator:

> The crocket-like floral postiches on the ridges of her head-gear looked crisped down in a threatening way: her nodular pink veil was an apoplectic gristle round her stormy brow; steam came out of her lips upon the harsh white atmosphere. Her eyes were dark, and the contiguous colour of her cheeks of a redness quasi-venetian, with something like the feminine colour of battle. This was surely a feline battle-mask, then; but in such a pacific and slumberous spot I thought it an anomalous ornament.
>
> My dented *bidon* of a hat – cantankerous beard – hungarian boots, the soles like the rind of a thin melon slice, the uppers in stark calcinous segments; my cassock-like blue broadcloth coat (why was I like this – the habits of needy travel grew this composite shell), this uncouthness might have raised in her question of defiance and offence. I glided swiftly along on my centipedal boots, dragging my eye upon the rough walls of the houses to my right like a listless cane. Low houses faced the small vasey port. It was there I saw Bestre. (77)

The narrator sees Bestre through the latter's kitchen window, from which Bestre is looking out. The narrator then describes Bestre's

> dumb bulk. His tongue stuck out, his lips eructated with the incredible indecorum that appears to be a monopoly of liquids, his brown arms were for the moment genitals, snakes in one massive twist beneath his mammillary slabs, gently riding up on a pancreatic swell, each hair on his oil-bearing skin contributing its message of porcine affront. (78)

The opening pages of Lewis's story escape Gissing's historical referents and their explanatory promise. That the "Frenchwoman" is a bourgeoise is quickly passed over. Instead of characterizing the woman, Bestre, and the narrator in a way that emphasizes class or time, Lewis introduces each of his protagonists as a collage of disparate things. Whereas Gissing's enumeration of the old man's clothes and person enlists our attempt to arrive at the human inside of the outward appearance, Lewis's catalog stays on the outside surface of things, insisting on externalization: the objectification of emotion as bodily gristle, for example. As for "bare humanity," in Lewis there is more bare nonhumanity than otherwise. "This composite shell" can apply to all the description, as well as to the narration. The vegetable and mineral elements in the narrator's clothing are made prominent – and grotesque; the insect boots add to the weirdness. The narrator himself is a nonhuman heap, whose very organs are not part of a unity: he drags his eye along as if it were a prosthetic device. Are the narrator and Bestre doubles? The clothes, the limbs, the bodies, and the selves in the scene are exchangeable or interchangeable parts.

It is a scene, of course, of eros and aggression, of drives as definite as the old man in Gissing is indefinite. Yet while love and hate are palpable, it is not at all clear what narrative, or what story, they suggest. Do they usher in a tale of the same Nature that Gissing refers to? Bestre is "porcine," meatily masculine, meatily feminine ("his mammillary slabs"), and simultaneously dissolute, a liquid. Self-contradictorily, liquid expresses itself in terms of human economy and manners; it is monopolistically "indecorous." Yet it is not aggressive: the waterside is "pacific and slumberous," whereas the first note of aggression in the story is sounded by the woman's architectural hat, an armory-like ally of the woman's "battle-mask."

Playing on the identification of humanity with savagery that characterizes nineteenth-century literary naturalism, Lewis revises naturalism by exhibiting the involvement of nature and artifice. He also revises realism, by constructing a descriptive language that dissociates itself from the historical terms that underwrite Gissing. Linguistic artifice is becoming an event in itself, or perhaps an invention of an alternative world. Construction of that alternative, in the form of the writer's treatment of his treatment (as it were), subordinates or replaces storytelling – and historical telling. Of course, while Lewis can, in this way, be seen to undo a Victorian novelistic mode, his description also replaces Impressionist streams of consciousness. He aims to make the reader figure language and art as an anomalous ornament and composite shell for the sake of the laughter-inducing "wild nihilism" that we have seen him identify with art.

Lewis's experimentation is the result of a struggle like Britling's – or Conrad's or Joyce's or Ford's or Woolf's – to leave behind stereotyped thought, emotion, and utterance. The good of it inheres in the possibility that *The Wild Body* corrects misleading views of the world. What if Gissing's (and the Victorians') enlistment of fiction for the purposes of intensifying historical awareness is not an ultimate way of knowing, or of explaining social order, or of "situating" the topics that concern us? What if it is not truthfully expressive? It is odd, to be sure, to think of fiction as revealing truth. We might say, however, that fictions furnish us with theories of what is true, rather than with truth itself, and that they remind us that we live our theories, perhaps unconsciously, but depending nevertheless upon their intermixture with our empirical concerns. If the experiments of modernist fiction cannot change those realities – because the latter are too formidable – the experiments might help us see them through. The ability or the promise of identifying the experiments is one of the strategic strengths of periodization.

Seeing through the Condition of Women

Inasmuch as we understand fiction to be a realistic register of historical truth, to which invention is subordinated (if we assume, in other words, that a Victorian paradigm of fictional "treatment" is applicable to modernist-era work), five novels about women – Arnold Bennett's *Anna of the Five Towns* (1902), E. M. Forster's *Howards End* (1910), May Sinclair's *Mary Olivier* (1919) and *The Life and Death of Harriet Frean* (1922), and James Joyce's *Ulysses* (1922) – offer us a mixed report on the historical actuality of women's freedom. Bennett's Anna is financially independent, but her wealth derives from her father, who remains (with the moral support of Methodist evangelicalism) a sleeping partner in all her dealings. She rebels against him, to the point of committing a financial fraud on behalf of a pair of debtors he is ruining – one of whom she is in love with. But her rebellion fails. Destroyed by patriarchal tyranny, Anna remains a wealthy woman, with multiple rooms of her own, but the bleakness of her existence is unqualified. Sinclair's Harriet is a like case. When she dies in 1912 (she was born in the 1840s), she has been clinging for decades to the security of Victorian upper-middle-class morality and comfort in which her parents enfolded her. They trained her to "always behave beautifully,"[4] and she has proudly exemplified beautiful behavior by not marrying the man she desired. Inwardly, however, she hates the self-sacrifice. It cripples her emotionally and intellectually.

Anna and Harriet should have been modernist women! But their fates have not been inevitable, or even typical, to judge by the three other novels. Mary Olivier, born in the 1860s, is early on, *pace* the difference between Victorianism and modernism, another feminist rebel. She defends her freethinking aunt against her father's censure. Doggedly educating herself and choosing an intellectual life, by 1910 Mary has placed her inhibitions behind her. A lyric poet and a translator of Greek tragedy, she has a liaison out of wedlock with a classics scholar, whom she loves. But she rejects marriage with him clear-sightedly: for her, neither eros nor marriage is the end of life, or its anchor. Forster's heroines in *Howards End* predict Mary's outcome. They are two deeply tried young sisters, who emerge as models of feminist achievement.

Initially, because their father is German, they have the advantage of his detachment from English mores; because he leaves them orphans, their independence has another head start. Ultimately, one sister becomes the owner of her businessman husband's estate, thereby disinheriting his bullying, imperialist-minded sons from his first marriage. The other sister is a single mother, proudly raising her illegitimate infant. These free women are both England's heirs in 1910 and its future. The most free of the fictional women, however, is Joyce's Irish Molly Bloom. She is an unqualified home ruler: loving her husband, mothering a daughter, and guiltlessly committing adultery. Joyce assigns her to 1904, an early date for her assured mix of domesticity, sexual promiscuity, and feminist power. Her roots, her modernist matrix, is Victorian.

If Harriet and Molly have hypothetical counterparts in reality, it is not easy to sort out which of them should be thought of as more historical, and which as more fictive. On the one hand, the represented lives confirm a clearly differentiating periodization; on the other hand, their imaginary histories blur the difference between what comes before and what comes after. That the history of the novel offers female types and antitypes within the same twenty years' span implies at least a complexly real social referent, at once conservative and revolutionary.

What we might gather most surely from the realist side of the novels is that women's historical achievement of freedom is as yet uncertain. That uncertainty persists in fiction in the 1930s. Three novellas by Storm Jameson, collected as *Women against Men* (1933), speculate that "People who were born a little before 1900 belong to no age. The old one had dried, and it split round them before they could accustom themselves to it, and the new one was not ready."[5] That is one reason why the stories evoke simultaneous premodernist, modernist, and post-modernist scenarios. The working-class protagonist of "A Day Off" had a better life before the Great War, even though her husband exploited her. Now a traveling salesman has been keeping her, but he and his checks are no longer showing up. The destitute woman, given her dependence on the power and whims of men, might as well be living in the previous century. But that is not at all the case for the protagonist of "The Single Heart." The daughter of a wealthy shipping magnate, she is a liberated modernist, contracting marriage with one man and regularly committing adultery with another, whose children she raises in her husband's home. When her husband dies, she marries her lover, a Labor MP. A convert to socialism herself, she works tirelessly to electrify slum dwellings, and to further her husband's career, including the career of his philandering – with her best friend, then with a female Tory. The latter liaison brings him to the brink of ruin, but his wife saves him. Under the strain, however, her heart gives out. For all her modernism, male-centered domination conforms her life to the grip of the patriarchal past.

By comparison, the first of the novellas in *Women against Men*, "Delicate Monster," more fully comprehends the unevenness of experiences that do not follow an expected progress of periods. Perhaps the title refers to what novels are: monstrous fusions of fiction and historical fact, yet delicately artful in their rendering of the amalgam. This possibility is justified inasmuch as the narrative is about two contemporary women novelists – that is, producers of such a genre. One of them, another likely match for the title, is glamorous Victoria, a best-selling author of sexy fiction, whose personal life is dedicated to sexual freedom (i.e., promiscuity). The other novelist (and also a literary agent), Fanny, is less successful and acts as the narrator. She and Victoria have been friends from childhood, when their lower-middle-class mothers brought them together. Their involvement surmounts a ten-year break that followed Fanny's discovery of Victoria's affair with Fanny's husband. When they reconcile, Fanny realizes that she is grateful. She had never really desired marriage, so Victoria's treachery gave Fanny an opportunity to write books and arrange her life in peace. Paradoxically, Victoria's promiscuity is retro-grade: "a reformed phallic worship," Fanny thinks, "with a different emblem and [thanks] to Dr. [Marie] Stopes" (the evangelist of birth control). The ancient worship was "both terrible and jolly," Fanny continues, "but what is there terrible or jolly about a lady novelist having a blood awareness of – say – a stockbroker?" (15). "Delicate Monster" thus portrays a sophisticated free woman as rather a throwback – Victoria-n, after all.

More surprisingly, the novella portrays the youngest generation of women as justly critical of their feminist mothers. Victoria's daughter at nineteen is giving up university and settling into married life. The mother finds her son-in-law as tedious as monogamy, and she labors to find a seducer of Camilla. Her plots don't succeed. Fanny accepts Camilla, but admits: "It still seems incredible . . . that a young quick-witted woman can be satisfied by a life only superficially different from the life of her Victorian grandmother" (57). Camilla's justifications appear trustworthy, however. She satirizes her mother's generation as "war wrecks who can afford to be immoral. We haven't the excuse of a war" (59). Moreover, her mother is "nearly out of date. I haven't the slightest ambition," Camilla adds, "to lead what you would call a full life" (5).

Camilla seems to want to dispart the intermingling of eras exemplified in the older women. A sign of their intermingling is their shared laughter about the men they have married. The merriment exemplifies the age-old setting of women against men. Yet it does not represent men against women, as Jameson's two other stories do. The female figures in "Delicate Monster" are stronger than the men in their world, and their lives do not fit a pattern of exploitation. Camilla also is a work in progress – or, rather, progressive retrogression. The historical patterning is "off," and, therefore, so is the explanatory pattern. That is one effect of Jameson's juxtaposition of separate novellas. Their non-unified collocation signifies a modernist treatment. Fanny mocks modernist fiction. "If . . . you cease to be intelligible," she says sarcastically in describing the novel-writing of her experimental contemporaries, "so much the better. You will have avoided the meanness and shabbiness of a plain narrative" (41). One assumes that Jameson sees herself as writing plain narrative; that, predicting Cyril Connolly's criticism of Mandarins, she reverts to an earlier mode – shabby compared to Woolf's or Joyce's. Yet at the same time, Jameson, to judge by the external narrator's assessment in "The Single Heart" of "the stupidity of nine out of ten of our masters" (157), is on the progressive, anti-Victorianist side of history.

Modernist treatments do not make transparency easy to come by if one wants to see fiction through history or through simplifying versions of literary history. To be sure, if experimental form suggests a perspective outside of historical explanation – for example, outside of an intelligible genealogy of the ills suffered by an entire class of actual persons – an impaired prospect of amelioration might arise. Such a loss is broached in the novel *Quartet* (1928) by Jean Rhys, whose novels usually are identified as a feminist protest on behalf of women (on behalf of colonial women, too) against men. But *Quartet*'s heroine, Marya, suggests an ahistorical human ill.

Marya is an English chorus girl who marries a raffish Polish émigré in Paris. He deals in stolen goods, for which business he is imprisoned for a year. During that time Marya is taken up by an Anglo-German art dealer and his English painter wife. The legitimate man of business is no more licit than the criminal husband. With results that will be fatal, he makes Marya his mistress. She resists this relationship, then desires it; it makes her feel "absorbed . . . without thought perhaps for the first time in her life. No past. No future. Nothing but the present."[6] A stranger once frightened her by telling her that her face predicts her victimization, and that victims are necessary "so that the strong may exercise their will" (162). But neither that "explanation," nor a gender-conscious or genetic one, seems adequate. Marya's ensnaring personal quartet seems to express "How terrifying human beings were" (160). Her reason recognizes the terror, but can do no more than remain in shock at it: "She began to think how ridiculous it all was . . . [began to] think that she only imagined the love and hate she felt for those two [her lover and his wife], that she had only imagined that such emotions as love and hate existed at all" (181). If love and hate are not bedrock realities, then Marya's thinking might be said to strike at some of the securities of our existence. Fiction is an apt vehicle for expressing such troubling thought, not because the thinking is illusory but because other discourses – about morality or politics or history – obscure or foreclose its possible truth.

Whether troubling or not, indeed whether anchored in fact or not (the Impressionist method, for all its mimicry of instantaneous life, is an artifice), novels make it possible for a reader to get free of existing versions of worldly thought and judgment. That freedom, for those who value art's autonomy, is an end in itself, even though it is available for more practical use. We already have seen Woolf's effort to surpass other discourses, even the novel's, and even those (such as feminism) whose biases favor fiction's ameliorative intervention in history. Another foremost female author of modernist-era British fiction is Dorothy Richardson. Her experimental writing, a series of thirteen novels, *Pilgrimage* (1915–1963), precedes Joyce and Woolf's more famous work. Exemplary of modernist paradox, Richardson relies on her reinvention of fiction to make a transcendence of history possible and plausible.

To be sure, the material history of gender difference informs the series. The fourth installment, *The Tunnel* (1919), characteristically asserts, in the voice of Richardson's protagonist Miriam, the struggle of men against women. "Books were poisoned. Art. All the achievements of men were poisoned at the root. . . . [E]ven [in religion] there was no hope. . . . No future life could heal the degradation of having been a woman."[7] Miriam, reflecting on a performance of *The Merchant of Venice*, thinks Portia

> ought to have gone through all the law courts of the world; showing up
> the law. . . . The knowledge of women is larger, bigger, deeper, less
> wordy and clever than that of men. . . . Women do not respect law. No
> wonder, since it is folly, an endless play on words. . . . [Portia] had been
> invented by a man. There was no reality in any of
> Shakespeare's women.   (188)

Miriam's feminist scorn is fueled by her employer, the eligible bachelor dentist Dr. Hancock. The pair has worked together with great sympathy; outside of work, Hancock has introduced Miriam to leading intellectual circles in London. Then their friendship, a possibility of something more, is strained by the dentist's kin. Miriam and he are of the same class – but, after all, his kin sneer, she is a "secretary"! Hancock's receptivity to his family's snobbery alienates Miriam. The snobbery is for Richardson an offshoot of male vanity's gender organization and its companion, female complicity. Miriam's best emotional and intellectual resources are a pair of women friends who live unperturbed in an apartment dwelling owned by a mixed-race madam, whose sex workers also live in the building.

At her most combative, Miriam is self-critical. "Harshness must go," she thinks, because "I am like a man in that, overbearing, bullying, blustering." She needs to remember that "I am something between a man and a woman; looking both ways" (186). Nevertheless, the world feels "enclosed" (202). "Its terms were terms on which she could not live" (203). It comes to seem to her – and to her reader – that all social life amounts to a false "social method" (175), inauthentic personal and class "positions" (209). "There is something that is untouched by positions" (209).

Where is that "something," and how does one see it through to realization? Richardson's experiments with language and formal treatment open a modernist novel's pathway to answers. Miriam experiences what is untouched by positions ("something beyond the everlasting innuendo of social life and the everlasting smartness of business life" [26]) as a joyful surge of being, as a self-possessed freedom. "There is something more than anything that anybody says, that comes first, before they speak ... ; everybody in heaven without knowing it" (255, elisions in original). The joy of being endures; it shows itself in moments that have "no beginning or ending. ... In each one she had felt exactly the same; outside life, untouched by anything; free" (213). Hancock would never recognize Miriam's eternal moment of being, her "heaven" (107). He would need it rendered as "statements, things that had been agreed upon and disputed and that people bandied about, competing with each other to put them cleverly" (107). Miriam's alienation from society and history, from language-as-statement, is her advantage: it keeps her closer to cosmic essence.

Narrative fiction can be open to that essence only if its language, its eventfulness, and its narrative agents are radically revised. Like Wells (who was Richardson's lover for a while), Richardson is appalled by the prospect of a tinpot style. Language "is the only way of expressing anything and it dims everything" (99), Miriam thinks. To render what Miriam experiences, Richardson must transport language to the limits of its dim expressive capacity, and to all but omit events. One might think that, like explicit positions and statements, explicit events might clarify the compromises that ensnare men and women and life. *Pilgrimage*, however, implies that they falsify and obscure: they get in the way of "the something more" that is a domain of radical freedom. Likewise, a narrating self can get in the way. Thus, *Pilgrimage* sometimes, incalculably, employs Miriam as an *I*-narrator, sometimes employs an external narrator, and sometimes shares the narration between external and character-bound perspectives. These metamorphoses complement on a formal level Miriam's refusal of "positions" on the topical level.

To disclose – and invent – an essential reality, apart from what is ordinarily real, requires Richardson's innovations of fiction's "grammar." These innovations are the means of her quest (apt in a pilgrimage) for a doorway out of history. It takes thirteen novels, published over nearly fifty years, for the pilgrim Miriam's "story" to advance from the turn of the century to a point still before the Great War. If her progress occurs in slow motion, it is because *Pilgrimage*'s essential movement is not a matter of dates or eras; instead, what counts is the position-less reality behind those markers. Its "heaven" is the measure of the failure, even the hell, of gendered order in the historical world. If only the latter were more aware of the measure, and more trustful of the claim by Richardson's fiction that we are already in touch with it.

How the Working Class Comes Through

The material poverty of laborers seems scarcely attenuated between 1900 and 1930. At the same time, class mobility intensifies – both in upward directions and, for the classes above, in downward ones, in part because of the democratizing effects of World War I. Conflicting perspectives, in regard to stable and unstable working-class identity, shape much of modernist-era fiction. Should workers swear allegiance to what the Labor leader and novelist Ellen Wilkinson calls "working class patriotism,"[8] even if the patriots improve their conditions and move up in the world? Should political activists and theorists, and novelists, no matter their class origin, take a like oath as a prerequisite for historical engagement?

Without answering such questions, D. H. Lawrence's narratives provide a paradigm of possible attitudes toward them. When the sons of a coal miner in Lawrence's *Sons and Lovers* (1916) reject mining as their future, and pursue white-collar jobs or military service, their social mobility alienates their sire. In an early version of the novel, Lawrence imagined the father being moved to filicide in response to one son's disassociation from working-class identity. In the finished text the bloodshed is omitted, but the protagonist Paul, in part thanks to his artistic talents, vanquishes his father emotionally by rising above him in terms of learning and work. Lawrence mostly draws his reader into sympathy with Paul's rise. Nevertheless, Paul is guilt-ridden by the distance it puts between him and his father's labor and class. Paul might have been happier to share an equivalent of the fate of one of the daughters in

Lawrence's "Daughters of the Vicar" (1912). When she falls in love with a miner, against the grain of her genteel family's class prejudices, she insists on marrying the man. Her choice fuses eros with her sense that respect for labor is an obligatory act of social justice. In marrying downward in class terms, however, she forecasts the life of Paul's mother. She also married "below" her, for worse rather than for better, inasmuch as she comes to enact a higher-class contempt for her worker husband. The children tend to side with their mother against their father, as if wanting to reverse her descent. The resulting material and educational improvement of their lives can be read as a tale of class treachery.

How the working class can see its deprivations "through" inspires contrastive pictures from Wells and Bennett. The hero of Wells's *Kipps* (1905), an assistant in a draper's shop, discovers that he is the bastard of an aristocrat, who at the end of his life decides to leave his wealth to Kipps. Kipps prepares to become a lord, and affiances himself to a schoolteacher who grooms him for his new status. But the closer he comes to marriage and his inheritance, the more he feels self-alienated. He breaks his engagement – his fiancée is snobbish, and Kipps does not approve of life cast in the terms of a gentry wannabe. He refuses the legacy. In essence, Wells's narrative amounts to a model picture of working-class self-possession, and of the evils and unhappiness of social mobility – evils that include an unequal distribution of wealth. In contrast, the hero of Bennett's *The Card* (1911), Denry Machin, the son of a washerwoman, ends up as a self-made rich man and the mayor of Bursley (the hometown of Bennett's Anna). With a daredevil economic shrewdness that makes him a "card," a popular entertainer in effect, Denry reinvents himself profitably from moment to moment. He is a generous Midas who never does harm, however. Nor does his wealth corrupt his idea of a suitable spouse – he rejects a woman who is a social climber.

"What great cause is he identified with?" a local citizen wonders about Denry. Can it be the good of the working class to which Denry "patriotically" gives back as he soars upward? The narrator says that Denry's great cause is that of "cheering us all up."[9] The answer implies that Bennett is also a card – or that any novelist is like Denry, inasmuch as a fiction writer takes the barest occasion for invention (Denry is nothing, and has nothing, to begin with) and so thoroughly develops its interest that it becomes an antidote to financial and emotional depression. Moreover, it emerges as an antidote to class-consciousness, at least of the kind that insists on workers' patriotism.

Bennett intends Denry's good cheer, along with his comic wit, to call a truce to sociological conflicts. The Great War's effect on the novel's modernist era appears to do the opposite. It intensifies the desire to respect the working class's position, and to use narrative to stabilize its identity. Fictionalized versions of the battlefield assert the class patriotism as well as the pathos of the lower orders. In Henry Williamson's *The Patriot's Progress* (1930), John Bullock, a bank clerk descended from farm workers, endures the horrors of the front, intensified by his hatred of the strategists and politicians in charge. Bullock survives the war but loses a leg. His disability marks one gain: solidarity with the soldier workers who have been swindled by allegiance to their "betters." The commitment to resist "betterment" is pivotal in Fredric Manning's *The Middle Parts of Fortune* (1929). Manning's protagonist, Private Bourne, resists pressure to take up an officer's commission. He does not want to break his union with the common soldiers, the equivalents of the pre-war lower social ranks. They share anger at the all-determining authorities; yet, at the same time – and despite their rebelliousness – they share a conviction that "war was only the ultimate problem of all human life stated barely, and pressing for immediate solution."[10]

Another working class is also treated in British fiction of this era: the non-British working subjects of British imperialism. Some of those subjects turn novelists, and use fiction to report on labor conditions and class mobility (and immobility) under the colonialist's thumb. What they are to feel patriotic about, what class they belong to, defies simplifications.

Mulk Raj Anand's *Untouchable* (1935) is the story of one day in the existence of Bakha, a young Hindu outcaste who cleans latrines for a living. He is at the bottom of Hindu religion's ordering of society and at the bottom of British imperialist hierarchy. But like Denry, Bakha wants to move up. He assumes that dressing like the English, or playing at their sports, or not blowing on one's tea to cool it is his key to improvement. Despite his impulses to identify with those in power, Bakha's untouchable state retains an advantage: it defends him against total identification with the "white man," even though the latter "had treated him as a human being."[11] The division is painful, however, and pressures Bakha to look for a way out from the contradictory allegiances – indeed, the contradictory countries – that inhabit him. The divide is also between Hindu and Muslim. Bakha looks askance at Muslims, as if Muslims were Hindu outcastes, both from his Hindu perspective and from his personal version of British-identified superiority. All his perspectives are at odds with one another. When Gandhi appears in Bakha's city on the day of the narrative, and delivers an address that declares the need to overturn the caste-class system, Bakha feels that deliverance is at hand. Still, it is a wary feeling. Anand shapes the novel so that it ends inconclusively with unsettled debates about Gandhi's ideas. Bakha needs more than just Gandhi's resistance to imperialism to be free; he also needs modern toilets, so that he can be liberated from his abject labor as well as his abject class. That means a dependence on modernizing Western technology, no less than the quest for freedom from the West.

An African equivalent of Bakha is the postwar Nigerian teenager protagonist of *Mr. Johnson* (1939) by Joyce Cary, who was himself a British colonial administrator until 1920. Johnson is another "card" – wildly imaginative and impulsive, yet also shrewd. The product of a mission school, he makes himself an indispensable ally of the British district officer's desire to forge a motor road that will open the district to commerce. That project promises upward mobility for the young man, too. Not that Johnson wants to be mobile for material gain; indeed, he seconds his superior's desire for adventure more than for profit.

Johnson must juggle forces that are impossible to reconcile: the British colonial administration, the native Muslim government, and hard economic realities that brook no escape. All this burden rests on the back of a single representative of a native working class. Johnson "solves" the problem by twice devising illicit financing of the road work and creative accounting for it. Without the chicanery, as the administrators and the native government recognize, budgetary red tape would block the "new civilization"[12] that, for better or worse, the road represents. Nevertheless, Johnson, despite being the worker-architect of the path of progress for everyone, is humiliated and dismissed. This time his derring-do leads him to murder a bullying white storekeeper. Johnson must be judged by the district officer, who condemns him to death.

At one moment in *Mr. Johnson*, Cary personifies the road, which is a synecdoche for Johnson, by assigning it a warning to the empire. "I am the revolution," the road says. "I am giving you plenty of trouble already, you governors, and I am going to give you plenty more. I destroy and I make new. What are you going to do about it? ... You made me, so I suppose you know" (169). The irony of "I suppose you know" means that the imperialists cannot afford to know, and cannot allow those whom they rule to gain the independent mastery that native labor seeks to achieve. Hence working-class patriotism abroad will become post-colonial nationalism – and anti-imperialist intransigence. Even though *Mr. Johnson* does not save its hero, it uses the resources of fiction to insist on the knowledge that imperialism misses, or represses.

One of the best measures of the fictional supply of knowledge about the working class, or of treatment of that knowledge, is provided by novelists' response to the 1926 General Strike. This event marks a turning point – along with the 1945 Labor Party victory – in the history of the British workforce's revolutionary potential. The impact of modernist experiment on ways for readers to see the strike, and its aftermath in the next decade, might best be gauged by comparing a pair of novels that reduces the profile of "treatment" of the proletariat with a pair that heightens form in the pursuit of adequately expanded expression.

John Galsworthy's *Swan Song* (1928) and Ellen Wilkinson's *Clash* (1929) illustrate lesser emphasis on form than on topical realities that fictions copy (or appear to copy) from history. Galsworthy, whose novel is the sixth of the nine that constitute *The Forsyte Chronicles* (1906–1933), foregrounds his middle- and upper-class characters' attitudes toward the strike. The perspective that most matters in *Swan Song* is that of the MP Michael Mont. Although neither a member of the working class nor a Labor Party delegate, Mont sympathizes with the Trades Union Council's (TUC's) demands that the entire British workforce cease its labor until coal miners win improved conditions and salaries. Yet Mont is skeptical about the motives for the strike (he thinks it is about saving face on each side more than about social good) and baffled by the opponents' refusal of reasoned compromise. In historical fact, in May 1926, thousands of citizen volunteers – strike breakers, in effect, on behalf of the government – rushed in to do what the workers withdrew from doing. Whether because of that action, or because of the government's claim that the strikers' action was anti-constitutional and anarchic, or because the TUC lost its nerve (fearing it had let loose revolutionary extremism), the General Strike collapsed within ten days. Galsworthy's Mont intends, nevertheless, to be a non-working-class working-class patriot by initiating a minimally profitable investment company, funded by upper-class magnates (including his father-in-law Soames Forsyte), that will clear London slums and provide electrified low-income housing to the mean streets.

Galsworthy portrays Mont as representing for the upper urban classes a newly vital ethic of social responsibility. His cousin Jon Jolyon, representing the upper middle classes of agricultural England, commits himself to farming, seeing it as an effort to help the nation toward a self-sustaining economy, and thereby to disentangle it from imperialism. Galsworthy's title does not refer to Mont's and Jolyon's new beginnings, but instead to the demise of the Forsyte line, which, in the person of Soames, has exemplified the rapacious Victorian past. The working class does not appear in the novel, but labor and amelioration of its condition are the wave of the future – what the upper and middle classes are called to underwrite in all decency.

Clash has no such indirect relation to the working class or the General Strike. The novel's heroine, Joan Craig, is a child of the slums who became a munitions factory worker and a union organizer. Her story celebrates a refusal to allow the failure of the General Strike to slow the effort at revolution. Class patriotism remains her inspiration during the strike and thereafter (as it remained Wilkinson's: in 1923 she became the first woman member of the Labor Party to be elected to Parliament). Thereafter she also finds herself beset by a love dilemma. Shall she marry her already-married lover, a fiction writer with close ties to the literary and artistic world of Bloomsbury (Woolf and her circle), or a World War I veteran pilot (scarred and lamed by combat)? Joan chooses the airman: her other suitor wants her to surrender her activist commitments in exchange for an ideal marriage and for "writing," whereas the veteran wants to be her equal in "the detailed planning that is wanted"[13] for socialist reorganization of industry.

The straightforwardness of Wilkinson's treatment – Jameson's meanness and shabbiness of plain narrative – moves the reader of *Clash* away from fiction's potential for suspended reference to the world, and toward practical politics. The representatives of literature as Wilkinson portrays them are dangerous because of their apparent disinterestedness. One of Joan's Bloomsbury allies, donating to the workers' causes with repeated generosity, wants Joan to be the leading "heiress of the [women's movement]. Someone who could really be a rallying point for [post-suffrage] women" (95). The air ace, however, warns Joan definitively against her. He includes her among the exponents of detachment: "They are bored with their own crew, so they stand outside the struggle, like keen spectators at a boxing match, and cheer the workers on to victory. But they are never *in* the fight. And if you go with that crowd, Joan, you will be out of the fight too" (296). Joan's last furious fight in the novel, against "that crowd," corroborates the warning.

"Forgive me, Joan. . . . We are absorbed in our little arty schemes" (23). So speaks the Bloomsbury friend Joan is warned against. Can fiction – above all, fiction that is artily schemed, more formally inventive, and allied with modernist experiment – foster activism? One answer might be that the contrast between plain narrative and complex narrative is overstated; arty schemes are inevitable in fiction. There is a self-reflexive thread in Galsworthy's plain tale that argues in favor of art's value for progressive reform just because it can take a detached, even comedic, view of present-day conflicts. Cary experiments with narrative by telling Johnson's story in a continuous present tense: in the history of fiction, relative to 1939, it is an arty choice, and motivated politically, as Cary's road attests.

The first of our two contrasts to Galsworthy's and Wilkinson's plainness is the Scottish novelist Lewis Grassic Gibbon's *Cloud Howe* (1933), the second unit in the trilogy *A Scots Quair* (1932–1934). The most powerful of General Strike–related novels, it is the ne plus ultra of working-class patriotism, yet arty influence from Joyce, Ford, Woolf, and Richardson operates prominently there. The narrative is a collage; it has no unifying narrator. (In pre-modernist fiction, multiple narrators would have taken the form of exchanges of letters or entries from diaries. Modernism dispenses with such motivation.) An external narrator who deploys free indirect discourse to convey the inner life of Chris, the female protagonist, is juxtaposed with monologues (innovatively cast in the form of *you*-narrations) by citizens of the ancient Scottish town of Segget. That the narration uses Scottish speech rhythms and dialect might be said to tether the au courant literary influences to an ancient vernacular, not to a modernist idiolect. Yet for non-Scottish readers, the language's estrangement from standard "British" diction (another tinpot) shares in modernist combat. The novel's resistance to English is also an investment in "Devolution for Scotland" (177; i.e., Scottish national independence from "Great Britain").

Segget from its earliest days is a site of imperialist conflicts and class wars. Its founding lord was an Italian adventurer (to be associated in 1932–1934 with Mussolini). The tilt of Segget's feudal history toward modernity occurs when a jute-spinning factory is established there during the Industrial Revolution. Ever since, the working-class spinners and the town's gentry have hated each other. Chris, the widow of a Great War soldier, arrives in Segget because her new spouse Robert, a Church of England minister, is taking up his appointment as vicar. Unlike Joan Craig, Chris already has accomplished her choice of lovers. What lies before her, albeit obscurely, are political choices. Robert is a sign of that. His experience as a war veteran whose health has been permanently undermined by exposure to poison gas has made him a Wellsian. He hopes to organize a local league that will agitate for a cooperative world order. In the face of the misery of Segget's working class, however, Robert alters his purpose, and allies himself with a communist. Robert and the communist believe that the General Strike initiates an era that will at last do justice to workers. The strike's failure shatters Robert. He withdraws from Chris and the world, and rallies his radicalism only one time more: in a sermon, delivered just before he dies, that condemns the TUC leaders for having betrayed Christ's "promise in Man."[14] Robert's communist colleague will also enact the betrayal: becoming a National Labor candidate for Parliament, he will promote *"The Country* ['Great Britain,' not Scotland] *First"* (199).

In making Chris's ways of seeing and judging predominate in *Cloud Howe*, Grassic Gibbon uses a modernist-Impressionist treatment to communicate first sympathy with Robert's radical goals, and subsequently aversion to his post-1926 resignation. Chris is the vehicle for expressing the change. She distances herself from a reliance on Christ that afflicts Robert's mind in the aftermath of the strike. She also repudiates the political incoherence that she sees distorting the mind of Segget. A monologue – by the town's shoemaker Hogg – applauds the General Strike's failure, blesses the town's mill owner and first citizen, and excoriates the departure from Segget of the communist millworker who had joined forces with Robert. He calls the organizer's departure from Segget "just the kind of the thing you'd expect from socialists and dirt that spoke ill of their betters, and yet powdered and fornicated like gentry" (160). In one and the same utterance, the middle-class voice praises the gentry and derogates it ("powdered and fornicated like gentry"), without registering the contradiction. Chris's consciousness maintains a steady, whole way of seeing things that a reader is made to feel is superior to the hate-filled irrationality environing her. In the trilogy's conclusion, *Grey Granite* (1934), under the leadership of Chris's son Ewan, the contradictions will be resolved, not by socialist compromises with capitalist class structure, but by a working-class dictatorship. Ewan commits himself to this dictatorship at all costs – including politically motivated murders of traitors to the cause.

Grassic Gibbon imagines Ewan as a Scottish Stalin. That he uses modernist-Impressionist means to arrive at such a figure is not without major irony. Ewan subscribes to an absolutist mode of politics. Fiction's Impressionist method, such as shapes the presentation of Chris, here seems fully opposed by Grassic Gibbon to objectivity-based directive impulse, indeed to the hard definiteness of absolutes. *Cloud Howe* depends on Impressionism's hazy means, so that its author's treatment of his treatment can steadily wear them away. The novel's four parts are named for cloud formations. The purpose becomes clear when Chris associates Robert's post-strike spirituality with "the Fear . . . he'd be left with no cloud to follow" (172). In retrospect, the narrative has told a story of persons wandering in the mists of the Howe, mistaking them for the shapes and essences of things. Chris's way of seeing turns out to be the right one: "she followed no cloud, be it named or unnamed" (173), because she sees "the end forever of creeds and faiths, hopes and beliefs men followed and loved: religion and God, socialism, nationalism – Clouds that sailed darkling into the night. Others might arise, but these went by, folk saw them but clouds and knew them at last" (187). One name does not denominate cloudiness: communism, which sees only granitic realities. Chris's Ewan ("he refused all clouds and all dreams" [165]) and his comrades are the ultimate justifiers of working-class patriotism. Inasmuch as a new prominence of cloudy meanings characterizes modernism, Grassic Gibbon uses it only as an instrument to gain an antithetical political end. A punitive disciplining of fiction, an authorial self-violence, is thereby suggested, to affirm the time when Ewan and the workers' "great black wave [will come] flooding at last, up and up, swamping the high places with mud and blood."[15]

Undoubtedly Grassic Gibbon's desire for justice and for keeping the working class true to itself explains his lean toward violence, given the global reach of what is at stake. If the violence includes the humbling of the formal side of modernist art, so be it. Yet Wilkinson's and Grassic Gibbon's fictions do not annul the possibility that novels might present a more contemplation-oriented rather than activist- or violence-oriented treatment of class without betraying workers, or worldly political relevance, or innovative narrative forms. By comparison, Henry Green's post–General Strike *Living* (1929), a novel about the owners and laborers of a Birmingham iron works, combines modernist experiment and realistic treatment to exhibit the intricate entanglements of class relations. It is perhaps the most formally innovative vision of labor since Conrad's.

Living immediately communicates the self-consciousness of modernist fiction. As if Green must assert within the text itself a periodizing difference, he employs two ways of narrating – an old way and a new one. The novel's first sentence follows a dateline that suggests the text conforms to journalistic convention. But the sentence itself is unconventional: "Thousands came back from dinner along streets,"[16] it says mysteriously and clumsily. Came where? Why "along streets" instead of "along the streets"? Direct telling is being made indirect, artificial. The characters speak a vernacular that sounds historically and sociologically authentic, but the narrative sentences that surround the speaking are not vernacular, as in the following: "Works manager, and Mr. Dupret's son were going about this factory. They went through engineer's shop. Sparrows flew by belts that ran from lathes on floor up to shafting above by skylights" (208). Again the narrator omits definite articles where ordinary usage would include them – and also inserts a deictic *this* where it seems unwarranted. Why Green chooses to create the stylistic split between vernacular and artifice as a way of telling *Living* remains to be seen.

In its immediate content, and in line with pre-modernist historical fiction, *Living* portrays working conditions in terms of conflict between owners and proletariat. The owners of the iron works are the wealthy Duprets; the laborers are the works' unskilled and skilled hands. The class terms are adequately descriptive – up to a point: the point at which the class divide is presented by Green as simultaneous with the intersections that bridge it. The Dupret paterfamilias is dying, and his callow son is taking over. The junior Dupret initiates changes in the workplace and shakes up its administrative personnel, in rebellion against his father's modus operandi, as if he were on the workers' side. Rebellion also is simmering among the workers: not only against the Duprets' paternalistic plant manager (significantly named Bridges), but also against the fatherly authority of Craigan, an iron foundry artisan whose craft and moral stature are stainless. Craigan has been an iron worker for fifty-seven of his sixty-five years. Although a bachelor, he has created a family by housing under his roof his less-skilled foundry partner, Joe Gates, along with Joe's daughter Lily, and Jim Dale, a young laborer whom Craigan has picked out for Lily to marry. In his own household, Craigan is a boss-owner. Gates and Dale chafe (in differing ways) against his domination. The one who chafes least and yet is the most proletarian member of the "family" is Lily. Although she is treated with Craigan's utmost respect, until she falls in love with a worker from outside the Craigan home, she does not realize how she is less free than the others. The likeness of the contrastive sides extends to the upper class women: young Dupret's mother, and his prospective girlfriend, are reduced to mere servants by the men of their circle. Lily, despite her working-class servitude, has more initiative, deliberates her fate more, and enjoys life more than her superior counterparts. Nevertheless, across their differences, the characters all seem potential proponents of a general strike against the prevailing socioeconomic order. The novel uses their similarities, to which they themselves are blind, to demonstrate the limits of easy suppositions about fixedly distinct class characteristics that might underpin class conflict.

The novel's finale, however, seems to restore those assumptions by consolidating the distance between young Dupret and his employees. The young man's office intrigues in the name of better management and better conditions for the workers cannot withstand an economic slump. Dupret callously retires Craigan and other older hands, and he sacks Bridges. As if in revenge, the narrative retires Dupret. It leaves him out of its last third, even though the effects of the firing operate there. By enlarging the gulf between the owner and his workers, the narrative exhibits its working-class patriotism. The reader is compelled to remember the workers' marginalized and defeated state and Lily's complementary fortunes: she elopes with her lover to Liverpool, but he abandons her, in effect sending her back to jobless Craigan. When Lily is on the verge of being abandoned, Green's narrator intrudes a blistering attack on the middle class, exemplified in the novel by the company managers, designers, and accountants. who, at odds with Dupret and with each other, blindly contribute to their own frustration and to the workers' misery. "Each life dully lived and the life next it, pitched together, walls between," the narrator mercilessly declares of the sociological middle. "Each house had generally a mother and complacent father, procreation, breeding, this was only natural thing there in that miserable thing home, natural to them because it was domesticated" (355).

Nevertheless, the chasm between the owners, the middle class, and the workers does not encompass all *Living*'s elements. The aggressive passage cited previously is a momentary outburst rather than a final judgment. The characterization of Bridges, if he is included in the attack, does not match the dullness charged against his kind. *Class*, an explanatory marker, promises to make society intelligible. For all *Living*'s sociologically explicable portrayals, however, what also looms are enigmas. The malevolence that Craigan stirs in some of his fellows – in a relentless troublemaker named Tupe, for example, and in his own helpmate Gates – suggests an impenetrable human malice; the failure of Lily's lover to act responsibly in his relation to her even as he *intends* to act responsibly constitutes another puzzle. Desire, too, is perplexingly obscure. "Craigan was imprisoned by his love for Lily, he was tied down by it. Miss Gates chained him to her father and this he had never seen" (369).

Another chain, an obligation for all classes, is work. What *is* work's relation to living? There would seem to be no mystery there. It is the means to life; it *is* life. That Craigan sees his decades of labor amounting to "nothing" (380) is explicable as the raw deal guaranteed by capitalist ownership. Yet this biological and social compulsion overlaps with the strange necessity – to recall Rebecca West – that constitutes the relation of artworks to our existence. Craigan addresses his labor as more than a means to life: he treats fabrication as an end in itself, an opportunity for perfection, as if he were producing art. Art's role in living, one might argue, includes the ability of fiction both to conjoin itself to class analyses and to estrange us from them, for the sake of vitalizing other ways of seeing, other modes of modeling the world.

Living's narrative is perhaps self-reflexively projected by Green when he describes a delicate job of metal work on a lathing machine. The job equilibrates oppositions. "[R]evolving so many turns each second, now [the metal] had a stillness more beautiful than when actually it had been still. On the small surface of it was sheen of light still and quiet" (334). The description is applicable to the novel because it narrates a revolution in the lives of all its figures, but does not register the change as if the transformation – including the final one – has a thoroughgoing definitiveness. The lives that turn within revolving days are simultaneously a stillness in the light of Green's treatment. It makes motion and stability, personal life and class structure, relative rather than distinct phenomena. They meet and exchange each other's characteristics and meanings (Craigan the working-class hero is also a governor, young Dupret the innovative manager is managed by his underlings), so they require in the reader thinking that remains flexibly comprehensive.

Indeed, for a reader to follow Green's text requires a constant taxing attention to an intricate formal web of plots, counterplots, and contingencies – scarcely less demanding of agile concentration than is a reading of *Ulysses*. How might such sentences as the following – variants in the middle of the novel of those on the opening pages – practice a reader in suppleness of feeling and judgment?

> Here factories were and more there, in clumps. She [Lily] saw in her feeling, she saw men working there, all the men, and girls and the two were divided, men from women. Racketing noise burst on her. They worked there with speed. And then over all town sound of hooters broke out. Men and women thickly came from, now together mixed, and they went like tongues along licking the streets.   (277)

The narrator is speaking a dialect of his own: an idiolect that furnishes a counterpoint to the dialects spoken by the characters, and that opposes tinpot uses of language. The idiolect reminds Green's audience of the text's formal distance from life, despite the novel's title. Flexible consciousness begins, such writing proposes, with a self-conscious halt of attention. One must meditate on the narrative's laborious sentences, so as to consider (if not grasp) their direct and indirect meanings, and their relation to other ways of telling, speaking, and working in the text. The reader's engagement with this idiolect, along with scrutiny of the relations among Green's characters, events, and conflicts, is obliged to negotiate slowly, even haltingly, complex difficulties, whether those difficulties are stylistic or sociological or political.

Indeed, to work hard at reading *Living* makes the reader, in response to the textual material object, rehearse multiple class positions: a laborer toiling at it, a manager and owner of it, a worker inevitably on the way to retirement from it. By replicating the roles that are *Living*'s content, the reader is able to imagine movement past as well as through them, and thereby to glimpse an autonomous life beyond the horizon. Might this constitute preparation for a revolution, if not a revolutionary turn in itself? The forecast of liberty from class and class conflict would be less available for feeling and thought if experimentation on routinized sociological categories and on conventional literary form were absent from Green's novel.

Seeing Modernism through Romance

In the modernist era, the uses of romance are less calculable than is conveyed by most commentary. Romance is a mode that might epitomize fiction; its use in the modernist era participates in modernism's "period" self-conscious explorations of the nature of artistic discourse. In this section, it also stands for the modernist expansion of utterance beyond established conventions of usage and meaning. It thus involves itself with modernism's aim to break free from heteronomous obligations. Some of the texts about to be examined, such as Kipling's *Kim* (1901) and J. R. R. Tolkien's *The Hobbit* (1938) scarcely depend on the formal markers that would qualify as modernist. Nevertheless, they are not immune to unintended likenesses. Moreover, the romance pattern they employ provides a measure of what modernist experiment will copy, vary, or oppose.

If we take *Veiled Women* (1913), a novel by Marmaduke Pickthall, we can see the potential of Ralph Fox's color, fantasy, and irony – characteristics he identifies with romance – to serve revolution: against British imperialism and against European values. Pickthall's vehicle is a narrative about Islamic women's life in a harem. On the face of it, the topic promises to be reactionary (in Western eyes), opposed to modernity and to modernism (women's freedom from patriarchy, or secularism). Yet one of the novel's contentions is that women are freer in the harem than they are where women are seeking rooms of their own. The novel's heroine is an English woman who in 1860s Egypt converts to Islam, takes the name of Barakah, and marries an upper-class Turco-Egyptian subject. She discovers that "the world of women [in the harem] was ... a great republic, with liberties extending to the meanest slave" – including the liberty of married women to hold property (in the 1860s, a feat as yet unachieved in Victorian Britain). The Muslim faith and its social order are also progressive: it "disown[s] all race prejudice,"[17] as the racial mixture in the novel's harem attests. Hence, in Pickthall's version of Islam – as a translator of the Koran, he knew Islam well – an ancient faith and order seems both anti-modern and modernist. Its rebellious side is up to date.

The novel's historical referent is Ali Arabi's revolt in 1879–1882 against British rule of Egypt. Barakah's son participates in the conflict, during which he is killed by his own men. They have retaliated against his authoritarian manner – a result, the narrative demonstrates, not of Islamic mores but of his mother's English ways, which have spoiled him and made him imperious. Pickthall's story is his way of reminding the British, whose rule of Egypt was consolidated by the defeat of Arabi, of current anti-imperialist animus in the Empire, and of women's share in the animus. But the realism of historical fiction is not Pickthall's only way of treating the reminder. He enfolds his narrative in a Muslim legend about women's place in the world. Allah has yet to decide, the legend goes, which gender should have freedom of choice in regard to marriage, and which should have multiple spouses. Repeated at the novel's end, the legend expresses unresolved suspense about the status of women, within Islam – and, by analogy, within Britain. In the light of the legend-derived fantastic coloring, the women of separate cultures equally maintain the possibility of undoing the phallocentric order. Romance, even if it does not see patriarchy through to its end, keeps Fox's "revolutionary imagination" alive.

Kim, Kipling's orphan hero on the brink of adolescence, is Anglo-Irish by birth, but has grown up in India as if he were Indian. Although he is bilingual, he thinks in Hindi. What then is his identity, or what will it become? The question organizes his story, which at critical moments focuses on his own bafflement. "I am Kim. I am Kim. And what is Kim?"[18] is a reiterated motif that appears again within a few pages of the novel's conclusion – and as the accompaniment of something like a nervous breakdown. It is also something like the dissolution that "character" undergoes in modernist ideas of fiction, and that Lawrence accepts as an inevitable bafflement – for better rather than for worse, because it opens up alternative possibilities of being.

In Kipling's novel the breakdown results from its protagonist's involvement in the kind of quest action that characterizes romance narrative. Two antithetical quests pressure Kim, each of which is unsatisfying or even impossible to fulfill because it contradicts the other. The first quest is religious, committing Kim voluntarily as the spiritual apprentice of a quixotic Tibetan lama who is seeking redemption from the sinful illusions of the Wheel of Life. Kim does not freely choose the second quest. Without his knowing it, the British imperial government has earmarked him to take up his identity as a white sahib and to undergo training as a British intelligence agent. When that alternative vocation is made clear to Kim, he reluctantly allows himself to be enlisted, on the condition that he can rejoin the visionary during the intervals of his training, and even for a while thereafter. Once Kim begins to move between the sahibs' world and the lama's, his identity crisis becomes crystallized. One might categorize his dilemma as a peculiarly modernist one: constrained by religious and secular-historical attachments, favoring the less worldly and more detached one, but desiring liberty (a further detachment) from the nets of both. The instability of identity points, however anxiously, to a transcendent articulation.

Generations of critics have solved Kim's crisis by arguing that he is a white man's creation, and that Kipling's pro-imperialist politics lead the character to a resolved identification with his British calling. No rebellious modernism in content or treatment here! But romance looms too large in the history of the novel genre, including the modernist novel, to justify dismissals of it as merely a retrograde aspect. Romance in *Kim* remains the promise of deliverance from the imperialist history to which Kipling is said to be tied. In the novel's penultimate chapter a Russian spy manhandles the lama. The lama confesses to Kim that he wanted to strike back; in other words, he wanted to betray the values of his other-worldly quest. The lama's desire reminds him of warfare he undertook in his youth. He was then a partisan of one guru abbot opposed to another, and he fought to determine "which Abbot shall bear rule in the valley and take the profit of the prayers they print at Sangor Gutok" (260). The religious conflict is an imperialist one in miniature, bound to both power and profit. The lama's self-accusation distresses his disciple intensely. It sets off Kim's collapse, as if resulting from Kim's internalization of the lama's struggle over who or what "shall bear rule."

The text might have done without the lama's retrospective revelation. Apparently Kipling wants the reader at this point to not settle into pro-British sympathy, but to feel instead that unworldliness is better than worldly rule. In the same chapter Kipling also requires the narrative to witness the hypocrisy of the British imperialist "game." He invents an attractive figure, the Woman of Shamlegh, a native polyandrous ruler who helps Kim and the lama on their journey. Kim's looks remind her of a former sahib lover, a missionary who converted her, Europeanized her, and promised marriage. "He went away – I had nursed him – but he never returned. Then I saw that the Gods of the [Christians] lied, and I went back to my own people" (264). She is an exotic figure, certainly; however, Kipling could have made her help Kim, and kept her merely exotic, without including her history. Its inclusion casts another shadow on Kim's imperialist future, which will inevitably entangle his practice of rule with ingratitude and lying. The unworldly aspect of romance, in the person of the Woman of Shamlegh, conveys the warning. It suggests Kipling's relevance to modernism because of its suggestion that an autonomous realm, neither sacred nor secular-historical, but at once fictive and truthful, might open the way beyond self-division and deadlocked allegiances.

Modernism does not escape a necessary double vision – namely, the novelist's way of seeing in the light of both realist and romantic modes as a way to discover new perspectives on the topics under novelistic treatment. *Kim* exemplifies this binocular view. E. M. Forster's *A Passage to India* (1924) surely has *Kim* in mind as its antitype, however, because realism seems to govern Forster's text. The story concerns a sexual assault allegedly perpetrated by an Indian on an Englishwoman, Adela Quested, who has recently joined the Anglo-Indian community that governs the city of Chandrapore. The assault on Adela turns out to be imaginary, but the narrator decidedly assaults the connotations of romance (although one might gather from Adela's surname that a quest is interwoven with the novel). The scene of the supposed crime is the caves of the Marabar hills. "These hills look romantic in certain lights and at suitable distances."[19] Nearness undoes the look: the approach traverses an unintelligible wasteland. "Nothing was explained, and yet there was no romance" [i.e., in the mysterious nature of the site] (125). Once in the hills and the caves, "no one could romanticize the Marabar, because it robbed infinity and eternity of their vastness, the only quality that accommodates them to mankind" (134).

Perhaps Kim's attachment to the lama humanizes infinity and eternity. Kim's – or Kipling's – quest seeks to see an Anglo-Irish-Indian hybridity through to the point where it will figure the equal – utopian – "mankind" of its constituents. Forster's Adela, as well as her prospective mother-in-law Mrs. Moore, the young Muslim doctor Aziz, and the English principal of the Chandrapore college Fielding might all be said at times to be in quest of a mankind that surmounts its divisions. When Aziz is tried as the perpetrator of the assault, Fielding defies Anglo-Indian racism in Aziz's defense. But the alliance between Muslim and Briton is a merely temporary friendship. The narrative's outcome and the narrator declare that it is not time for unions or alliances. The romance-driven visions of utopian politics are useless. As for visions that transcend politics, "Visions are supposed to entail profundity but – Wait till you get one, dear reader!" the narrator scolds. "The abyss also may be petty, the serpent of eternity made of maggots" (188).

In exorcising romance-laced vision, however, Forster's novel – or its reader – runs the risk of replacing such vision's ties to cosmic coherence with a correspondent incoherence. The risky complementarity of romance and anti-romance shows itself when Forster's narrator meditates on the things of cosmic romance – "that huge scenic background of stars, fires, blue or black air" – and then argues that

> All heroic endeavor, and all that is known as art, assumes that there is such a background, just as all practical endeavor, when the world is to our taste, assumes that the world is all. But in the twilight of [a] double vision, a spiritual muddledom is set up for which no high-sounding words can be found.   (187)

Centering on the muddledom, an inhuman indeterminacy, in which Muslim, Hindu, and British are caught, Forster's novel seems to block the modernist aim at expanded expression.

Yet Adela and Fielding are touched by something that transcends exclusive worldliness and mere muddling indeterminacy, something whose articulation belongs to Forster's own favored mode: fiction's fantastic–prophetic axis. For all its attachment to disillusion, Forster's novel is like self-divided Kim. In the scene of Aziz's trial, Adela does the unthinkable: to the outrage of Anglo-India, realizing on the witness stand that Aziz did not assault her, that perhaps no person initiated the panic and emptiness set off in her by the caves, she declares the doctor's innocence and drops her case. Her resistance to Anglo-Indian bias against natives at such a moment is, one is tempted to say, heroic – a romance refusal of muddle. The narration resists this temptation. It treats her action as rational, sane, and mature: if it were heroic, it would not be realistic. After the trial Adela and Fielding agree that real practical life, however temporary and mixed up, trumps all else. But the narrator comments on their conversation: "A friendliness, as of dwarfs shaking hands, was in the air. Both man and woman were at the height of their powers – sensible, honest, even subtle" (240). The narrator sees this zenith; the characters suddenly occupy it. It is "as though they had seen their own gestures from an immense height" (240). The characters hereby observe reality from the perspective of a romance elevation. The narrator goes on: "the shadow of the shadow of a dream fell over their clear-cut interests, and objects never seen again seemed messages from another world" (240).

Messages from another world haunt *A Passage to India*. After Mrs. Moore dies, she becomes a minor deity – a spectral inspiration for Aziz, and for Chandrapore's populace. Of the novel's three parts, the first and third – "Mosque" and "Temple," respectively – are named for sites that are thresholds of divinity. During the courtroom scene, the body of a low-caste Hindu who pulls the cord of the punkah fan "stood out as divine," according to the narrator. "He seemed apart from human destinies" (196). The latter are "the scene of [a] fantasy," whereas "the beautiful naked god" (209), surmounting fantasy, is real. He is a romance figure, nevertheless. His naked presence contributes to a lyric refrain about the reality of divinity provided from the novel's start by a Hindu professor, Godbole. Godbole's imploration of a god to come to earth and redeem worldly confusion frames "Temple." The narrator there equates godhood with "this approaching triumph of India . . . a muddle (as we call it), a frustration of reason and form" (258). But at this point in the novel the muddle is accepted, however ironically, as a coming victory. It takes a contribution from the elevated romance background to adjust the narrator's ironic – modernist – sight, and to help him see through an obscuring medium of frustration – *to* a hopeful end.

Had Forster foregrounded visionary-prophetic perspectives more, the clash between reality's problems and attempts to transcend them, and thereby to arrive at an ultimate issue, would have intensified. A demonstration of this kind of probability is provided by a colonial novelist from Africa: William Plomer, in *Turbott Wolfe* (1925). Plomer's topic is incendiary in 1925: interracial eros and miscegenation in British and Dutch colonial territory, and interracial marriage's possible attachment to communist revolution. In *A Passage to India*, sexual relations between brown and white, or black and white, are taboo and provocative of violence; even so, the topic of those relations is nudged aside when the court case against Aziz is dropped. Moreover, other than the politics of anti-imperialist nationalism, Forster's ensemble of characters does not include socialists or communists.

Wolfe's retrospective story is a portrait of himself as a young artist. Having emigrated to Africa for health reasons, Wolfe set up a trading station in Lembuland (a fictitious country) and an arts studio wherein he drew and sculpted representations of local blacks, played music with them, and collected their folklore. His atelier became a scandal to the whites. Potentially more scandalous was his falling in love with a native woman. His evocations of the hypocrisy and aggression of his white neighbors (their violence includes the castration of a black man) make Forster's nasty Anglo-Indians seem almost congenial.

When a missionary named Friston appears on the ugly scene, an agent of romance vision enters Plomer's text. Overturning irrelevant Victorian values, Friston announces his modernist relevance: "the white man's day is over . . . the world is quickly and inevitably becoming a coloured world . . . it is the missionary's work now . . . to prepare the way for the ultimate end."[20] The quests of the lama, Kim, Adela, Aziz, and Fielding do not touch this height. "My prophecies belong," Friston says to Wolfe (and to readers who might think Friston is not inspired by a romance background), "as I myself belong, to the world of dreams, which is the actual world. The world we live in simply reflects part of the truth from that other, the actual world of dreams" (138). Friston is unable to see his vision through. He goes off to a distant village, where he is planning a Bolshevik-inspired sabotage of the government and where he is murdered.

Friston leaves behind, and Wolfe's text publishes, Friston's verbal picture of a new historical type: "The Politico-Aesthete." Wolfe and Friston both have enacted an attempt to jettison the world's social equivalents of miserable tinpot style. Friston's "politico-aesthete" devises a new vocabulary for it. The type "is divided by a thin red line drawn down the middle. On the right hand he is politico, on the left aesthete" (212). The bisection reflects back on Plomer and his text. In Wolfe and Friston (they are variants of each other) and in the nested narratives, visionary impulse, projecting a redeemed world, moves restlessly: across the color line, across the communist red line, and across the boundary between reality and dream. There seems no place in the actual world where the vision has a "politico" purchase that can be seen through, so only fiction (the aesthetic) can keep open the possibility of expressing and establishing a revolution outside of dreams. The miscegenating inspiration of eros (it is called the "sexophone" [212]) contributes.

Making eros salient in romance (as we nowadays expect), other modernist-era fictions promise enlarged accommodation of desire's link with "politico." Seeing the promise through to its realization still depends on antagonism to empire. In Ronald Firbank's novels, a romance world fully assumes an anti-imperialist ideology.

Stylistic experiment is an essential helper. Firbank descends directly from the paradoxes with which Wilde equates earnestness and verbal artifice. The first sentences of *The Flower beneath the Foot* (1923) typify the equation: "Neither her Gaudiness the Mistress of the Robes nor her Dreaminess the Queen were feeling quite themselves. In the Palace all was speculation. Would they be able to attend the *Fêtes* in honour of King Jotifa, and Queen Thleeanouhee of the Land of Dates?"[21] At once expressive of familiarity and irony, the opening puts Firbank's reader in the same disoriented state as his characters. What exotic kingdom (or state!) is this, where is the Land of Dates if it is not out of this world, and what do the honorific titles suggest about the narrative to come?

Firbank will unfold a speculative fiction – that is to say, a romance endowed with the usual split reference to reality. The world of this novel is a monarchy, in southern or southeastern Europe, named Pisuerga. It is imaginary, but Firbank conjoins it to real Great Britain. There is to be an Anglo-Pisuergan alliance, a result of the imposition – for mutually exploiting purposes that include an international monetary loan – of British Princess Elsie on native Prince Yousef. The Empire rules to crushing effect even in Firbank's fantasy space. Pisuerga already is worried by "the Eastern question" – or the Middle Eastern question – that surely includes the Land of Dates; now it will have to "not feel quite itself" by alliance with the Northern power. Britain treads the prince's intended native bride underfoot, and British hegemony indirectly threatens the workforce of a flower shop whose laborers are migrants or refugees (mostly Muslim). The flowers themselves speak, expressing the imperious hierarchy above them ("I'm glad *I'm* in a Basket!" says a lordly blossom), and the pathos of those whom the Empire displaces ("Life's bound to be uncertain when you haven't got your roots") (81).

Displacing history's global powers onto his mimic universe, Firbank provides a vantage point from which what exists for real can be seen critically, and history can be acknowledged as, in comparison, a state of misery. The reader's Pisuergan distance from reality – if we might so name the effect established by Firbank's invention – finds expressive identification in Prince Yousef's rejected bride Laura. She adopts an ascetic vocation and immures herself in a convent. (Laura, we are told, will become a saint.) The convent, shutting out the reality that its inmate can only observe from afar, might figure Firbank's text: a visionary place – what we expect from romance – and hence removed from the world; an exile, in line with Firbank's identification of himself and his novels with the migrants and rootless flowers.

But fictional romance artifice can see uprooting through to a curative revenge. Firbank's homosexuality was one motive for the author's interest in uprooted figures. He was always liable to imprisonment should he act on his sexual desires. As if to flout that prohibition, Firbank employs his novels to turn the tables on the regulative order that perhaps made him feel homeless – or a colonized subject – in his native place. Pisuerga is replete with polymorphous perversity: queer figures of diverse nationalities pass through on their way to rediscover Sodom; a lesbian seduction occurs in a boat at sea and is spied on by an aroused voyeur; man–boy love is practiced; the florists are gay. Laura, cast off by the prince, contemplates adjustment to life in the convent of the Flaming-Hood, under the guidance of Sister Ursula:

> She felt she had never cared for Yousef as she had for Ursula. . . . Sister Ursula's talk was invariably pointed, and often indeed so delicately that words seemed almost too crude a medium to convey her ethereal meanings. . . . And the infinite tenderness of her last caress! Yousef's lips had seldom conveyed to hers the spell of Ursula's.   (53)

Ethereal meanings, bisexual sensuousness, innocence: Firbank's interweaving of them, so that his words seem too subtle for definite meaning and yet are pointedly clear, is an antitype of shabby, plain narratives. For depicting such "perversity" *Ulysses* was banned, and in 1928 Radclyffe Hall's *The Well of Loneliness*, the history of frustrated lesbian love, became the object of a sensational obscenity trial. The modernist sexualities of Pisuerga, however, escaped condemnation. Because Firbank has forged a newer mode of expression (with Wilde's "Victorian" inspiration), he is able to portray officially condemned sexualities without raising a courtroom eyebrow.

"Non-normal" modes of eros refresh the quest narrative by another conjunction with communism in J. C. Powys's *The Glastonbury Romance* (1932). According to romance legend, Glastonbury is the site to which Joseph of Arimathea brought the grail cup from the Last Supper and the Roman spear that pierced Christ during the Crucifixion. But the grail and spear disappeared, thereby provoking centuries of quests to rediscover them. In Powys's version, the class struggle in contemporary Glastonbury replicates the grail quest, which now pursues economic democracy. The town's most influential capitalist and factory owner is successfully opposed by a communist–anarchist coalition, including a husband–wife communist pair whose surname is Spear. The coalition re-creates Glastonbury as a workers' commune after it elects John Geard as its mayor. He is a miracle worker: he apparently raises a dead boy to life; he does heal a cancer patient thanks to a "terrific upheaval of phallic force," the plunge of "that Bleeding Lance of his mind" into the "octopus-like" disease.[22] The intellectual Bleeding Lance, allied with the Spears, is polymorphously eroticized: Geard's love of Christ is described as homoerotic and undergirded by sadistic eros. When the communist Red Robinson delivers an oration that initiates Geard and the commune, Powys simultaneously focuses on another character, a sexual sadist who is listening to the speech and at the same time reading Malory's narratives about King Arthur. Red wrests the reader's attention away from Malory and turns it toward revolution. Romance and revolution are complementary. After all, sadism is a double-edged sword (as is romance): it unites eros and death – but so does revolution, which seeks to redeem a fallen community and must do so with aggressive means. As for some objects of redemption, their receptivity to revolutionary aggression is likened by Powys to erotic masochism, which the narrative also portrays honorifically. It is encapsulated in the experience of a red fellow traveler whose vision of the grail is associated with "what he felt to be a gigantic spear . . . struck into his bowels and struck from below" (939). Along with sadism, masochism, and homosexuality, redemption of the social order is allied with anal eroticism: a modernist innovation of Marxist–Victorian conceptions.

In the end, Powys shows the Glastonbury workers' commune – and the capitalism they oppose – to be at the mercy of contexts that are natural and cosmic. A disastrous flood carries Geard away and arrests the revolution. "Liquidation" is a Stalinist-era euphemism for executing political enemies, and the novel includes a character who describes himself as a "lickidater" (766). In Glastonbury the flood is the ultimate "lickidation." It gives Powys an occasion to declare that realistic fiction does not plumb the anarchic, destructive depths of nature. To do so requires a demon-like power of expression. Powys is the specific demon agent here, but the generalized demon that adds its own nature-exceeding touch is modernism – and is also romance.

In *The Hobbit*, a purer example of the romance mode, and one more legible as a foil to modernism than any other texts considered here, the hobbit hero Bilbo has, like Kim, a mixed pedigree. An individual of his nonhuman species, he also has the blood of an alien fairy race in his veins, and so harbors that race's adventurous streak. This genetic endowment serves him well when he receives a vocation from the wizard Gandalf (an equivalent of a holy man). Bilbo is called to be a redeemer: to recover, from a usurping dragon, the mountain homeland of an exiled clan of dwarves, whose treasure of metal and jewels is now the dragon's stolen property. Bilbo never knows why he is the chosen one in regard to this quest, but he sees it through, heroically. It is an anti-imperialist adventure: a dispossessed native population must be restored to self-determination. Tolkien vindicates Ralph Fox's desire to fuse epic, fantasy, and revolutionary vision!

The anti-imperialist thrust is further facilitated by *The Hobbit*'s treatment of humanity as only a marginal element in an ecosystem that includes natural history. A post-war modern utopia is one of the romance's horizons. Yet the more Bilbo becomes immersed in the dwarves' repatriation – it sets off a virtual world war – the more he longs for domestic reality, not "this bitter adventure" at the front.[23] Bilbo must turn thief, taking it upon himself – without consulting the dwarves – to steal a superlative gemstone from the dragon's hoard in an effort to dislodge the dragon's territorial hold. His motive is his foresight of difficulties to come. But the theft remains the kind of action – Realpolitik – on the basis of which real imperialism is established. To steal or not to steal what has been stolen; to appropriate or not: on the eve of World War II, the perplexing conflict between revolutionary means and ends worries *The Hobbit*.

Moreover, when Bilbo arrives home, he is "held by all the . . . neighborhood to be 'queer'" (285), a romance figure on the quotidian scene, suspended between contrastive worlds, and marginalized, despite his pivotal heroism. Who or what is Bilbo? Where does he belong? If Bilbo does not know what he is, that is because neither he nor the reader understands the larger circumstances that only Gandalf comprehends. That ignorance reduces the liberty Bilbo achieves to a local instance – and to Bilbo's ultimate confinement. On the one hand, the romance depends on an obstruction of knowledge. On the other hand, more knowledge and more freedom depend on more romance: *The Lord of the Rings*, which Tolkien published after 1950. But the end of *The Hobbit* is a retreat from the fantastic component in Bilbo's blood. We scarcely think of Tolkien in the context of the Joyce era, but Bilbo's final dislocation – despite the happy ending for the dwarves – echoes the alienated condition that literary modernism deliberately pursues.

It is unclear if Samuel Beckett's *Murphy* (1938) and Flann O'Brien's *At Swim-Two-Birds* (1939) are to be read as modernist renewals of romance, or as dark and giddy parodic retreats from it. The signs of *Murphy*'s corrosive modernism are immediately prominent. Beckett's female protagonist, Celia, is introduced, non-narratively, as a double column of 20 items of her physical appearance that include measurements of her wrist, knee, and instep. On the novel's second page, the narrator declares that Murphy's mind matters to him more than his body, "as described in section [chapter] six."[24] The implicit direction to the reader to proceed to the latter chapter makes the middle of the book part of the start. An annotated transcription of the moves of a chess game played between Murphy and a psychiatric patient named Endon is one of the novel's climaxes. The foregrounding of the treatment is continuous.

That is because, as Beckett said about Joyce, the writing is not about something outside of itself (as emotional response to it might assume). It advances expressiveness by being that very something. Murphy's story is also a purgative process, during which he undergoes many trials. They begin with his heart, which uncontrollably oscillates between extremes of contraction and expansion. Seeking a happy medium, he must engage a further ordeal: working for a living in England. Employment becomes the object of his quest. It is fulfilled by the Magdalen Mental Mercyseat, "a hospital for the better-class mentally deranged" (52). Murphy is able to sign on there as a nurse. "Here was the race of people he had long since despaired of finding" (102). What he also has searched for, and finds at M.M.M., is "self-immersed indifference to the contingencies of the contingent world which [i.e., indifference] he had chosen for himself as the only felicity" (102).

Is it excruciatingly funny that Murphy's fulfilled quest leads to his abandonment of Celia and, within days, to his own death at the Mercyseat? His demise comically frustrates a group quest that constitutes a subplot in Beckett's modernist play with romance. In Ireland, Murphy's native land, four other characters have initiated a search for Murphy. The involved erotic and economic foolery of their pilgrimage appears to satirize Murphy's journey. But the latter, however tinged with parody, is also presented as a desirable antithesis to the other. "The patients" at M.M.M. are described by their doctors "as 'cut off' from reality" (107). Yet "the nature of outer reality remained obscure" (107), and *Murphy* bitingly suggests that the outside world is the real merciless madhouse. The ambassadorial pilgrims are proof! Why not a quest for an alternative obscurity?

Murphy thinks there is "no dark quite like his own dark" (55). His quest's final object, therefore, is his grasp of himself as "a mote in the dark of absolute freedom … a point in the ceaseless unconditioned generation and passing away of line" (68). By "line," Beckett means defining shape, including the storyline of quest, which *Murphy* both solicits and obscures. Again, we see modernism move away from narrative: a lyric meditation on darkness would be more expressive than clearly articulated events or statements. If it is not easy to translate the obscurity, nevertheless it abets a desire for "absolute freedom" – radical autonomy – including the freedom of fiction to not be what we expect.

Beckett's desire for adequately expressive utterance depends upon such paradoxical asceticism of treatment. But surely a less punitive aim can trust fiction's ebullient inventions of romance – for so very long in literary history the heart of the novel – to see a modernist freedom through to an alternative adequacy. *At Swim-Two-Birds* is proof. It is the story of an Irish undergraduate (another version of Joyce's Stephen!) who lives under his mocking uncle's roof, confines himself to his bed when he is not out drinking, and invents stories as a way of escaping his studies. His idea of fiction is that of "One beginning and one ending for a book I did not agree with."[25] The protagonist-student sees that aim through to realization by constructing four or more stories at once, in addition to his own autobiographical one. One of the stories narrates the quest of an Irish mythical hero who, magically transformed by a curse into a bird, searches ceaselessly for a comfortable nest. There is none to be found, not least because the nesting of stories within stories in O'Brien's text offers no fixed stability.

The fountainhead of most of the stories in *At Swim-Two-Birds* is a novelist, Trellis, who illustrates "aestho-autogamy," the "very familiar phenomenon in literature" (55) of an author's giving birth to offspring who are already fully grown. Trellis is the student's aestho-autogam; most of the other characters are Trellis's, but they also number a set of Dublin cowboys (sic) who are the creations of another writer (named Tracy). Eventually the characters decide to attack Trellis, for having invented them along *his* lines and consequently leaving them no absolute freedom. They drug him; they then enlist his aestho-autogamous son Orlick to devise tortures for their shared progenitor. Once the tortures are ended, they tear the author apart – in a ritual Dionysian dismemberment – yet Trellis must also undergo a juridical trial. In a counterpoint to Trellis's failure at his trial, the undergraduate succeeds at his: he passes a crucial university exam. His dragon of an uncle, as well as the scholastic test, are overcome.

To judge by the revolt against Trellis's authority and authorship, the student will not serve anything established, or anything that intends to define or limit him. He makes fun of Irish mythology and heroism in his rendition of the bloated, interminable laments – expressed in bathetic lyrics – of the bird-man Sweeny. Like the net of Irish heritage, the net of working-class patriotism is looked at askance. Another poet, Jem Casey, "The Workman's Friend," is part of the narrative. His verses are as bad as Sweeny's. The way the text ridicules Sweeny's and Casey's poetry skewers *The Portrait of the Artist's* metamorphosis of narrative into lyric – even as O'Brien repeats the experiment. Laughter tears apart everything – topic, theme, treatment – and O'Brien's own self-conscious modernist gaming. The all but hysterical fun of it speaks of a freedom of fiction from any settled truth, and of fiction as an absolute state of free invention. And if *At Swim-Two Birds* suggests that such freedom is also a fiction, it nevertheless tries to see even that idea through.

The realization of escape from tinpot thoughts and styles is perhaps a phantom object of an interminable quest, always more fiction's future achievement than its realized one. In a futural light we come full circle back to Wells. In his *The Shape of Things to Come* (1933), the anti-novelist must still rely on a novel of sorts – a scientific romance – to push the envelope. The fictional vehicle is "the book of Dr. Simon Raven," a narrative of world history from a point in time at the end of the twenty-first century. There "the modern state" is in control of life: "the struggle for material existence is over. The need for repressions and disciplines has passed."[26] The years between 1933 and 2059 proved overwhelmingly the need for arriving at such an achievement – hence the usefulness of Raven's record. Nevertheless, records of the present can offer a like utility. "What is really happening? If one knows what is really happening one knows what is going to happen." Interpretation of the present, including novelistic interpretation, it seems, can be carried "on to prophecy. It is a logical development" (18). Here, again, is a convergence between Wells and the ideas of the modernist novelists he opposed because of their alleged indifference, on behalf of art, to the world's prospective improvement. Raven is sure that after we absorb his knowledge of the crises of the years before 2059, the art of fiction will finally come into its own. A "real dread of aestheticism" had "haunted" the Council ultimately responsible for 2059. That dread overpassed, "the struggle for truth and that indescribable necessity which is beauty begins now" (393). Our "period" imposingly reasserts itself: in the strange necessity whereby Wells remains compelled to write fiction "now," in 1933, and to see the struggle for truth and beauty's adequate expression through to its modernist–romantic realization, immediately, as well as in the temporal distance.

Short Stories by Rudyard Kipling and Katherine Mansfield

Kipling's Diversity of Genres

Conjoining the names of Rudyard Kipling and Katherine Mansfield amounts to a provocation. Surely the modernist era does not include Kipling! History presents us with strange conjunctions, however; literary history does the same. Whether "periods" are historical or literary-historical, they intermingle, as well as eat away at each other. Kipling the "Victorian" writes until his death in 1936; Mansfield, an icon of British modernism, dies in 1923. The two writers can be viewed in the light of differences as distinct as their genders and their places of origin: Kipling's roots are in imperial Anglo-India, Mansfield's in colonial New Zealand. Nevertheless, this interchapter considers the experimental address to prose narrative fiction that is common to both writers. If modernism means a revision of past patterns of fiction, then a decided turn away from the longer prose form is the enterprise the two figures share. Certainly, they belong to an international flowering of the short story (for example, as demonstrated by James, Maupassant, and Chekhov). But it is remarkable that in his fifty-year career Kipling authors only three novels (and co-writes a fourth); prose short stories, narrative verse, and lyric verse account for the majority of his work. Mansfield's five volumes of fiction contain prose short stories only.

Verse distinguishes itself by its compression of prose's unregulated voicing of meaning. Brevity for Kipling plays the role of a restrictive meter, enforcing measure on the novelistic material that he submits to the story form's constraint, as if for the sheer difficulty of it. In line with such artifice, verse is part of almost every Kipling story and collection of stories. In the wartime *A Diversity of Creatures* (1917), fourteen tales are paired with fourteen poems (and a verse epigraph to boot). In "The Village That Voted the Earth Was Flat," the lyrics to a song become a summation of the story's elaborate intrigue, which ends with the entire House of Commons singing the refrain. *A Diversity of Creatures* contains "Regulus," which mimes a Latin class's construction, word by word, of an English translation of an ode by Horace.

The mimicry enforces on a reader the contrast between lyric states of mind or feeling and narrative's conjunction of subjective elements (the teller's perspectives) and objective elements (the told). The contrast emerges even as the reader realizes that he is reading simultaneously, and sorting out, Horace's poem (the Latin is generously quoted), its translation, and an additional translation of it into a narrative (one of the schoolboy translators enacts an equivalent of the Roman hero Regulus's integrity). Kipling appends to the story another modernist turn: his own "translation" of an ode by Horace. In fact, no such ode by Horace exists: Kipling has made it up. He playfully involves Regulus's model integrity with the betrayals of integrity perpetrated by authorial subjectivity, literary history, "translation," and fiction.

The prominence Kipling gives to self-consciousness about genres is typically modernist. The self-reflexive mixture of earnest and game receives reinforcement from the fantastic component of Kipling's generic diversity. The fantasy, as we'll see, pushes Kipling's distasteful political views, as we know them from outside the stories, off their conservative base and into alignment with modernist perspectives. A case in point is the utopian science fiction, "As Easy as ABC," that leads off *A Diversity of Creatures*. In 2065, democracy has been superseded, to the planet's great relief. Twentieth-century democracy, according to one of the lyrics that flanks the story and is quoted in it, buttressed the nation-state, which unfailingly produced war in the all-sanctifying name of "The People." Now the globe is no longer nation-centered, and the earth's populations (rigorously practicing birth control, and consequently well off economically and physically) are dispersed into zones that guard against "invasion of privacy" by "Crowds," those exemplars of "The People" and their superseded ideology. Nevertheless, occasionally the Crowd-spirit starts up, and it invokes "The People" as a motive for unreasoning, violent discontent with the new world order. The global administrative body is the ABC – the Aerial Board of Control – a planetary information and transportation network that in an emergency can step in to quench reactionary populism. Doing so in this story, it controls the uprising by unleashing apocalyptic auditory, visual, and electronic effects that bring the crowd to its knees. The malcontents are transported to London, where they are sentenced to perform superannuated politics – the process of electioneering "first by crowd-making, next by talking to the crowds made, and lastly by describing crosses on pieces of paper"[1] – in a kind of educational vaudeville for audiences curious about history.

Given such a story (originally published in 1912), what could seem less aligned with modernist progressivism than Kipling and his fiction? Yet, considering the context of the story's reissue during the Great War, the tale seems appositely critical of the illusions about democracy that contributed to the conflict. Moreover, the ABC world order is neither a despotic empire nor a violent one. Its disarming crowd control causes no physical harm, and it is appalled by the pyrotechnical display of power it is obliged to enact. The team is an international group of technicians, in which no nationality dominates – it is egalitarian. The world it administers is egalitarian, too: the inhabited zones are both self-sustaining and self-possessed. Most importantly in regard to the story's politics, the crowd's populist violence is explicitly identified with the burning alive of American blacks in the Jim Crow United States. There is a statue of such a horror, dating from the good old days of "democracy," at the scene of the story's uprising – Chicago. Preserved by the ABC as an artwork representative of an earlier time, the statue may be viewed only once a year. Now, as a rebuke to the malcontents, the ABC destroys the statue, as an insurance against a resurgence of mob rule. The destruction of the racist statue suggests that artworks, Kipling's fiction included, have no right to survive if they glamorize aggression and injustice.

Thus the story's reactionary surface covers an antiracist, democratic core. It is not the only story in the 1917 collection that contradicts a conservative or reactionary line of thought. Perhaps something autonomous and unruly in the nature of fiction sends Kipling toward sympathy with modernism. "My Son's Wife" (a title that derives from a song lyric) begins by making fun of its modernist protagonist, Midmore, for representing the "Immoderate Left" and for being "an experimenter in Social Relations" (334). Midmore's experimentation includes modernism's liberated sexual relations. Suddenly, however, Midmore is thrown off his ideological track. After inheriting a country house, he is exposed to practical responsibilities, above all to the management of a virtually lawless tenant farmer. His exposure shows how merely theoretical his leftism has been. At this point the story seems to revise its object of satire: the target is abstract theorizing about social conditions, not modernism or leftism. The tenant newly socializes Midmore by enforcing on the landlord a personal respectful response to a man of a lower class and of dissimilar (diverse) traditions.

In practical terms, the landlord becomes a better modernist and leftist than he was. Kipling underlines the change by landing Midmore again amid untraditional sexual relations. The tenant is polygamous, and Midmore's housekeeper is the mother – by the obstreperous tenant – of an illegitimate child, now grown up and doing well in local business. London modernism is a pale shadow of rural liberty and license, which the country persons treat matter-of-factly, without political or moral (or literary) fuss. Midmore learns to do the same. If he represents conservatism, it is conservatism paradoxically appreciative of lawlessness at the same time as it seems responsible to order.

Lawlessness is what Kipling's stories often applaud. They depend, after all, on their author's insubordination against laws regulating generic distinctions – say, between narrative and lyric. Yet the discipline Kipling brings to the short story form, and his self-subjection to its constraints, is the reverse of antagonism to rule. He gives with one deregulating hand what he takes back with the other, balancing sympathies with law and sympathies with lawlessness.

The lyric component of Kipling's generic repertory plays its role in the stories' give and take between conservative reaction and proto-modernist liberty. In *A Diversity of Creatures*, the lyric "Jobson's Amen" expresses an English soldier's response to imperialist jingoism ("Blessed be the English and all they make or do") and racism ("Cursed be the Savages that prance in nakedness") that refuses to bless and curse likewise. "Where I mean to die," Jobson fiercely says, "Is neither rule nor caliper to judge the matter by" – and that means he will die beyond the reach of "blessed" English values (237–8). Jobson's intransigent lawlessness echoes an earlier lyric in the collection, "The Land," which expresses the crafty endurance of English yeomen in the face of centuries of imperial conquerors. "English" imperialism happens at home, in other words, and Kipling's poem is on the side of the subalterns. "The Land" succeeds "Friendly Brook," a story in which a flooding brook drowns an extortionist – as if the brook were the ally of the persons undergoing the extortion. The land refuses domination. The story's blend of realism – evoking ordinary rural life – with preternatural phenomena again exemplifies Kipling's experimental treatments, including their implicit conformity with modernist formal transgressions.

Indeed, each of the stories might be read as a single compacted impression of a situation – as evidence, therefore, that Kipling's method is modernist-Impressionist. When Kipling presents a character's immediate situations and sensations without at once telling what those situations or sensations are "about," his compositional method is in line with what literary history associates primarily with Conrad and Ford.

Delay or deferment is essential to the technique: the reader must wait for comprehension or explanation of the surface impressions. The deferring treatment is writ large in "Mary Postgate," a wartime story from 1915 placed last in *A Diversity of Creatures*, as if it is the opposite pole of "As Easy as ABC." Movingly verisimilar as "Mary Postgate" is, however, one can read it as yet another self-conscious Kipling experiment: his probing of the theoretically indissoluble pairing of realism and fantasy. Mary keeps house for a single elderly woman who has raised an orphan nephew, Wynn. Wynn joins the army Flying Corps and meets his death in a trial flight. Almost immediately thereafter, a German aerial bombing of Mary's village occurs, and Mary witnesses the death of a child killed in the attack. Now, when she is about to incinerate Wynn's effects in a secluded outdoors spot of her employer's property, she discovers at the base of a nearby tree a fallen airman, the perpetrator of the bombing. Alive but broken-necked, he asks for help. Mary refuses the request, and listens for the airman's death rattle. Then, having quitted the funeral pyre, she returns to the house, where she makes a strikingly novel impression on her employer. "Scandaliz[ing] the whole routine" of the household by taking "a luxorious bath" before tea, she appears "lying all relaxed" on a sofa and "looking . . . 'quite handsome!'" (441).

The narrated impression does not explain what causes Mary, whose surname denotes her emotional rigidity, suddenly to relax and look handsome, nor does it tell us that Mary recognizes the change. One probable explanation – which one must supply because the narrator (Mary-like) defers it – is that her conduct toward the German has avenged both the death of the child and Wynn's casualty. Her own aggression has been released, and the directness of release – utterly abnormal for her – puts her in a glow. Yet this directness is just another indirection. One is led to deduce that Mary, without ever telling herself the truth, has been in love with Wynn. She received the news of his death perfunctorily. Yet the narrator does allow one telling remark – even though the remark is rendered, with Mary-like indirection, impressionistically, and in a subordinate clause. Mary discovers the fallen airman "as she lit the match that would burn her heart to ashes" (436) – her heart thereby being identified as Wynn's property. Mary's relaxation and victorious air is another displacement, a form of not-telling, of not expressing her passion.

The Impressionism of "Mary Postgate" is, as literary Impressionism means to be, a hyper-refinement of realism. Wynn's clothing and possessions, amassed for burning, are detailed by the narrative in a full-page inventory. But in fiction, such details, which constitute the stuff of realism, are only "realist" in appearance. Kipling heaps together Mary, the German, the incinerator, and Wynn's effects not by accident – even though it all *looks* like an accidental conjunction – to reveal an essential meaning about Mary that, were she a living person, might never be seen or told, or even obtain. Thus, realistic artistic treatment transforms into fully interrelated, fully meaningful components things that in life are only arbitrarily and meaninglessly side by side. Only in fiction perhaps do we find such repletion of interlinked significances. Although we desire them to be real, they are more likely fantastic.

The way Mary is seen in the last moments of "Mary Postgate" suggests that Mary is more alive than previously. Yet the perspective is an impression, a surface reality that displaces and defers a deeper one: desire. That Mary breaks the surface of routine with a mysterious afterglow probably means that she has momentarily realized a fantasy of (as it were) flying with Wynn. Given what has been destroyed, however, her break with habit is a dead end. Her desire is no more likely to emerge directly (or again) than Wynn is likely to come back to life. Insofar as surface realism delays and defers fantasy, and insofar as realism (figuratively speaking) kills desire, Kipling evokes the pathos and horror of the killing. His stories' transgression of the confines of realism, their fantastic flights into generic lawlessness (on lyric wings, beyond realism, beyond "the novel"), constitute their defense of desire – and of fiction.

Mansfield's Suspended Moments of Being

When Kipling assigns his fantasy realms a densely detailed existence, he makes them all the more totalized alternative realities. Mansfield experiments in the opposite direction. That is, she represents fragments of existence, passing moments of consciousness, minute events. Those evanescent phenomena might be felt by their subjects as bigger than they appear; nevertheless, Mansfield keeps her readers' attention on limited experience. If her stories solicit *history, empire, gender,* or *class* for framing fiction's treatment of life, they also undermine those large-scale frameworks. Novelistic tradition made those frameworks commonplace, and historical discourse and analysis have underwritten them. But the commonplaces, Mansfield's stories imply, have been only crude preliminaries. Anti-imperialist writers of Kipling's era wanted to withdraw fiction from the illiberal politics attached to historical references. Such an impulse might motivate Mansfield's art. It suggests that the big topics fail us; that is, they insufficiently express the unrealized desires, fragilities, and inabilities that might constitute life, and that fiction might disclose.

What *is* "life" to Mansfield? It is hard to define, and in Mansfield's work, as in the work of Woolf and other modernists, it escapes capture even when Mansfield's stories invite readings in terms of class conflict and class oppression, which figure in "The Garden Party." In that story, a wealthy New Zealand family, preparing to host its annual social fête, learns that a young workman neighbor – living in poverty nearby – has been killed in an accident. Laura, one of the family's daughters, thinks that the party should be cancelled – even though the family does not know the man and maintains a strict taboo against contact with the lower orders. Nevertheless, once the garden party is over, Laura's mother suggests that Laura take leftover food and flowers to the widow. Although Laura has earlier protested "absurd class distinctions,"[2] her excursion to the site of class difference fills her with shy dread. But when she is forced to see the corpse, she is amazed by the dead man's beauty and apparent repose. "All is well, said that sleeping face. This is just as it should be" (261). "But all the same you had to cry," the narrator reports (261). Laura, sobbing, suddenly asks the dead man to forgive the garden-party hat she is wearing. When she returns home, Laura cannot explain to her brother what she has experienced. She appeals to "life": "'Isn't life,' she stammered, 'isn't life –.' But what life was she couldn't explain. No matter. He quite understood" (261).

So much for life and understanding! The story leaves both a blank. The blank might be offered ironically: isn't life only too obviously intelligible as capitalist exploitation and the solipsism of the rich, an intelligibility Laura and her brother cannot face? To answer affirmatively is to remain within the framework of the conventional reasonings. Yet what cannot be understood or explained – the sleeping face that says, according to the external narrator as well as Laura, "All is well" – stretches beyond the relevance of "class."

The same refusal of motivating explanation shapes "Marriage a la Mode," in which a wife has insisted on a country home for her and her children, forcing her husband to commute from London to his family on weekends. She also has cultivated a circle of chic bohemians, who freeload on her hospitality, occupy the house while the husband is "visiting," and make fun of him. Attempting to reverse his marriage's breakdown, the husband writes a post-weekend letter to his wife, pleading for attention while praying that he not "be a drag on [her] happiness" (320). The wife reads the letter aloud to her friends, and mocks it as they also do. Alone for a moment, she feels guilty for making an intimate relation into an opportunity for public satire; nevertheless, she recommits herself to her snob set. Superficially a sociological report on the modernist era's superannuation of marriage and family, "Marriage a la Mode" is more: a study of an inexplicable perversity – in the wife's friends as well as the wife – that is interwoven with what might be otherwise regarded as a "progressive" historical change in manners and morals.

"At the Bay," the lead story in *The Garden Party*, best exemplifies Mansfield's use of the short narrative form to exceed – in its very condensation – the history that guides us when we are not reading fiction, and the historical topics that we turn into facile "themes." "At the Bay" evokes, in twelve juxtaposed segments, an entire New Zealand summer "colony" (207) by concentrating on one day in the life of the Burnell family and its neighbors. Such a short story derives from a tradition of regional sketches that harks back to the early nineteenth century. Yet Mansfield reclaims the tradition for modernist experiment with her narrative's first segment. Instead of representing a definite locale or definite persons, it presents a fantastic world of mists and bay waters, "as though one immense wave" had erased the boundary between beach and sea. "[I]f you had waked up in the middle of the night you might have seen a big fish flicking in at the window and gone again" (205). Disorientation rather than location is the introductory keynote. Wandering sheep and a distracted sheepdog, entering this sleep-drowned world, emphasize the dislocating movement: what are they doing in this story, and what purpose do they serve? Although a shepherd appears out of the mist, the narrator names the Burnells's cat Florrie as the colony's "first inhabitant" (207). A dialogue ensues between Florrie and the sheepdog, and the segment closes with the disappearance of the sheep and the shepherd. Is the directive shepherd an authorial figure? Are the sheep readers waiting for direction? If so, direction is obscured by Mansfield's indirect opening, as if to announce that more indefiniteness and drift are to follow.

They do follow, as the human actors pass across the field of vision. No matter how rigorously purposeful the actors are (in contrast to the night's floating fantasy or the morning's errant sheep), they and their thoughts and feelings, caught up in obscurity and perplexity, appear suddenly and dissipate just as suddenly. Linda Burnell, a young wife whose husband is a hard-driving business man, has been displaced from her native Tasmania by her marriage, which she feels is a burden. The heaviest burden is motherhood: "she did not love her children" (223). Notably, she resents the youngest, an infant boy. Yet, in a segment that portrays her with the infant, Linda finds herself suddenly enchanted by the child. Will that moment, changing her settled indifference, become her historical turning point? Mansfield does not let us know. Suspense, which a novelist must maintain over a great length of text, is equally in play in Mansfield's moments of being. In the seventh segment, Linda's daughter Kezia suddenly realizes the fact of death; thinks she can avoid it; then, panic-stricken, declares that her grandmother must not die; and finally forgets death entirely. Because metamorphic intermingling of contrastive feelings, of certainty and uncertainty, pervades the characters' "lives," each of them is a world of suspense, each of them repeating Laura's stammering inconclusiveness.

Mansfield, echoing Kipling, makes the short form straddle the supposed divide between realism and imaginative flight from reality. The last segment of "At the Bay" dissolves the realism that appears to anchor the story after its misty start. The dissolve begins with Florrie the cat expressing her thanks that the extensive day is finished. Florrie's vocal return prefaces a radical change in the voice of the narration: the narrator speaks in the second person (as she speaks momentarily on the first page) to convey what Beryl, Linda's sister, tells herself as she prepares for sleep. Mansfield makes the reader unsure of who is speaking, unsure which thoughts are Beryl's, and unsure of what is truly happening. Beryl sees a couple embracing in the middle of her room. They can't possibly be there – yet the narrator tells us they are – the same narrator who reports what a "sorrowful" bush in the garden speaks aloud in Beryl's hearing (242). Beryl then sees outside her window the disreputable young husband of a woman friend who earlier has been shown to desire Beryl sexually. Now the husband lures Beryl to come to him, past her garden gate. Once she has joined him, however, she struggles to escape. Neither we nor she seems to know why she has ventured so far. More importantly, neither we nor she seems to know if the episode of seduction (and perhaps rape) is real. We are left in suspense about what has happened. The story breaks off by noting the ocean's vague, "troubled" sound (245). Unresolved by the author-narrator, "At the Bay" is the equivalent of the sea, its sounding words a simultaneous limit of articulation.

What good does a fiction do us if, by using refinements of artifice, it arrives at a point where uncertainties suspend its resolutions, and words suspend its sense? The ideas about fiction and the modernist experiments our chapters have been "seeing through" forge the novel and the short story as the necessary special discourse that even Wells, along with his contemporaries, felt compelled to discover. The suspense of resolutions in modernist fiction does us good, one might argue, by resisting custom-deadened reference to the world as we know it already, and inadequately.

Chapter 4

British Fiction amid Nonfictional Discourses in the Era of Modernism

Readers are not to take on faith a claim that pervades the previous chapters, which have followed the novelists in asserting a special nature of fiction. The present chapter and Interchapter 4 test that claim by comparing and contrasting examples of modernist-era thought – in aesthetics, anthropology, psychology, science, and history – with novels that might be said to align themselves with the discourses proper to those intellectual realms. That the other discourses intermingle with fiction, and that fiction writers cultivate the merger, is obvious. But does the alignment resist or confirm fiction's independent character or authority? The extent and limits of the interminglings are proposed in what follows.

Aesthetics and Modernist-Era Fiction

T. S. Eliot's *The Waste Land* (1922), the essential modernist poem, is the focus of the "Conclusion" of *The Principles of Art* (1938) by the distinguished Oxford University philosopher and historian R. G. Collingwood. According to Collingwood, Eliot's poem represents a new turn in creative artistry. The fin de siècle writers – Wilde and James, for example – were committed, Collingwood argues, to "individualism, where the artist's only purpose was to express 'himself,'" and to do so in terms of a "literature whose interest depends not on its subject-matter, but solely on its 'technical' qualities."[1] Formal "treatment" would no doubt qualify as "technical." Despite the prominence of Eliot's innovative treatment, for Collingwood *The Waste Land* essentially, and most importantly, evokes an urgent communal topic: "the decay of our civilization" (334). For Collingwood, *The Waste Land* essentially evokes an urgent communal topic: "the decay of our civilization" (334). "The poem depicts a world where the wholesome flowing water of emotion, which alone fertilizes all human activity, has dried up" (335). The virtue of the poem is that it articulates the dryness in a manner that makes readers newly conscious of the drought. "No community altogether knows its own heart" (336). "The remedy" for such lack of knowledge "is the poem itself" (336).

Collingwood differentiates art "itself" from multiple other things. It is not, Collingwood argues, despite overlaps with alternative activities, identical with craft; nor is it a "representational" endeavor; nor is it religious and political propaganda; nor amusement; nor make-believe. Those multiple distinctions are perhaps best illustrated by the one between craft (connoting "making" or "fabricating") and "creating." When one makes or fabricates a thing, Collingwood says, one imposes a plan on material reality, and the plan is an instrumental means to the realization of that more important purpose. This is where technique matters. Nevertheless, techniques are subordinate to the more valuable process of creation. Freedom of expression from instrumentalizing uses marks authentic art.

To use art to produce a likeness of an external reference is to submit creation to mere mimicry According to Collingwood, an artwork subordinates outward appearances to emotional expression. Collingwood also thinks that to employ art for political purposes is to misuse it. Inevitably politics reduces art to propaganda, which willy-nilly identifies art with magic, because magic attempts to control or influence the world for certain ends (another instrumentalizing aim). And politics (or magic) depends upon previously existing ideas that render art a mere repetitive (or cliché-ridden) illustration of them. In 1938 – in the era of the rise of fascism, the Spanish Civil War, and the advent of a World War II – the confusion of art with politics has created a "new magical literature," and hence another servile allegiance: "no longer of imperialism but of communism" (71). "The peculiar tragedy of the artist's position in the modern world" is that it is repeatedly "forced aside from its own original nature and enslaved to … an end not its own" (33). Clearly, Collingwood favors art's autonomy.

Art's leading principle is a mode of consciousness – Collingwood uses the venerable term *imagination* for it – that gives "new form," and newly expressive language, to "feeling," without sacrificing intellect's comparatively abstract, non-sensory mode of articulation. He targets a contemporary example of erroneous dissociation in the philosopher and linguist I. A. Richards' claim (in *The Principles of Literary Criticism* [1926]) that a scientific use of language is opposed to an emotive use of language, which Richards says defines works of verbal art. Both uses, Collingwood argues in response, are imaginative and, therefore, emotional. Thus a poem or a fiction "may be described as expressing the intellectual emotion attendant upon thinking in a certain way" (and philosophy expresses "the intellectual emotion attendant upon trying to think better") (297); it will lead a reader to grasp the same "intellectual emotion" in the specific terms and language of the writer's imagination.

Given Collingwood's differentiation of art from what it is not, perhaps it is surprising that he ends by theorizing the presence of imaginative expression in every discourse. It is because of his desire to argue art's communal nature that Collingwood universalizes imagination's presence. The artist communes with his predecessors and his colleagues, and he collaborates with his audience, because every person, Collingwood thinks, undertakes a shared dialogue with his fellows. The artist tests the possibility of sharing what he imagines, in order to become certain, in the light of others' responses, that his unfolding consciousness "is not corrupt" (317). Every community, as well as every individual, inevitably experiences corruption of consciousness. The artist's engagement with an audience exposes the extent of corruption, and frees the art – and the audience – from it. Nevertheless, one's explanation of "standing in relation to others" cannot be completed. "There is no point at which a man has finished becoming aware of himself as a person" (317). In sharing the artist's imagination, the audience realizes that it cannot reach or express an absolute awareness any more than the artist can.

The shared inconclusiveness of the process exemplifies Collingwood's desire to draw distinctions, even as he strikes a balance among them. While insisting that art is a collective give and take, he declares that the imaginations of artist and audience are always individualized. Yet he refines that claim, too: in art, each individuation (of selfhood, of emotion, of expression) "is an experience in which the distinction between what is due to myself and what is due to my world has not yet been made" (288). The intellect alone makes those distinctions when it seeks to "argue" or "infer" truth that it deduces from the imagination (287). Purely intellectual deduction does not constitute the only truth, however. Art, too, "is . . . essentially the pursuit of truth" (288).

Collingwood proposes the lack of difference between self and world in the service of his reaffirmation of the communal vocation of *The Waste Land*. The artist must tell his audience what the collective would deny: his role is that of a prophet. Surely Collingwood could have named D. H. Lawrence – an exemplar of fiction's fantastic–prophetic axis – along with Eliot as exemplars of his thought. When Collingwood asserts that "there is no point at which a man has finished becoming aware of himself as a person," he echoes (if unknowingly) "life's quivering uncertainty" and Lawrence's contention that "I shall never know my me." The very title of Lawrence's novel *The Rainbow* (1915) implies a wasteland, a decay of civilization, in need of the help of

Lawrence's artistic vision. Taking on "community" as a topic, portraying its heroine's resistance to the drying up of emotion, *The Rainbow*'s art forecasts consonance with the philosopher's principles.

The unfathomable character of "my me," and of life itself, pervades Lawrence's narrative, which traces the history of three generations of an English Midlands family, the Brangwens, between (roughly) 1840 and the first decade of the twentieth century. The inconclusiveness of personal self-awareness is a reality for Lawrence's figures. Tom Brangwen, chronologically the first of the novel's male protagonists, marries the Polish widow of a Polish fighter who died in the wave of European revolutions in 1848. Tom's marriage represents his attempt to know "my me" by searching for it beyond his native place: a revolutionary aim itself, because traditionally in his native place his gender, according to Lawrence, does not look beyond the domestic horizon for fulfillment. That quest has been the woman's province. By reassigning the search to a male figure, *The Rainbow* begins with a suspense of gender identity, a complement of the uncertainty of selfhood. The suspense continues, to Tom's later grief. Neither his break with tradition nor his partial attachment to it substantiates him. "Was his life nothing?" he thinks, as he takes stock on the day of his step-daughter Anna's wedding to her cousin, Will Brangwen. Hating to give his Anna away, he exclaims, "What weariness! There was no peace, however old one grew! One was never right, never decent, never master of oneself!"[2] Yet Tom has had a happy marriage and a good life. Will Brangwen's marriage also will be happy, but he comes to feel the same self-alienation and lack of finish. Both Tom and Will believe their wives (and daughters) do not suffer such incompleteness. In truth, that is not the case. Will and Anna's daughter Ursula, whose story dominates the second half of *The Rainbow*, undergoes a constant indetermination. "One was not oneself," Ursula thinks, "one was merely a half-stated question" (264). "How to become oneself" (264) seems to her an unanswerable problem.

Lawrence might be said to predict Collingwood's claim that art must remind us of how even our individuation evades purely intellectual grasp. History also for Lawrence is a phenomenon that at no point becomes a finished mode of awareness. The narrative dramatizes Ursula's fight – and apparently the novel's own fight – to enter into history, to "hold her place . . . in the world of work and man's convention" (377). Ursula's struggle is preceded by her discovery of her grandmother's history, which soothes Ursula's fears about her "something-nothing" (264) self by making her "know the tiny importance of the individual within the great past" (242). Entry into history is simultaneously entry into worldly community. Even if the great past dwarfs the present individual it nevertheless seals the individual's communitarian ties, his or her social belonging: the consummation of self-definition and knowledge.

Yet Ursula's author also shapes history against the grain of certainty. The experience of Ursula's parents and grandparents, occupying the novel's first half, is made by Lawrence's treatment to slip away, despite the intensity of its initial impact. The eponymous rainbow, one must remember, is a promise of the future rather than a revelation of past historical meaning. Moreover, although Ursula in the last pages looks to the rainbow as a sign of her enlarged importance among things to come, the reader is unlikely to forget an alternative view – Ursula's own – of the phenomenon. She loves Genesis, but reading through (in the novel's chapter XI) the description of the aftermath of the flood, which includes God's setting His bow in the cloud, she mocks the episode and the rainbow's donor. The trustworthiness of the sign under which Lawrence's novel unfolds, or the novel's informal covenant to deliver fully resolved historical meaning, is shaken by the narrative's contradictory uses of the rainbow – in effect, contradictory uses of its very self.

The contradiction confirms the cogency of Collingwood's identification of art with a dynamically unfinished search for expression. Art takes the lead in that search, with the aim of revealing and castigating what is, for Collingwood, society's disavowed reality: its failure as a collective. That act of leading is popularly resented, Collingwood points out, because it rejects easy solutions: magical thinking, on the one hand; "political remedies" ("shooting capitalists or destroying a social system" [335]), on the other hand. Collingwood's trust in the veracity of Eliot's portrait of "a present where there is nothing but stony rubbish" (334) is corroborated by Ursula's continuing sense of frustration, given the world's unslaked state. She triumphs as a teacher, over brutally unruly students and a dictatorial male school administrator; she exchanges home life for a university education, resisting parental pressure that she conform to domesticity. She becomes another woman who did.

Nevertheless, Lawrence also represents her as feeling that her new status in social existence, her entry into history, is a hollow triumph. Her university education, she comes to believe, is "only a little side-show" (403) to industry, which she figures as a "sham workshop" for which the university is a "sham warehouse." Ursula is painfully certain that her New Woman's liberty is returning her to confinement, to a "dead unreality" (404). Her alternative is marriage with her distant cousin Skrebensky, who is posted to imperial army service in India, and who will take her with him. She engages herself, but is overwhelmed by what she takes to be Skrebensky's submission to another sham warehouse: the Empire. She breaks with him, even though she suspects that she has conceived his child, and will become an unwed mother. Ursula thus becomes Lawrence's delegated prophet, a vehicle for expressing an adequate knowledge of the present order of things, and, as Collingwood puts it, "a medicine for the worst disease of mind, the corruption of consciousness" (336).

Collingwood's brilliant discourse about aesthetics and Lawrence's fictional discourse thus stand shoulder to shoulder. However, if only for the sake of debating fiction's conformity with other discourses, I propose one potential fissure in the convergence. Collingwood's argument turns on his trust in art's prevailing communitarian character. But what if Lawrence allows the resources of fiction to propose a profound skepticism about the value of social being? Collingwood would likely judge such a possibility as a sign of the novelist's corruption.

However it might be assessed, Lawrence's imagination makes Ursula's resistance to the historical warehouse appear valuable, because her dissatisfaction opens on an alternative dimension of life as we know it. The alternative is not sociable; indeed, it is scarcely communicable. Ursula's mother Anna "knows" it before her daughter does. Anna is early "aware of another, freer element, in which each person was detached and isolated. Was not this her natural element?" (185). It is an unnatural element – alien and barely coherent – when Ursula enters it. Ursula's passion for Skrebensky in its early stage leads her to believe that she will obtain "a sense of his own or of her own maximum self" (281). Later, she changes her mind and prefers "a sense of the infinite" (281). Comes a time when both the finite and the infinite seem overdefinite. In a nighttime scene, under a full moon, Ursula simultaneously makes love to Skrebensky and destroys him emotionally, in a way that makes her motives unintelligible. "A strange rage filled her, a rage to tear things asunder. Her hands felt . . . like metal blades of destruction" (297). Her lover feels to her like a "blind, persistent burden," as does the rest of humanity. Rejecting both, Ursula identifies with "the coolness and entire liberty and brightness of the moon," and wants "the moon to fill in to her" (296). The same alienating dimension, promising more life than deathly industry and empire do, hovers over the novel's final pages. That strange dimension is the rainbow's promise! Historical "progress" from Victorian Britain to the brink of global war has not been a worthwhile development. Collingwood's "standing in relation to others" cannot be completed in *The Rainbow* not because incompleteness is the fate of every artwork, every person, and every society, but rather because "standing in relation to others" is proposed as the original corruption. The break-up of sociable community, rather than another invocation of shared interests, is what in *The Rainbow* will satisfy *The Waste Land*'s dryness.

For better or worse, *The Rainbow*'s creative rigor might inhere in its use of fiction to reverse the usual values attached to community and isolation. Anna and Ursula's "freer element," in comparison with public-minded leanings, is uncomfortable and unhelpful, and therefore – paradoxically – is the path that life should take. The promise of that path (its new rainbow) is the aggressive "treatment" Lawrence applies to traditional storytelling and characterization. Shattering the coherence of Ursula's identity, and of narrative continuity and surface realism, the scene of Ursula's rage against her lover and social order ("He was the dross, people were the dross" [296]) contradicts the "warm world of the commonplace" in which "she was a kind, good girl" (300); it contradicts as well the warm world of commonplace novelistic tradition. We might think that "the nothingness" Ursula feels with Skrebensky and others is a "horrible" (299) aberration, to be subordinated by the storyline overall, and "never for one moment allowed to be possible" (299) as anything but a temporary unhealthy emotion – and a momentary narrative experiment. Yet Lawrence does not make things so intelligibly psychological – or so easy for us to evaluate formally. His artistry insists on the actuality of the dimension in which Ursula "was cold and hard and compact of brilliance as the moon itself, and beyond [Skrebensky] as the moonlight was beyond him, never to be grasped or known" (297). That "beyond," Lawrence's novel implies, is what the self-deceiving human heart needs to recognize and know, but wants to refuse knowledge of. The innovative treatment brings that knowledge to the fore. It is not socially or communally oriented. Collingwood would judge the antisocial implication to be a misguided one on Lawrence's part. And perhaps the evidence for it in Ursula's moony rage is not conclusive. If not, then *The Rainbow* remains in line with Collingwood's rationally expounded and eminently sociable aesthetics, despite the fact that fictional discourse (not only Lawrence's) permits itself unreasonable flights.

Modernist-Era Fiction amid Anthropological, Psychological, and Sociological Discourses

The first readers of Naomi Mitchison's novel *The Corn King and the Spring Queen* (1931) would have recognized in its title a reference to one of the era's most famous books, *The Golden Bough*, a multi-volume work by the anthropologist Sir James G. Frazer. A one-volume abridgment of *The Golden Bough* appeared in the same year (1922) as *The Waste Land* and *Ulysses*. Frazer's study, which influenced multiple modernists, documents ancient (or so-called primitive) humanity's universal use of magic to foster nature's bounty and humanity's collective well-being, even at the cost of scapegoating and slaying the fostering agents. The agents are magicians, or priests, or kings, who are appointed to lead their communities, to bless them, and to die for them. The death, as necessary as the change of seasons, is anciently believed in, according to Frazer, as a preliminary to life's resurrection.

Corn Kings, and their female doubles or accomplices, occupy a large swath of Frazer's text. But despite the cues Mitchison's audience could take from *The Golden Bough*, that work would not orient readers to other of the novel's threads. Mitchison's Spring Queen, a Scythian young woman living at the end of the third century B.C., uses one of the annual Corn King ritual magics as a mask for a revenge murder she perpetrates on her father. Having killed him, however, she becomes penitent, as well as a tabooed outcast. Clearly the murder overlays self-divided impulses. The Spring Queen traverses the Mediterranean for five years in search of expiation. In the centrality to the text of the Spring Queen's ambivalence, contemporary readers would have recognized another of the novel's references: Freudian psychology's overlay of anthropology.

Freud's *Totem and Taboo* (1913, English translation 1918), draws heavily on Frazer's work, but revises it by psychologizing the ritual slayings Frazer assigns to magic and religion's invocation of renewed life. Freud hypothesizes a family drama prior to a religious-magic one: the slaying of a father-king, a patriarch, by a primitive group of sons who love their father but also resent his power. The murder, either as historical fact or as permanent human fantasy, is the origin for Freud of collective life, not least because of the ambivalence that results. Freud hypothesizes that, after the slaying, the sons' divided feelings about what they have done (or want to do) establishes itself universally as a system of totemic institutions and prohibitory taboos that generates all psyches and social forms. This system, which is permanently marked by the sons' original ambivalence, and designated in Freudian shorthand as the Oedipal conflict, is inevitably a war of unresolved, self-contradictory desires and aggressions.

The Corn King and the Spring Queen's story, despite its temporal distance from 1931, when women are advancing into a post-patriarchal state, rehearses a narrative that builds on the Freudian explanation and on Frazer. Mitchison agrees that ancient motives still underlie modern life. But there is a further involvement of Mitchison with Freud. Freud's work opened the door to a tolerance of erotic phenomena hitherto considered abnormal, homosexuality and bisexuality prominently among them. Erotic male–male love is a norm in

Mitchison's depiction of ancient Sparta, which is another of her novel's settings. The novel's second female protagonist is a young Spartan woman, who tolerates the fact that her husband is the lover of the king of Sparta. When the king and his lover are about to die, Mitchison shapes the episode so that the men recall their having fallen in love years before – a memory that the author lingers over as tenderly as they do.

Unqualified liberty to discover and to discuss sexual desires and practices is essential to modernist discourse's revolt against the conventions of the past. Along with the prominence Freud gave to alternative sexualities, he made incest newly topical. In *Totem and Taboo*, the band of brothers whom Freud imagines violently eliminating their father are motivated by erotic rivalry. They desire their mother, or her surrogates, whom the patriarch, priest, or king forbids possession of. But the sons subordinate their unruly desires and themselves to the father-figure's taboo on incestuous impulse and enactment. Hence the taboo against incest is part of Freud's picture of society's origin in Oedipal conflict. When we turn later to another novel, Ivy Compton-Burnett's *Brothers and Sisters* (1929), the fact that the story is about a marriage between brother and sister, and about their offspring, who can barely conceal their hostility to their all-controlling, hence male-like, mother, demonstrates another involvement of fiction with Freud.

For a literary history to broach interdiscursive involvements such as these is to undertake a complex operation. When novels borrow substance from nonfictional discourses, their borrowing is not simple and unidirectional, if only because the loan sources are not. In the first three decades of the twentieth century, the intellectual disciplines indicated by anthropology, sociology, and psychology were far more intermingled than they became in later years. The intermingled sources were also at odds with each other – simultaneously. Claims for the autonomy of fictional discourse face stark opposition here. When we approach the cross-currents environing the novelists' versions of anthropology and related disciplines by beginning with the 1922 volume by Frazer, we are already in the middle of things. So are the novelists. A complex intersection involves them not only with Freud's similarity to and differences from Frazer, but also with the oppositions to Freud and Frazer established by 1922 in the work of two young anthropologists-sociologists (one English, and one a Polish immigrant to England), W. H. R. Rivers and Bronislaw Malinowski. And there is more to consider: the feminist cultural anthropology of the classics scholar Jane Ellen Harrison, eclectically negotiating Freud and Rivers, and the female-centered revision of Freud by the Freudian analyst Melanie Klein. Their perspectives are woven into the intellectual cloth of Mitchison and Compton-Burnett's narratives – for example, in Mitchison's replacement of the Freudian brothers' murder of the patriarch with a daughter's slaying of him, and in Compton-Burnet's construction of her mother-figure as equal in power to a patriarchal tyrant.

A temporary detour is required to evoke the contest of ideas about psyches and societies to which the fictions are linked. Rivers and Malinowski, drawing on their anthropological–sociological field work in Melanesia prior to the Great War, opposed Frazer's and Freud's universalizing assumptions. Both also judged that Freud's fascination with sexual desire had led him astray. On the possibility that their criticisms of Freud might influence a certain detachment in the novelists from the very Freudian discourse the novelists also depend on (what an occasion for ambivalence!), we should remark on the anthropologist-psychologists' contentions.

Freud argued that dreams express – under the distorting censorship of the dreamer's matured ego – the ever-active desires of infantile sexuality, including anal eroticism, fetishism, masochism, and sadism, that do not conform to the taboos imposed by religious and social proscription. Rivers countered that sleep and dreams exemplify a less advanced stage of neurobiological development rather than the distorted significances Freud assigns them. That primitive developmental stage is nevertheless valuable because it includes a drive for self-preservation at all costs, and for inclusion in the human collective. Hence, for Rivers, dreams stay close to the problems of waking life, and are attempts to solve them. In 1915, Rivers was assigned to London hospitals for wounded soldiers. The troubles of Rivers's soldier patients, Rivers declared in 1920, were sexual in origin only in "few and far between" cases; they were instead the products of history's "social censorship" – external to dreamers – whose "existence points to something unhealthy in the social order."[3]

Freud's other antagonist, Malinowski, insisted that Freud's idea of "the Oedipus" and its global reach was merely a projection of Freud's white middle-class and upper-class Western European environment. The provincial limitation of Freud's theorizing is proved apparently in Malinowski's *Sex and Repression in Savage Society* (1927) by the alternative family and social order that Malinowski studied in the Trobriand Islands. Social organization there, as also expounded in Malinowski's *The Sexual Life of Savages* (1929), is founded on matrilineal "mother-right . . . the man in no way contributing"[4] other than as a primary caretaker and maternal adjunct who is inferior in status to the mother and the mother's brother. The matrilineal structure is free of Oedipal conflict, Malinowski contends. To be sure, the maternal uncle constitutes a greater paternal figure than a Trobriander's biological father; moreover, struggles develop between maternal uncles and nephews.

At the same time, the matrilineal order includes taboos, against brother–sister incest above all.

Freud's rejoinder to Malinowski was adamant: the matrilineal taboos and the uncle's authority are variants of the Oedipal conflict, complemented by another prohibition of incest. Malinowski agreed that all cultures are marked by incest taboos, but he contended that the structuring of the taboo varies from culture to culture, and functions differently in each. Accordingly, when in *The Sexual Life of Savages* Malinowski reveals that one of the most popular Trobriand island myths is about a brother–sister incest, he wonders if this taboo-breaking tale signals a specific culture's "incredible inconsistency" (539) – and is a point in favor of Freud's universal Oedipus complex. He decides that it is not, because the myth's function, he argues, is to explain to young Trobrianders their culture's magical practices that have eros as their object. It would be a mistake to see it projecting a communal yearning for incestuous transgression and a simultaneous communal repression of that yearning.

Malinowski's patrolling of sociohistorical boundaries repeats Rivers' criticism of Freud's emphasis on non-normative drives in the human sexual constitution. The Trobrianders allow children free sexual play (except for the taboo against brother–sister relations) before puberty, and promiscuity before marriage. Malinowski represents the children's license thusly: "Genital manipulation and such minor perversions as oral stimulation of the organs are typical forms of [their] amusement" (55). Having criticized Freud for universalizing a culture- and class-bound theory, is Malinowski now importing his own white European taboos – against so-called "perversions" – into his science? If the Trobrianders have any likeness to European eroticism, Malinowski thinks the similarity is with "the peasant and proletarian child," because the latter's habits are "less clandestine, less associated with guilt, hence less immoral, less 'anal erotic' and more attached to sex."[5] "Sex" apparently means genital intercourse. Even as Malinowski applauds the Trobrianders' accommodation of infantile sexuality – an applause that marks his modernist subversion of Western mores – he also seems censoriously Victorian, at odds with Oscar Wilde as well as with Freud.

The view of homosexuality in Mitchison's novel, as we will see, enlists the antagonistic views of contemporary discourse, as if to allow their lack of resolution, and to exploit the dissonant alternatives when and where the independent needs of fictional discourse require. We might say something of the same for Compton-Burnett. For Mitchison, the dissonance does not affect either her attachment to "primitive" matriarchy or her implicit alignment with discursive attempts such as those of Harrison and Klein to resolve, or at least redirect, the controversies that exercise their male counterparts. Harrison's attempted resolution celebrates matrilineal order, in agreement with Malinowski; yet in *Epilegomena to the Study of Greek Religion* (1921), Harrison avows her indebtedness to *Totem and Taboo*, to Frazer's work, and to Rivers to boot. She finds it "easy to see," along with Freud, that taboo "takes its rise in ... the fiercest of human impulses in sex jealousy"[6] – that in Greek Olympian religion, the shaping of social impulse became a patriarch-centered theology (Zeus as the supreme father-king-ruler). But Harrison's *Themis* (1912, revised 1927) expounds the pre-Olympian religion, in which Themis is the goddess of the human collective. "Not religion, she is the stuff of which religious representations are made" (485). The "stuff" is "the matrilineal type" (514). For scholars and readers, to be recalled to matriliny is to return to the origin of religion and society. Thus Harrison recovers for Europe the same social organization that Malinowski and Rivers found current a world away. In doing so, she contradicts the anthropologists' criticisms of universality.

The figure of the mother, heiress of the matrilineal type, is given her supreme due in the psychological sphere of modernist-era anthropological–sociological–psychological discourse. Melanie Klein, emigrating to England in 1926, theorized Oedipal conflict anew, in effect dislodging the primacy of the father in Freudian doctrine, even as she continued to be a Freudian. For our purposes, the bearing of Klein's revision of Freud affects this chapter's interest in the nature (special or otherwise) of fiction. Before we can engage her relevance to art, a final preliminary summary of her thought is required.

Neither a male nor a female child, according to Klein in "Early Stages of the Oedipus Conflict" (1928), experiences emotional ties with its father without first experiencing a complex of responses to its mother, above all to its mother's body. The mother is the bodily fount of its nurture, and the infant feels lovingly identified with her flesh. But when the infant feels that nurture is withdrawn, or when the infant is being toilet-trained and resents its mother's demands, its lack of understanding drives it to fantasize retaliatory responses: harm, even to the point of matricide. At the same time, the aggression fissures the child's identification with the mother, so the violence appears to be a self-splitting. A boy infant's intimacy with his mother's body and her will, Klein theorizes, creates a "femininity complex" in the child: feeling one with her, he assumes that his mother's breasts, her generative organs, her power vis-à-vis males, are also his. Nevertheless, "anxiety associated with the femininity-phase drives the boy ... to identification with the father."[7] But that parent becomes a source of rivalry for the boy. The girl child undergoes complementary conflicts. For both genders, there is no direct approach to a father without primary access to mother: she encloses or harbors the father's phallus.

The mother is, for the infantile mind, both a good figure and an aggressive one. According to Klein, as any child grows, and as any adult life unfolds, it will repeat in its relation with others the original patterns of response it adapts to the maternal center: returning its goodness with goodness, or raging at its apparent persecution, or repairing mutual aggressions with compensatory desires and actions.

Our excursus into nonfictional discourse now can be halted so that we can gauge how the novelists might be using the thinkers who are not novelists. We have noted that, like Freud, Mitchison treats as essential the self-division that succeeds antipatriarchal aggression, but that she makes her Spring Queen, Erif Der – a daughter, rather than a son – the aggressor. Erif Der's father wants to exploit his daughter's position as the consort of the life-giving Frazerian Corn King of Scythia, Tarrik, in order to install one of her brothers in Tarrik's place. A Freudian supreme patriarch, the father kills Erif Der's first child as part of his dynastic scheme. Her murder of her father, in turn, is a maternal revenge. It suggests more than a personal motive, however: it implies a repressed matrilineal social order struggling to reclaim its centrality. Echoing Malinowski, Harrison, and Klein, Mitchison's narrative enfolds her male figures in a story that first and last focuses on mothers. Erif Der's wanderings will issue in a climactic reunion with her long-lost mother in Egypt. It comes about during her penitential visit to a temple of Isis, the supreme mother of the Egyptian pantheon. Thereafter she is released from tabooed status and guilt. Mitchison's other heroine, the Spartan Philylla, loves the queen consort of her King Kleomenes (the lover of Philylla's husband) even more than she loves others. The struggles among the novel's men, and the relations of the women to them, are therefore resonant with Klein's idea that both genders take on their identities and histories in the form of a primary encounter with maternal power.

Mitchison pursues a course also in line with Rivers's and Malinowski's antagonism to the ahistorical nature of the others' research. The unevenness of historical development, the degeneration of primitive folkways, and the ascent of innovations are all left out of *The Golden Bough* and *Totem and Taboo*. Putting them back in, Mitchison's tale – it is nominally a historical novel, based on real events in the Mediterranean between 228 and 187 B.C. – appears to have grown out of a meditation on how the religious magic dependent on ritual slayings would have been historically modified by the very cultures practicing it, and by the environing civilizations. Mitchison's Scythians are not isolated savages: they have economic and cultural intercourse with the Greek city-states, which have developed in democratic and rational directions that influence Tarrik. Indeed, Tarrik has an ethnic Greek heritage as well as a native Scythian one, and he is increasingly affected by the cosmopolitan rationalism of a visiting Greek Stoic philosopher. The Stoic's ideas cause Tarrik to develop an ambivalent consciousness. Because of his position, he believes he is a god, but he wants only to be a man. He travels to Sparta to learn a way of ordering society that is liberated from totemic and tabooed structures. (He has a Frazerian–Freudian psyche, one might say, and wants a Riversian one instead.)

The whole of Mitchison's world is changing historically. Sparta, another version of Tarrik's split, takes on a double consciousness, at once old and new, because King Kleomenes subscribes to the dual monarchy of Spartan tradition, but suspends it anyway; even more revolutionarily, he initiates a classless communism. Far in advance of Scythian magic, this is an entirely new way of governing natural increase and distribution. Unhappily, Kleomenes's "New Times" creates a political reaction. A Greek anticommunist league crushes his political experiment, although it ultimately will sow a progressive seed in Tarrik's city-state.

Mitchison's Sparta suggests a flowering in her own historical era – namely, Stalin's contemporary Soviet Union. A political nonfictional discourse adds itself to the other discourses in the novel. But Stalinists would not have fancied Mitchison's picturing them in terms of homoerotic liaisons. Those are legally tabooed in 1931, and perhaps anachronistically projected into the past. That is not to say that Mitchison portrays homosexuality as a uniform constituent of polymorphous Freudian eros. We have already noted a dissonance in this regard. *The Corn King and the Spring Queen* respects historical determinations of eros. In Mitchison's Sparta, homosexuality is fostered by a liberating social movement, transforming the character of both genders, as well as foregrounding one aspect of a bisexual ancient humanity. Significantly, it is when Kleomenes is losing his ideological battle that he forsakes his male lover for the apparently reactionary pleasures of sex with a captive female slave, whose erotic charm is a submissiveness antithetical to revolutionary Spartan womanhood as well as to the egalitarianism of Spartan male–male love. After Kleomenes flees to post-defeat exile in Egypt, he, his family, and his followers suffer from the mounting tyranny of the Egyptian ruler Ptolemy, who is fated by tradition to marry his sister, and who is gay. Suddenly it is as if censorious Malinowski had taken over Mitchison's Freudian typewriter. The reader is manipulated into feeling aversion for the same eros that is a virtue in a revolutionary Spartan context, and that garners sympathy again in the final pages about Kleomenes's sexual love for Philylla's husband. Mitchison's point – which Rivers and Malinowski would appreciate – is that sexuality changes its functional or normative value, as well as its psychological profile, under the pressure of differing conditions.

But if the differences of conditioning are all-determining and prevailing, how can there be exchanges between cultures, and what good is the ancient past to the present-day concerns of 1931? After the Spartans in Egypt rebel unsuccessfully against Ptolemy, Philylla stoically submits to her death sentence (the sort of action unexplained by Rivers's survival instinct). Mitchison represents her loss as a lamentable disappearance from the world stage of the communist hope to which she is devoted. History seems the sign of irreversible discontinuity in human experience, and of the uselessness of redemptive recovery.

Nevertheless, alongside Mitchison's ideological aims, and the earnest discourses that her novel threads, her fiction contains marked romance elements – Erif Der's quest for healing, for one – that disrupt the reader's reading of history as a prefiguration of the present at the expense of reading the novel as a verbal artwork. Giving her novel's allusion to Stalin yet another turn, Mitchison pictures Kleomenes, on the eve of the insurrection against Ptolemy, as convening a last supper for the twelve most favored members of his retinue. The meal, inspired by Osiris – a variant of the Corn King who is killed and comes back to life – "is one of the Mysteries. ... The God becomes corn, becomes bread. He is taken and eaten by the Initiates."[8] Is Mitchison's reader to think of Tarrik, Kleomenes, Stalin (or Lenin), Osiris, and Christ as king-priests who die or who will die efficaciously for the people? Are they all one? If so, romance is overtaking history. It overtakes it thoroughly when we find that Erif Der's mother in Egypt is no longer a woman: she is changed into a bird, and in her avian existence she reunites with her daughter. Erif Der herself undergoes a supernatural metamorphosis: she turns into a snake to protect the body of the slain Kleomenes. The priestess of Isis tells Erif Der that a person's life is divided between "one's own image that is always separate" and a "spirit" that can "enter other bodies or make itself a body to do its will" (685). Because Mitchison's leading protagonists are not integrated selves (or even, given their bird and snake forms, integrated bodies), it is unlikely that Mitchison wants to assert unqualified identities between her characters and Christ or Stalin. The splits characterize another ambivalence – about the novel's relation to the world. It refers to historical reality, and suspends the reference.

In doing so, it foregrounds Mitchison's conscious meditation on art – on the discourse of fiction itself – in her novel; and suggests her coincidence with Klein, whose theory of art can now be brought forward. Klein hypothesized in a 1929 essay that an infant's love and rage in regard to the objects – and the persons – it depends upon are the roots of creative impulse. After aggressively attacking the source of its nurture, the infant mind seeks to repair the damages caused by its aggressions. The production of artworks repeats, in a finer form, such reparative recreation. In *The Rainbow*, for example, the sign of the repair of Lawrence's aggression toward society and novelistic tradition might be his text itself. In Mitchison's work, Berris Der, Erif Der's brother and Philylla's lover after her husband returns to the king's bed, is an artist and illustrates Klein's idea. He begins his artistic career as a proto-modernist abstractionist or cubist, forging nonfigurative metal ornaments that are detached from the world of recognizable images. The detachment, one might argue, is a form of aggression against the world that, despite being a mother-like source of his nurture, is unable to satisfy him. Then Berris becomes less detached: visiting Sparta with his penitent parricide-sister, he joins Kleome-nes's revolutionary troops and revises his art in a figural direction, becoming a socialist realist ahead of his time. His succeeding move to sculpture, mixing realism and abstraction, suggests Mitchison's own restless position among formal artistic possibilities of treatment. She gives Berris a formula for her work when the Stoic philosopher urges him to break up a statue he has made of Philylla and Death. "My statue is meant to be disturbing," Berris responds; "it is meant to break up all kinds of little realities which ordinary men and women have made for themselves, and little calmnesses which philosophers have made for them" (698). "My novel is meant to be disturbing in the same way," Mitchison might be imagined as saying.

One of the effects of Berris's proto-modernist iconoclasm (aggression reinforced by his sculpture's emblem of death) is to identify "little realities" with illusions. By doing so, Berris's artwork, or (from a Kleinian viewpoint) any artwork, including narrative fiction, revives in the viewer or reader a version of the infant's uncertainty about the nature of its nurturing source. Mitchison's entanglement of history and romance provokes a like uncer-tainty – aggressively. What is the source of the fiction? Life? History? Fantasy? Is the source destructive or creative? Raising those questions is only the starting point. After breaking up recognizable appearances, the artwork substitutes in their place – reparatively – a new objective reality: its own, which provides its audience with a material intellectual nurture. Like magic, the fictional work satisfies, or at least charms and pacifies, whatever hungry and divided desires the audience brings to it. The satisfaction or charm is a contemplative one: novels such as Mitchison's give readers an opportunity to meditate the dissonances – the clash of intellectual paradigms, the conflict between realities and fantasies – that amid actual life and prevailing nonfic-tional discourses are less available to reflection.

If *The Corn King and the Spring Queen* satisfies in this way, the satisfaction offered by Compton-Burnett's *Brothers and Sisters* is more uncertain – less charming and more biting. Returning us to the Freudian Oedipus, the novel also contradictiously enlists the emphasis on maternal-female power that Harrison and Klein recover. Compton-Burnett's antipatriarchal revolutionists are Sophia and Christian, who have been raised as if they were brother and sister, although Christian is an orphan adopted by Sophia's father, Andrew Stace. The young people rebel against Stace when he taboos their marriage, on pain of their disinheritance. As if their will to marry were lethal, Stace dies as soon as the couple insists on their purpose, with Sophia in the lead as the violator of male power. But ambivalence follows: having in effect killed her father, Sophia then in effect resurrects him, or encloses him, in her maternal presence. When her daughter and two sons are grown (more than twenty-five years later), she still infantilizes them – dictating their routines and retaining their governess to spy on them. Ruling her husband Christian as well, she insists on being a center of attention and superiority. The children seethe with resentment. They attack her verbally – aggression and criticism are their métiers – to her face as well as behind her back. But she remains their tyrant.

The children acquire additional reason to be unhappy. Dinah and her brother Andrew want to marry, probably as a way of escaping Sophia. They court, respectively, a brother and sister newly arrived in the neighborhood. But it is discovered that the mother of the new arrivals is also Christian's long-lost own mother. Dinah and Andrew are on the verge of marrying their grandmother's children: their uncle and aunt! They test their fiancées' inclination to break off their engagements – and the break ensues. They do not as yet know the identity of Christian's father, because Christian's mother does not name him. But they will learn that Stace lied: Christian is Stace's son, a result of an extramarital affair. Stace's confession of the fact was in a document that Sophia knew was locked away, although she thought – or tried only to think – that its contents were about a different legacy.

Christian dies of a heart attack when he discovers that his wife is his sister. Dinah and Andrew have just affianced themselves to another brother–sister pair, with the brother being the parish rector. As the news of the incest circulates, the rector and his sibling break their engagements. They varnish the event with talk about tragedy, following the line of Dinah's prior suitor, the uncle she escaped marrying. According to him, he and his sister (who was to marry Andrew) "are beginning to leave off feeling branded, but all our friends seem shy of us. It is all too like an ancient tragedy for them."[9] Likewise, it is all too like for the speaker, who, in alluding to Oedipus as if he were above branding Dinah and Andrew, belies his likeness to "our friends."

The rector later renews the sophistications about "tragedy": "I hardly even envy [Dinah and Andrew] their credit for behaving well in tragedy; though tragedy is by far the best background, and every one behaves well in it" (267). The rector apparently behaves well by dropping Dinah and engaging himself to Andrew's newfound aunt. There is something deceptive and self-deceptive in such responses, if only because the young people's betrothals have all along been lukewarm or opportunistic. They really don't want anything to do with marriage or family! The "tragedy" provides them a convenient, although temporary, escape.

Lying, and the shaming of scapegoats so as to divert attention from lying, seems in Compton-Burnett to be the origin of society. Stace originally exemplifies it, and Sophia's announcement of the facts to her children recapitulates it. "So I am Father's sister," she says. "Well, I am not troubled about that. It only seems to draw us closer. But you must not think of it, my dears. You must not know it. ... Just forget it. ... Really be unconscious of it" (209). Really be unconscious, in other words, of anything – such as the truth – that gets in the way of assertive self-approval, not to speak of self-deception and the deception of others.

Once they are left without fiancées, Dinah wryly remarks to her brother: "You and I will be wedded to each other, Andrew. That sounds dubiously in accordance with family traditions" (270). Facing his "wedding" with his sister, Andrew wonders, "Shall we be able to bear the spectacle of all our best friends normal and prosperous and married to each other? ... Can we be so great?" His sister's reply, "We need not be quite" (269), punctures the value of the normal "spectacle" and the heroic pathos of bearing up. The wryness also faces the incest matter-of-factly, without moral repugnance and without making it (once more) an "unconscious" secret.

"The Oedipus" for Andrew and Dinah is only an accidental life-occurrence. Their mordant humor about it, even as they are caught up in it, are of a piece with the characteristically critical perspectives their author assigns them about their mother's and other characters' illusions, as well as their own. The biting aspect of their registrations of their world suggests that their author too does not unquestioningly subscribe to visions of totem and taboo, patriarchy and matriarchy, and Kleinian mothers and fathers, because those visions and their visionaries can be impositions upon us, dictatorial discursive Sophias. Perhaps only Rivers's downplaying of eros and incest would not qualify for the aggressive dark humor to which the novel, it might be argued, subjects the nonfictional discourses. To be sure, *Brothers and Sisters* can exemplify Klein's idea of the origins of art in the artist's attack on reality, and his subsequent reparative objectification of it in his work. Nevertheless, in this case the reparative character seems hard to tell apart from the antagonism that inspires it, from the hostility the unwedded (yet "wedded") siblings persistently voice, from first to last. The simultaneity of destructive and reconstructive impulses gives an unusually unsettling quality to Compton-Burnett's practice of fiction.

Whereas Sophia and other characters prefer to live by lies, suppressing the difference between truth and fiction, and whereas the real world also suppresses it, Compton-Burnett makes clear to her readers that her novels do not. They are emphatically fictive. The author demonstrates their fictive nature by flaunting her modernist experimentation. Because most of her pages are dialogue, her narrative redirects narrative toward drama, analogous to the way that modernist fiction turns stories into lyric texts. The treatment undoes differences between tragic and comic modes, as well as between genres. Oscar Wilde has been called in, it seems, to encounter the tragedy of Oedipus, to rewrite it, and to make it funny, however horribly – all the time behaving well in the process. Moreover, as another Wildean derivation, the dialogue is taxingly noncolloquial, sequences of aphoristic cerebral exchanges that emphasize the text's artifice. The artifice abets the distance of the story from historical reality. Compton-Burnett makes the Staces' dilemmas unfold in a village world, before the time of the automobile. Abstraction from ordinary reality, not local color or periodization, is the motive. The abstraction makes it possible for the fiction to constitute an autonomous world unto itself, and for a reader thereby to take up an imaginative distance from actuality, one where the reader can think more freely – and more critically – about the nonfictions, even the most earnest and world-determining ones, that shape knowledge and experience.

Modernist Fiction, Modernist Science

Scientific technology, political activism, mysticism, and narrative fiction are in conflict – indeed at war – with each other in Aldous Huxley's novel, *After Many a Summer Dies the Swan* (1939). The technology is being applied to an experiment in longevity, funded by a southern California real estate tycoon, in the hope of realizing his mantra: "God is love. There is no death."[10] The scientist in charge will discover a formula for "well-fed bod[ies], forever youthful, immortally athletic, indefatigably sexy" (12). A junior scientist in the lab worries about the new possibility's relation to democracy and economic justice. He desires "happiness and progress through science as well as Socialism" (133). He has recently fought against fascism in the Spanish Civil

War. His desire is assessed adversely by another protagonist, William Propter, a historian who has become a mystic. He regards the research project as symptomatic of a will in modern science, essentially sadistic, to dominate life and death. Moreover, he judges the immortalizing project to be a violation of the determinism that rules life. "On the strictly human level no acts are free," he argues. He, too, wants social justice – he has initiated a sustainability project in aid of local migrant workers – but for him there is a cosmic dimension, "the highest cause of all" (134), that is ignored and even violated at "the strictly human level" by science and politics. The role of art, whether verbal or visual, in relation to such perspectives, and to mysterious aspects of the universe or of existence, is problematic.

The conflicts in Huxley's fiction emerge amid the same conflicts in the revolutionary scientific discourse of the modernist era. What relation has that discourse to religious and mystical views of the universe, to determinism, to politics, to art? Thirty years earlier, John Masefield's *Multitude and Solitude* (1909) rehearsed answers. Masefield's writer-protagonist Roger does not think that an author of novels or plays or poems should be primarily a political activist or propagandist. Nevertheless, Roger is about to lose his faith in fiction. "What you had better do," says one acquaintance, "is, give up all this 'obsolete anachronism' of art" for the sake of yet another modernism. "Science is the art of the twentieth century."[11]

Roger decides that "Science, so cleanly and fearless, was doing the poet's work" (172). If Roger is to continue writing, however, he must first undergo "the discipline of action, thought, or suffering" (190) in an arena outside of literature. A medical researcher – Lionel Heseltine, who wants to develop a cure for sleeping sickness – strikes Roger as the poet's heir: the scientist-hero. He goes with Lionel to Africa, in the hope of discovering a cure. After they both contract the illness, Roger, at death's door, concocts the antitoxin and rescues them. Nevertheless, during the time they have been near death, the antitoxin has been discovered elsewhere. Roger's story witnesses the life-giving force of science anyway. He agrees with Lionel that "Science is not a substitute for religion but religion of a very deep and austere kind" (330). Hence science absorbs poetry and religion, and reestablishes their purpose and authority in its own discourse.

Two historically real scientists of the modernist era, the British astrophysicists and mathematicians Sir James Jeans and Sir Arthur Eddington, discuss their objects in ways that borrow from the vocabulary associated with novels, poetry, and religion. "The waves which form the universe," Jeans writes in *The Mysterious Universe* (1930), "are in all probability fictitious. ... And yet they are the most real things of which we have any knowledge or experience, and so are as real as anything can possibly be for us."[12] Again, when Jeans affirms that "the simplest conceivable event" in the universe is "when two electrons meet," he hastens to add that "the meeting of two electrons is fictitious" (129). One basis of science's fictional character is the revolutionary "uncertainty principle" that the German physicist Arthur Heisenberg, building on Albert Einstein's theories of cosmic spatio-temporal relativity (1905, 1915), introduced by demonstrating "that nature abhors accuracy and precision above all" (28). The waves and electrons are possible and probable rather than surefire fact, because they are calculable only in mathematical and abstract terms. The very title of Jeans's book suggests a romance realm. As we might expect in a romance, the line "between realism and idealism becomes very blurred indeed" (147) in the new science.

Eddington's *The Nature of the Physical World* (1928) originates the note that Jeans repeats. "We are haunted by the word *reality*," Eddington complains. It is useless for science to attempt to tie down its meaning, or the entity that goes by the name, in a single-minded way. *Reality* and *existence* are "conventional term[s]" that help us make discoveries, but are not separately identifiable – or certainties – in themselves. Hence "It has become doubtful whether it will ever be possible to construct a physical world out of the knowable," Eddington writes.[13] Eddington likens the physicist, in his relation to atoms or electrons, to the artist, "who tries to bring out the soul in his picture [but] does not really care whether and in what sense the soul can be said to exist" (316).

The fiction-like indeterminacy principle inspires the scientists because it means that our machine-based accounts of cause and effect do not rule the elementary operations that compose us. According to Eddington, we need not admit more than a limited operation of cause and effect, because neither the electron nor the atom nor the cosmos admits more. "We may note that science thereby withdraws its moral opposition to free-will" (318). It even withdraws its opposition to religious thought, inasmuch as the latter suggests the plausibility of mysticism in response to the mysterious universe.

So far, it seems, scientific discourse converges toward what Propter (the historian turned mystic) in Huxley's fiction stands for. But Huxley's young socialist wants the universe to be accountable for terrestrial justice, as do Eddington's and Jeans's fellow scientists on the left of the political spectrum. The biologist and geneticist J. B. S. Haldane (brother of Naomi Mitchison) shares Eddington's emphasis on human freedom from external determinations, but at the same time resists assigning that freedom transcendent possibilities. "The truly scientific attitude," Haldane concludes in *The Causes of Evolution* (1932), "is a passionate attachment to reality as such, whether it be bright or dark, mysterious or intelligible."[14] The difference between that statement and Eddington's resistance to being haunted by "reality as such" is a measure of modernist science's intra-discursive disagreements. Yet the disagreements share opposition to causal determination. Despite its very title, *The Causes of Evolution* both accepts Darwin's evolutionary theory and rejects (a sign of its modernism) much Victorian deterministic thought in which Darwin was entangled, including Darwin's "survival of the fittest." Most biological fitness, Haldane demonstrates, travels the road to extinction. Writing in 1932, Haldane thinks that degeneration and extinction is humanity's prospect "unless [it] takes conscious control of evolution within the next few thousand years" (167).

In his 1932 text Haldane aligns himself with Samuel Butler, H. G. Wells, and Huxley. In his 1939 *The Marxist Philosophy and the Sciences*, Haldane aligns himself with Marxism, because "It claims to enable us to understand change and development of all kinds, ... and by understanding to influence and to control them."[15] If Haldane resists determinism, however, he also resists indeterminacy. He emphasizes the conclusive knowledge that science establishes, hand in hand with historical materialism. The "same fact which gives us the uncertainty principle," he writes to illustrate Marxist dialectical thought about science, "gives us an immense amount of verifiable deductions ... which add to our knowledge to such an extent that we might legitimately speak of a new certainty principle" (89). A scientific certainty principle is empowering, in other words, because it solidifies our power to direct our fate.

In the philosopher Bertrand Russell's study, *The Scientific Outlook* (1931), the topic of directive empowerment becomes central. The ensemble of perspectives that is gathered into Huxley's novel implicitly includes Russell's view, which absorbs the other scientific reflections. Because human empowerment is not on Propter's horizon, how might Russell's summation bear on Huxley's fictional discourse? To begin with, Russell appreciatively avows science. Pavlov is one of his heroes for discovering how conditioned reflexes can be "as capable of scientific treatment" – that is, of directed determination – "as the behaviour governed by unconditioned reflexes."[16] Unlike Rebecca West, however, Russell does not ally Pavlov with "the strange necessity." Science and art are equals in the pursuit of truth, Russell says, but he also repeats Masefield's emphasis on the superiority of science when it comes to practical matters: "[B]ecause science gives us the power of manipulating nature ... it has more social importance than art" (xxiv). Russell also sides with Haldane against the physicists' bias toward the mystery of matter. Their bias is retrograde: they "lose faith in knowledge," which is the "better faith" of the "unyielding rationalist" (95).

Yet the scientific outlook has become one of our troubles! Indeed, preparing the way for Huxley, the last third of Russell's book presents – dialectically – an alternative to the celebratory view of scientific rationalism that precedes it. Power is the trouble. "All modern scientific thinking ... is at bottom power thinking; ... the fundamental human impulse to which it appeals is ... the desire to be the cause of as many and as large effects as possible" (128). In medical science, power thinking has been the cause of cures that Russell believes outweigh the destruction produced by the modern science of weaponry. Yet science depends on expertise – and such expertise, Russell predicts, as it expands over all areas of life, will inevitably become a means of domination. Russell can imagine a worldwide scientific oligarchy that is utopian in character. At the same time, he thinks that "the price [humanity] will have paid for" Utopia might not be worthwhile (180). It will occasion an extreme class divide between technical workers, who will be the progeny of science-derived experts, and nontechnical laborers. Should the latter think of revolting against the oligarchy of their superiors, science will provide a technology of entertainments whereby rebellion can be pacified and diverted. "In such a world, though there may be pleasure, there will be no joy" (192). And there is an even higher price to pay: "Science has more and more substituted power-knowledge for love-knowledge, and as this substitution is completed science tends more and more to become sadistic" (198). A society that is dominated, managed, and made into an economy by scientific techniques will be inevitably an agent of willful harm.

"If knowledge consists [of] the power to produce intended changes, then science gives knowledge in abundance" (196). But knowledge has another form, exemplified in "the mystic, the lover, and the poet," Russell declares. "In all forms of love we wish to have knowledge of what is loved, not for purposes of power, but for the ecstasy of contemplation" (196). In a turn against Masefield and Haldane, and reversing his own previously expressed antipathy toward the mysteriousness of the universe, Russell concludes that "the lover, the poet and the mystic find a fuller satisfaction than the seeker after power can ever know" (199).

So, by way of interdiscursive coincidence, Russell comes to be echoed by Huxley's Propter, minus the latter's doubt about the satisfactions of "the lover" and, as we'll see, the value of "the poet." The young scientist who has returned from Spain, Pete Boon, is blindly in love with the tycoon's movie starlet mistress, who also happens to be the willing erotic object of the senior researcher, Dr. Obispo. The sexual taste of Obispo, as Russell would have predicted, is sadistic. Propter continually warns Pete against eros. It combines, Propter argues, "loyalty to your physiology" and "loyalty to your higher feelings," but the combination amounts to just "being loyal to yourself." "You couldn't be loyal to yourself," Pete comes to realize in Propter's light, "and loyal at the same time to the highest cause of all" (135). The highest cause transcends the fact that "every psychological pattern is determined . . . within the cage of flesh and memory" (208). The tycoon's desire for immortality seeks to live forever in the cage. There is only one supreme escape, Propter says: it bears the name of "God." According to Propter, God is present only in the absence of what we call our humanity, which erroneously regards "the ego or its social projections as real entities" (210). A not-so-distant echo of Lawrence is audible in Propter's antisocial animus.

Propter's derogation of individual selfhood also echoes the artistic–critical discourse about impersonality that modernist novelists want to substitute for traditional novelistic "character." Those novelists include Huxley. Yet Huxley's attitude toward novels is startling, even ferocious. Countering his fellow novelists no less than discursive trends about fiction and art evidenced in the work of Jeans, Eddington, and Russell, Huxley's novel favors a spiritual realm withdrawn from science, from theology, and from the poet's and novelist's realm – a withdrawal from literature. Literature, Propter thinks, is

> just a huge collection of facts about lust and greed, fear and ambition, duty and affection; . . . and imaginary facts at that. . . . It helped to perpetuate misery by explicitly or implicitly approving the thoughts and feelings and practices which could not fail to result in misery. And this approval was bestowed in the most magnificent and persuasive language.   (173–174)

As for literary historians and critics, Propter derides "the astonishing nonsense talked by those who undertake to elucidate [literary art's] hodge-podge of prettily patterned facts and fancies!" (173). The nonsense includes contextual historical explanations of literature: "The real conditions at any given moment are the subjective conditions of the people then alive. And the historian has no way of finding out what those conditions were" (218).

Thus, in this novel, fictional discourse is presented as different from others, and as having a special nature, of the worst kind and of the worst effect. Its discourse is all but anathema. Huxley's anti-literary, anti-novelistic, and anti-fictional animus is located in another researcher-character, Jeremy Pordage, a literary critic, literary historian, and archivist. He arrives at the tycoon's castle because he is hired to catalog a new addition to the tycoon's staggering collection of world artefacts. The new treasure comprises the family papers of an English aristocratic family, whose most intriguing descendent, the Fifth Earl of Hauberk, is a diarist from the era of the French Revolution, and whose sexual appetites make him an English equivalent of the Marquis de Sade. As Pordage works through the journals, he begins to realize that its writer was unusually long-lived – and was regularly feeding himself on carp intestines. That is the very nutrient Obispo is testing as the agent of longevity. Obispo's experimentation, as Pordage delightedly reports, had been confirmed – and scooped! – by a previous sadist scientist.

By making the man of letters Obispo's helper, Huxley makes fiction and literary discourse complicit with the will to power that animates the tycoon and his paid allies. How can Huxley the novelist deride the very genre, narrative fiction, that he produces? Is this another modernist anti-modernism? If so, Huxley exceeds Wells's precedent: he seems to want to erase his storytelling altogether, in exchange for mystical polemic. Indeed, he seeks to turn his novel into a nonfictional manifesto, an entirely other discourse. In the latter part of Huxley's text, one of the chapters begins with three pages of condemnation of "the arbitrary, purely human order that comes from the subordination of the swarm to some lunatic 'ideal'" (209) – including the apparently sane political ideal that Pete fought for in Spain. Here the author exhorts the reader directly: to hell with prettily patterned facts and fancies, and their entrapping contributions to flesh and memory! Nevertheless, at the end of the three pages, we discover that the author's thoughts are simultaneously a free indirect discourse report of what Pete is thinking. The fictional character, and the fictional context of the exhortation, resumes its sway. The sway is powerfully intensified in the novel's finale, which includes an encounter with the horrifying results for longevity of piscine intestinal flora. The sadistic proto-scientist the Fifth Earl, at least two hundred years old, is still alive and residing, and hiding, in secret caverns under his ancestral home.

The encounter and the Fifth Earl belong to fantasy, to a romance world that fiction provides us. In other words, in the novel's conflicts among science, political commitments, religious vision, and fiction, fictional discourse does not merely succumb to Propter's strictures. Indeed, although Huxley writes into his narrative an attack on literary art, he also writes into it a metaphorical encomium. He evokes a painting by the seventeenth-century Dutch artist Jan (Johannes) Vermeer to reflect on the nature of all arts. The picture turns up, and is impersonally described, at a moment in which the tycoon, frenzied by jealousy, is on his way to murder the scientist, whose dalliance with the starlet has been discovered. Before the killing, the tycoon passes the Vermeer, without regarding it. But the narrative regards it. It portrays a young woman in blue satin, looking out "from her universe of perfected geometrical beauty ... into that other universe in which [the tycoon] and his fellow creatures had their ugly and untidy being" (204–205). In regard to those fellow creatures, the mysterious universe of art, of narrative fiction, has, after all, a role to play. It produces a version of Russell's ecstasy of contemplation. "Within the frame [of the picture] nothing could have been different; the stillness of that world was not the mere immobility of old paint and canvas; it was also the spirited repose of consummated perfection" (206). Propter, against the grain of his witting discourse about literature, has been persuading Pete of the value of just that repose, and of just that perfection. Huxley, despite his criticism, uses fiction – and its romance dimension – to persuade the reader of the same. Russell and some of the scientists help him to do so; and Huxley himself attends, if only momentarily, to the special nature and value of art – his own art included.

British Fiction's Ideas of History, 1923–1946

This volume's title exhibits the customary dependence of histories of fiction on real history. But what real history *is*, and what meaning of it should be adopted when literary history refers to nonfictional historical discourse, perhaps is taken for granted by us, and therefore is not always clear. Modernist-era novelists do not take it for granted, but instead they experiment with ways of writing, knowing, and valuing it. Their experiments are subtended by irony: they originate in fiction's new autonomy in relation to the historical record, in the freedom that develops for fiction a history of its own – of a periodizing that depends on treatments internal to the practice of novel writing, or on the nature of fiction regardless of its historical context. As we will see in what follows, even when Lytton Strachey and George Orwell produce versions of historical discourse, they draw on aesthetic inspirations rather than on historians' practice to shape their narratives. Do they write real history, then, or a fictive alternative to real history? To guide this interchapter's examples of address to history by modernist literature, and our usage of the term *history* in its nonliterary sense, we can again begin with the comprehensive thought of R. G. Collingwood.

Inspired by the Italian modernist philosopher Benedetto Croce, Collingwood's *The Idea of History* (1935–1946) argues that history is "an intuition of the real" (193).[1] "[T]he real ... falls inside the sphere of the possible, not outside it, and thus history as narration of the real falls inside art as the narration of the possible" (192). The historian's research and discourse begin in the historian's imagination of what might be. The novelist's "research" and discourse also begin in the imagination of what might be. Historians and novelists share visions of characters and events "developing in a manner determined by a necessity internal to themselves" (242). "Both the novel and the history are self-explanatory, self-justifying, the product of an autonomous or self-authorizing [imaginative] activity" (246).

Collingwood thus brings together discourses that historiography traditionally divides. He will not leave out the subjectivity of the historian – a component of his individuality ("individuality ... is just that out of which history is made" [150]) and imagination. The historian's individual imaginative intelligence is "not concerned with events as such [i.e., as purely external objects] but with ... events brought about by the will and expressing the thought of [an] agent [in the past], and [the historian] discovers this thought by rethinking it in his own mind" (178). The historian tears past minds and events from their context, Collingwood bravely claims. If we "cannot know [thought] except in the context in which [it was] thought, [we thereby] restrict the being of thought to its own immediacy ... and so deny it as thought" (299).

For all the convergence of history with novels, however, a crucial difference is insuperable: "the historian's picture is meant to be true." "Purely imaginative worlds," Collingwood writes, "cannot clash and need not agree" with anything extrinsic: "each is a world to itself. But there is only one historical world, and everything in it must stand in some relation to everything else" (246). The historian's imagination must propose rational possibilities for knowing and understanding such relatedness – and its objective truth. His mind is simultaneously at one with the past and different from it, because rational rethinking of past action is the mediating counterweight to his personal immediacy. There is a further mediation: the historian is organizing more than his own consciousness; he is sharing it with humanity's ever-expanding self-knowledge.

History and philosophy, Collingwood concludes, because of their equal dedication to knowing ourselves comprehensively, are one and the same. Despite his reconciling purposes, however, he designates two swaths of life that history cannot include. "Reflective acts [such as the historian's] [are] the acts we do on purpose, and these are the only acts which can become the subject-matter of history" (309). Those acts cannot serve a historian's distorting investment in one or another ideological commitment (politics or economics, for example) that would direct the presentation of the past at the expense of his respecting one thing's ties to everything else. Nor can reflective acts serve mere consciousness, "a succession of immediate feelings and sensations." They are not purposeful (188). Consequently, "many human emotions are bound up with ... bodily life in its vicissitudes ... but this is not history" (304). Indeed, a narrative genre that might seem a branch of history – namely, biography – which records "biological events" and its subject's unstructured "tides of thought ... [also] is not history. ... The record of immediate experience ... [a]t its best ... is poetry; at its worst, ... obtrusive egotism; but history it can never be" (304).

Collingwood's assertion of what history "can never be" marks a dissonance between his advance-guard historiography and modernist fiction. For one thing, proscription of immediate experience and bodily vicissitudes (unless they are counterbalanced by a mediating rationality) goes against the grain of Impressionism, which all but Wyndham Lewis among the writers we are about to consider – Lytton Strachey, Rose Macaulay, George Orwell, and Ralph Bates – employ as a mode of treatment. That mode, risking irrationality and error (and vainglory) by making fiction compete with fact, might plausibly contest the separation of history from some novelists' ideas of authentic immediacy. (And we have seen Ford sort Impressionism with objectivity.) Moreover, Strachey, Macaulay, Orwell, and Lewis employ fictional and nonfictional discourse alike to question history's claim to be (along with philosophy) the definitive center of human self-knowledge.

Nevertheless, the power of Collingwood's assertion is the enduring challenge it hands to the fictional discourse of his time. A candidate for meeting it might be Strachey's *Elizabeth and Essex: A Tragic History* (1928). Experimentally crossing the border between history and fiction, and proposing their hybridization, Strachey takes up the biographical genre Collingwood resists, and "novelizes" it by transgressing the possibilities of evidence. *Elizabeth and Essex* provides numerous "reports" of immediate feelings, such as Elizabeth's emotions when Essex barges in on her after he fails to repress insurrection in Ireland: "She was surprised, she was delighted – those were her immediate reactions; but then, swiftly, a third feeling came upon her – she was afraid. What was the meaning of this unannounced, this forbidden return?"[2] There is no documentary warrant for this penetration (or deduction) of Elizabeth's responses. Modernist Impressionism, and the novel's genre, has taken over the historian's job.

An objectifying counterweight is Strachey's proposal that Essex exemplifies a pre-modern mode of conduct, and that Elizabeth represents a modernity that is incompatible with a man, and a class, of his superannuated kind. Yet the differentiation made by the "tragic history" between pre-modern and modern characters pales in comparison with the irrationality of the exponents of both sides. For example, outwardly Robert Cecil, Elizabeth's Secretary of State, seems a consummately rational actor, but Strachey concedes that what motivates him remains an "enigma," "almost entirely unknown ... we can only obscurely conjecture at what happened under the table" (111). Despite the free indirect discourse transparencies that fill Strachey's pages, obscurity overbalances them. It intensifies because, Strachey says, Essex, Bacon, and Elizabeth do not know themselves, making it all the harder for Strachey and us to know them.

Queen Elizabeth "made her mysterious organism the pivot upon which the fate of Europe turned" (7). To bring Elizabeth to the bar of rational understanding, Strachey proposes Freudian-influenced intuitions about her gender identity and sexual desires. "She was a woman. . . . But she was something more. . . . Was she a man? . . . She had read of Hercules and Hylas [Hercules's younger same-sex beloved]" (29). Essex was perhaps her Hylas, Strachey suggests, so that her masculinist desire for him is a queer love rather than a heterosexual one. Or, in beheading Essex, Elizabeth perhaps was avenging her mother Anne Boleyn's execution by Elizabeth's father. Nevertheless, Freud does not solve Elizabeth's mystery. Strachey suggests that history is the record of "contradictory convolutions" (186) that overwhelm intelligibility.

Collingwood would reject the idea. "Mind . . . realizes the presence in itself of elements that are not rational," he agrees. But "these irrational elements are the subject of psychology. They are the blind forces and activities in us which are part of human life as it consciously experiences itself, but are not parts of the historical process. . . . Our reason discovers them, but in studying them it is not studying itself" (231). Collingwood's point tells heavily against Strachey. The possibility that history is a record of inexplicable forces is something we can entertain in novels; but can that be true of the true past? It is plausible to think that Elizabeth's reign, whatever its passions, realized rationality more than it does in Strachey's pages. Fiction's thrusting itself into history's place is here perhaps a failed rebellion.

What might provoke such rebellion is history's claim to supreme human self-knowledge. Macaulay's novel *Told by an Idiot* (1923) suggests that respect for history as a master discourse is scarcely as rational (and philosophical) as Collingwood might make us think. Macaulay fights fire with fire: all but a few of her characters – members of the Garden family – are obsessed with being "historical." Month by month, year by year, decade by decade, Macaulay's characters "periodize" their lives – beginning with father Garden's modernism, which sends him from one religious creed to another, forever critical and unsatisfied. Macaulay practices the periodizing, nominally. She divides her tale into historicizing segments, just as we still do in literary history as well as in history proper: "Victorian," "Fin-de-Siècle," "Edwardian," "Georgian." The last category is itself subdivided ("Circus," "Smash," "Debris"), an unintended forecast of literary historians most recently differentiating among "high modernism," "interwar modernism," and "late modernism," even though the years at issue seem too few for such distinctions.

The Garden family's young members take such distinctions to heart. Victoria, arguing against her mother, proclaims, "I'm a late Victorian, and we do what we like." Her mother corrects her (in the late 1870s): "A *mid*-Victorian, I hope, dear."[3] Thus begins a definitional sparring about who belongs more to history and whom history most possesses over the course of forty-plus years. Another daughter, Stanley (named for the historical explorer of Africa!), beginning as an aesthete of the Wilde kind and as an advocate of New Women Who Can, moves – duplicating her father's search for salvation – from one history-minded progressive cause to another. At issue in all the struggles is a rage to enlarge "freedom." Maurice, one of the siblings, opposes all idiocies that betray rationality and human self-knowledge as well as freedom. He is intransigently in revolt, a modernist in the name of historical progress.

Yet Macaulay does not portray attachment to history as inescapable. She is using fiction's capacity for playing with history, for being detached from it, as a way of attesting to an alternative reality. Three of her female figures, and her narrator, escape by not chaining their minds to historical discourse. Mrs. Garden and Macaulay's narrator have little time for periodizing real life. Countering assertions of youth's break with traditions in the 1870s, the narrator deceivingly intrudes "the actual words of a writer of the [1920s]" (14) to describe the "break" of fifty years before. They are a perfect match. They argue the indistinctness that subverts separate "historical" situations. Repetitiousness, rather than change, marks the march of time. The Great War enters the narration under a chapter title, "Sound and Fury." But it doesn't mark for Macaulay the generational divide claimed by historicizing ballyhoo. It's "more interesting," Macaulay's narrator says (as well as "unscientific, sentimental, and wildly incorrect"), to "class groups" according to historicizing rubrics than to treat "merely a set of individuals" (186). Nevertheless, the novel insists – uninterestingly, as it were – on the mere set of individualities, which don't seem caused by their "time." Assigning those constants to historical and temporal uniqueness appears to abet aggression. Mrs. Garden's granddaughter Imogen, growing up in a hothouse of historicizing ideas, imagines life on a technologically up-to-date battleship as the best one possible. As Imogen matures, her imagination drops away from her time. An aspiring poet, she flees to the South Seas, pursuing the possibilities of romance rather than history. Imogen's development respects, the narrator says, "the advantage that the conscious must always have over the unconscious" (277). It also respects the advantage that fiction's transcendence of history's pressures might carry with it.

In alliance with Macaulay's fiction, conscious mind – the faculty most valued by Collingwood – is here turned against Collingwood's object. The most conscious of Macaulay's characters is Rome Garden. She is continually taunted by her siblings as a traitor to history and a cop-out in regard to its causes. But hers is the leading reasoning and impartial mind in the novel. The narrator advocates for Rome, because she "eschews the heat and ardour of the day" (66). Macaulay offers her historical novel as a place of refuge from the heat of the historical day. The latter makes Rome suffer: when she is about to embark on the one love affair of her life, the man is stabbed to death by a Russian anarchist-terrorist. History horrifically intrudes.

The loss of Rome's lover implies the impossibility of making contact with the past: the impossibility that Strachey adumbrates – perhaps as the tragic part of the history – and that Collingwood refutes. Nevertheless, Macaulay's final vision – or Rome's and the narrator's – is not tragic, but instead mixes Rome's detached rationality with a generous sense of comedy or at least of stoic cheer. Even if life is a tale told by an idiot, "and not a very nice idiot at that," the teller has "gleams of genius and fineness. The valiant dust that builds on dust – how valiant after all, it is … not contemptible nor absurd" (313) – even if it does not measure up historically.

Macaulay's very title, derived from Shakespeare, implies that the history that matters to her is fiction's history. Nevertheless, to measure up historically, to get out of fiction and into history, became ever more the demand of the 1930s. George Orwell's nonfiction *Homage to Catalonia* (1938) records Orwell's first-hand attempt to engage the historical record. He went to Spain as a volunteer fighter on the side of the Spanish republic – on the side of its socialist-anarchist wing. The book is a homage to anarchism more than to Catalonia. "The thing that … happened in Spain," Orwell writes, "was … not merely a civil war, but the beginning of a revolution" whereby workers were to win control of industry and superannuate parliamentary "democracy."[4] The revolution was concealed by communist-inspired malice against the anarchist militias. From the time of anarchism's origins in the early nineteenth century, and despite its perversion by terrorists, anarchists constituted the leading leftist opposition to Marx – until the communists' betrayal of their ideological kin brought an end to it.

Having devised verbal Impressionism as the sign of emotions bound up with sensations (and with thoughts), modernist narrative fiction is responsible for the form of Orwell's account of anarchism's loss to the world stage. The account is a history, yet simultaneously explicitly resists being one, because Orwell, too, identifies history with sound and fury. Nevertheless, like Rome, Orwell finds a source of optimism in the valiant dust (which has the same outsider status in relation to history that fiction does). If bodily life in its vicissitudes is not history, so be it, Orwell seems to say. As he portrays them, those vicissitudes constitute an essential egalitarian endowment to which social, economic, and political order – history proper, in sum – must be justly responsive.

The note of its anti-historical component is struck when Orwell advises his reader, after forty-five pages, to skip reading portions of his text. For at this point Orwell says that he will attempt to explain the political content of the conflict. The explanation is inseparable from the conflict's history. Nevertheless, the political-historical component is not responsive to egalitarian impressions. Orwell would rather that he and his readers ignore "the political side of the war," because it is all "the horrors of party politics" (46). He repeats this advice at the end of chapter X. He himself does not skip ahead, because it is "necessary to try and establish the truth, so far as it is possible" (149).

By wanting to skip politics, Orwell's history consorts with Collingwood's idea that a historian's political bias will violate the interrelatedness of history's components. Yet Orwell falls back on pure immediacy as the proof of truth. After all, Orwell seems to think, the Impressionist novel vindicates such a way of proving things. Arriving in Barcelona from England, Orwell meets an anti-fascist militiaman and feels an unreasoned bond: "Queer, the affection you can feel for a stranger! It was as though his spirit and mine had momentarily succeeded in bridging the gulf of language and tradition and meeting in utter intimacy" (3–4). Orwell skips objective confirmation. "To retain my first impression [of the militiaman] I knew I must not see him again" (4).

Collingwood's historian would never queerly suspend the intuition in Orwell's deliberate – and modernist fiction-inspired – way! Nevertheless, Orwell's queer Impressionism works a saving grace on his most critical moments. When the anarchist–communist infighting erupts in Barcelona, Orwell feels "concentrated disgust and fury" (137) "at the folly of it all" (130). "When you are taking part in events like these," he comments, "you ... ought by rights to feel like an historical character. But you never do, because at such times the physical details outweigh everything else" (139). Yet their weight counters disgust and fury. Even when Orwell is shot in the throat (near fatally), even though it is "very hard to describe what I felt," the "whole experience of being hit by a bullet is very interesting" (185). Impressions, mattering more than politics, displace the "historical character" of things, and transform it. "The prevailing mental atmosphere" expressed "disbelief in capitalism" and breathed socialist–anarchist equality. "The effect," even of the folly of it, "was to make my desire to see Socialism established much more actual than it had been before" (105). He was "hardly conscious" of that desire at the front; he was "chiefly conscious of boredom, heat, cold, dirt, lice, privation, and occasional danger" (105). Yet "this period which then seemed so futile ... is now of great importance to me. ... [I]t has taken on the magic quality which, as a rule, belongs only to memories that are years old" (105).

At the end of chapter VIII, Orwell remembers "incidents that might seem too petty to be worth recalling." Their "magic quality" introduces shades of romance in a documentary remembrance of things only recently past. Real history, like the Communist party, might refuse the atmosphere that Orwell relies on; modernist fiction doesn't. Thus, Impressionism's detachment from the stakes of historical partisanship has in *Homage to Catalonia* a political impact, if only because of its having made "vicissitudes" a foundation of artful composition. Accepting their power as a creative form of treatment as well as a reality, Orwell is even able to forego enmity. After failing in a desperate effort (as suspenseful as a novel) to liberate a comrade from unwarranted imprisonment, Orwell has an exchange with a police supervisor – in effect, an antagonist – that ends in a handshake. At once spontaneous as content and artful as treatment, it complements the handshake on Orwell's opening page. "Curiously enough" – in another "magical" turn – "the whole experience has left me with not less but more belief in the decency of human beings." The author concedes that "it is difficult to be certain about anything except what you have seen with your own eyes, and consciously or unconsciously everyone writes as a partisan" (230–1). Warning readers against his partisanship, as well as that of others, *Homage to Catalonia* echoes Conrad's preface-manifesto of forty years earlier. It hopes to "make you hear, to make you feel ... to make you *see*" that human solidarity, liberated from invidious social, economic, or political distinctions, is "all the truth of life."

An Impressionist-derived equanimity such as Orwell's is a mode of resistance to side-taking, and an instance of "indifference" to historical discourse as the leading human truth. There is no indifference to the idea of history in the communist writer Ralph Bates's fiction about the Spanish Civil War, *Sirocco* (1939), nor in Lewis's novel about it, *The Revenge for Love* (1937). But lack of indifference, we will see, covers a diversity of "historical" visions.

Bates, a *Left Review* confrère of Ralph Fox, and another veteran of the fighting, brings together in *Sirocco* novellas and stories about the transitions – from monarchy, to republic, to civil war – that mark Spain's early twentieth-century history. The individual stories are decipherable as virtual allegories of the entire nation in each of its changing states. In the eponymous novella the protagonist Andreu, by virtue of his family past (an unhappy pairing of a politically reactionary father and a liberal-left mother), is born into the struggle for and against revolution. He begins his own political career (as a Communist partisan in a failed uprising in 1934) as a revenge for the death of his uncle, a revolutionist who assassinated a Catholic cardinal, and who was murdered in turn by Andreu's father.

Bates's treatments of personal–political–historical lives depends, we find again, on Impressionism. Such treatment is adaptable, clearly. In the work of Strachey and Orwell, it is a medium critical of history's way of recording things; in the novellas of Bates, it is a medium of attachment to history, especially through moments in which violence is enacted or suffered by his figures. The "Sirocco" novella also implies that the attachment to history must exchange the immediacy of violence for the immediacy of love. "Once it was revenge I sought," Andreu says in his narrative's conclusion, "then the carrying out of an [ideological] idea. It is no longer a mere plan, an ideal pattern that I love, but a country of villagers. There are so many of us who love now that at last we must win."[5]

Accordingly, the Impressionism of *Sirocco*'s stories seems motivated by Bates's desire to absolve Spanish communists of initiating aggression. After all, Impressionism, modeled on being impressed, suggests receptivity more than initiative. The narratives imply that repressive powers have forced communists away from love and into a reluctant counterviolence. Andreu, after the miscalculated uprising in 1934, hides out in a fishing village, where he becomes the boarder of a family whose loves and hatreds typify local life. He is drawn into the family's generational conflicts and erotic entanglements; he is also drawn into the town's seaborne labor, which he will come to organize into a collective. Surrender to his environment undoes his previous aggression. Growing distanced from his assassin uncle, he says that he has "fought . . . against the infantile anti-clerical deviation in the workers' movement" (158). Later the village is stirred to anti-clerical rioting and church-burning by an anarchist, against whom Andreu inveighs for inciting "a fierce sirocco of passion" (219). Here is the communist view of anarchism! Nature, too, is anarchistic. A terrific storm, an outward form of emotional sirocco, pulverizes the village. But the storm's force is also withstood, by the spontaneously communist constructiveness of the survivors. Opposition to natural and political–historical violence is summed up in Andreu's love for a "country of villagers."

Bates uses Andreu to repeat (unintentionally) Collingwood's reconciling of historical imagination with reason. The anarchist, Andreu says, undermines "the success of our revolution, [which] depends upon reason, upon serenity, upon discipline, cleanness of mind" (222). But although *Sirocco*'s Impressionist method proffers love as an immediate innate radicalism, the reason and cleanness of mind on which communist revolution depends, according to Andreu, seems more a political abstraction than can be conveyed by Bates's use of Impressionism – or fiction. The abstraction perhaps results from Bates's fear that, *pace* love, nothing but violence can mediate the gap between radical rational plan and bodily vicissitudes, including the body's fierce siroccos of passion. Bates's fear in regard to violence might, if we consider it from a Kleinian perspective, inhibit his artistry: creative impulse in art (and perhaps in politics) necessarily involves destruction. Nevertheless, if *Sirocco* promotes love as the clean and serene antithesis of violence, Bates perhaps wants to use fiction itself with instrumental violence: to forcibly fuse imagination with history, so that both can be empowered to effect actual historical change.

What if fiction, by its very distance from real history (and even though it has a history of its own), cannot achieve such instrumental efficacy? *The Revenge for Love* rebukes advocacy of political violence, and at the same time accepts its lamentable inevitability. The doubleness of the perspective signals Lewis's disbelief in the possibility that fiction can surmount an inevitable distance between art and life. It can only lay out, in relation to real life, a complex volatility of judgments, of detachments and partisanships. In the penultimate chapter one of the modes of treatment is an Impressionist merging of narrator and female protagonist – even though Lewis's idea of fiction is an anti-Impressionist one. How he combines his use with a revision of it must be preceded by a look at how his invented narrative bears on the topic of actual contemporary history.

Contemporary life in *The Revenge for Love* seems characterized by a universally agreed-upon identification of history with politics – an all-determining identification of the kind Collingwood warns against. A movement in this direction was already visible in Macaulay's characters. Lewis's communists exemplify it. For them, everything historical is political, and everything personal is historical because it is political. Everyone is presumed to have a "historical" responsibility to take sides in regard to Spain. And if one resists side-taking? The result of resistance is fatal for two of the novel's leading characters: Victor, a down-and-out Australian artist living in England, and his devoted lover Margot. They die as a result of their being drawn into gun-running on the side of communist fighters in Spain, even though they are not partisans. The risks of the young couple's journey seem to them offset by their temporary leader, the seasoned communist veteran Percy Hardcaster. But Hardcaster, tethering Victor and Margot to his aggressive making of history, bears responsibility for the couple's demise. On the basis of Lewis's characterization of Hardcaster and his circle – chicly radical, they are a new species of snob – analysis might claim that *The Revenge for Love*, until at least midway in the narrative, is exclusively an anticommunist polemic.

Yet Lewis's fictive mode of constructing the reader's knowledge of characters, and of engaging sympathy or antipathy toward them and their ideologies, continually changes. His narrator presents the preeminent female communist, Gillian Phipps, as a cerebral phony. As she becomes more prominent in the narrative, a reader who recoils from her will look to some other figure or to the narrator for a standard by which to judge her. The narrator offers us Jack, a "natural" noncommunist instead of a fake. But the narrator has already shown us that Jack is a pugnacious philanderer. Juxtaposed with Jack, "Jill" is suddenly more to be sided with, because she is what the harassing Jacks of the world have made of women. Yet Jack also is presented as a rather harmless sensual clown. Gillian's high-handed provocation of him (sexual as well as intellectual) alienates the reader once more. Can the narrator supply a trustworthy alternative perspective to both characters? No: the narrator turns abruptly into a buddy of Jack's. If, this narrator says, you consider Jack a thuggish hog, well, "I'm telling you what he's called by others, and I'll let you judge for yourself. But how about that beam in your own eye, brother?"[6] (112). Such alienating chumminess begins the reader's baffled search for side-taking all over again. In a sense there is nowhere to go, no securely justifiable partisan base. If history means taking political sides, then Lewis's treatment of his narrative suggests the untrustworthiness of fixed alliances with any objects, personal and political. Nor will fiction provide a trustworthy bridge of the difference between it and present-day historical materials.

Collingwood is corroborated once more: when politics equals "history," the interrelationship of things is betrayed. At the same time, neither Lewis's narrative nor his reader can trust any founding historical "intuitions." "History" in Lewis's work is Strachey's opacity and Macaulay's obsessional madness; it also is a reconciler of immediacy and mediacy, and then again it is not. Surprisingly, the novel's finale sorts out the complexity of "historical" partisanship in a way that exculpates the communist side, at least in regard to Hardcaster. The narrative shapes the reader's ultimate respect for his working-class patriotism because his last adventure in Spain honors political integrity. He preserves – as does the narrative – advocacy of the exploited objects of all leftist ideologies, whether socialist, communist, or anarchist. Victor and Margot, too, are the (unemployed) working class, the persons whom the revolutionists are, or ought to be, fighting for. In the end Hardcaster surrenders his own liberty in an attempt to avoid a sacrifice of them. Belatedly, he discovers that his and the lovers' enemies are not the parlor revolutionists back home. The gun-running is a facade for international opportunists, who have adopted a left-liberal mask in London to exploit the sale of armaments. The capitalists behind the scenes profit from the arms sales that underlie gun violence on all history's fronts. History, in Lewis's portrayal of it, is an unending violence. That is its summa of human self-knowledge.

Lewis's use of Impressionism in a scene noted earlier renders a desperate car ride in which Victor and Margot attempt to escape a police ambush. As the fleeing car careens down a mountainside, Margot's moment-by-moment distensions of time and feeling as she suffers the violent descent, in a spray of bullets, is described by the narrator as a "crash of images" that "cinemato-graphically" usurps "the picture-house of [Margot's] senses" (314). Lewis expresses Margot's bodily vicissitudes by reference to cinema because he wants to align the art of Impressionism with modernist-era mechanical technologies. Impressionism, Lewis reminds us, is an artificial, directive way of making a reader see reality, not reality itself. He also implies that the immediate operation of the senses is no longer possible, because the senses – and life – have been fused with fabricated extensions or mechanized alterna-tives, superior and irresistible directive forces. They have become "contrap-tions," to use one of Lewis's words for mechanisms – and for bodies. An epitome of them is the automobile, "that muscular vehicle," which Margot detests, because "it carried her forward, she knew, by means of unceasing explosions" and must use "*her* organs, . . . as well as its own" (314). History is another careening vehicle, a supremely attaching, organ-consuming force. Modernist fiction's treatments of life are co-opted, Lewis implies, by the "unceasing explosions" of material production, whose technologies – whether capitalist or communist or something in between – impose their domination on the world, dignifying the imposition with the august name of history.

Lewis inculpates his own art-vehicle in this global contest for power. His novel might be valuable for that reason. Collingwood's historical discourse respects knowledge, not power. The finale of *The Revenge for Love* proposes at least some knowledge to offset power. One can know, from the novel's finale, that runaway historical explosions are something of a check on the planful minds of their fabricators. They get away with murder, nevertheless. But why should anyone go to fiction for such knowledge (or its lack), when other discourses – such as history – offer inspiriting knowledge, not to speak of truth, with certainty? Lewis seems to foresee the question. Before Margot is overtaken by the grand historical organ (and by death), Lewis describes "[t]he passionate, the artificial, the unreal, yet penetrating, voice" (336) that belongs to her. The description suggests the voice of Lewis's fiction, and of fiction generally. Possibly, for all its distance from historical reality or its lack of power or of certainty vis-à-vis other discursive ways of knowing the world, fiction maintains a penetrating efficacy.

Chapter 5

Entertaining Fictions

Readers of Chapter 4 might protest: whatever ideas novelists have about fiction, whatever discourses they engage, aren't novels also entertainments that escape the world as we think about it or know it? Certainly, ever since we followed the careers of The Woman Who Did and Stephen Dedalus, we have traced fiction's desire for flight from things as they are. Adventure is one such flight. Because historical or political transformation of the world has appeared to be the aim of novels such as those by Grant Allen and Joyce, their adventure component is subordinated or disguised. However earnest modernism might be, its romance elements point to escapism. Indeed, its earnest claims to autonomy point to escapism! That is one reason why, in what follows, aspects of the perennial (history- or time-escaping) bias of fiction toward autonomy are interwoven with specimens of modernist-era writing. But even if the meaning of entertainment in fiction is prejudicially reduced to mindless amusement, all the invented stories of 1900–1950 have some relation, for writers as well as readers, to killing time for the fun of it. And hasn't this always been a function of fiction, so that its purely amusing character transcends "period"?

And yet, in the escapism afforded by modernist-era crime novels and spy novels, comic novels, science fictions, and fantasies and gothic tales, all of which this chapter surveys, entertainment value is not untouched by a demand for analytic effort on the reader's part. Disciplined thought becomes part of the adventure of reading, becomes escape as well as resistance to escape.

Modernist Adventures of Detectives and Spies

Early twentieth-century stories about detectives and spies conjoin entertainment with a demand that readers scrutinize every word of those narratives: how else for the reader to follow the path of a mystery's solution, or to discover the treachery that might underlie intrigue? The instigation of heightened scrutiny on the part of readers might be due to the Victorian novel: Charles Dickens, George Eliot, and Henry James demanded of their audiences an unusually close attention to the novelists' prose and structure. Modernist experimentation with fiction also might have heightened the profile of the detective mode, for modernism directs a reader to take up a detective-like interrogation of the motives of all aspects of narrative treatment. And by demanding a reader's detachment from the world – for the sake of attention to treatment as well as topic – modernist fiction also might have stimulated the interest of writers and readers in the figure of the spy or the double agent. A novel is like a double agent, betraying its identity as fiction by delivering us information about reality, betraying reality by playing a game with "intelligence," which the novel – and the novelist – elaborates for sheer fabrication's sake.

Modernist-era detective and spy fiction, one might argue, emerges from, and revises, another Victorian matrix: adventure narrative. If the detective or spy of narrative fiction is an action hero, his kind of activity – or inactivity – takes shape under the pressure of changes in stories about adventure as the nineteenth century closes. These changes affect romance, which also informs the character of fictions about detectives and spies. Indeed, romance, which previous pages have suggested as exemplary of modernist fiction's independence from other discourses, will be seen in later parts of this chapter to be a means both of asserting literary autonomy and of chastening it. Comic and fantasy fiction assert it. Horror fiction might chasten it. Perhaps in dark stories about the animacy or inanimacy of the cosmos, what is at stake (below the narrative surface) is a modernist worry about whether fiction, which is not a literally living thing, can possibly have an autonomous life of its own. The question gets mixed in with, and projected through, theologically oriented tales. Is there, they seem to wonder, a freely creative maker of the cosmos, one who models and inspires fiction's autonomous makings? Is the universe alive, or is it a universe of death? If the latter, does fiction's autonomy share in the morbidity?

Putting such questions aside for now, we first focus on adventure. Critics have convicted the Victorian adventure story of complicity with Western imperialism, and have named it "imperial romance." They have done so because the British adventurer outside of fiction is white and male, and his historical setting is likely to be the non-Western places of the earth and their peoples, whom he expropriated. John Buchan's adventure and spy fictions conform to the critical view of romance's support of historical empire. In Buchan's *Prester John* (1910), the young Scottish protagonist sets out to defeat the eponymous Zulu, a leader of a movement of "Africa for the Africans." For all his anti-native zeal, however, the Scot has a moment in which he feels "a mad desire to be of [Prester John's] party," indeed to be mastered by the heroic native. The youth's surprising wish makes him panic, for it undoes, he says, "the difference between white and black, the gift of responsibility, the power of being in a little way a king."[1] The Scot resists what he calls his "passive," even "overwrought" madness by recovering his will to govern.

Yet being undone, being unable to govern events or persons (including oneself) or fortune, even in the Victorian "period," is essential to adventure, which inevitably encounters, and surrenders to, the unknown. Buchan's Victorian predecessor H. Rider Haggard produced a series of novels (starting in 1885) about the romance quests of his hero Allan Quatermain and of his heroine, a 2,000-year-old demi-goddess named She. Although Haggard's fiction is also regarded as an imperialist instrument, the fact is that Allan and She are not self-possessed enough to be "little kings." In the series' last installment, *She and Allan* (1921), Allan laments that "We are not always the same," that "Different personalities actuate us at different times," ungovernably. Moreover, "Everything rules us in turn, to such an extent ... that sometimes one wonder[s] whether we ... rule anything."[2]

Buchan's work after *Prester John* increasingly cedes its protagonists to the passive aspect of adventure, as we will see later in his *Mr. Standfast* (1919). Adventure's capacity to undo action shows itself in another Victorian precedent: the romance narratives of Anthony Hope, wherein the adventurers who interest us as the generators of detective and spy figures withdraw from the name of action after their initial success as actors. Rudolf Rassendyll, the hero of Hope's *The Prisoner of Zenda* (1894), bored by an aimless uneventful life, decides to visit his ancestral Eastern European home, Ruritania. There he discovers his uncanny resemblance to Ruritania's royal heir apparent, also named Rudolf. When, on the eve of the prince's coronation, His Highness is abducted and made a prisoner by his brother-rival, the English Rudolf is persuaded by the legitimate heir's partisans to impersonate him, as a way of holding the true ruler's place, until he can be rescued. Such doubling, in which one figure disguises himself as another, is the ancient stuff of romance, and reappears centrally in detective and spy fiction. In Hope's novel, Rudolf improvises the king's role brilliantly: his improvisation, typifying the gamble with the loss of control that even deliberate action must face, is the adventure. He improvises so well that he exhibits a better potential for rule than the prisoner does, and he wins the love of the king's intended. Thus, in impersonating the king, he becomes the king's rival – a double of the king's rebellious brother, at the same time as he opposes the brother.

The outcome, once the real king is rescued, turns the successful action into an occasion for reversing its achievement, and for resigned melancholy. English Rudolf must disappoint the followers who have transferred their allegiance to him, and abandon the queen whom he loves and who loves him. Detective and spy fiction characteristically are shadowed by melancholic associations. That, too, becomes part of their romance aura. The same finale is repeated in Hope's sequel, *Rupert of Hentzau* (1898).

One of the narratives that might most qualify as imperial romance by virtue of its setting is A. E. W. Mason's *The Four Feathers* (1902), yet there, too, one finds a retreat from masterful action. It is a story about soldiers whose regiment is ordered to the Sudan to fight for the Empire against Muslim insurgency. One of them, Harry Feversham, afraid that fear will cripple him in battle, resigns his commission. Repudiating his cowardice, three comrades, and his own fiancée, award Harry white feathers, markers of shame – and of broken engagement. Harry's best friend, Jack Durrance, does not repudiate him, but, as he achieves success in military action in the Sudan, remains perplexed by Harry's motive for withdrawal. Meanwhile, Harry, deciding that he must dominate his fear, sets out for Africa as a private citizen, in an effort to do whatever he can to revoke the four feathers. His adventures, which include his taking on disguises to hide his identity, become his romance quest for redemption.

As Harry's ability to act gains ground, Jack's ability begins to lose it. He is made blind by over-exposure to the sun. As a consequence, the man of action becomes the man of inaction, and his disability becomes Mason's narrative center – and a redemptive romance value in itself. Jack's perceptions are sharpened by blindness and passivity; it is "a delight to him to make discoveries which no one expected a man who had lost his sight to make."[3] Solitary, detached from the world thanks to his injury, he ultimately returns to the Middle East and Africa to undertake research about the Sudanese war. The contemplative man, divorced from action by his blindness, becomes the capable historian.

Sir Arthur Conan Doyle's stories about Sherlock Holmes feature *adventure* in their very titles. Yet the shift in the nature of adventurous action that we have traced is exemplified in Conan Doyle's imagination of Holmes's genius. Criminals act; Holmes solves crime by means of intensively contemplative reading of the action of others. When he does act – usually by enlisting the disguises that are characteristic of romance adventurers – his aim is to confirm the truth he already has deduced. "Do you mean to say," Holmes's sidekick, Dr. Watson, asks him in *A Study in Scarlet* (1887), "that without leaving your room you can unravel some knot which other men can make nothing of, although they have seen every detail for themselves?"[4] Yes, is Holmes' career-long answer. It makes Holmes a new hero of a new kind of escape from realism, even though Holmes's deductions are all apparently reality- and materially-based. Despite the materialism, from first to last (*The Casebook of Sherlock Holmes* [1927]), the detective is, according to Watson, a "necromancer" (*I*, 14), an engine of "stimulating . . . thought that can only be found in the fairy kingdoms of romance."[5] His magical power derives, as Watson describes it in *The Valley of Fear* (1914), from "the asceticism of complete mental concentration" (*I*, 194).

Such is the intensity of Holmes's mental concentration that he solves the murder mystery in the novel-length *The Valley of Fear* at the narrative's halfway point. This would seem to be an excess of asceticism. The second half redresses the excess, inasmuch as it tells the compound-complex – and fantastic – history of the killer and the murdered person. The former has been an American police official, working as both a detective and a spy – as a double agent as well, because he pretends to be a member of a terrorist organization in the western United States that, falsely in the name of American coal and iron workers, has become a mafia. The official's mission was to bust the organization. Having done so, he has fled the United States to be safe from avengers of his betrayal, and he has had to add a third identity to his two former ones. The killing he executes is justified self-defense: his victim belongs to the terrorist gang that is hunting him. To throw other avengers off the track, the killer, with the help of his wife and a friend, pretends that the murdered man (whose facial features have been destroyed by gunshot) is himself. Holmes penetrates the complex masquerade (another romance doubling) after one night of thought, and before hearing the American police agent's history. The action adventure of the second half of the novel satisfies the old romance emphasis on the importance of outward deeds, but it makes the American policeman-spy's actions of secondary interest, compared to Holmes's wizard reading of the crime scene.

For a producer of narrative fiction to create a detective who is a hero-reader as well as a romance figure, and who makes the fascination of actions and events secondary to acts of reading, amounts to flattery of Conan Doyle's consumers: they can see themselves in Holmes. What a way for a fiction writer to master the entertainment market of print media! Nevertheless, if Holmes's assertion, "I am a brain, Watson, the rest of me is mere appendix" (*II*, 505), is a marketing ploy, it raises the intellectual level of the merchandise. It also makes a reader believe that the fantastic, irrational world of romance is compatible with, and indeed a double for, braininess.

Erskine Childers's *The Riddle of the Sands* (1903) and Chesterton's Father Brown stories (1911–1935), in which a Roman Catholic priest – decidedly "ascetic" – is the detective, further exemplify the adventure that reading becomes in the twentieth century's first half, and that promotes it as the brain's match for romance externals. Childers' protagonist, Carruthers, an English Foreign Office employee, accepts an invitation to join a yachting expedition with a former schoolmate, Davies, amid the shifty coasts of Holland and of Germany's eastern Frisia. The expedition soon presents itself as an unfathomable mystery to Carruthers: what is Davies *doing*?

Davies is reading maps and charts of the coastal geography, and making his reading ever more precise: an exercise that the reader, along with Carruthers, compelled by the narrative and by the maps and charts included with it, is also obliged to undertake. This adventure in closely observing the spaces of the narrative, and coordinating them with events, leads to a spy story. Davies is tracking another yachtsman, whom Davies suspects is a native British citizen masquerading as a German and conveying to the Germans intelligence about the British navy. The Germans, too, are reading the shifty geography – as part of planning a future invasion of England. Carruthers's holiday from the Foreign Office thus merges escapism and the interests of his job. The merger of adventure and responsibility to reality, with a focus on the strategic use of "intelligence, not ... brute force or complicated mechanism," as the way to read and solve the mystery-riddle of the sands, is repeatedly termed by Carruthers "our quest," inspired by a personified female figure of "Romance," "the ancient inspiration which, under many guises, ... is always the same."[6] Always the same, indeed: Childers's narrative includes such romance commonplaces as a sunken treasure ship, and characters, including Carruthers, wearing material disguises. Even without dressing up, Carruthers and Davies are spies in masquerade: there is a deep logic at work in their final discovery that their object is a double agent, because he doubles their duplicity, as they do his.

Carruthers and Davies are on the "right" side of romance and duplicity, of course – inasmuch as the right one, for British readers, is the nationalist English side. Yet the adventurous spies and detectives of fiction stubbornly court the wrong side, and their identities shade into it. Romance, as we saw in Hope's novel, is productive of such ambiguous blends. When Sherlock Holmes in "His Last Bow" (1917) captures a German master spy on the eve of the Great War, the German calls Holmes a cursed "double traitor!" (*II*, 455). He is not one, yet even during his anti-German national service he remains intellectually and morally detached, in a way that undercuts simplified identities and side-taking. Holmes's cocaine addiction is an example of his own lawlessness. In "The Adventure of Charles Augustus Milverton" (1903), he says that he "always had an idea that I would make a highly efficient criminal" (*I*, 798), and rejoices that he can flout the law in order to enforce it. His separateness from the official policing institutions, whose personnel he mocks as well as helps, is a mark of the outsider status to which he clings.

Holmes "loathed every form of society with his whole Bohemian soul," Dr. Watson attests in "A Scandal in Bohemia" (1891) (*I*, 209). His interest in crime is in the intellectual challenges it sets for him. "I play the game [of detection] for the game's own sake," Holmes declares ("The Adventure of the Bruce-Partington Plans," [1917], *I*, 363). Holmes's arch-enemy, the king of a global crime syndicate Professor Moriarty, is admitted by Holmes to be his "intellectual equal. My horror at his crimes was lost in my admiration of his skill" ("The Final Problem" [1892], *I*, 646). To serve the cause of intellectual power, Holmes is antisocial and amoral, traits that suggest modernism's contamination of conservative impulses. Childers's and Conan Doyle's nationalisms would not be as intriguing or entertaining without an element of subversion in their proponents.

As if to cover up the detective figure's share in autonomous fantasy, the novelists seek to anchor their romance heroes to real historical referents. Agatha Christie's detective Hercule Poirot, another outsider (a Belgian, a celibate), exclaims at the start of his adventure in *Murder on the Orient Express* (1934) that he wishes he "had ... the pen of a Balzac! I would depict this scene" of the train's passengers, "representing all classes and nationalities."[7] That would make Poirot an ally of realism. Nevertheless, Poirot's reading of clues splices necromancy and modernist moral transgression. Having discovered that a group of vengeful conspirators on the Orient Express has murdered a heinous criminal among them, Poirot justifies the murder, arrests no one, and offers the police a fictive (but plausible) solution. The real solution, explaining events that are essentially a romance flight from plausibility, is what readers are to take as fact, even though it is consonant with a fantastic reality that will remain hidden from the authorities.

Christie's other famous detective, the amateur Miss Marple (a spinster), also seems preternatural: she "can tell you what might have happened and what ought to have happened and even what actually *did* happen. And she can tell you *why* it happened!"[8] That uncanny penetration is characteristically at work in *A Murder Is Announced* (1950), wherein Miss Marple, reviewing evidence collected by a police professional, thinks over the crimes that occur in a post–World War II rural village. The policeman acts, but her brain makes all the action intelligible. The historical medium in which she thinks is less

fantastic than her brain. "Realistically," it represents real classes and nationalities. The village has been transformed by an influx of refugees from war-
torn Europe and around the globe. Christie has Miss Marple speak with
eloquent pathos about how it is that, under the influx of immigrants, "the
subtler links that had held together English social rural life had fallen apart"
(127), so that identities as well as histories have become untrustworthy. Yet
the murderer is homegrown English, and a German refugee is instrumental
in bringing the mystery to a solution. Miss Marple, herself intellectually
detached from immediate reality and history, is at home with strangers and
estrangement, and is therefore, paradoxically, all the more sociologically
comprehensive an intelligence.

Dorothy Sayers might fulfill Poirot's Balzacian aspirations more than
Christie. Her mysteries represent cross-sections of contemporary life – the
advertising industry in *Murder Must Advertise* (1933); institutions of higher
learning in *Gaudy Night* (1936). Against the grain of modernist art's pursuit
of autonomy, Sayers's redirection of the romance of detective fiction toward
sociology and history includes her use of the periodizing that literary history
cultivates. Her novels dramatize – and make fun of – modernists and modernism as historical elements of contemporary culture.

The novels objectify modernism by distancing it from identification with
Sayers's detectives, Lord Peter Wimsey and Harriet Vane. In *Strong Poison*
(1930), the milieu from which Miss Vane emerges is bohemian-modernist. Is
modernism the strong poison of Sayers's title? Harriet is a detective novelist,
and she has been the lover of another novelist, a modernist one, whose books
are described as of "an 'advanced' type" because they are ideologically corrosive. "They preached doctrines which may seem to some of us immoral or
seditious, such as atheism, and anarchy, and what is known as 'free love,'"[9] a
legal expert complains. Harriet, after living with her paramour for a year,
broke with him. Shortly thereafter he was poisoned, and Harriet put on trial
for his murder. Miss Vane has been another woman who did, and who
consequently has been vilified. Yet modernist feminism, if it participates in
the dangers of "advanced" types, is not scapegoated by Sayers. Harriet broke
with her lover because in gender relations he reverted to Victorian male
norms. Lord Peter vows to purge the poison that smears Harriett. But it is
two female associates of Wimsey, women with rooms of their own, who in the
novel's second half take over the narrative and work to liberate the accused.

Wimsey wants to marry Harriet as well as free her, but she refuses: she has a
modernist distrust of marriage as well as of male superiority. Sayers's sociological treatment of detective fiction, from a feminist perspective, achieves
an enlarged scale in *Gaudy Night*. An Oxford women's college – epitome

of women's liberation from male-centered education – is threatened for months by poison pen letters to the scholars, anonymous attacks on the college library, and mayhem that falls just short of the murder of Harriet. A graduate of the college, Harriet is asked to solve the mystery. In the process, she and her author assemble a comprehensive picture of corporate university life. Its sociological thrust includes Harriet's attempt to solve another case: her divided feelings about marriage and Wimsey. The solution is keyed to the modernist-feminist independence that the women's College must preserve against assault.

The university setting of *Gaudy Night* returns detective work in fiction to its bias for adventurous detachment. Wimsey worries that Harriet's immersion in Oxford means that she has "retired from the world to pursue the contemplative life."[10] His métier is worldliness. That, too, threatens Harriet's freedom. Yet Wimsey originally planned to be an academic historian. Moreover, when he returns to Oxford to help Harriet, he is struck by his sudden liberation from "unsound, unscholarly, insincere" ordinary life (278).

Wimsey's ability to maintain analytic distance from ordinary life underwrites the sociological aim of *Murder Must Advertise* – and its version of modernism. The death of an employee during working hours at a London advertising agency causes the agency's owner to hire Wimsey as a private investigator. He gives Wimsey cover by employing him (under a pseudonym) as a new copy writer for the firm. While the detective gathers evidence that the death was a murder, he and Sayers canvass the business and its ninety-one personnel in terms of comprehensive social realism. At the same time, Wimsey's masquerade – whereby he conjoins detective and spy stories – shows his creator's attachment to romance tradition: in the novel's course Wimsey assumes three disguises. Fusing romance and modernism, he initiates one disguise as a pierrot – a quintessential emblem of modernism (for example, in the paintings of Pablo Picasso) – at a costume party populated by a bohemian-modernist crowd that has become the collective victim of a dope-dealing syndicate. The syndicate is behind the advertising agency murder. Modernism's association with "strong poison" seems to be reestablished, but it is thanks to the fictions made possible by Wimsey's disguises that the truth is revealed. In accord with such distance, the criminal is punished – with the criminal's consent, and at Wimsey's direction – outside the law, and thereby antisocially, in rebellious modernist fashion.

A self-distancing reflection on detective fiction also marks Sayers's text. Wimsey is a superb copy writer. His genius for slogans spills over into the imitation-advertisement titles of the novel's chapters. Thus detective writing's relation to advertising in print media becomes germane to the shaping of

Sayers's book. Moreover, Wimsey sees "a subtle symmetry ... which is extremely artistic" between dope and advertisements.[11] Sayers explicates the symmetry: murder mystery stories must advertise, too. They are caught up in the doping. Even as she inculpates her art, however, Sayers also uses it to blast a contemporary world that demands "Advertise, or go under." That demand is the chilling last line of the text. *Murder Must Advertise*, criticizing the betrayals of truth that make advertising this detective novel's alter ego, contributes a characteristically modernist self-consciousness to entertainment.

Sayers might be another case of anti-modernist modernism. Perhaps the most remarkable case is Buchan's detective-spy hybrid, *Mr. Standfast*. Its protagonist, Richard Hannay (hero of two previous books), undertakes during the Great War to capture an enemy mastermind. To do so Hannay must masquerade as something he loathes – a British pacifist – and pal with a modernist crowd that includes conscientious objectors, "arty" devotees of avant-garde painting and Russian novels, "ten varieties of Mystic," and diverse political radicals ("Africa for the Africans"; "academic anarchists"). Hannay considers the crowd's modernism and its detachment from the armed conflict to be "puffed up with spiritual pride and vanity."[12] A native South African and booster of the Empire, he fears "the world is getting socialism now like the measles" (289). The villain, who uses modernist circles as a front for his penetration of English intelligence, is Maxon Ivery. He is "the superbest actor that ever walked the earth. You can see it in his face. It isn't a face, it's a mask. . . . He hasn't got any personality either – he's got fifty" (284). With such an antagonist – a new Moriarty, Ivery is said to be responsible for all the war's troubles, including the Bolshevik revolution – the narrative's historical referents are fused with romance. Hannay is a match for the magical shape-shifter Ivery, however: his own facility for disguise soon leads him to adopt "three names in two days, and as many characters" (339).

Although Hannay brings down Ivery, his confidence about consciously directed action ("what a tonic there is," he says, "in a prospect of action" [363]) undergoes a surprising turn. He comes to respect pacifism in the person of a conscientious objector, significantly named (speaking of romance) Launcelot. The impact of Launcelot Wake on the activist hero reminds us of the revision of adventure in the direction of passivity we have noted as a modernist "period" thread. Launcelot Wake first appears amid the "arty" enclave that Hannay loathes. He is resolutely "against your accursed war" (325), but he also loathes treason – and Germany. He and Hannay keep crossing paths, by sheer chance, as if by the grace of adventure rather than by deliberate plan. As they become intimate, Wake explains himself to Hannay

in self-abasing terms: he says that modernist pacifists are antisocial individu-
alists, incapable of communitarian spirit; that in their detachment they find it
easier to die than to have the courage to live. Whether or not the character's
analysis is to be taken in earnest remains unclear. But the fact is that
Launcelot saves Hannay's life on a treacherous Alpine height. Later, when
he becomes a noncombatant messenger for Hannay's troops on the French
front, he dies for the sake of bringing a crucial communication through the
lines of combat.

In Buchan's last chapter, Hannay remains on the side of action: "I have
always found patience and standing still the most difficult job to tackle" (469),
but Wake has fled the "tonic" of action as it is exemplified in the impatient
protagonist. By surrendering to action more than by commanding it, Launcelot demonstrates that passive alienation is as redemptive as any alternative. "He was the Faithful among us pilgrims, who had finished his journey
before the rest" (470), Hannay concludes, alluding to the protagonist of
the seventeenth-century religious romance-allegory, *The Pilgrim's Progress*
(wherein Mr. Standfast is a character).

There is a second Faithful, and a second sacrifice, in *Mr. Standfast*. Hannay's most loved friend, a South African airman who substantiates the name
of action even more than Hannay does, contributes to the relief of Hannay's
ground troops by winning a pitched aerial battle overhead – and dying in the
encounter. Hence the narrative makes heroes of its consummate pacifist and
its consummate activist. But, because both heroes die, what they each epitomize takes on a melancholy, mournful cast. We return to the affect that we
have seen inherited from the adventure tradition (as in Rider Haggard,
Hope, and Mason) by modernist detective and spy stories, even when their
protagonists have an invincible air.

Loss is the other side of the story of the canny penetrators of mystery. The
police forces attempting to counteract the international terrorists in Edgar
Wallace's *The Four Just Men* (1905) are not as brilliant as the eponymous
four, who plan to kill a government minister because he wants to ban the
entry of refugees into England. Both sides, however, are beaten by a technological glitch, a chance mistake. Accident, an undergoing of uncontrolled
phenomena, defeats action. Likewise, chance, in combination with emotionally induced miscalculation, defeats the artist-detective Trent in E. C. Bentley's *Trent's Last Case* (1913). Bentley's referential realism expands the crime
story: the murdered man is an American tycoon, whose death seems devoutly
to be wished by entire social classes, across international borders. At the same
time the commonplaces of romance elbow in: even the corpse wears a
disguise. Trent must take all of this in. His work is acute, but entirely misses

the mark. Although he wins the love of the victim's widow, the defeat of his intelligence is a bitter pill, in part because his passion is a blinding agent.

The defeat of active intelligence, and the blindness of passion, are treated as ironic comedy by Wallace and Bentley. In contrast, they are treated as tragically melancholic in Joseph Conrad's *Under Western Eyes* (1911) and Liam O'Flaherty's *The Informer* (1925). The life of Conrad's Russian protagonist, Razumov, is usurped by his involuntary relation to a terrorist assassination of a state minister. The assassin impulsively makes himself and his deed known to Razumov. Razumov, although his conscience is torn, believes that he must inform the government and stand up against "revolutions with their passionate levity of action."[13] Once he becomes an informer, however, his own power to act is cancelled. Now he is forced by the authorities to become a double agent. Masquerading as a terrorist, he is to penetrate incendiary cells in Geneva. By horrible chance, the expatriated mother and the sister of the assassin, who is executed because of Razumov's informing against him, are living there. And Razumov falls in love with the sister! He must hide his identity, his story, and his treachery not only from the terrorists, but from her. In Conrad, the adventures that constitute spying and detection transform action into passional suffering.

As if to emphasize the melancholy undoing of mastery that pervades even such adventure narratives as *The Four Feathers* – Razumov is a cousin to Mason's blinded Jack – Conrad doubles the story of Razumov's pain in another character. The narrator of *Under Western Eyes* is an English teacher of languages who has gained access to Razumov's journal, and it is he who transmits the Russian's story. That is fitting: just as Razumov's life is imposed upon by the assassin's, so the narrator's life is imposed upon by Razumov's. The narrator, too, has fallen in love with the sister. Like Razumov, he has no hope of realizing his love in active form; he must submit to inhibition instead. He must also, like Razumov in Geneva, submit to being a stranger among strangers. That both Conrad's men are distant from their national origins seems an additional brake on their ability to act freely.

The protagonist of O'Flaherty's *The Informer*, Gypo, also suffers from estrangement and exile, although he lives in his native Dublin, during the time of the Irish Civil War. The melancholy of the spy's detachment, as well as of his compromised agency, again comes to the fore. Gypo's emotional exile is an effect of his having been cast out of the "Revolutionary Organization" that opposes continuing political ties between Northern Ireland and Great Britain. Although the Organization is committed to violence, it has proscribed Gypo for being trigger-happy. Gypo still believes in a fully liberated Ireland, but isolated and stone broke, he informs on an Organization buddy to collect the reward money from the police. The buddy, cornered, commits suicide. Gypo is conscience-stricken, and then betrayed for money (in turn) by his girlfriend prostitute, and killed by the rebels with whom he continues to identify.

The unresolved tension between attachment and detachment that in Razumov's and Gypo's cases inhibits action's "levity" in association with melancholy is not without value. The value is illustrated in W. Somerset Maugham's collection of stories, *Ashenden: The British Agent* (1927), based on Maugham's experience as a spy during the Great War. In "A Trip to Paris" and "Giulia Lazzari," Ashenden is assigned to entrap an Indian nationalist who is, as Ashenden's supervisor describes him, "bitterly hostile to the British rule in India" (92) and "concerned in two or three bomb outrages."[14] But Ashenden defends Chandra Lal's "courage to take on almost single-handed the whole British power in India." The supervisor calls this a "morbid" response: "You," he tells Ashenden, "look at [espionage] like a game of chess and you don't seem to have any feelings one way or the other" (101). Ashenden agrees. His detached response is not morbid, however, but modernist. "People sometimes thought him heartless because he was more often interested in others than attached to them, and even in the few to whom he was attached his eyes saw with equal clearness the merits and defects" (144). Thus Ashenden can sympathize with the enemy – the Indian whom he must entrap "is aiming at freedom for his country" (100), he says feelingly. Later, in "The Traitor," when Ashenden leads the eponymous figure, "who enjoyed his treachery" (151), to his death, the British agent is sickened by the firing squad execution, which Maugham powerfully evokes. The last page of the tale does not celebrate a national triumph over an enemy, but instead records the desolation that the enemy traitor's wife is left to face.

The impersonal disinterestedness that Ashenden exemplifies, mixed with attachment to the underdog, even if the latter is an enemy, is, one might argue, a modernist virtue. It instantiates modernism's worth as a criticism of a world committed to aggressions at any cost. In a 1941 retrospect, Maugham remarks that his stories about Ashenden "purpose only to offer entertainment," which he still thinks, "impenitently, is the main object of a work of fiction" (9). As we have seen, entertainment as a main object of fiction is as compatible with seriousness (or melancholy) as Maugham the entertainer is compatible with Maugham the earnest student of philosophy.

In Eric Ambler's *The Mask of Demetrios* (1939), we find a consummate example of modernism's world vision, of its self-consciousness about art, and of its compatibility with crime fiction and spy fiction. The novel immediately calls attention to the kind of fictive thing it is, even as it exhibits its ability to transcend what it is. Its protagonist, Latimer, is a former economics professor who has become a successful crime novelist. On a vacation trip to Istanbul, he meets a Turkish police official who claims that real criminals are unlike what one finds in fiction. In the face of this assertion, Latimer is inspired to pursue a nonfictional "experiment in detection"[15]: a disinterested historical research into the past of a real criminal, "Demetrios," recently deceased, whom the Turkish policeman thinks of as an epitome of criminal mind. What might have made this criminal tick, Latimer wonders. As he undertakes a quest for the answer, the novel that is about a writer's vacation from his chosen genre becomes an instance of the genre. Latimer's research ensnares him, to all but fatal effect. In the end, he returns to plotting a new crime fiction, relieved at the thought of inventing something simpler, and more formulaic, than the real story he has just lived.

The one he has lived conforms to the romance adventures from which Ambler's entertainment springs: Demetrios turns out to be yet another master of aliases and disguises; Latimer's "experiment" is aided by his being unmarried, in celibate detective fashion; he also is enlisted to impersonate others. At the same time, the "real" process of detection Latimer lives through and undergoes – an obsessional process that he insists is not "impersonal" but nevertheless is "unaccountable" (140) – foregrounds the mystery of crime's stubborn presence in real social and political history. The chapters of research on Demetrios's past evoke European history from 1922 to 1938, and uncover the criminal's involvement in a gamut of intrigues that include world-historical ones. Besides being a gun for hire, a thief, a drug lord, a human trafficker, and a murderer, Demetrios has helped governments spy on, and steal, each other's military secrets; he has meddled in the internal politics of one or another nation; he has aided the illegal laundering of moneys for offshore businesses. It is the mind behind such things that Latimer wants to get at. "Merely to label [Demetrios] with disapproval was not enough. I saw him not as a corpse in a mortuary . . . but as a unit in a disintegrating social system" (82–83). Latimer's conclusion turns out to be impersonally detached, and, in a modernist way, beyond our conventional moral terms. "It was useless to try to explain him, in terms of Good and Bad," Latimer thinks. Instead, he ought to be explained in money terms: "Good Business and Bad Business were the elements of the new theory" (252). In those terms,

> Demetrios was not evil. He was logical and consistent; as logical and consistent in the European jungle as . . . poison gas . . . and . . . shattered bodies of children killed in the bombardment of an open town. The logic of Michelangelo's *David*, Beethoven's quartets and Einstein's physics

had been replaced by that of the *Stock Exchange Year Book* and Hitler's *Mein Kampf.*   (252–253)

Demetrios turns out to be still alive, as "logical and consistent" as the shattered bodies and the bombardments. Ambler–Latimer does not mention, on the side of the logic of art and physics, the logic of narrative fiction. Perhaps the kind of entertainment that springs from fiction's discourse offers terms that the world in 1939 might consult to best explain itself. The power of the stock exchange or fascism to replace alternatives might have been (or might remain) even more formidable without their portrayal in crime and spy fiction's fantastic adventures.

Comic Entertainments

In the English comic novel of 1900–1950, we meet witty characters whose ingenuity in solving dilemmas is unfailing. Their wiliness triumphs over life's ordinary constraints. It is as if the wizard detectives return in a new form, and the adventurers too, but in versions that are scarcely touched by melancholy, and certainly not by defeat. If more ordinary figures appear in the comic narrative, the authorial treatment of them encourages their unrealized desires, and celebrates their flouting of convention if it obstructs what they want. When the comedy shades into satiric aggression, that also is a sign of the fiction's and the reader's victory over conventional thought and feeling. Just as the modernist idea of autonomous fiction finds an epitomizing ally in romance, it finds the same in comic novels. Such works make it possible, once again, to treat the exponents of modernism in their narratives as objects of ridicule – and simultaneously as self-conscious portraits of their own reality-surpassing artifice.

No comedy-compromising touches are included in P. G. Woodhouse's tales. His heroes – Psmith, a middle-class youth improvising his future, and Jeeves, the clever valet of Bertie Wooster who extricates his employer from countless scrapes – surmount obstacles ebulliently. Psmith in *Leave It to Psmith* (1924) superficially loans himself to crime. Desperate to escape his family's wholesale fish business, he publicly advertises his availability for any employment ("Someone to Assassinate Your Aunt? / PSMITH WILL DO IT/ CRIME NOT OBJECTED TO").[16] He thereby becomes attached to a hare-brained burglary scheme in which the heir of Blandings Castle plans to steal a diamond necklace from his aunt to pay off gambling debts. But the bait for Psmith is not crime: it is the Castle's new female librarian, Eve, with whom he is smitten. To be near her, he participates in the crime plot. As part of that plot, he impersonates a poet, who is supposed to be a guest at the Castle, and who fortunately doesn't show up. But a practiced criminal, impersonating the same poet, does arrive, with ensuing complications. They include Psmith's bravura lies to Eve – pure inventions – about his former marriage to a woman whom Eve knows, although Psmith doesn't know that she knows. No matter! In the end Psmith unmasks the criminal and the criminal's female accomplice, wins Eve, and selflessly obtains rightful funds owed to Eve's best friend. Psmith's mastery of disguise, lies, and criminal mischief save the day for his dreams.

Jeeves saves the day for others by less outwardly dramatic actions. Pure intelligence is his métier. Moreover, he is remarkably learned. His conversation and advice is full of quotations of Shakespeare and a gamut of English lyric poets; he is also a Latinist, who teaches Bertie Latin phrases. His favorite author is the seventeenth-century philosopher Spinoza, who celebrates the contemplative mind. In Jeeves, contemplation is not tinged by sadness; it animates, producing only happiness in others. "There is something about the mere sight of this number-nine-size hatted man," Bertie says of Jeeves, with a notice of his valet's brain capacity, "that seldom fails to jerk the beholder from despondency's depths in times of travail."[17] In *Joy in the Morning* (1946), thirty years into Wodehouse's stories and novels about the valet, Jeeves must rescue Bertie from finding himself miserably engaged for a second time to a woman he didn't want to marry the first time. How will Jeeves, who is said to be superior to Napoleon as a strategist, solve Wooster's problem – and solve another: a marriage between a pair of Wooster's friends that is blocked by a crusty guardian of one of them? His solution depends on sending the principals to a masked ball, so that they can sort things out with the help of their disguises, and on Jeeves's clever last-minute, impromptu lying.

Psmith and Jeeves are characters whose archetypes are ancient and yet timeless, and Wodehouse's comic world is a romance one, as is indicated by the disguises, coincidences (two impersonations of the same missing poet!), and obstructed but invincible loves. The pattern of their action is also ancient. Nevertheless, Woodhouse (like Christie, in regard to her magical detectives) wants to tie his fiction's autonomous timelessness to some historical specificity. Rather than referring to historical events, he makes modernism, especially modernist media or aesthetics, thicken the plots that Psmith's or Jeeves's ingenuity will rise above. It is another example of a modernist-era writing fighting fire with fire.

On the one hand, what is thoroughly modern is approved: Psmith's self-advertising search for employment exemplifies his freedom from his class and class prejudice, even his freedom from morality. Psmith's Eve is admired for a charm that goes along with "the broadmindedness of the modern girl" (167). On the other hand, mixed feelings about modernism are in play. Movies inspire the Blandings Castle heir to think of the diamond necklace heist; indeed, they shape his idea of law, his occasional prudence, his very vocabulary. The result is not bright. The poet impersonated by Psmith is mocked because he is a modernist: no one can understand the experimental use of language in the poet's *Songs of Squalor*, one line from which becomes a running gag in the novel. In *Joy in the Morning*, the dilemma in the story is made "modern" in divergent ways. The male in the couple whose marriage is threatened by the elder tyrant (a staple of ancient comedy) is a dramatist on his way to Hollywood, where he will write screenplays. In this case Bertie and Jeeves are on the side of movies, and hence on the side of modernity. But Bertie's objectionable fiancée is a novelist (her latest book is *Spindrift*) who is described as "one of those girls who look on modern enlightened thought as a sort of personal buddy, and receive with an ill grace cracks at its expense" (148). It is Bertie's cracks at his fiancée's modern thought that help break his latest engagement and return him to celibacy – and his pairing with Jeeves.

Perhaps Wodehouse's fiction engages a modicum of modernity only to provide the cracks made at its expense. Nevertheless, one might argue that his protagonists represent an essential modernist endeavor. Modernist experiments with fiction depend upon their authors' wily, unconstrained, and free manipulation of formal possibilities and "thematic" contents: compositional hijinks, so to speak, that are like the freedoms of invention exploited by Psmith and Jeeves. Among the novelists who are most Psmith- or Jeeves-like, or who even make those figures' mischievous freedom of invention pale in comparison, are Max Beerbohm and Saki (the pen name of H. H. Munro).

Performances of authorial zaniness dominate Beerbohm's *Zuleika Dobson; or an Oxford Love Story* (1911). Zuleika, a stunningly beautiful young woman who makes a living as a third-rate magician, comes to Oxford to visit her grandfather, a college warden. Zuleika can fall in love only with someone who does not reciprocate. She experiences love at first sight for the most celebrated Oxonian of the day, the Duke of Dorset, who has never previously been moved by a woman's charms. Alas, he falls in love with Zuleika, which means she cannot return the feeling. With nothing left to live for, the Duke vows to drown himself in her honor. Meanwhile, the entire Oxford undergraduate body falls in love with her. It pledges to imitate its leading exponent, Dorset. And so, as a climax to an Oxford boat race, Dorset commits suicide, and mass suicide follows, depopulating the university. Zuleika, feeling somewhat guilty, plans to move on to Cambridge.

The mere summary of "what happens" in Beerbohm's story should make clear that the content is over the top, and that erotic perversity (reciprocity forbidden!), eros-related morbidity, and even death are being laughed at. Lest we be diverted into thinking that the earnestness of love and death cannot be mocked, Beerbohm's narrator – or Beerbohm the author – constantly reminds the reader of the autonomous artificiality of fiction, and of the authorial clown – a super-Jeeves – who manipulates the artifice and makes the most serious topics into an occasion for fun. The Duke tells Zuleika, who "hardly ever open[s] a book," that her speech has "a literary flavour." "Ah, that is an unfortunate trick," she says, "which I caught from a writer, a Mr. Beerbohm, who once sat next to me at dinner somewhere. I can't break myself of it."[18] The Duke also seems to have sat next to his author. The literary flavor of his public announcements of suicide, because he is "enslaved to Miss Dobson," is patent: "The iron has entered into my soul. I droop. I stumble. Blood flows from me. I quiver and curse. I writhe. The sun mocks me. The moon titters in my face. I can stand it no longer. I will no more of it. Tomorrow I die" (78). A fellow student (on the dense side) asks, "Do you mean you are going to commit suicide?" "Yes," said the Duke, "if you choose to put it in that way" (78).

The reader's interest is intrigued by the many rhetorical ways in which "Mr. Beerbohm" can put his story. He maintains the rhetorical inflation, so that it becomes an interest of its own, a reason to keep reading; but it is equally fascinating to see him practice deflations. When some undergraduate followers of the Duke jump out of an upper-story window because their hero finds that exit more expedient than a doorway, one of the students, says the narrator, "fell headlong, and was, I regret to say, killed" (80). The curtness of the regret is as ridiculous as the opposite literary flavor. But there are more than two modes of the storyteller's comic performance. He sometimes scolds readers for raising questions about the narrative: "Please don't interrupt again. Am *I* writing this history, or are you?" (128). At other times he comments on his formal treatment: "I am loth to interrupt my narrative at this rather exciting moment – a moment when the quick, tense style, exemplified in the last paragraph but one, is so very desirable" (171). As if he were committed to realism, he debates with himself about whether "just once to fob off on his readers . . . one bright fable for effect," and thereby make Zuleika's magic look less dismal (95). He has no trouble reporting as historical fact that, when the Duke is playing a farewell piano performance at a pre-suicide gala, the shades of Chopin and George Sand appear, comment on the musician's bravura, and express Sand's postmortem interest in the beautiful young man. Soon after, a central chapter is devoted to a fantastical justification of how the narrator is incontrovertibly a historian. Thanks to special help from Clio the muse of history and a dispensation from Zeus, the historian of *Zuleika Dobson* is allowed to share the special privilege of novelists (especially Impressionist ones) – that of "a presence invisible and inevitable, ... equipped with power to see into the breasts of all the persons whose actions he set himself to watch ... , with a flawless memory thrown in" (106). In other words, this historian is given the privilege that distinguishes fiction from history, yet is allowed to be trusted as a historian rather than as a novelist. Novelists in general have the privilege of being utterly factitious, even as they appear utterly veracious. We like to see the trickery of fiction exposed, we like to admire its means of deception, and we like to believe in it. The comedy of our relation to novels is not to be underestimated.

Oscar Wilde's modernist ideas of fiction, and Wilde's aphoristic wit, are inseparable from Saki's tales and novels. What is also intermingled with their comedy are British nationalist polemics, grisly tolerance of violence, and Wellsian scientific romance. The mixture is jarring, but turns the reader's attention to the authorial performance, and intensifies an overall comic effect. To be sure, in the foreground of *When William Came* (1912) one encounters the prominence of the polemic and the future-directed fantasy in the service of patriotism. Saki's novel imagines a German colonization of Britain by Kaiser William. Receptive to every foreign influence, cosmopolitan London adjusts itself to becoming a German colony with surprising ease. Social-climbing ambitions also inspire it to collaborate with the invaders. As Cicely Yeovil, the female protagonist and apologist for those ambitions, says to her outraged husband, "We may arrive at ... being the dominant factor in [a foreign German] Empire, impressing our national characteristics on it, and perhaps dictating its dynastic future and the whole trend of its policy. Such things have happened in history."[19] Meanwhile, accommodation must be the order of the day.

Cicely's position is so reasonable that it resists the lack of "sufficient insight" (751) the narrator rebukes her for. Besides, such things as the coming of Dutch William to the English throne in the seventeenth century and the subcontinent of India's accommodation to Victoria's rule have happened in history! The Yeovils' more discontented contemporaries are finding that emigration to India is the solution to their political oppression. But Murrey Yeovil imagines that if he stays at home he can become an incendiary leader of a movement that will recover Home Rule. Withdrawing to the country and to fox-hunting, however, he discovers, against the claims of his political conscience, that the rural sporting life is exactly right for him.

The thrust of Saki's narrative is critical of Yeovil's retreat. Yet there is one actor who, not withdrawing from the cosmopolitanism that is marked as treacherous, seems able to remain faithful to the Fatherland: Saki the author-narrator. Thanks to his bravura juggling of genres that upsets a reader's expectations of a unified tone as well as a unified content, *When William Came* is centered in a style that derives from the very aesthetic culture – the *modernist* aesthetic culture – that Saki makes appear a hysterically funny object of derision, politically nefarious, and yet a source of his own way of expressing things.

Wildean aphoristic sayings, whoever utters them and whatever their content, matter to the author and his narrator at least as much as patriotism. We read that "People were willing to worship the Golden Calf, but allowed themselves a choice of altars. . . . [One worshiping couple] kept open house in such an insistently open manner that they created a social draught" (739). Socialism is no better than the Golden Calf: it is "made for the greatest dullness of the greatest number" (767). But conspicuous consumption is also to be deflated: an aspiring socialite "had attained to that desirable feminine altitude of purse and position when people who go about everywhere know you well by sight and have never met your dress before" (738). As bon mots decorate Saki's text, Wilhelmine London is agog over the modernist innovations of dance introduced by one Gorla Mustelford. The narrator is less moved. "The dancing . . . did not seem widely different from much that had been exhibited aforetime by exponents of the posturing school" (743). His review of the performance continues: "The highly imaginative titles that she had bestowed on her dances, the 'Life of a fern,' the 'Soul-dream of a topaz,' and so forth, . . . [i]n themselves . . . meant absolutely nothing, but they induced discussion" (744). Such sarcastic drawling is characteristic of the treacherous cosmopolites. Saki devotes a late chapter of the novel to a scene in a Turkish bath, in which two languid youths discuss an Anglo-German masked ball of the previous evening. The chapter is meant to contrast them to the dignity of noncollaborationists. But Saki's imagination of their dialogue comes from the resources of a rhetorical drollery that is the modernist root of his art's mercurial turns.

Some literary historians in our day argue that "modernism" has been constructed retrospectively: that it did not recognize itself, or was not recognized contemporaneously, in the identifiable terms claimed for it by our periodizing habit. Yet as the butt of comic novels, modernism seems to have borne from the start the characteristics we are familiar with. It is a prime object of laughter in Stella Gibbons's *Cold Comfort Farm* (1932), although, as in Saki, its animating spirit participates in the very thing it mocks.

The mockery begins in Gibbons's preface, where she dedicates her book to a novelist (an imaginary one) whose language challenges ordinary usage and meaning – and therefore is highly modernist. Having herself achieved modernist heights, Gibbons says that she will mark her most artful pages with asterisks, so that ordinary readers can be sure "whether a sentence is Literature or . . . sheer flapdoodle."[20] The starred passages are flapdoodle modernist. But such language is not Gibbons's only literary target. The heroine of *Cold Comfort Farm*, Flora, is a young sophisticated Londoner who, orphaned and impecunious, migrates to Sussex because she must throw herself on the kindness of her stranger-cousins, the Starkadders. They are a peasant clan, primitive, unwashed, without civility, in no way modern, let alone modernist. Their life at Cold Comfort Farm is a relic of prehistoric matriarchy (shades of Harrison and Klein!): an all-controlling figure, Ada Doom Starkadder, rules them with an iron fist, even though she is bed-ridden. Gibbons's imagination of this clan's figures seems to parody the rural characters in Thomas Hardy's novels and those in the best-selling contemporary novels of Mary Webb (*Gone to Earth* [1917] and *Precious Bane* [1926]). The connection between this realist-naturalist material and modernism is revealed by Gibbon's snarky inter-identification of the latter with religious mania, and of both with primitivism.

The inter-identifying link is Amos Starkadder, a revivalist preacher of a sect of his own. His audience's religious mania makes Flora realize a likeness of the congregation "with audiences she had studied in London; and particularly an audience seen once – but only once – at a Sunday afternoon meeting of the Cinema Society." Devoted to "the progress of the cinema as an art," the audience suffers from intellectual mania. But,

> not content with the ravages produced . . . by the remorseless workings of its critical intelligence, . . . [it] had sat through a film of Japanese life called 'Yes,' made by a Norwegian film company in 1915 with Japanese actors, which lasted an hour and three-quarters and contained twelve close-ups of water-lilies lying perfectly still on a scummy pond and four suicides, all done extremely slowly.   (93)

The laughable additional involvement of modernism with primitivism as well as old-time religion comes in the form of Gibbons's take-off on D. H. Lawrence. He appears in the guise of an ex-Londoner and writer named Mybug, who haunts the Cold Comfort neighborhood. Gibbons characterizes Mybug especially in the light of the sexual candor (and some of the dialect) of Lawrence's banned novel *Lady Chatterley's Lover* (1928). Mybug even "quotes" Lawrence: "D. H. Lawrence was right when he . . . said there must be a dumb, dark, dull, bitter belly-tension between a man and a woman, and how else could this be achieved save in the long monotony of marriage?" (206). The character's rhetoric recalls visionary patches of *The Rainbow*. He also writes a kind of absurd literary history (he *knows* Branwell Brontë is the real author of the Brontë novels) that Gibbons probably intends as satire of Lawrence's critical writings.

Gibbons's spoofing also includes nonliterary modernist discourse. Ada Doom Starkadder is a pseudo-Freudian study in hysteria: as a child, the narrative reveals, she was traumatized by something nasty she saw in the woodshed – and, thanks to that primal scene, never to be made explicit, she has been invalided (and all-powerful as a victim!) ever since. It is her happy fate to be cured by Flora, who liberates all her cousins from their retrograde state. She accomplishes that by thoroughly modernizing them. In Gibbons's novel, we come again to the anti-modernist modernist. Flora is a latter-day can-do New Woman, who evangelizes in the name of "civilizing" (Flora's term) and progressive improvements. She frees the cousins' womenfolk from abjection. She wangles a movie contract for her cousin Seth (he has matinee idol looks). She cures Ada Doom by flying her to Paris and committing her to a long stay in a chic hotel. That is one kind of avant-garde therapy! Flora plans to marry a cleric, but she admires him most for his commitment to airplane travel. If these instances of tidying what Flora calls "messes" do not seem to justify calling them modernist, then one remarkable action of the heroine's does. Marie Stopes's ground-breaking *Married Love* (1918), a manifesto of planned parenthood, is a foremost example of modernist discourse. Early in Flora's stay at Cold Comfort Farm, she instructs one of the farm's leading bearers of illegitimate children about the facts of contraception. Her auditor is shocked by what Flora communicates "carefully, in detail, in cool phrases, . . . exactly" (69). Such wicked, unnatural advice! Yet the unwed mother thinks she will try it out. It is a sign that, for all Gibbons's criticism of modernism, Flora accomplishes a modernist mission.

That modernist fiction takes in stride the laughter it solicits at its own expense is one measure of its autonomy. In some of its practitioners, the comedy of its vulnerability to criticism is contained by imaginations of utopian or romance places where rebellious modernist values are the order of the day, and, despite contrary antagonisms, establish their rule. Such modernist transhistorical romance kingdoms, which ultimately ally themselves with comic vision, are constructed in Norman Douglas's *South Wind* (1917) and Compton Mackenzie's *Extraordinary Women: Theme and Variations* (1928).

Douglas's kingdom is the Mediterranean island of Nepenthe (a fictitious version of Capri), a cosmopolitan crossroads of nations and ethnicities. The novel's eponymous wind represents modernist inspiration: it corrodes all certainties, including trust in reality. Above all, it overturns established values. Of the two wise characters whom Douglas makes in effect the wind's spokesmen, Count Colaveglia and Mr. Keith, the Count answers the question, "What is the outstanding feature of modern life?" by asserting "The bankruptcy, the proven fatuity, of everything that is bound up under the name of Western civilization. Men are perceiving . . . the baseness of mercantile and military ideals"; even more, Keith claims, they are perceiving that old laws, especially religiously instituted ones, "are inappropriate for modern life; their interest is purely historical."[21] The outstanding need of modern life is to change, radically, from what it has been. Nepenthe is beset by a history of ruthless and bloody rule, still operative in its judicial order. It is also the scene of current-day violent conflict between local customs, governed by the Roman Catholic church, and an exiled Russian sect of religious mystics. The iron-fisted law and the religious contentions represent the bankruptcy and fatuity of Western civilization (including Russia). The unfortunate past encroaches on the scene of the advent of "a fresh body of ethics" (25).

An ancient island oracle has long predicted the need for that freshly liberating vision of conduct. On its behalf, Keith's exhortations are composed of an aphoristic eloquence that again shows Wilde's enduring impact. He finds accepted morality to be largely a matter of sentimentality – and "all sentimentalists are criminals" (280). While Keith respects justice, one of his precepts is that "Trying to be fair-minded is generally a mistake" (279). "Any child can grasp the morality of its period," he says. "Why should I pretend to be interested in what a child can grasp? . . . All morality is a generalization, and all generalizations are tedious. Altogether the question that confronts me is not whether morality is worth talking about, but whether it's worth laughing at" (223).

Keith's most impressionable listeners find it difficult to think of morality as a laughing matter. One of them is an Anglican bishop, the other an English undergraduate. The bishop feels alarmed that his values are being decomposed by his experiences on Nepenthe. But he also bravely, and acceptingly, senses that his values are being shaped into attractively "fresh and unexpected patterns" (201). That means another trouble: loss of his identity. Yet he acknowledges the opportunity to newly "find himself" (201). The undergraduate is more troubled. His self-discovery is merely a prospect. At one point, looking for guidance, he descends into the Cave of Mercury, a haunted place that promises him a visionary experience, but it does not deliver, which deepens his depression. The episode points forward to Forster's baleful Marabar Caves. Yet the bishop and the student come through in the end.

Their search is something that Keith knows well, and its issue promises to generate equivalents of the comprehensive wit that he exemplifies. Nepenthe is the modernist romance space that enables personal metamorphosis, and perhaps a global south wind, too.

Mackenzie reiterates that magic space, by adapting Capri as Douglas did. He re-creates it as the island of Sirene, and he populates it with lesbians, whose loves and jealous rivalries are the narrative's substance. Homosexuality is prima facie a modernist matter, partly because of Wilde's martyr-like imprisonment for his exemplification of "queer" desire, and partly because homosexuals' demands for social and legal rights constitute a major rebellion against religious and moral tradition.

Mackenzie's novel might have escaped prosecution for its scandalous content because it appears to treat its cosmopolitan crowd of lesbians satirically. Any female who comes to Sirene and who is recognized as an object of desire by its femme fatale, Rosalba, automatically solicits her will to dominate. What does Mackenzie want us to feel or think about that? The narrative seems to indulge the likable bisexual young woman, Lulu, who is the novel's first focus. It might be because her fluid eros does not play a power game, whereas the unwavering fixity of Rosalba's desires is ruthless. The ruthlessness, not the desire, is the object of the satire. To twenty-first-century taste, however, unmitigated hostility to same-sex love, and not to eroticized one-upsmanship, might underlay the narrator's question: "Of what is Rosalba the portent? What signifies this boy-girl . . . in the curve of a civilization?"[22]

The narrator proposes some answers. One is that Rosalba returns civilization to a time when only the present moment mattered. In the curve of civilization, then, her sexuality signifies a lapse of culture's time-sense: escape from thinking about gender's rigidly defined history and from thinking about a reproductive future. Another answer comes from the native Sirenesi: they think the "extraordinary women" are products of the Great War's having made men more scarce. There is also a striking feminist answer (in a free indirect discourse moment): "Women of [Rosalba's] temperament had a sense of justice denied to the cowardly slaves of men's desires. They knew when they were in the wrong and could admit it" (150). Finally, one response to the question about portent is another question. The narrator, in alliance with Rosalba's staunch and all-forgiving lover Rory, asks: "Why should Rosalba be tamed? Such a process would reduce their sublime love to the level of a suburban marriage." The meaning of "this boy-girl" is allied to modernism's attack on marriage – a significant "curve."

Nevertheless, Rosalba is never likable. Because of that, what is interesting is the intense extent of Mackenzie's imagination of her intrigues. Rosalba is a powerful narrative driver – indeed, is the narrative drive itself. She weaves and unweaves complications in the way we have seen comic characters and their authors do (Zuleika is like her). Without liking her, Mackenzie allows her to take him over. That is not a method for facilitating satiric detachment. It leads the author and the reader to look for less aggressive evaluations of Rosalba. The least aggressive is that of Sirene's other protagonist, Rory. Although she is charmless, and ridiculously submissive to her beloved Rosalba, Mackenzie allows her passion unusual dignity. "It is because I believe my love is something beyond ordinary love, being creation not procreation," she says. "I regard myself as privileged to be constituted as I am. I regard myself as the evidence of progress, not as a freak" (167). Rory's patience with Rosalba's provocations *is* freakish. But Mackenzie's modernist island offers readers the opportunity to practice patience toward what they might find too trying for their sympathy. Moreover, the loves on Sirene are freakish not because they are lesbian, but because they are loves, and entangled in social demands for empowering approval and recognition. Those demands, *Extraordinary Women* proposes, "queer" love more than eros does.

In Nancy Mitford's *Love in a Cold Climate* (1949), despite the coldness of the English, the heat of love in all its varieties assumes revolutionary force. Mitford does not create a self-conscious representational island to channel the force; instead, her treatment is straightforwardly realistic, referring to the interwar period as we think of it historically. The novel's narrator is a lively young woman who, both during her adolescence and before it, has love on her mind continually. Her erotic inclinations are commonplace, however, in contrast to those of two other leading protagonists. The first is Polly, the gorgeous only child of Lord and Lady Montdore, present owners of a great estate, Hampton. The estate is entailed to a male heir, a Canadian, but no one knows him or has searched for him. In part to compensate for the passing of Hampton to a stranger, Lady Montdore expects Polly to make a brilliant marriage. Polly lacks all interest in her exalted prospects. Since an early age – scandalously early – she has been in love with an older married man – an uncle – whose philandering involves underage girls, Polly included. When her uncle's wife dies, Polly proposes, and is accepted. Her mother is outraged – not least because her uncle has been her mother's lover. Polly is disinherited, but, against all the forces of censure, she independently and triumphantly realizes her desire.

Not that the realization lasts. At the end of the novel, she is happily committing adultery with a new love. Her affair is being facilitated by the cleverness of Hampton's heir, Cedric, who has been discovered in Paris, and has become the ruling spirit of the estate. Immensely charming and drolly witty, Cedric replaces Polly in Lady Montdore's heart, and wins the affection of Lord Montdore as well. But there is an anomaly. Cedric is gay – flamingly, publicly so. The Montdores' neighbors, the Boreleys, are revolted. "The thing they could least stick in the world were 'aesthetes – you know – those awful effeminate creatures – pansies.'"[23] The neighbors' reaction proves that they are provincial. "London society, having none of the prejudices against the abnormal which still exists ... in country places, simply ate Cedric up, occasional echoes of his great success even reaching Oxford" (436). Cedric, a more glamorous Jeeves, is a member of the underclass who steps into aristocratic tradition, and makes it his own.

A woman who has married her uncle/mother's lover, and who becomes an adulteress, and an openly queer man are unqualifiedly approved by Mitford's narrator. What an anti-Victorian transformation of values! "I thought the whole thing simply splendid, since I like my fellow-beings to be happy and the new state of affairs at Hampton had so greatly increased the sum of human happiness ... yet the Boreleys were disgusted. They must indeed be against the human race, I thought, so to hate happiness" (412). It is a romance world happiness, despite the historical references, and modernism has fostered the comedy. Mitford's imagination of Cedric is only twenty years beyond Woolf's *Orlando*, Radclyffe Hall, and *Extraordinary Women*, and years ahead of the historical decriminalization of homosexuality in Britain. For some of those who are locked out of history, fiction creates ahead of time (or outside it) an autonomous place of entry.

Fairy Tales, Fantasies, Horrors, and Romances

Debatable Boundaries

Any claim fictions make to occupy a contemplative, autonomous space separated from our ordinary discourses and actions can be characterized as an illusion – a fairy tale. Fairy tales, and fictions in general, are all well and good, we might say, but they are not to be isolated from their involvements with nonfictional phenomena. Surely their real place, despite their Nepenthes, Sirenes, and suspension of our daily purposes and probabilities, is in a nonfictional world.

But an impatient attachment of fiction to nonfiction runs the danger of prematurely assuming an answer to a question that remains open: what *is* the proper place of the far-fetched realms that imagination unendingly generates, and that modernism's autonomizing of fiction abets? Arthur Machen, a leading British producer of fantastic and macabre texts, and hence a candidate for placement on fiction's prophetic axis, proposes that "literature" is different from "mere reading matter" because literature produces and promotes "ecstasy." In *Hieroglyphics: A Note upon Ecstasy in Literature* (1905), he suggests that ecstasy is synonymous with "desire of the unknown, sense of the unknown, rapture, adoration, mystery, wonder, withdrawal from the common life."[24] Certainly we are entertained (if not made ecstatic) by fiction's withdrawals into unknown worlds. Not that those worlds offer exclusively painless pleasures. Nor do they, and their producers, avoid keeping open questions about the relation of fantasy to what's real. As we'll see in an initial sample, fantasies and fairy tales can divide their narratives between real and fantasy places, even though what they designate as real, for the sake of contrast with explicitly designated fairy realms, is yet another fantasy. In such contradictory proliferation of contrasts, what is at stake is whether reality can draw a hard-and-fast boundary line between itself and its radical fictive alternative, or whether one form can dominate the other. This question is yet another facet of the relation of fiction to nonfictional discourse.

The young protagonist of Machen's *The Hill of Dreams* (1905), Lucian, experiences an initial ecstasy at the site of a hilltop ancient Roman fort. It includes some sort of intercourse with a faun and a wood nymph. The rapture of this experience begins his alienation from ordinary life. His way of enacting his estrangement is to become an imaginative writer – but not a novelist: he detests George Eliot as an epitome of Victorian fiction, with its "long follies of 'character-drawing,' 'psychological analysis,'" and so on (145).[25] "The fancy that sensations are symbols and not realities hovered in his mind" (116), and he wants to materialize in writing the visions he conjures up of an entire Roman colony at the fort (they include lesbian love-making).

The London literary world rejects his work, however. Lucian takes it as a confirmation that "He could not be human" (167). And now he experiences an alternative ecstasy, but one that terrifies him. He stumbles into a working-class quarter where an orgiastic celebration is under way: a witch's Sabbath. "[H]e was suspended in the void between two worlds" (179). It would be more precise to say that he is suspended among three worlds. The middle world, the ordinary human one, is the void. The others are substantial: the fairy alternative at the Roman site and the Satanic sphere in London. Belonging more to the antithetical fantastic realms rather than to reality, Lucian cannot choose between them and commits suicide. Machen's novel cannot choose between its two fantastic worlds either, but it presents them as superior in ecstasy, pain, and substance to ordinary life, whose value it evacuates. As a realist text, one might say, it commits suicide, or it kills off reality because it prefers the alternatives, as if fiction too cannot be human.

The dilemma-fraught choice between fairy magic and human reality is repeated in Lord Dunsany's *The King of Elfland's Daughter* (1924). It begins with a decision by the parliament of an earthly city, Erl, that it wants its constitutional monarchy to be ruled by a magic lord. Erl borders on magical Elfland, a territory that humans enter at their mortal peril. But at the parliament's wish, Prince Alvaric, with help from a border witch, penetrates the other country, in a quest to bring back as his consort Princess Lirazel. Her domain is in every way different from reality. Elfland is timeless. When Lirazel agrees to Alvaric's suit, she does not realize that she is subjecting herself to time. After she produces an heir, Orion, her fears of growing old make Lirazel persuade her father to grant her wish to return home. He does so, but then radically contracts Elfland's boundaries, so that Alvaric cannot find them and pursue his wife. Alvaric spends decades questing for an entry point. Unlike his father, however, Orion has Elfland in his makeup. During his father's absence he brings trolls and will-o'-the-wisps over the border, in fulfillment of parliamentary demands. He brings in so many magical elements, in fact, that the politicians decide they have had enough. Unfortunately for them, Lirazel wants to see her son. She persuades her father to invade Erl, and contain it entirely. Again he agrees, and magic engulfs the city-state. Losing forever the fields it knows as its human home, Erl disappears from history.

The narrative climax whereby a shining line of light, the bounding edge of the magic kingdom, advances into the human space, is a tour de force of treatment. What is amusing is that both sides are the same "elfland" entities – purely fictive, referential to no reality other than the narrative, and to what the narrative pretends is real rather than magical. Dunsany seems to nudge the reader's awareness that all along we've been having our fictive cake and eating it. "And some," the narrator says,

> translating [Lirazel's] bitter need [to return to Erl] into pitiless earthly words, may say that she wished to be in two places at once. And that was true, and the impossible wish lies on the verge of laughter, and for her was only and wholly a matter for tears. Impossible? Was it impossible? We have to do with magic.[26]

The magic of fantastic fiction is partly a result of its ability to make us think that there is no alternative to it, that reality and enchantment are contained in one and the same autonomous enclosure. Hope Mirrlees's *Lud-in-the-Mist*

(1926) makes the point in another border story. Lud, the capital city of Dorimare, lies next to Fairyland (just beyond the Debatable Hills). An ancient revolution walled off the domains, but their separation is illusory. Fairyland's natural product – fairy fruit – is being smuggled into Dorimare, undermining the established division. In Dorimare, fairy fruit is condemned. It, and indeed all Fairyland, is said to be delusional, "a sort of magic, moulding reality into any shape it chose."[27] Nevertheless, some citizens long for the banned substance and the place. Mirrlees's protagonist, Chanticleer, has heard since childhood an uncanny music that evokes "an ever-present sense of insecurity together with a distrust of the homely things he cherished" (6). The music is a Fairyland sound. Chanticleer's son hears it so insistently that he escapes to the other country. His father must undertake a quest to recover him.

The end of the quest is, as in Dunsany's finale, another takeover. Fairyland invades Lud. Chanticleer leads the invasion, and Lud receptively capitulates. The ending drives home an insight of Chanticleer's: the distinctions that have kept, or keep, Fairyland separate from reality, are arbitrary and illusory. Chanticleer early saw "a curious parallel" between the law and "fairy things." Against the latter, "the men of the revolution" – the anti-fairy-ists – "had substituted law"; yet the law was only another magic, "moulding reality into any shape it chose." For better or worse, "All our dreams got entangled" (13), Chanticleer thinks, and they will continue to do so. Everyone eats fairy fruit, and everyone is consumed by it, even when he or she eats, discusses, and digests something thought to be different.

Mirrlees clearly means the fruit and its place of origin to figure fiction – "lying words . . . in a feigned voice," as her book's last paragraph puts it, with sudden caution. Fairyland feignings exemplify imagination's, and fiction's, and modernism's freedom from reality and its laws, and their opposition to the latter. Yet Fairyland's autonomous realm is also operating when it makes Chanticleer nostalgic for what he already possesses: like realistic fiction, fairy fruit estranges us from "the fields we know" (a refrain in Dunsany that means *home*) to help us repossess them cognitively, and retain our immediate attachments. Nevertheless, even in Mirrlees's novel uncertainty continues. Chanticleer, "I fear," Mirrlees's narrator notes, "did [not] cease to be the prey of melancholy" after his triumph. Although the division between the kingdoms was a mistake, Chanticleer worries that the intermingling of real and fictive realms might yet "mishandle . . . the sacred objects of the Mysteries": life and death (269).

Whether the division between fiction and reality, and modernism's treatments of it, can handle those mysteries, and whether the division must be as stark as it is in Machen's novel or as fluid or dialectical as it is in Dunsany's and Mirrlees's tales, remains open to contest. Literary history lives on the Debatable Hills. Sylvia Townsend Warner's *Lolly Willowes, or The Loving Huntsman* (1926) is a newly complex intermingling of reality and fantasy. For four-fifths of her novel, Warner keys the narrative to realism: marks of reference to modernist-era social norms and history, including the Great War, abound (no such references appear in the novels by Machen, Dunsany, and Mirrlees). Lolly is a spinster aunt who suffers from her brothers' families the condescension, mingled with misogyny, that unmarried women in pre-suffrage days (and after) undergo. Then she breaks away, deliberately isolating herself – in an attempt to find herself – in Great Mop, a rural place deep in Buckinghamshire. Great Mop is her version of Nepenthe or Lucian's Roman fort, but, again, Warner breathes no hint of a novelistic transgression of realism. And then it happens: Lolly participates, almost by chance, in a ritual that she thinks might be a witch's Sabbath, a rural holdover from ancient days. When she is kissed by a masked figure who claims he is the devil, she brushes it off. But the masked man *is* the Devil.

Unlike Machen's Lucian, Lolly is not traumatized by diabolism. Her happy conversations with Satan occupy the remainder of the novel. Yet the fantastic dimension is presented as also plausibly real: no essential difference bounds them. Satan is there; Lolly is talking to him. And the content of the fantastic conversations is realist, referential, historical – and modernist: it is Lolly's declaration on behalf of women's rights. After the Sabbath she has become a witch, not for the sake of harnessing magic or riding broomsticks, but "to have a life of one's own, not an existence doled out to you by others."[28] The condition of women is potentially explosive: women "are dynamite and long for the concussion that may justify them" (243). History will set off the explosion, even though in this text history and the supernatural seem to be equals. Satan is the immortal, but Lolly, who is merely human, evinces a bravery in becoming a witch – "to show our [women and witches'] scorn of pretending life's a safe business, to satisfy our passion for adventure" (242) – that is superhuman. Warner seems almost to think of her modernist magical realism as a thing that must and will do practical, fully enabling, and downright supernatural things for us – once, like Lolly, fiction gets sufficiently over the border of reality's entrammeling circumstance.

But *Lolly*'s last pages, crossing back into the fields of circumstance, also acknowledge the protagonist's mortality, from whose confines her witchery and autonomy cannot free her, and from which the Devil will not save her. In contrast to Lolly's acknowledgment, an assurance that magic and fiction will face down ultimate mortal limitations is found in Forrest Reid's *Uncle Stephen* (1931). It avers that time's flight can turn backward and that age, too, is reversible. The novel's protagonist, Tom, is orphaned at fifteen. Alienated from the relatives with whom he has been residing, he flees to his grand-uncle Stephen, whom he has never met or corresponded with, and who is a recluse living down some sin or failure or tragic loss. Tom has a dream-vision of him that prompts his flight. The meeting of Tom and the sixty-three-year-old is a success, and Tom is taken into the household. But what companionship other than his uncle's company can Tom find? He discovers a contemporary in an old garden Uncle Stephen had mentioned – "a separate enclosure within the main grounds."[29] In a dilapidated house there, before which is a weed-choked fountain surmounted by a statue of a naked boy holding an urn, the other young man secretly resides. Tom gets the impression that "he was on the boundary-line between two worlds. . . . In there was the unknown – mystery – romance" (83).

Mysterious indeed: the other adolescent is Uncle Stephen in his youth, re-embodied as he was then. Time's boundary line is erased. At first young Stephen palms himself off on his grand-nephew by calling himself Philip. When Tom figures out who Philip really is, he wonders what Philip-Stephen knows about the future. "It was really very queer and confusing. Uncle Stephen for Philip was . . . , *Philip's* future, and of course you can't remember the future" (173, emphasis original). The resulting dilemmas for Tom's friendship with his rejuvenated uncle must be read to be believed. "All the past was dreamland," Tom concludes; "it was only the present moment that wasn't" (254). But the narrative makes uncertain where the reality of time and change leaves off and fantasy begins.

The movement of Reid's fiction from reality to fantasy land and back again is wilder than that present in Warner's novel. Perhaps it is wilder because Reid's transgressions of temporal reality insinuate sexual transgressions less available to public discussion than Warner's feminism. They suggest male–male love that does not conform to legal definitions of the age of consent. Tom requires his uncle's physical touch. Uncle Stephen's bedroom includes a broken statue of Hermes, whom the uncle identifies as "he who cares for boys,' and his statue was put up beside that of Eros in the palestra. . . . But he is also . . . the prototype of the Christian Good Shepherd, and you can be his young ram" (121). The young ram twice passionately kisses on the lips the stone boy of the secret garden's fountain – the second time when he thinks he has lost young Stephen. He sleeps with the latter in his uncle's bed – that is, he sleeps with his uncle, cuddling him, then admiring the naked body of his uncle's youth. The different temporal dimensions that Tom and young Stephen inhabit, the perverse queerness of the fantasy, all seem solved by reading – by diagnosing – *Uncle Stephen* as a mask for a taboo desire.

Nevertheless, to read it all as a mask for something we can define and prosecute reduces fiction to what it is not. Certainly it curbs the adventure, the romance, and the autonomy of fictional discourse. Even to read *Uncle Stephen* as what it licitly might be – an exploration of male psychic dynamics that are not identical with Oedipal or homosexual desire – would reduce the fiction by submitting it to real-world "psychological analysis." The reduction, resisting what Erl and Lud also opposed, holding tight to the territory that is the near side of reality, might trigger yet another invasion by fairy forces.

Animating and Limiting Autonomy

One of the motives for writers' and critics' ideas about fiction's autonomy, insofar as the previous subsection and the pages on comic novels suggest, is a desire to enlarge human powers by dreaming of fantastic extensions of them, or of mergers with nonhuman or inhuman forces. A demand for a cosmic increase of animation, testing to the limit the prospect of augmenting the life of everything from objects to the cosmos, seems to motivate the autonomizing impulse. Among the limits to be tested are death and God. What if fiction's modernist experiments could convince us that death is only apparently limitary? As for the Supreme Animator, doesn't the idea of art's autonomy provide us with a substitute for Him, or – appropriately for a modernist frame of mind – relocate His power where it has always been at home, in imagination? An affirmative answer is plausible. But we remember Dr. Moreau's lack of success in pursuing modernist experiments on life, or Chanticleer's unresolved fear that the intermingling of real and fictive realms might mishandle life and death. In this section I consider fantasy fictions that, it is arguable, are self-divided. Although they are rooted in imaginative freedom, they also counterweight autonomy, projecting modernist fiction's depression of its creative power, even as they draw upon the latter's inventive resources.

The difficulty of telling the difference between animation and death constitutes part of the interest of Bram Stoker's *Dracula* (1897). Its famous vampire, according to one of the novel's heroes, Dr. Van Helsing, is evolving. In him the Un-Dead, creatures who inhabit an interval between life and death, are trying to come fully to life; they are also trying to develop their still-immature brains. Thus their deadly aggression has enlarged vitality and intellect as its object. The physician continues his surprising apology:

> What more may he [the vampire] not do when the greater world
> of thought is open to him. He that can smile at death as we know him;
> who can flourish in the midst of diseases that kill off whole peoples.

Oh! if such an one was to come from God, and not the Devil, what a force for good might he not be in this old world of ours.[30]

Nevertheless, the more-evolved "are pledged to set the world free" from the less-evolved. Only a few pages away from the back-handed praise of the monster is Dracula's demise at the hands of the doctor's associates.

Still, the drama of the narrative's struggle of life against death, and of the vampire's possible siding with life, solicits attention. It is as if Stoker is unsure which side of the difference is served by fiction. Does fiction feed on life? In the novel's first half, the engorging of blood or a body fluid appears to be life-giving. Transfusions from Lucy Westenra's male friends reverse her sapped vitality, and Dr. Van Helsing once had the poison from a potentially mortal wound sucked out by another man. Soon afterward, however, the vampire focuses such exchanges as death-dealing. And yet they remain life-giving. A mad patient under the care of another of the novel's doctors is diagnosed as "a zoophagous (life-eating) maniac; what he desires is to absorb as many lives as he can, and he has laid himself out to achieve it in a cumulative way" (95). This patient and his site become an entry point for Dracula's appearances. He is a double for the vampire, but he significantly also resists him, hence duplicating Dracula's opponents. The plotters against the fiend – abetted by their Un-Dead-like helpers the typewriter and the phonograph – excite us because they will absorb death by defeating it in the person of the vampire. But fiction too is zoophagous, absorbing as many lives and deaths as it can in pursuit of more life, increasing animation in the universe, but strangely both living and dead. It is, like Stoker's patient, more than a bit mad, and double-edged. It opens itself to Dracula, who figures the bite of invincible mortality, but like the fiend, fiction "can smile at death as we know him." At the end of the novel life triumphs over the horror, death – even though outside of fiction, everyone is bitten, not to animating effect. Does Stoker's novel, rooted in independence from actual life, defeat its autonomy by killing off Dracula, who might be an emblem for itself? No wonder that the vampire lives on in countless stories, because fiction, the vampire's life blood, betwixt and between life and something not alive, never meets a limit or an end.

Nevertheless, fiction's intermediate state between life and death might also hamper its autonomy and its own animating force. One of fiction's curious missions, against the grain of its freely life-giving impulse, is to entertain us by representing the implacably disabling character of death. Walter de la Mare's *Ding Dong Bell* (1924, 1936) collects his stories about graveyards (cemeteries are secret gardens, too) and their epitaphs. De la Mare is as experimental as any canonical modernist: he treats the place of the dead, the utmost edge of life, to test the possibility that autonomous fiction can animate it. A renewal of animation is proposed by a graveyard visitor in one of the stories – it's not clear that he is a live visitor – who says that "when we are nearing the end . . . what may be called the real takes on another colour."[31] That color, it would seem, is of spectrality. Does it promise an alternative life? In "Winter," the "very air" in the cemetery, "cold and ethereal and soon to be darkened, seemed to be astir with sounds and shapes on the edge of complete revelation. Such are our fancies" (207). But the revelation is still-born; termination is all. One of De la Mare's narrators, being scrutinized by another cemetery visitor, feels that he is already being read, as if an epitaph. We are such stuff as epitaphs are made on, so the animating aim of fantasy is drastically limited by mortality. Fiction's autonomy stops – even as it flourishes – here.

Humanity and fiction's animating forces together are marginal in a modernist universe of death, if we take seriously the cosmos of William Hope Hodgson's *The House on the Borderland* (1908). It renders the content of a diary written by the new owner of an ancient vast house dangling at the edge of a geographical abyss. Soon after taking possession the owner undergoes visionary experiences, in which he floats over a landscape inhabited by gods and goddesses of death. There is no Supreme Animator. The visions of the deadly gods fade, however, and the owner is back in his house. Then he discovers that the house's grounds harbor a population of interspecies beings – half human, half swine. The swine-men lay siege to the habitation, but temporarily they are held off. In the interim, the diarist suffers another transport, bringing him to the entropy-determined end of the world. He is once more returned to the house, where everything has long crumbled into dust. A hostile organism extending from a scratch on his wrist, a wound from his fight with the swine-men, begins to cover him; it is about to overwhelm his face. The diarist contemplates suicide as the swine-men break in, and the house falls into the chasm. The diary survives in the upper layer of debris. Although its writer's history includes a sister, a lover, and a faithful dog, those human relations are momentary and meaningless. The journal figures the human record: puny, fragmentary, and incredible, in comparison with the more plausible eons of cosmic hostility and lifelessness behind and around it. The modernist autonomous imagination that licenses Hope Hodgson's imagination envisions thereby only its own prospective (and present) impotence.

We might think, on the basis of such stories, that the darkest fictions serve thought, rather than desire for freedom from determination; that they mean to remind us of where the gaps in knowledge of life must be filled in – and at least achieve that filling in, for better or worse. That would be an optimistic way of considering M. R. James's ghost stories and tales of horror, as they frequently make brainy researchers and inquiring historians their protagonists. Perhaps rational inquiry – one of the sources of modernist discourse – can model resistance to engulfments by magic and death; can keep vitality on the right side of the grave, and maintain the autonomy of reason, if not that of imagination. Alas, James's investment in the value of brainwork is overbalanced by his demonstration of reason's limitations. In "Casting the Runes" (1911), Edward Dunning, an expert scholar of the history of alchemy, adversely reviews a *History of Witchcraft* by another claimant to expertise. Unfortunately, the latter kills adverse reviewers. His murderous medium are the runes he casts against those who have offended him. Dunning and a friend do the research work that makes them understand the reality of the threat. The knowledge is no shield. One night Dunning gets into bed, puts his hand under his pillow, and "touched . . . a mouth, with teeth, and with hair about it, and . . . not the mouth of a human being."[32] To save his life he must redirect the runes against the other man. He succeeds, but his success proves that his rationality is powerless on its own, without the superior aid of magic. Another scholar, a Cambridge University librarian in "The Tractate Middoth" (1911), also must undertake research to identify what turns out to be a murdering ghost. In this case, the ghost indirectly helps the librarian toward a happy marriage and new wealth. But the macabre comedy does not flatter the mind's capacity to penetrate darkness.

The animating influences remain beyond human life. James's "The Story of a Disappearance and an Appearance" (1913) is a detective story – but the work of detection belongs to a nonhuman agent. The story's protagonist has joined a community effort to discover the whereabouts of his missing clergyman uncle. The knowledge arrives, but only by transmission from an inhuman animating power in the protagonist's dream of a grotesque Punch and Judy show. He wakes to find the dream real. A traveling Punch and Judy exhibition, offered to the town on Christmas Day, reveals that the cleric was murdered, and includes his effigy in the entertainment. Intellect is dwarfed by the puppetry, whose dead–alive "animation" belongs to something unfathomably stranger than whatever is available to human cognition. James's late tale, "An Evening's Entertainment" (1925), claims that modern storytelling amounts to instruction in science, whereas pre-modern entertainments were inspired by ghosts and hideous bloodletting. Of course, James's story is old-fashioned. It maintains fantasy's anti-scientific subversion – its bleeding, so to speak – of disciplined intelligence.

But is it any wonder that fiction produces stories that remind us to believe in what resists reasoning? In such an upside-down and self-serving way, fiction's hope in autonomy springs eternal! The reminder fascinates, even when it mostly says that death and pain, as well as creepiness, prevail. If this assertion is true, and we can be diverted by fiction's proposal of it, then the premise of Hugh Walpole's *Portrait of a Man with Red Hair* (1925) is plausible. It pictures a madman who believes that "life [is] never so intense as when we [are] suffering."[33] He insists on making his son, his daughter-in-law, and Walpole's tender-minded protagonist undergo torture as a testament of his love for them. The idea of the involvement of pain and love runs fantastic fiction up against theology. Walpole's red-haired sadist is inspired by God: "[T]he whole of His power is derived from the pain that He inflicts upon those less powerful than Himself. ... It is plainly for our good that He torments us" (166–167). The maker of the stars and their worlds thus is a virtual fabricator of gothic fictions that convince us of pain's potency, its alliance with death, and its radical constraint of intelligence and pleasure. Our only consolation is that a supreme free agent is out there in the cosmos, even if it is not humanity's own.

If such a view comes closest to truth, it indicates a nightmarish cosmos, wherein the difference between animating and life-destroying principles is blurred. The possibility is riskily entertained in G. K. Chesterton's *The Man Who Was Thursday: A Nightmare* (1908), where modernist doubts about religious orthodoxy again are at work. A self-proclaimed modernist poet in Chesterton's story asserts that "the lawlessness of art and the art of lawlessness" are the same, and that modernists are violent anarchists who "have abolished Right and Wrong."[34] Autonomy indeed! The assertion provokes a counter-claim from another poet, Syme, who insists that he and poetry stand for freedom-inhibiting law, order, and moral distinctions. Syme also happens to be a detective, and aims to hunt down the anarchist leaders. His opponent is about to become one of them under the code name Thursday. Thursday is bravely modernist-impersonal in deciding to help Syme penetrate the organization – not to betray it, but to expose him to its cogent motivation. What Syme discovers is that the anarchists are themselves detectives, who pretend to be lawless as a strategy for infiltrating and undoing the forces of mayhem. Modernism is thereby exposed as a mere fantasy of radical autonomy – a mere misrecognition of an illusory independence. Nevertheless, the president of the "anarchists," Sunday, remains mysterious, and he leads everyone on a wild pursuit that terminates in an awed vision: the supreme anarchist Sunday is God.

Given such an identity, the universe is animated by a radically autonomous maker, but its essence would seem to be the very disordering of life that Syme opposes. We saw earlier how Chesterton's ideas of fiction and faith tend to turn inside out the oppositions, such as the one between modernism and orthodoxy, that he relies on. During the chase after Sunday, Sunday diverts his pursuers by throwing at them written messages that are absurd in themselves and irrelevant to the moment. Are the messages (they seem to predict passages in *Finnegans Wake*) figures for God's customary communication to mortals? The gap between them and understanding is laughable, and Chesterton's God is less a monster than a clown. To have a clown preside over the cosmos is not much different from thinking of it as James's Punch and Judy show. Syme says that he has "been suddenly possessed with the idea that the blind, blank back of [Sunday's] head really was his face – an awful, eyeless face. . . . Shall I tell you the secret of the whole world? It is that we have only known the back of the world. . . . If we could only get round in front –'" (170). If we could only get fiction round in front, it might discover how the author of all makes sense, and is not funny by virtue of being unintelligible. But that we can't get it round in front says little for the power of modernist fiction after all. Chesterton's jokester, anarchist God might as well be a modernist, yet the autonomy is all His.

The suggestion that God is a monstrous creative agent is taken up once more in T. F. Powys's novels and tales, where the treatment of the Maker retains the humor that plays through Chesterton's vision, and nevertheless is lacerating. Powys's *Fables* (1929) enlists fiction's animating principle to personify and make speak the lowliest, least likely objects – dish cloths, fence posts, clocks, seaweed, spittoons. Powys's *Unclay* (1931) even animates Death, making him an engaging character. But perhaps because fiction only deceives itself and us by its animating impulse, Powys's fiction permits readers a vicarious revenge for the mortality God has cursed us with. Powys figures God as a lowly itinerant, Tinker Jar, camping at the edge of a town named Dodder. In Powys's "The Only Penitent" (1931), Dodder's clergyman decides to reinstitute individual auricular confession as a sacrament. Tinker Jar is the eponymous penitent.

"I crucified my son," he confesses; "Twas I who created every terror in the earth, the rack, the plague, all despair, all torment. I am the one who rips up the women with child, every foul rape is mine act, all pain and all evil are created by me." He wonders if his confessor can still love Him, especially inasmuch as He also admits to destroying all men: "I cast them down into the pit, they become nothing." The holy man is incredulous. He forgives Jar's sin, pardons all His evil, and credits and strengthens His goodness – "and," he concludes, "bring you to everlasting death."[35]

An anti-modernist God who is a clown, a God who is justly condemned to death argue for fiction's capacity to amuse us with blasphemy. It has that much autonomous power. Of course, it has more. All the narratives just considered, whether they represent a divine autonomy that disallows human possession of a creative equivalent or emphasize death's supreme power, are examples in themselves of unconstrained fictive invention. Free fantasy thereby imagines its lack of freedom. Those narratives, contradicting their own animating independence, allow fiction an occasion for self-divided play. When fiction's dark terrors or shocks absorb us, we overlook the way in which the play is self-reflexive: an exhibition of the license that only in appearance is being denied.

The self-reflexivity is prominent in Charles Williams's *Many Dimensions* (1931). Williams's novel returns divinity to a more traditional characterization, although it also emphasizes the terror that God is, and again dwarfs human aims that might be symptomized by desire for worldly might. An English traveler and archeologist has purchased in Persia a remnant of the crown of King Solomon, which contains a remarkable stone, engraved with the name of Allah. The stone is thus Judeo-Christian and Muslim at once. It is also an agent of the divinity: it can transport its possessor from one space to another, or one time to another, or one mind to other minds; and it can heal disease. No less wonderfully, it can be divided and multiplied, without being diminished. Its purchaser decides to profit from it, to sell its duplicate "types" to industrialists and to the British government, to employ it for the sake of an orgiastic advance of secular power. A near-chaos results nationally; and the Islamic world, which wants to repossess what has been alienated from it, comes to the brink of tumult.

A British Lord Justice and his female assistant, Chloe, along with a Muslim cleric, are appalled, and work to rescue the stone – and its duplicates – from exploitation. The Lord Justice describes the stone's effect, when it is not being coerced, as a state of "profound repose," not "altogether governed by time. . . . I am sure that state never comes while I am concerned with myself, and . . . that in some strange way that state was itself the Stone."[36] It is absence of will, and of active manipulation, that the stone exemplifies. The mode of rescuing it also must be will-less. Chloe comes to enact the inactivity that protects the object. Even when she undergoes mortal threat as a result of an attempt to seize the "type" in her possession, she surrenders to what it wills or does not will. That surrender confirms a dream the Muslim cleric has had of her: "I saw the name of Allah written on her forehead." She becomes the climactic conduit whereby the stone and its types, "that mysterious visibility of the First Matter of creation," "returned to the invisibility from which it had been summoned" (262).

Williams makes *Many Dimensions* reflect on itself as fiction in relation to the high theological matter it broaches. One evidence of the self-reflection is a description of the Lord Justice as "at once in contact and detached, at once faithless and believing," beholding the fantastic things in the narrative "in the light of that fastidious and ironical goodwill which, outside mystical experience, is the finest and noblest capacity man has developed in and against the universe" (194). Whether or not the capacity at issue "in and against the universe" is as exalted as Williams's rhetoric, it is hard to resist seeing the characterization of the judge as a portrait of any reader of fictions. Their reader is rehearsed repeatedly in attached and detached states of faith and doubt in the face of myriad mysteries (inside of mystical experience as well as outside). Indeed, a reader might contemplate fiction (the core of fantasy), and modernist fiction above all, as a type of Williams's stone (or vice versa). Like the stone, modernist fiction takes us wherever we want to go, offers us infinitely extended powers, yields to our interpretations and checks them, confronts God and the death of God, and celebrates and condemns our animating desires. All the while it remains in repose, inventing actions and agitations to provoke in us contemplative attention and response. Even though Williams did not divorce himself from religious faith, his fiction emphasizes the same things modernists do.

Quests and Collectives

A political revolution – the post-war construction of the British welfare state, which it is plausible to think of as revolutionary – lies just beyond our survey of entertaining fictions. The election of a Labor government in Britain in 1945 might have represented an unusually collective-minded commitment to historical change as well as a modernist-inspired one, as we will see in Chapter 6. Preliminary to that chapter, in this section I examine a few additional modernist-era romances, more or less conformable to quest narratives – for their address, or their lack of it, to collective experience and values.

The utopianism implicit in these fictions is allied with their autonomy-inspired separation from the "actual" state of things. However, an immediate problem for fiction's aim to imagine collectives seems posed by the novel genre's habit of focusing on individual consciousness, and playing that off against a sociologically rendered group. Stories of minority–majority conflict ensue, and they accord superior value to personal, even isolated experience. For example, in W. H. Hudson's *Green Mansions: A Romance of the Tropical Forest* (1904), the frustrated love of Abel and Rima foregrounds Abel's sensations and ideas about his discovery and his loss of the young woman. She is at once ordinarily human and a sprite of the forest, expressing herself in everyday words as well as in a wordless language that belongs to the forest's birds. Abel desperately hopes for unity with such language and Rima: it brings "a sense of an impersonal, all-compromising One who is in me and I in him."[37] His longing for an impersonal mode of being would include unity with Rima's grandfather and the environment's Indian tribes.

It appears, then, that the union which figures collective existence is the narrative's desire as well as Abel's. Nevertheless, the narrative also assigns disastrous consequences to the quest for unity. Abel is originally a revolutionary nationalist. Disillusionment with that collective effort initiates his retreat to the forest, the blessed threshold of Rima and wordless language. Her own retreat – from her own mystical threshold – begins the disaster to come. She wants to return from her isolation to her native place, to recapture the identity of her mother's people. But the long trek to that place of solidarity has a barren issue. Her people are gone; the community is a phantom. Collectivity reigns only among the Indians, and it expresses itself first as one tribe's slaughter of Rima, and then as Abel's murderous alliance with the tribe that in effect avenges Rima's death.

Abel's singleness – another possible figure for autonomy – is the center of grief in *Green Mansions*, but collectivity as a practice or ideal is only a destructive alternative to sorrow. To pursue that alternative, and to redeem it, remains an urgent ideal but is inevitably compromised, if one judges by the outcome of the effort in another fantastic history: Fr. Rolfe's *Hadrian the Seventh: A Romance* (1904). In this narrative, an obscure English candidate for the priesthood is – miraculously – elected to the papacy. His assumption of the throne, and his conduct of his office, is a global scandal, not least because he retains the eccentric individuality – and "quixotic impossible idealism"[38] – that long kept him from ecclesiastical acceptance. One of his singularities is his apparent homosexuality. A modernist pope indeed! That he promotes "infinite difference . . . not equality, but diversity" (181) aligns with his cherished queerness, as does his fierce opposition to the entire spectrum of political ideologies. But then Rolfe imagines the new Pope Hadrian as dedicated, neo-socialistically one might say, to the collectivity of the Italian state. He sells off the Vatican treasury of art and learning, and turns over the proceeds to the Italian nation, as an endowment of a social welfare scheme.

Clearly Rolfe's romance is driven by a utopian hope that collective good, and the conservation of ancient institutions such as the Catholic Church, be compatible with intelligent liberty from clichéd or rigid partisanships. And, for all its emphasis on the value of Hadrian's personal uniqueness, the novel proposes that, *pace* individualism, a person is a composite being, first and last. Hadrian exemplifies modernist fiction's idea of allotropic states of self. In effect he says so when an international media campaign exposes compromising facts of his early life, and begins a smear campaign against his youth's assumption of multiple personae. "There were four of me at least," Hadrian admits. "Most people have only half developed their personalities. That a man should split his into four and more; and should develop each separately and perfectly, was so abnormal that many normals failed to understand it" (392). "Normals" fail to understand that a modernist self need not be unified and, Rolfe implies, that its separate parts can survive creatively, in effect constituting a model collectivity that reconciles idiosyncrasies and commonalty. Ironically, the socialist collectivists in the novel, resisting Hadrian's reconciling model, incite his assassination.

Rolfe went on to write *The Desire and Pursuit of the Whole* (1934), a fantasy about transgender eros that retreats from the earlier novel's imagining of collective possibilities. Yet in quest fictions generally, in the era that concerns us, "the whole" remains the desired object of pursuit. The romance of David Lindsay's *A Voyage to Arcturus* (1920) seeks to tell us, by means of the adventures of its hero Maskull, what underlying story or principle gathers the scattered parts of the universe into a unity. Is the maker of its collective identity the deity known as Shaping? Is Shaping an alter ego of the supreme cosmic ruler Crystalman? Do Shaping, Crystalman, and another being, Surtur, constitute a holy trinity? If they are One, then earth and the cosmos are.

That unifying fit will be advanced when Maskull will bring back to earth, from the planet Torrance in the solar system of Arcturus, revelatory illumination from a mystical source called Muspel. The merger of earth and alien life is rehearsed by Maskull's body, when arriving on Torrance and moving from one environment to the next, he accrues or loses multiple organs. The metamorphoses promise a unity among radically diverse entities. Separate worlds interlock: existence, relation, and feeling are, he is told, "three gods, . . . mutually antagonistic. Yet . . . somehow united."[39] But "somehow" overstates. The mergers of idiosyncratic things constitute the hope but also the torments of the Torrance romance. The whole keeps falling apart. Although some identities merge into others – Shaping and Crystalman are the same – their very union is an evil (as we might expect in a modernist cosmos, where selves are not fixedly integral). Antithetical worlds, Maskull discovers to his horror, exist on earth and the other planet simultaneously: the real and the unreal, so that "reality and falseness are two words for the same thing" (165). The two things are kept together by what the narrative calls "sports" (accidents) or "forkings" (divided rather than conjoined paths). And Maskull is a victim of another story, one that has been hidden from him and the reader: a cosmic conflict between Crystalman–Shaping and Surtur.

Lindsay's cosmos, a war of heterogeneous essences, scarcely affirms humanity's potential for collective existence or efficacy. Yet art's inventive power, if given its head as modernism tries to do, can make *reality* and *falseness* be two words for the same thing: fiction. The sports and forkings keep promising the possibility of integrated narratives and communities. That is borne out in James Stephens's *The Crock of Gold* (1912). At first glance, not even a hint of collectivity appears in its content or – given the heterogeneity of its content – in its treatment. Stephens's treatment of his tale depends on discontinuities of the kind one finds in the most notorious modernist experiments (it clearly engenders its heir in O'Brien). Book I announces "The Coming of Pan," which is not consonant with a focus on either the opening chapter's protagonists, two pedantic philosophers at war with their wives, or on the initial event: the theft of the crock's gold. The crock's stolen gold (a treasure amassed for centuries) appears a subordinated narrative matter. The thief is a farmer who takes the treasure as part of a contretemps with the gold's owners, local leprechauns. But what has that to do with Pan's advent? Pan will captivate the thief's daughter. He talks modernist discourse to her: "Right is a word and Wrong is a word . . . these words . . . have no meaning."[40] Ancient-modernist Pan's relation to the young woman will lead to the intrusion of another god, an Irish one, who announces that he is called Infinite Joy and Love – whereupon Pan says that those are his names, too.

The conflict of gods, the suggestion that words and the things they stand for are the equivalent of Lindsay's "sports" or "forks," the throwing together of life forms – human beings of different classes (philosophers, farmers, urban policemen), Greek gods, Irish gods, talking cows and flies, the Fairy Host – makes *The Crock of Gold* resemble an adventure on an alien planet. The narrative depends on diversity; how can it support community? The leprechauns find their own corporate identity a burden. They "were unable to organize a direct personal hostility against their new enemy" – the philosopher who had pointed out to the thief where he might dig up something notable – because the philosopher's wife belongs to a fairy collective with which the leprechauns are allied. Nevertheless, by the end of the romance, both the Irish god and his human beloved (previously Pan's object of affection) attest that "until there is a common eye" – "the duty of life is the sacrifice of self" – "no one person can see God," or, no less, experience freedom (221). "Released from the hard bondage of self-hood . . . these people, though many, were one . . . , organic with a simultaneous understanding, a collective action" (225–226).

The means of this transformation, one might say, is a relaxation of differences, enacted by the narrative's refusal to make any one generic treatment prevail over another; by its carelessness about which divinities rule the world; and by its indifference to the invidious distinctions between reality and error that torture Maskull. The narrative ends with a collective dancing and singing that "took the Philosopher from his prison, even the Intellect of Man they took from the hands of the doctors and lawyers, from the sly priests, from the professors whose mouths are gorged with sawdust, and the merchants who sell blades of grass" (228). Stephens reverses what we expect as an ending to a narrative. We expect a narrative to begin with characters in a relative state of innocence, and to end with them in a relative state of experience. In the Stephens novel, the ending is a triumph of mass innocence.

It can easily be objected that *The Crock of Gold*'s utopian finale allies fiction with romance sentimentality: we have only to think of the actual fate of collective action during the years of Anglo-Irish conflict in which editions of *The Crock of Gold* were continually reprinted. Stephens is popular entertainment for children or, at most, "young adults"! To say so, however, is to continue literary as well as psychological distinctions that are invidious or factitious. It is not childish, fiction (whether modernist or not) tells us, to expect such reconciliations of realism and romance, and to expect them in the name of truth as well as history.

The fortunes of collective life in fiction bring us finally to the prewar and wartime treatment of Arthurian romance in T. H. White's tetralogy *The Once and Future King*. Its first two installments, *The Sword in the Stone* (1938) and *The Queen of Air and Darkness* (1939), in dogged service to pacifism, stress the need for resistance to the fracturing that afflicts humanity. *The Sword in the Stone* prepares the collectivist ideal in the succeeding novel by rooting it in the boy Arthur's education. It is all magic, the essence of fiction's autonomy. Arthur's learning includes, thanks to Merlyn, his magical participation in nonhuman societies, first among ants, and then among geese. The ants are a military organization forever involved in internecine battles, exactly as humanity is; the geese are scandalized to think a species would commit itself in effect to civil war. Arthur favors the sociable, pacific feathered tribe. "Passive resistance" as "a new weapon"[41] will interest him in the third novel, *The Ill-Made Knight* (1941), where it is relevant to the ideological troubles, and the games-mania (combat devolved into bloody competition for triumph and celebrity's sake) that plague the Round Table.

The fairy tale aspects of Arthur's youth, directed toward community values as White and Merlyn point them, are influenced by the traditions we've been traversing. At the same time as White is a fantasist, however, he avoids generic purity; that is a sign of an invasion of his romance by skepticism toward it. The skepticism unsettles the utopian unity that the protagonist stands for. Indeed, it unsettles Arthur's place as a protagonist. The third novel's title names ugly and psychologically unbalanced Lancelot. It might also identify White's narrative with the curious cobbling, perhaps ill-made, of ancient and modern or modernist elements (Merlyn's time machine–enabled ability to discuss Hitler; Freudianism). The ill-making, if it is White's deliberate modernist experiment with his materials, begins jovially enough with the comedy of King Pellinore's hunting of the Questing Beast, which entertains us over the course of two novels. But the entertainment is satirizing the quest pattern, without which we wouldn't have Arthur and all the rest. Making us laugh at the very thing we are absorbed in, the buffoonery constitutes a proleptic ridicule of the Holy Grail quests, which, as Arthur will realize, are an ill-made project. There is a shadow even over the valuable human–animal fusions. Merlyn surmises that human language derives from the shrieks of animal prey. If language thus imitates and develops sounds that connote death, the speech whereby collective communication transpires permanently echoes mortal vulnerability.

The skepticism that most worries the quest for a collective utopia is the modernist psycho-analytic one. White utilizes it, to begin with, in the episode of the ugly slaying of a unicorn by the sons of Morgause. They present the dismembered beast to their mother in an effort to gain her attention, which she has diverted to suitors. Cutting off the life of a beautiful phallic substitute for rivals of their mother's love, and presenting the unicorn horn and themselves as replacements for the rivals, the sons enact an Oedipal drama. White reinforces the Oedipal dimension when he discloses, at the end of the second volume, that Mordred, Arthur's bastard son, is the result of Arthur's sleeping with Morgause, who is his sister. Even though Arthur was unaware of his relationship to Morgause, "It seems, in tragedy, that innocence is not enough" (312). The tragedy is extended, and made more complicated, in Lancelot's relation to Arthur. It is described as a love no less intense than Lancelot's love for Guenever, so that a forbidden homosexual component, a drive to be wedded to Arthur, is ill expressed but operative in Lancelot's passion for the Queen. Lancelot's religious mania, we are allowed to think, might be driven by his need to escape his love for Arthur, which can't be fulfilled any more than the Grail quest can.

The desire and pursuit of a communal wholeness comes to grief in White's narrative. Its modernist romance thereby suits the real global conflict into which it emerges. The ants in *The Sword in the Stone* are said to speak of things *done* and *not-done* where we would speak of *right* and *wrong*. Arthur's

Round Table and the religious quests hope to get things right *and* done, but every realization of the hope is somewhat wrong and not-done. If that is all White's fiction, free from historical realism, can tell us – however thoroughly it lays out the difficulties of bringing together might, right, law, religion, eros, and psyche – perhaps actual history does better than autonomous fiction, and tells us more. After the next Interchapter, Chapter 6 will bring us back to what history does.

Entertainments: Graham Greene, E. F. Benson, and Olaf Stapledon

Graham Greene's *Orient Express: An Entertainment* (1932)

A character in Graham Greene's *Orient Express: An Entertainment* (1932) says that a novelist is "a spy," because he has "to see everything and pass unnoticed."[1] The character, Savory, is a novelist himself, on his way, via the Orient Express, to hunt material in Istanbul. He also claims that insofar as a novel is "founded on the author's experience, the novelist is making a confession to the public," and hence "puts the public in the position of the priest and the [psycho]analyst" (106). In reading novels, therefore, the public contemplates sin or crime or repressed secrets: the essentials of mystery writing.

Savory makes his pronouncement in a novel – an "entertainment" in its author's parlance – that certainly evokes the adventure matrix of spy fiction and crime fiction. The train passengers include an elderly Bulgarian communist revolutionist who has been living in England disguised by an alias; a female journalist who, detective-like, pursues the truth of the revolutionist's identity; and a murderer who gets away with murder. At the end of the novel a business associate of one of the protagonists disappears, perhaps the victim of a different killer. The elements we expect to find in Conan Doyle, Sayers, Christie, and Ambler are all present. Yet Greene plays with the elements. No detective – no Holmes, Poirot, Marple, or Wimsey – arrives or emerges as the central investigator and explainer. There are no "solutions." As for the journalist's detective work, it is only a sidetracking aspect of the story. In a bitterly laughable turn of events, the climax of the narrative takes place at an unforeseen railway stop – on a siding. Perhaps Greene thinks of his novel as entertaining because he expects his readers to be amused, or amusingly shocked, by his reversal – or *his* sidetracking – of the expected treatment.

Greene's tie to modernist experiment shows itself in his game with established patterns. A chapter of disconnected fragments of conversation or thought echoes a like unit (grander in scale) in *Ulysses*. Joyce might also be responsible for a fusion of interior monologue and dream with which Greene early in the novel "treats" his characterizations, especially that of his Anglo-Jewish businessman protagonist, Mylatt. The interiors and dreams are woven into the external narration that sees everything. That interweaving reinforces Savory's assertion about how a reader's response is shaped by a novel's "confessional" resonances. The reader is invited to become a psychoanalyst of the dreams, in order to uncover their relevance to the entire narrative; to become also an investigator of the mind of the author, inasmuch as the authorial mind, passing unnoticed, is immanently detectable in his characters and events; and to be a confessor-priest assessing morality's applicability to the actions of the characters. The latter assessment is especially important because in this text the communist, whose fortunes are pivotal for the narrative, is punningly named Czinner. Not least of what the reader must investigate is the state of the contemporary world. Greene, like his contemporaries the more straightforward detective and spy novelists, wants the elements of mystery writing to serve a realist-oriented treatment of sociohistorical conditions.

What the characters enact under those conditions becomes in effect the mystery of *Orient Express*, because their actions exceed accountability. Czinner for years has been living in disguise in England because he is on the lam from a death sentence in Bulgaria for his political activities there. Now he returns to the scene of his "crime," because a new revolutionary rising, portending his exoneration, is expected. But while Czinner is journeying toward Bucharest, the revolt occurs, only to fail. Apprised of the defeat, he has the opportunity to detrain. Not taking it, he deliberately goes "home" to undergo, albeit at an unscheduled stop, his execution under counter-revolutionary martial law. What motivates him appears to be fidelity to his cause, and the decency of fidelity. The same decency governs the conduct of Coral, a showgirl who, on her way to a job in Istanbul, is thrown together with Czinner, and stands by him through his final agony. Yet no good comes from either Czinner's self-sacrifice or the young woman's alliance with him. It results in her losing her job, and in her being "rescued" by the predatory journalist, a lesbian who is not interested in the girl's freedom. No wonder that, at the moment of Czinner's death, Coral thinks, "I'm tired of being decent, of doing the right thing. Her thoughts were very close to Dr. Czinner's when she explained to herself that[decency] didn't pay" (168). "But she knew too well that it was her nature, she was born so and she must make the best of it." Nevertheless, she remarks that her capacity for fidelity is also "stupid."

"She wondered for a moment whether ... Czinner's case was not the same; he had been too faithful to people who could have been served better by cunning" (169).

No reader-analyst can help but approve the selflessness of Czinner and Coral. They are sinned against, rather than sinning. The name Greene has given the communist seems not to cohere with his conduct. But there is more coherence than meets the eye. The character's fidelity, even though it is part of his virtue, is, as Coral suggests, a trespass, if only against rational sense. Had Czinner gotten off the train after he learned of the failure of the revolt, he would not have given his opponents their chance to prevail over him. Decency doesn't pay, a reader might argue, if the condition of its enactment merely confirms its capacity for ineffectual idealism. It has a more effectual capacity, surely. The spontaneity of Coral's tie to Czinner seems less a matter of "stupid fidelity" (169), and more pragmatically effective.

Nevertheless, the spy-narrator (to echo Savory) and the reader-spy-detective-cleric can see that Coral is, unfortunately, stupidly faithful. She began the train journey a virgin; she surrendered herself to Myatt, in part because she wanted to console him for the anti-Semitism that her fellow passengers shamelessly evince. But Myatt is not worthy. Even before Coral is wrongly taken off the train with Czinner, Myatt is becoming interested in another woman. So Coral, the narrator tells us, "was aware all the time that there was no quality in Myatt to justify her fidelity; it was just that she was like that and he was kind" (169). Memory keeps faith with its objects, and Greene's narrative frequently brings memory forward as a topic. In doing so, however, it suggests memory's capacity for fading as well as faithlessness. Myatt exerts himself to rescue Coral, but is prevented by a lie that the train passenger who is a murderer tells about her whereabouts. Within two days of losing sight of her, however, Myatt's fidelity lapses, and he cannot remember her face. There is a like lapse in Coral's sense that fidelity to Myatt makes her feel "strangely tied to a memory which lacked all conviction" (137).

Unfortunately, in 1932 the conditions of life – anti-Semitism, unemployment, international business (as opportunistic Myatt illustrates it), sexual "liberation" (Myatt and the lesbian journalist callously swap partners), and murderous violence enacted by states as well as individuals – are begging to be cured by the decency and fidelity that we see (in Czinner and Coral) are available in the world and yet deprived of strength. Why there is no cure for the conditions, when the novelist can discover, and make the reader feel, the absolute need for it, is baffling. One of Greene's favorite books, Conrad's *The Secret Agent*, ends with a refrain describing the personal and sociohistorical catastrophe it represents as "an impenetrable mystery ... hang[ing] forever over" phenomenon that defy explanation.[2] If the contemplation of such mystery is "entertaining" at all, it might be because it provokes a reader's ironic sense of the gap between fiction's acute diagnosis of the world's ills and the world's blindness to its own condition. The irony moves Greene's reader to take on, and interiorize, the detached contemplative melancholy that looms in the romance and adventure traditions underlying *Orient Express* (and developed further in Greene's subsequent novels).

This melancholy does not contribute to the reader's worldly empowerment. It aligns the reader with Czinner and Coral, and with all their failings – including their "decency" and its weakness. But why pursue power in a world that destroys sinners and innocents alike, and in which autonomy outside of art belongs most of all to those who use it to crush their opponents? *Orient Express*, and the reader – or the ideal reader – whom the novel solicits, exemplify a distance from the mighty. The distance perhaps provides a compensatory measure of freedom: a paradoxical (or ironic) powerless autonomy. As evoked by Greene's fiction, the powerlessness, and the detachment on which it depends, are not without value.

E. F. Benson's *Mapp and Lucia* (1931) and *Trouble for Lucia* (1939)

An exuberant contrast to the dark sides of adventure is provided in six comic novels by E. F. Benson about Lucia Lucas Pillson and Elizabeth Mapp-Flint. Consummate enactors of schemes to dominate the towns they live in, Lucia unofficially rules her Cotswolds town of Riseholme, while Mapp unofficially rules her South Downs city of Tilling. Neither can endure incursions on her spheres of influence. When Lucia decides to move to Tilling, the stage is set for an epic struggle.

Not that it is epic in fact; realistically considered, the struggle is a tempest in a teapot. It is essential to Benson's comedy to make us realize, and yet simultaneously to disregard, the smallness of the scale. When in *Mapp and Lucia* (1931) Lucia takes over the role of Queen Elizabeth in Riseholme's annual pageant commemorating the town's Elizabethan heritage, her directive skill makes her appear larger than life. She has a supreme ability to animate her environment. She seems to epitomize history's driving force: Queen Elizabeth indeed, or Napoleon (she has a "Napoleonic eye for detail"),[3] or, ominously, Lucrezia Borgia. In the sixth novel, *Trouble for Lucia* (1939), Lucia becomes Tilling's mayor. Mapp the native Tillingite will not be outdone by the empress-usurper. She claims that every mayor, no matter his or her gender, must have a mayoress, and she volunteers to be it. Lucia concedes, but only as a matter of Machiavellian strategy: she does so, she says to her husband Georgie, to "dope" Mapp's "malignant propensities" (521). The concession illustrates a habit of "vindictive forgiveness" (663) that both women employ. Mapp chastises Lucia for being "rather prone ... to plot or intrigue in a way we regret. And a little superior sometimes" (631), but she herself is a little superior always. She is not satisfied with being mayoress. As part of her vindictive "forgiveness" for Lucia's rise, Mapp competes with Georgie for a seat on the Borough Council. She wins, thereby gaining two public voices to the mayor's one. Not that Lucia can be outdone. She adopts "[b]rave cheerfulness" (647) in the face of defeat, while she seeks new resources of absolute command. Napoleon failed to make a successful come-back, whereas Lucia *will*.

Georgie notes in the 1931 novel that an initial combat between Lucia and Mapp is a version of the Great War's onset in 1914. By 1939, Benson's comparisons of Lucia with historical figures extend to Mussolini, and liken her mind to "a modern army attended by an air force and all appliances" (633). Nevertheless, although the intensity of historical actors and movements is rendered in Benson's novels, it is shorn of involvement with history's power to hurt. Despite wounded egos, there is essentially never any harm done by Lucia and Elizabeth's combat with each other or with the partisans they enlist and reject by turns. Comedy frees characters and readers from what history would yoke them to. Like the heroines' fellow citizens, readers, avid for "combat without quarter" (203), can watch the women's war in Benson's series not for the pleasure of endorsing aggression, but for the "unbounded ingenuity" (599) with which the heroines elaborate their conflict. Until Lucia prevails, Tilling roots for her; when she overdoes her success, Tilling wants the contest evened out. Readers can see themselves in the Tillingites: "[t]hough Miss Mapp was no favourite, they would have liked to see her score. But there was little partisanship; it was the sporting instinct which looked forward to witnessing an engagement between two well-equipped Queens" (147).

Benson's artistry is indispensable to the sport. How the antagonists sur-mount the self-entrapments that their schemes become calls the reader's attention to the thrills and spills of Benson's own plotting. Inasmuch as modernist works self-consciously remind their audience of how fictions are shaped, Benson does not escape his period. To be sure, Lucia rejects "that horrid [modernist] thing which Freud calls sex" (86), even though she has not read Freud; she also refers to "that huge horrid book [*Ulysses*] by Mr. James Joyce" (607). Despite her distastes, Lucia's cherished friend and most ardent supporter is a lesbian modernist artist, Irene (usually denominated "quaint Irene"), whom we might see as one of Benson's transgendering self-portraits. Irene declares that she is "the only person in this petty, scheming world of Tilling who acts on impulse" (551) – by which she means she is not a schemer, that she is disinterested. Nevertheless, Irene's artistry in *Trouble for Lucia* becomes a fulcrum of the plotting. She plans a mural for the front of her house that will update Botticelli's famous *Primavera,* which depicts a naked Venus rising from the sea. A minutely realistic depiction of Tilling will be the background of the mural; a modernist version of Botticelli's mythological figures will be the foreground. Alas, the Town Survey Department won't license the fresco. Irene is infuriated by what she lambastes as Victorian prudery and interference with art's autonomy. She transfers her plan for the mural to a satirical painting in which Venus and Venus's attendant, the South Wind, become stuffy, over-dressed Victorian figures. She puts Mayoress Mapp's face on her Victorianized Venus, and the face of Mapp's blowhard husband on the South Wind.

But there are two divergent ways in which Irene's painting is received. The picture earns the Royal Academy's designation as Picture of the Year. In London, Irene's Botticelli and her outmoded Victorians are legible as modernist satire of both. But in Tilling, Mapp and the citizens read the picture as a sign of the mayoress's laudable celebrity, and a defeat of Mayor Lucia. To even the score, Lucia commissions Irene to do her portrait, which Lucia intends for permanent display in the Town Hall. But Mayoress – Town Councilor Mapp blocks the publication of the picture (so to speak). Nevertheless, in effect the match between the contestants has already been resolved – most significantly by a novelist, another of Benson's self-conscious projections. Susan Leg, a female fiction writer of "worldwide" fame (626) whose pen name is Rudolph Da Vinci, has come to Tilling to research, for a future book, "this little centre of provincial life" (626). Miss Leg/Mr. Da Vinci, falling in with Mapp, imbibes intense prejudice against Lucia. But when the novelist sees quaint Irene's portrait of the mayor (which is in turn a portrait of the artist Benson's portrait of his heroine), she realizes that Mapp is untrustworthy. She finds the picture brilliant, and asserts that Lucia "might be the Key to Tilling" (640).

Irene's take-off on Botticelli aptly likens Benson's protagonists to divinities, who defy mortal limitations. Shockingly, in *Mapp and Lucia,* Benson sends the two women to their death. They are swept away in a flood. They are not heard from for three months, and a cenotaph is erected in their memory. Then they come back to life, as if miraculously resurrected. With this outrageous turn, Benson rejects the realism of Victorian fiction (the loss of the protagonists to a flood parodies the finale of George Eliot's *The Mill on the*

Floss [1860]), and he violates the plausibility his narrative has seemed to honor. What it honors far more is Lucia's imagination, which is invested in "cloud-castles in the sky, forming and shifting and always elegant": "fairy edifices" (644). No matter how often those autonomous edifices are on the verge of collapse, Benson's heroines restore them.

Olaf Stapledon's *Star Maker* (1937)

"Novel and miraculous vision" (377) of the cosmos is afforded the narrator of Stapledon's book. So compelling is it that one feels almost wrong to associate his vision with entertainment. After all, scientific romance (Stapledon's work advances Wells's genre) and the imaginative weird texts that we have surveyed solicit our earnest belief in them and their objects even while they divert us. We readers must do the entertainment – in the sense of entertaining the truth of fantasy. *Star Maker* and its kind propose fiction as a mode of access to truth because truth and reality are not necessarily the same. The truth made available by entertainment might be strangely necessary to our vital interests.

Everyday life hides those interests, to judge by the experience vouchsafed to Stapleton's narrator. His starting point is a moment of dark depression, in which he experiences "horror" not only at his own futility but also at humanity's "unreality, and ... at the world's delirium"[4] (255) in the era of interwar fascism. The narrator wonders if it is possible that human mind, or a being that is "minded," might underwrite our ordinary conditions, and make them meaningful rather than bitterly "planless" (301). Desperate to know that the cosmos is planful, the narrator is given the chance of testing mind's presence in interstellar space by being taken out of his body and his time, and lifted into the mysterious universe.

He first probes the fortunes of mind on a planet that is like another earth. Although its inhabitants' bodies are radically different from ours, a likeness to human intelligence structures their existence. Unfortunately, the narrator discovers, the fortunes of body and mind on Other Earth have had historical and technological effects that lead the narrator back to his pessimistic starting point. The mind of Other Men is involved with the bodily distribution of their taste organs. They have a site in their genitals. Hence the evolution of sexual practices on Other Earth has developed along diverging lines of taste. The divergences became invidious class and race markers, and those in turn became exploited nefariously by Other Earth's version of capitalism. To rectify, or obscure, those differences of sexual taste and class, Other Men put their minds to work on the curative potential of radio and television. They invented pocket radio-like taste receptors as a means of democratizing pleasurable communication among all persons. They succeeded: "Such was the power of this kind of entertainment that both men and women were nearly always seen with one hand in a pocket" (278). "Sexual broadcasting" (278) and "sexual receiving sets" were also developed to allow the satisfaction of sexual tastes in virtual reality, free of the inhibiting factors of its material alternative. The media revolution made Other Earth governments happy. They discovered that "the principle of radio–brain–stimulation"

> gave them a cheap and effective power over their subjects. . . . Strikes
> and riots [for example] could . . . be broken by the mere threat to close
> down the broadcasting studios, or alternatively by flooding the ether
> at a critical moment with some saccharine novelty. (279)

And yet, despite the inventive intelligence that brought about such transformation, the new media led to new conflicts, including a reaction in favor of religious fundamentalism, and ultimately a disastrous global war. The narrator leaves Other Earth while it is in the midst of the war, which he equates with insanity.

The Other Earth's capacity for sound mind is not wiped out totally. The narrator has made a friend of a thoughtful Other Earth man, Bvalltu. He and the narrator, abandoning Other Earth, are able to intermingle their intellectual beings. "Our union of minds brought into being a third mind, as yet intermittent, but more subtly conscious than either of us in the normal state" (298). Subsequently that "third mind," continuing its cosmic research, telepathically penetrates multiple planetary cultures, experiences life on simultaneously different timelines, and finally discovers signs of mindedness in the nebulae out of which stars evolve. Can all this testify to a supreme animator of the cosmos, an originary, planful, and meaningful Star Maker? It would seem to. Nevertheless, every planetary history, as the intertwined narrator–Bvalltu observes it, achieves an ideal state and then comes to grief, either from a dynamic within its own perfection or from an antagonism that it has inspired. It seems that a Star Maker, if it exists, creates worlds that participate in the Maker's intelligence, and then, with apparent indifference or mindlessness, allows those worlds to go smash, or does the smashing itself.

To arrive at Star Maker's attitude toward its own mindful caprice, and to discover the narrator's attitude toward Star Maker's mind, become the final objects of Stapledon's quest romance. The Maker's attitude, the narrator decides, is that of a scientist's or an artist's impersonal disinterestedness. Star Maker makes real lives – real planets and stars, not fictive ones. Each is one of the Maker's "mere thoughts" (429). The Maker both tyrannizes over those thoughts and plays with them. The result shocks the narrator:

> Here [in the Maker's making and unmaking] was no pity, no proffer
> of salvation, no kindly aid. Or here were all pity and all love, but
> mastered by a frosty ecstasy. Our broken lives, our loves, our follies,
> our betrayals, our forlorn and gallant defences, were one and all calmly
> anatomized … with complete understanding. … But sympathy was
> not ultimate in the temper of the eternal spirit; contemplation was.
> Love was not absolute; contemplation was. … All passions … were
> comprised within the spirit's temper; but … icily gripped with the cold,
> clear, crystal ecstasy of contemplation.   (429)

Surprising both himself and readers, the narrator decides that he can accept
the detachment, that he can even worship it, because it is all "a dread mystery,
compelling adoration" (430).

Stapledon's Star Maker sometimes seems an allegorical personification of
the author-creator of novels – or of modernism's autonomous fiction. Novels
constitute a galaxy of alternative life forms that remain in touch with the
human mind, yet also expand it. When Stapledon's narrator describes the
minds his own takes on – Bvalltu's is only the first – he says the coalescence is
"nothing more mysterious … than those many occasions in normal life when
the mind delightedly … discovers in confused objects a pattern or a significance hitherto unnoticed" (342). Novel-writing and novel-reading would be
among those occasions. As for the minds of stars, Stapleton's text reads them
as aesthetically directed variants of contemplation. "[T]he star's whole physical behavior is normally experienced as a blissful, an ecstatic, an ever
successful pursuit of formal beauty. This the minded worlds [i.e., the planet
worlds] were able to discover through their own most formalistic aesthetic
experience" (388).

Given the increasing possibility by 1937 of another global war, Stapledon
worried that fiction of his speculative kind, accepting "frosty ecstasy" and
adopting an all but passive religious attitude toward an impassive cosmos,
would seem less than responsibly engaged with history. But Stapledon rejects
any suggestion that his work is above political and historical urgency. "The
crisis does exist," Stapledon writes in a preface to his novel; it "is of supreme
importance, and concerns us all." Yet he sympathizes "with … those 'intellectuals'" – he says he is one of them – "who … have no useful contribution to
make to the struggle, and therefore had better not dabble in it." "The cause,"
nevertheless, "constantly, obsessively, holds our attention. But we are convinced by prolonged trial and error that the most useful service open to us is
indirect" (249).

The indirectness of all entertaining fictions, and their own aesthetic modes
of treatment, do not preclude their enlistment on behalf of any dimension of
"minded" service.

Chapter 6

Collective Welfare and Warfare

British Fiction, 1936–1950

With the coming of a second global war, pressure mounts on novelists, whether they are realists or fantasists, to treat the collective state of human affairs at home. Which ideas of political and economic order do they think should prevail nationally: leftist, or liberal, or conservative, or fascist, or none of those? How they represent Britain's character as a collective – or its potential to be one – is relevant to their answer.

History's answer, called the welfare state, emerges at the war's end, with the landslide election of a Labor government in 1945. The welfare state represents a compromise among the pre-war ideological divisions. It is defensible, nevertheless, as a victory for socialist-inspired collectivity. Its founding text, *Social Insurance and Allied Services,* is a 1942 blueprint for the post-war nation, devised – through a cooperative effort on behalf of the entire nation – by experts and civil servants under the direction of the economist Sir William Beveridge, and at the behest of Winston Churchill's wartime coalition government. The document implies that economic security for all members of a nation is a communal political and moral right. In this governmental form, H. G. Wells's forty years of promoting comprehensive planning for social welfare comes through. It is considered in this chapter, as is the contentious perspectives on it represented by two other economists, John Maynard Keynes and F. A. Hayek. Because both men's work still affects global economics, their thoughts about collective welfare, with the Beveridge scheme considered as a touchstone, demonstrate the continuing relevance of a past cultural moment, including that of its modernist literary component.

How the novelistic and governmental models of collective life play into each other, or against each other, is the concern of this chapter. Before we come to the Beveridge report, I want to extend, beyond the final segment of Chapter 5 (and with echoes of Chapter 3), notice of fiction's models of community in the run-up to the war as well as during the war. Providing a range of novelistic "treatments" of public welfare, a half-dozen specimen texts can serve as an entry point to the interplay.

Models of Collective Life

The communitarian imagination of David Jones's *In Parenthesis* (1937) tempers, even dissipates, the aggression it portrays. The book is about its protagonist Private John Ball's experience in the Great War. Yet *In Parenthesis* is dedicated, pacifically, not only to "my friends in mind of all common & hidden men," but also to "the enemy's front-fighters who shared our pains against whom we found ourselves by misadventure."[1] Its final segment, in which Ball is wounded during a desperate forest fight, becomes a fantasy in which "The Queen of the Woods" appears and awards honors to twelve soldiers, half of them German. A romance vision thereby overlays 1915–1916. Transforming the battleground into the sacred wood of Frazer's *The Golden Bough*, Jones identifies the war's action with Frazer's ritual king-killing, and with T. S. Eliot's use of Frazer in *The Waste Land*. Ball and his companions also repeat the stuff of Welsh and Arthurian legend. Here the text especially withdraws itself from combativeness. In Jones's preface to his work, he quotes approvingly a scholar's contention that "the conservatism and loyalty to lost causes of Western Britain ... has given our national tradition its distinctive character" (xiii).

The text's movement into a romance dimension of lost causes is part of its stilling of specific, immediately historical tensions. Jones's desire to make *parenthesis* a metaphor for nonmilitary life is another distancing movement. "This writing is called 'In Parenthesis,'" Jones declares, "because ... the war itself was a parenthesis – ... and also because our curious type of existence here is altogether in parenthesis" (xv). If history is parenthetical, and if we ourselves are, our partisanships remain bracketed by suspense: potentially all causes are lost. In that case, our assent to shared vulnerability would scarcely incline us to warlike antagonisms.

Few collectives are likely to adopt Jones's anti-triumphalist model. A modernist sublimity of vision underlies Jones's work, and produces on the surface another example of modernism's aim to transform narrative fiction into lyric utterance. Virginia Woolf's *Three Guineas* (1938) is equally modernist and visionary: an experimental fusion of polemical essay, documentary research, and fictive invention. It makes modernist treatment serve Woolf's idea of a new communal order – an extra-collective collective, which she calls the Outsiders Society – that is also a pacifist one.

The occasion of her text, Woolf says, is a letter soliciting her opinion about how war can be prevented. Simultaneously, she is being pressured by other requests: that she monetarily support a women's college; that she add to a fund in aid of working women; that she join a society "whose aim is to promote peace."[2] Each appeal represents an urgent historical matter. Yet Woolf decides that instant direct action will be insufficiently thoughtful. What circumstances underlie each plea, what relations the pleas have to each other, must be reasoned out patiently. The reasoning requires both temporary circumlocution and decided contemplation.

In the parenthesis (so to speak) of a contemplative suspense, Woolf achieves a diagnosis of a world that, albeit post-feminist, is suffused with resentful remains of patriarchy, expressing themselves in aggression at home and abroad. The father's power, in a newly disseminated form, inspires what Woolf calls "unreal loyalties" that promote modes of pride: "pride of nationality ... religious pride, college pride, school pride, family pride, sex [gender] pride" (80). Hence, "before us lies the public world, the professional system, with its possessiveness, its jealousy, its pugnacity, its greed" (74).

The matrix of pride seems to be collective being itself: society. "Is there not something," Woolf asks fiercely, "in the conglomeration of people into societies that releases what is most selfish and violent, least rational and humane in the individuals themselves?" When it comes to the status of women, the history of "society" intensifies the question; when it comes to twentieth-century armaments and war, it does the same. So the social collective, as we have known it, is a tyranny, repeating "the old worn ruts in which [it], like a gramophone whose needle has stuck, is grinding out with intolerable unanimity, 'Three hundred million spent upon arms'" (105). Given the intolerable old ruts, Woolf imagines an alternative, a collective working for unanimous ends – "justice and equality and liberty" – but a collective that is "outside ... society, not within" (106). This Outsiders' Society, dedicated among other things to disarmament and refusals of national allegiance, sounds utopian. But Woolf cites evidence of its current existence: the Mayoress of Woolwich publicly refuses to so much as "darn a sock to help in a war" (115) even though armaments are her town's industry; a female director of a women's sports league announces that the league will eliminate awards and trophies, and concentrate on play for its own sake; and a statistically demonstrable "experiment in passivity" (117) – a passive withdrawal of young women from the Church of England and Christianity – is under way. This last evidence of the Outsiders' collective rhymes with the suspense of immediate action that has shaped Woolf's text. "For [the experiment] seems to show that to be passive is to be active; those also serve who remain outside" (119).

The other texts about collectives that we now turn to do not bear (with one exception) the stamp of modernist treatment or visionary inspiration. The social collective, they suggest, is to be transformed from within, not broken with for the sake of a radical "outside" that remains to be constructed, along unheard-of lines. The realism of these fictions has a Victorian feel. But collective existence in them is of a piece with the progressivism of modernist culture.

The collective or "corporate action" of British local government is portrayed in Winifred Holtby's *South Riding* (1936). That the scope is local does not mean anything invidious: "Local government [is] the first-line defence thrown up by the community against our common enemies – poverty, sickness, ignorance, isolation, mental derangement and social maladjustment." "The war" against those things is "worth fighting" because, Holtby says, "we are members one of another"[3] (v–vi).

Unfortunately, according to her narrative, acknowledgment of the mutual membership also must be fought for. Holtby's pivotal figures –Mrs. Beddows, an alderman on the South Riding County Council; her fellow aldermen, Robert Carne ("a sporting farmer" [xiii]) and Joe Astell (a socialist); and the newly arrived headmistress of Kiplington High School for girls, Sarah Burton – are at loggerheads. The conflicts between Mrs. Beddows and Sarah reproduce what we've seen in Storm Jameson and others: a generational feminist divide. Mrs. Beddows, given her successful political career, can be regarded as a pioneer (like Ellen Wilkinson); yet when Mrs. Beddows prescribes patience for Sarah's attempts to improve the high school, Sarah is indignant: "We need courage, not so much to endure as to act" (215). Astell is an instant convert to a Council housing development and real estate scheme, yet he wants to be "fighting to change the system, not content to render first aid to its victims" (321), as he thinks he is doing in a chapter about "public assistance." Carne is a Tory obstacle to the Council's progressivism. Sarah finds him "reactionary, unimaginative, selfish, arrogant, prejudiced" (545). The problem with her discovery is that it complicates another: she has fallen in love with him. She has therefore made herself a rival to Mrs. Beddows, whose maternal feeling for Carne, her junior in age, is touched with eros.

We are members one of another, it appears, only by being at odds. Nevertheless, Holtby portrays the souring of cooperation only to show that it is temporary. Deeper unities exist; plans are not to be sworn off, but are to be replaced by better ones. Carne the conservative isn't the enemy. He reveals that the Council's town planning has been manipulated by another Council member, to the benefit of the manipulator's private profits. Soon after the revelation, Carne dies – perhaps because Holtby wants to kill off conservatism, no matter its virtues. Mrs. Beddows stands by them, however. At one with her author, she honors "just working together – us ordinary people, against the troubles that afflict all of us'" (545). One fruit of working together is illustrated by a result of the Council's allotment of funds for floodlighting the local hospital. When another of the novel's female characters, who is dying of cancer, comes to the hospital, "the beauty, the radiance of the floodlights pleased her. At last she had seen death illuminated, honoured like health and life with brilliance and dignity" (246). If authentic collective planning can transform the look of death, perhaps it can overcome less fatal community-disrupting divisions.

Whether uncompromised socialist formulations should model collective life comes to the forefront in Lettice Cooper's *National Provincial* (1938). That the question matters in "provincial" cities is important. According to one of Cooper's Londoners, the provinces are "the main body and we're the advance guard. An advance guard that gets out of touch with the main body isn't any more use"[4] (27). But the main body has trouble being in touch with itself. Whereas in Holtby's novel the narrative moves divisive elements in the direction of progressive coalition, in Cooper's novel the liquidation of past social forms is painfully unresolved. That collective change should be a slow process is the contention of Cooper's John Allworthy, an old-time (already, in 1938) Labor Party member and union organizer in the northern England city where the novel is set. He is broken with by his leftist successor, Tom Sutton, who scorns both the Labor Party and the unions for what he takes to be their reliance on loathsome interclass compromise. Working-class patriotism remains a critical sore point. Both Allworthy and Sutton are employed by one of the city's principal manufacturers, an anti-union authoritarian who has the same impoverished working-class origins as they do.

On the whole, the future of the national–provincial community is no more hopeful than the final condition of two of the novel's protagonists: Mary, a London journalist who has returned to her working-class roots in the northern city, and Stephen, son of one of the old-guard City Council families. As Mussolini invades Abyssinia in an attempt to initiate a fascist empire in Africa, Mary voices what she and Stephen have come to know, in part from their share in the Allworthy–Sutton battle, in part because of their increasing experience of deracination: "It won't be possible to be indifferent or neutral any longer. This has happened because we've left things drift for so long" (198). Mary and Stephen are lovers, but Stephen is married, and Mary doesn't want to force him into new commitments. Separating from "the main body," she returns to London. We are left uncertain if the constituents of "society" can be united, despite the impossibility of remaining indifferent to the collective state.

That a communist model would halt "the drift" is advocated in James Barke's *Major Operation* (1936), but resisted in Mulk Raj Anand's *The Big Heart* (1944). Barke's fiction is another national–provincial study: Glasgow is its setting, which Barke treats in ways derived from Joyce's handling of Dublin in *Ulysses*. But modernist form in Barke is subordinated to ideological content: the conversion to Marxism of an upper-middle-class coal wholesaler for whom the global economic depression is the beginning of political wisdom. He gains it from a heroic communist. "Among the bourgeoisie, especially the petty bourgeoisie, are many elements," Barke's communist-hero says, "who are preparing to identify themselves with the working class – with the progressive and liberating force in society. ... We must ... help them to liquidate their past."[5] The wholesaler also helps by sacrificing his life on behalf of the hero in the course of a protest march that turns violent.

Anand, representing an imperial provincial, throws doubts on the prospects for a communist redemption of the collective. His hero is Ananta, a one-time union organizer in Bombai and a native member of a community of coppersmiths in Amritsar. The artisans are under siege: their neighborhood now houses a factory mass-producing substitutes for their handiwork. It also is producing war armaments. Ananta believes that machinery is inevitable; he believes that if he can unionize his superannuated fellow workers, he can make them masters of the machines. But a local communist student and Ananta's more hot-headed associates turn violent, smash the factory, and cause Ananta's death.

Ananta figures for Anand a more revolutionary figure than the communist, because he exceeds ideological assumptions and guidelines, including those of the real-life revolutionary hero, Gandhi. A Sikh poet friend of Ananta articulates a Soviet criticism of Gandhi: he "never realized the meaning of the Russian Revolution for our country and went on believing in an unplanned, individualist, competitive profit-making industrialism."[6] But because a communist brings about mayhem in *The Big Heart*, the invocation of the Soviet experiment is qualified. Inasmuch as Ananta endorses the poet's views of the Indian leader or sympathizes with Russia, Anand makes him do so more intuitively than exactly. Ananta is less articulate or resolved but bigger-hearted than an exact and exacting ideological critic can be. He embodies "the audacity of the adventurer, the rogue, the lover, the rebel, the man who bore his life on the palm of his hands, as it were, and judged each situation as it came along" (30). We return, after all, to a romance outsider, who acts as the herald of "the new community with a new morality in which, and through which, men can live creatively" (136).

Does a romance outsider mean, in the context of a search for collective unity, that the latter is always more fantasy than achieved fact? Ironically, the fact of war, it might be argued, made it possible for fiction's visions of a newly socialized community to become actual. "The fact that we are at war has turned Socialism from a textbook word into a realizable policy,"[7] writes George Orwell in *The Lion and the Unicorn: Socialism and the English Genius* (1941). "Since a classless, ownerless society is generally spoken of as 'Socialism,' we can give that name to the society towards which we are now moving" (67), he proposes. Orwell does not adduce that movement as a result of a powerful tradition of fiction, but acknowledges that "Since about 1930 everyone describable as an 'intellectual' has lived in a state of chronic discontent with the existing order" (37). Nevertheless, the "English genius" that matters to Orwell is that of the people on the whole. It is no longer divided by class, and should not be: "This war, unless we are defeated," he predicts, "will wipe out most of the existing class privileges" (43). Moreover, English genius is no longer divided by unreal loyalty to unreal party labels: "None of the old classifications fit" (67).

The war must have revolutionary collective effects, Orwell argues, for two principal reasons. "What this war has demonstrated is that private capitalism ... *does not work*. It cannot deliver the goods" (47, emphasis original). Consequently, the wealthy and their ruler-partners ("artificially stupefied people") at last will learn that "[a] planned economy might be better than a free-for-all in which the worst man wins" (54). If the post-war condition were a return to "private capitalism" and invidious class distinctions, it would mean the betrayal of every life expended in the conflict. "What is wanted is a simple, concrete programme of action, which can be given all possible publicity, and round which public opinion can group itself" (75–76), Orwell advises. He wants the simple program to come from below, from "the people." For him, it cannot come from the Labor Party and the trade unions, because both are "directly interested" in protecting British capitalism and the profits of British workers at the expense of colonized laborers (68).

Orwell's forecast of a classless, ownerless nation, one might say, moves his evocation of England's "genius" toward Forster's visionary–prophetic axis, although Orwell's text is a nonfictional essay. However, all the texts we have traversed in this section aspire to "prophecy": that is, to a kind of second sight, which penetrates to the underlying deficiencies that the writers discover in their unreformed nation. Jones's anti-triumphalist community of lost causes, Woolf's antisocial society, are the most visionary of the prophetic expressions. Barke's communist hero, heroically self-possessed and invincible, is an unworldly romance paragon, just as Anand's Ananta is. Holtby and Cooper treat their novels' socio-historical content in terms of conventional realism, but they do so from a critical perspective that wants to see history transformed. They are less fierce versions of Woolf, who, accumulating documentary evidence in footnote after footnote of *Three Guineas*, grapples with the present order for the sake of a desire to overturn reality, rather than to submit to it.

Perhaps because "the people" are not critically visionary, they did not fulfill Orwell's hope that their genius would formulate the necessary program of action for collective change. The "simple program" instead came from intellectuals and their Civil Service counterparts. We now turn away from fiction, temporarily, and toward history's attempt to occupy a prophetic axis.

Social Insurance and Allied Services was given all possible publicity and became a best-seller. It announced a government plan whose introductory formulation sounds like a romance narrative about a new Pilgrim's Progress, a new collective quest. "Social insurance . . . is an attack upon Want. But Want is only one of five giants on the road of reconstruction. . . . The others are Disease, Ignorance, Squalor and Idleness."[8] The time for killing those giants has come, according to the report's review of the nation's schemes of public welfare since 1897. "Now, when the war is abolishing landmarks of every kind, is . . . [a] revolutionary moment in the world's history. . . . [It] is a time for revolutions, not for patching" (6), the report declares. The attack on Want, indeed its "abolition" (7), institutes "co-operation between the State and the individual" (6): "The term 'social insurance' to describe this institution implies both that it is compulsory and that men stand together with their fellows" (13). This standing together will guarantee retirement pensions for all; subsistence-level benefits for the unemployed, the sick, the disabled, the widowed, and the aged; universal health care ("without a charge on treatment at any point" [14]); maternity stipends, with thirteen weeks of financially supported leave for working mothers; and "recognition of housewives as a distinct insurance class, with benefits adjusted to their special needs, including . . . in all cases [marriage grant], maternity grant, widowhood and separation provisions and retirement pensions" (15–16).

"There are some to whom pursuit of security appears to be . . . inconsistent with initiative, adventure, personal responsibility" (170), Beveridge writes. On the contrary, one might argue on behalf of Beveridge, and against the "inconsistent" appearance, that the plan clearly seeks to make initiative and its adjuncts possible, because otherwise they are available only to those who can afford them. When shelter and food are safely secured, a person can pursue life's larger stakes, and risk – adventurously – whatever surprises the pursuit entails and effects. As for the adventurousness of the minds behind the plan, one also might be justified in ascribing to it a distinctly modernist character. Indeed, the ideology of the welfare state is a modernist turn of thought against the Victorian century, if we understand the latter to be the canonizer of "classical" economists (Adam Smith, T. R. Malthus, David Ricardo, J. S. Mill) and the seedbed of Marxism. Notwithstanding the plan's descent from the previous era's socialist ideas, when John Maynard Keynes, after consulting frequently with Beveridge in 1942, called the report "a grand document,"[9] he meant implicitly that the plan conformed to the supersession of nineteenth-century economics, including Marx's.

Keynes's close personal ties to Virginia Woolf, E. M. Forster, and their circle suggests that Keynes and his theories merit a modernist label. Keynes himself periodized: Marx had dated, he insisted, just as Marx's century had. (Wells made the same claim.) Should the collectivist-minded novelists have absorbed Keynes's discussion of Marx in *The New Statesman* in 1934? Keynes there asserts that "Marx's picture of the capitalist world, which had much verisimilitude in his day ... is unrecognizable ... three-quarters of a century later. [It] looks backwards to what capitalism was, not forward to what it is becoming."[10] Capitalism then was invested in powerful persons; now, according to Keynes, it is an impersonal diffusion, transcending class distinctions and conflicts. "Time and the Joint Stock Company and the Civil Service have silently brought the salaried class into power," he writes. "Not yet a Proletariat. But a Salariat." H. G. Wells was right, Keynes concedes, to argue early in the century that a Marxist revolution was not workable. Yet Keynes asserts (creditably) that by 1934 Wells, for all his dedication to a global collective, still had not found the specifics of what was "workable, or what must be made to work, to solve today's muddle" (34). The muddle is exemplified by the Salariat – yet the Salariat is the muddle's best chance for clarification. "The problem today," Keynes proposes, "is to concert good advice and then to convince the well-intentioned that it is good" (34). When "the right stuff" for a solution is discovered, Keynes predicts, "the public will swallow it in gulps – the Salariat quicker than the Proletariat" (34). The Salariat, of which Keynes implies he is a part, might even come up with a persuasive plan, "reasonable and disinterested" (36) and under the aegis of the Labor Party, of what is workable. He offered his own ground-breaking work *The General Theory of Employment, Interest, and Money* (1936), and later his approval of Beveridge's "grand document," as concerted, clarifying good advice for collective existence.

Essential to Keynes's thinking is the idea that the economic system is not self-regulating: "without purposive direction, it is incapable of translating our actual poverty into our potential plenty" (140). Yet the rightness and justice of purposive direction in economic planning became an occasion of controversy, one that remains a current source of discord. F. A. Hayek's *The Road to Serfdom* (1944) is the work of an Austrian refugee who became a colleague of Beveridge at the London School of Economics. Published two years after the Beveridge report, perhaps in an effort to head off the hegemony of the Labor Party in the immediate post-war years, *The Road to Serfdom* declares that economic planning inevitably becomes a form of totalitarianism (fascist, communist, or whatever), and that it is unjust and immoral because it violates initiative, adventure, and individual responsibility.

Hayek's position has increasingly prevailed in the ideology of global capitalism. That prevalence, I would argue, embodies an aversion not only to Keynes but also to the modernist literary and intellectual culture out of which Keynes emerged. For that reason, a further consideration here of Hayek and Keynes seems justifiable. Every chapter of *The Road to Serfdom* cautions against the danger of directive planning on behalf of collective values. A typical passage asserts that "in a competitive society, nobody ... can exercise even a fraction of the power which a socialist planning board would possess."[11] A competitive market system "is the only system designed to minimize by decentralization the power exercised by man over man. ... What is called economic power ... is, in the hands of private individuals, never ... power over the whole life of a person" (166). The individual matters above all because "individualist tradition ... has created Western civilization" (73). Hayek criticizes Wells for inconsistency:

> It is pathetic that ... [Wells,] a leading advocate of the most comprehensive planning should at the same time write [in 1939] an ardent defense of the rights of man [to become part of the Declaration of Human Rights adopted by the United Nations in 1948]. The individual rights which Mr. Wells hopes to preserve would inevitably obstruct the planning which he desires. (121)

Besides, "belief in the community of aims and interests with fellow-men seems to presuppose a greater degree of similarity of outlook and thought than exists between men merely as human beings" (161).

What of the individual lives that the market disables, and casts adrift from employment? With neo-Victorian moralizing gravity, Hayek praises the discarded worker for illustrating the hazards of freedom:

> In a competitive society it is no slight to a person, no offense to his dignity, to be told by any particular firm that it has no need for his services or that it cannot offer him a better job. ... [T]he unemployment or the loss of income which will always affect some in any society is

certainly less degrading if it is the result of misfortune and not
deliberately imposed by authority. However bitter the experience,
it would be very much worse in a planned society.   (137)

The Road to Serfdom closes by urging readers to turn away from "contemporary obscurantism" about a new world order – the utopianism that has led to fascism and Nazism – and return to "the liberal ideas of the nineteenth century." We still "have the opportunity to realize its ideals – and they were not mean" (238), he concludes about Victorian and pre-Victorian economics.

It is worth noting Keynes's putatively modernist, disinterested response. Having read *The Road to Serfdom*, Keynes congratulated its author with the same phrasing he had used to Beveridge: "It is a grand book" (XXVII, 385). Despite the praise, Keynes also puts his finger on the problematic license Hayek's argument gives to the alleged inevitable effects of planning. "Once the working of the free market is impeded beyond a certain degree," Hayek writes, "the planner will be forced to extend his controls until they become all-comprehensive" (137). "You admit here and there," Keynes rejoins, "that it is a question of knowing where to draw the line [i.e., between planning and initiative, between security and freedom]. You agree that the line has to be drawn somewhere, and that the logical extreme is not possible. But you give us no guidance whatever as to where to draw it. In a sense this is shirking the practical issue" (386). For all Hayek's reliance on risk, one might say, he shirks not only the practical issue offered him by the Beveridge report, but also the increased opportunity for risky freedom implied by it. The welfare state projected by the document, as I've noted, argues for the possibility that life – individual as well as collective – can be an expanded adventure. Once it settles accounts with Beveridge's giants, the welfare scheme aims, practically as well as theoretically, to secure possibilities that new private and public fortunes (not merely economic ones) can be hazarded by persons beyond the sphere of daily drudgery. It plans for the unplanned, for the prospect of surprise, even for the overturning of well-deliberated control, that is emphasized – innovatively so – in the modernist-era adventure narrative. It makes practicable the disinterestedness appealed to by fiction for those ordinary people who, without the scheme, cannot overcome the giants.

That the result of the Beveridge plan was more freedom rather than less for the collective (and the individual, too) is witnessed by the British sociologist and political scientist T. H. Marshall in *Citizenship and Social Class* (1950). On the basis of the post-war realization of the welfare state, Marshall argues that the twentieth century has added to previously established political rights – citizenship and suffrage – what Marshall calls "social rights": rights exemplified by social security and collective health insurance. Social rights are another element to be reckoned with in the prospects for either fusing security and freedom, or telling them apart. If only economists, sociologists, politicians, and fiction writers, either separately or collectively, could resolve where to draw the line! It seems no easier to do than Chanticleer's distinguishing the boundary between fantasy and reality in *Lud-in-the-Mist*. Keynes's and Hayek's quandary, one of the legacies of British history and of fictional representations of that history, remains undecided.

Fictive Wars

As fiction proposes new models of collectivity, and as actual persons try to realize new visions of community, the historical war menaces both. How does British fiction mirror or represent the battle? A summary preview (in two paragraphs) of answers provided by texts in this current section is in order. In a sense, British fiction scarcely represents the battle! Fictive wars and conflicts, in which imaginative invention rather than realism is the mode of treatment, are as much the object of novelistic practice during the war as is the real war. Of the three novels from 1941 that we will consider first, Rex Warner's is sheer fantasy, and Marjorie Allingham's displaces the anti-fascist struggle onto a fantastic detective tale. The third novel, by Patrick Hamilton, raises questions (relevant to the others) about connecting fiction to history. Hamilton suggests that the connection might be a mad, indeed schizophrenic, enterprise.

Wartime fiction's leaning toward fantasy, which includes surrealist writing (William Sansom, for example), issues in C. S. Lewis's famous work. There, as we'll see toward the end of this section, the very identity of England is uncertain. How can one nation be at odds with another when it does not know what it is itself, and therefore cannot know what it stands for? The most surprising aspect of British fiction in World War II is the uncertainty it exhibits about the grounds of the armed conflict. We'll see in Evelyn Waugh's *Put Out More Flags*, for example, that there is no difference between the domestic citizen and the alien enemy fascist. Such a conviction seems one motive for the fact that in Somerset Maugham's and Huxley's writing, even in the thick of the military struggle, the novelists celebrate the virtues of pacifism and of detached withdrawal from the historical world. Moreover, to judge by Henry Green's novel about London's Auxiliary Fire Service, despite the meritorious political stakes of the war's ideological conflicts, the holocaust that the stakes inflict upon individual lives seems more evil than can be justified on any basis. Whatever the war's losses and gains, however, utopian planning (indomitable romance!) survives in J. B. Priestley's fiction, and an exuberant return to realism triumphs in Denton Welch's. Nevertheless, realism, even in Welch's novel, is undergoing a startling revisionary "treatment." Indeed, throughout all the texts that we now engage, a constant self-reflection on the nature of fiction endures. History and war do not vanquish the persistence of that essential modernist element.

Rex Warner's protagonist, Roy, in *The Aerodrome: A Love Story* (1941) discovers at the end of the novel that reality's ordinary conflicts are more valuable than any plan to reform them. Those conflicts are represented for him by "perplexity," "despair,"" "disappointment," and "rankling conscience"; and by life, which he describes as "vague, amorphous, drunken, unwieldy, and unsatisfactory."[12] Despite those descriptors – indeed, because of them – Roy affirms life's "nobility and grandeur" (284). Characteristics that are distinct and that one expects to be kept apart – drunkenness and grandeur, or unsatisfactoriness and nobility – become fused for Roy, components of a vital medium.

That Warner's fiction should express a desire to join and exalt characteristics that otherwise might indicate despair is not surprising in the context of the bombing of London. *The Aerodrome* means to transform rhetoric and reality to heartening effect. It does so by accentuating the difference between separate worlds – invented and actual – before it dissolves the difference. Perhaps, because of the novel's aim to take flight from reality into a fictive conflict, Warner maintains a modernist self-consciousness about fiction's indirect path to visions of life's valuable messiness. We will see that other novelists who represent war likewise both heighten the difference between fiction and reality, and resist the line-drawing. It is as if novelists of the era must confront an equivalent of Keynes's and Hayek's difficulty in tracing the right boundary between freedom and security.

The Aerodrome's avant-garde air force has a strikingly modernist tenor. Fabricating an alternative to the British state, a new aerial government will expunge "the stupidity, the ugliness, and the servility of historical tradition" (178). Its spokesman, the Air Vice-Marshal, designates *parenthood, ownership, locality*, and *marriage* as a set of common nouns whose referents as well as meanings are to be superseded. The words are declared "wingless" henceforth. The Vice-Marshal, when he directs recruits to stop thinking about their parents and homes, announces that now "for good or evil you are yourselves, poised for a brief flash of time between two annihilations" (178). The enlistees must live in and for the instant, killing off tradition, and letting the future take care of itself.

Roy recounts the months when he abandoned the wingless words. His retrospect begins with a figurative annihilation of his familial past. At his coming-of-age birthday party, his father – a Church of England rector – announces that Roy is an adopted son. Roy later overhears his "father" confess to being a murderer and an adulterer. His subsequent break with the rector, and with "the rector's wife" (for 200 pages he cannot bring himself to call her "mother"), drives him to join the force at the aerodrome, where he becomes a favorite of the Vice-Marshal. "The intricacies of deceit in family life" (156) now are behind Roy. However, the Vice-Marshal turns out to be his real father! Roy makes the discovery just before the Vice-Marshal dies (or commits suicide, or is murdered by another of his illegitimate sons) in a plane crash. Thus, though Roy at the aerodrome thinks he is outside a family drama, he remains inside it – a complex Freudian drama. At one point he thinks his lover is his sister; during another stretch of the narrative, a different woman becomes the object of rivalry among him, his step-brother, and his father. Outside and inside are established as separate, but then revealed to be mutually annihilative – because they are the same. Similarly, the fictive aspect of *The Aerodrome* kills off real history, and real history returns the compliment, as it were. So, to instance its own brief interstitial character, the fiction must speak with a voice at once integrated and disintegrated. That is the remarkable voice devised by Warner for Roy. It is curiously flat, perhaps an effect of uttering contrary impulses and simultaneously throttling their antagonism.

The relevance of *The Aerodrome* to the actual war inheres in its suggestion that the distinct sides of the war's conflicts also are indistinct. Consequently, life valuably abides the partisan struggles that try to cleanse it of imperfections. To be sure, the Vice-Marshal can be read allegorically as a fascist leader, and Roy's story as the progress of a soul all but fatally tempted to join the enemy. But such a reading mitigates the possibility that the Vice-Marshal stands for attractive shades of Wellsian modernism (including post-war planning) or for the discipline necessary to fight a war (for which soldiers must be willing to surrender home and family). Warner's novel-fantasy also is less than an endorsement of unwavering aggression against ideological enemies. One cannot be sure of who or what they are. *The Aerodrome* faces its readers – at least those in 1941 – with an unsettlingly double vision of things. The line between antagonists is and is not one; the same goes for the differences between home and world, nonfascist and fascist (if that is what the novel's village and aerodrome represent), and fantasy and history.

Whereas *The Aerodrome* ends happily with the collapse of distinctions between antithetical meanings, and between fantasy-utopian and actual

realms, another novel of 1941, Patrick Hamilton's *Hangover Square*, dramatizes the urgent need for both making and maintaining distinctions – and yet
suggests those distinctions' very insanity. Hamilton's George Bone, a big-
hearted alcoholic, is obsessively in love with Netta, an aspiring film actress
who sadistically exploits him. Bone knows that Netta and her Nazi-like crowd
hold him in contempt; yet he does not want to know that he knows. Increasingly unable to distinguish who is an ally and who is an enemy, what is
fantasy and what is truth, Bone suffers a schizophrenic split. One self is
furiously clear about Netta's worthlessness. It plans to kill her and her
Hitler-like boyfriend. His other self, meanwhile, stoically patient, hardly
knows what his version of Mr. Hyde is up to. The climax of *Hangover Square*
is Bone's murder of his victims on the day of the British declaration of war
against Hitler in September 1939. Bone's tortured ambivalence finds surcease:
after the murders his non-aggressive alter ego commits suicide.

By involving with schizophrenia Bone's desire for clarified antagonisms
and resolution of them, Hamilton seems to identify warfare, the hoped-for
definitive resolver of conflicts, with mental illness. But the implication dis-
locates the novel from the supposedly sane national war effort, as if *Hangover
Square* itself crosses the line between loyalty and treachery. It also suggests
that the text is of two minds, suffering a schizophrenia of its own, about its
connection to historical reality. On the one hand, it offers Bone's madness,
Britain's long appeasement of Netta-like Hitler, and September 1939, as all of
a piece. There is no boundary between them to speak of. On the other hand,
Hamilton provides material that, attenuating the likeness between the tale and
referential reality, reasserts the bounding line. Bone's mental state might
originate in his love for his dead sister; that is, he murders Netta to displace
an incestuous desire, which he must destroy in the person of a substitute. The
link of such a possible motive to Britain's objective history is merely arbitrary.
Moreover, thanks to the intervention of an old friend, Bone is taken under the
wing of a group of decent theater people who give him every reassurance of
his lovable nature – exactly what he misses in Netta's circle. That outward
resistance to the insecurity that drives his self-division doesn't cure it, but
doesn't suit a reader's making George's story the representative of a national
condition. In other words, the novel can be aligned with the war effort after
all – because of the gap between its historical and nonhistorical components.

But the alignment wavers. The theater people are legible as representatives
of the world of fiction. They figure that world's generosity to those most in
need of it, as well as its lack of aggression (the theater world instantly
recognizes and rejects Netta's violence). Given its virtues, then, fiction doesn't
back the war effort. Not only that: Hamilton suggests its inefficacy. George

remains unhealed. And for the side of Hamilton that wants to make fiction efficacious enough to be a player in history, *Hangover Square* represents the murder of Netta in terms of a chillingly grotesque parody of fantasy's ambition to tie itself to actuality. When Bone prepares to kill Netta – he will drown her in her bathtub – he equips himself with reels of sturdy thread. After the murder he unwinds that thread around Netta's body and across the space of her bathroom, catching her in a net – in a gross form of punning. Bone does this so "nothing should be disturbed until the police came. It must all be in order for her." The threads put things in order for him, too. Of course, it is Hamilton (not Bone) who decorates the scene of the murder with this evocation of the way meanings belong to a crisscrossing network of connections, making it possible that "All the threads were gathered up,"[13] as Bone thinks they are. And yet this united network, much as characters in novels and their readers want it, is the hope in Hamilton of a deranged man. Within the confines of *Hangover Square,* connection, the solution to enmity, can be as deranged as the aggression it wants to cure. The line between connection and aggression undergoes erasure. And because it is murderous Bone whose weaving replicates fiction's supposed tie to history, perhaps that weave is not always desirable.

Tying things together succeeds triumphantly, however, in yet another 1941 novel, Marjorie Allingham's detective fiction, *Traitor's Purse.* It must overcome an initial dissociation as radical as Bone's. The gaps begin with the alienation of the novel's protagonist from his own name. When he wakes up in a hospital bed, utterly amnesiac, all that he knows is the clear line of his disconnection from everything. Persons present themselves who know him, without knowing that he does not know himself. He prudently keeps his ignorance a secret, intent on piecing together, from what is said to him, who he is supposed to be, and what he is supposed to know and do. He must be his own detective.

How can the detective make connections when there are so many boundary lines to cross? The very place in which he finds himself is named Bridge, a geographically isolated, ancient English town, with a governmental structure that makes it the landed equivalent of an island nation. A romance place, "its winding hill is like a part of an old fairy story."[14] Despite (or because of) its fantastic appearance, Bridge is the connector between the detective's suddenly unreal world and history. Bridge's County Council, the detective ultimately will learn, is a planning collective, masterminded by a Fifth Column pro-Nazi egomaniacal economist (who looks down on Keynes). He means to realize an elaborate fake welfare scheme, which will distribute counterfeit English currency throughout the country. To intervene against that way of building welfare, the detective must get past his amnesia.

He does it, significantly for Allingham's art, by trusting the variant of Impressionism that associates the latter with unbiased receptivity, and hence with a kind of objective immediacy, at once personal and impersonal. (The variant harks back to Henry James, who tests it in his nonfictional observations about the United States in *The American Scene* [1906], and in his unfinished novel, *The Sense of the Past* [1916], which is a model for the epistemology of *Traitor's Purse*.) The detective's objective Impressionism becomes his prime mode of deduction, and his prime weapon against treachery, which Allingham identifies with counterfeiting. Counterfeit money, welfare, and nationalism are resisted by the detective's openness to truth, and are resisted – of course! – by fiction's bridge to reality! Closing the gap between counterfeiting and truth, Allingham can conclude her narrative with patriotic fervor. The detective has turned out to be one indeed: he is Albert Campion, Allingham's version of Holmes, Wimsey, and Poirot. Praying for "sweet sanity! ... ultimate honesty and the final triumph of the best!" Campion recites to himself "the magnificent jingle from the end of [Shakespeare's history play] King John ... *'nought shall make us rue, if England to itself do rest but true'*" (212–213). If fiction, overleaping the line between itself and reality, do keep true, too.

Numerous fictive characters in wartime have difficulty keeping true. Another home-grown Nazi, Basil Seal, is one of the protagonists of Evelyn Waugh's *Put Out More Flags* (1942). Not formally a traitor, Basil nevertheless epitomizes the enemy. When he decides to help his married sister find rural billets for evacuees from London and other bombing sites, Basil turns it into an opportunity for extortion. He threatens eligible households, unless they pay him off, with quartering on them an obnoxious, destructive set of evacuee children whom he makes into his malicious sidekicks. After the billeting caper, he uses his talent for fakery to worm himself into the War Office as an informer. To showcase his skill, he frames as a spy an old university friend, Ambrose Silk – a gay Jewish aesthete and intellectual – and smears the reputation of Ambrose's publisher, whom he lands in jail. In the end Basil joins an elite military corps. Thus a blackmailer and impostor responsible for victimizing two innocent men, one of them a Jew and a sexual dissident, becomes a high-ranking official fighter against the victimizers of innocent Jews, gay people, and blameless others.

Basil is outrageous and reprehensible, yet Waugh makes us take pleasure at times in his nastiness. The citizens whom Basil exploits about billeting are more awful than he because they pretend to morality, whereas at least Basil does not. Yet Waugh also treats the narrative focalization so that we are made most sympathetic with the two characters who are antithetical to Basil: Ambrose and Cedric Lyne. Almost everyone in the novel finds Ambrose objectionable, for one thing because everyone is always "periodizing." They are history snobs of the kind we've seen in *Told by an Idiot*. Ambrose "belongs" to the literary-historical tradition represented by Wilde and by the modernism prior to the Great War, and shortly after. To the novel's youngest generation, Ambrose is passé and politically unacceptable. They decide he is a fascist because he won't talk Communist Party jargon, and also because he doesn't like surrealist painting.

If Ambrose is indeed "historical" and outdated, Waugh nevertheless draws a line between Ambrose's modernism and later cultural fashion, especially of the omnivorously politicizing kind, and he approves Ambrose's side. The approval is in part based on Ambrose's impersonal and impartial character as a writer – indeed on his denying himself, unlike his creator, "any hint of satire."[15] (240). Ambrose has had a German lover, Hans, who now is in a concentration camp because of his sexuality. Ambrose publishes Hans's life story, which includes an account of Hans's off-and-on involvements with his Nazi compatriots. The narrative makes clear how the fascists "shone in Ambrose's story as they did in Hans's eyes." Unfortunately, the honesty of the record becomes the occasion of Ambrose's undoing. Basil seizes upon its publication to argue that Ambrose's "great delicacy and precision" (240) about Hans's perspective is a cover for treacherously promoting Nazism.

Waugh's siding with Ambrose is remarkable for its respectful dissociation of the character from satire. It might mean that Waugh wants to assure readers that his own aggressive clowning – in multiple novels in the 1920s and 1930s – depends on a primary disinterestedness like that evident in Ambrose. Moreover, in effect Ambrose is a pacifist, so that Waugh's inclination for him, coupled with Waugh's creation of Basil as the unrecognized British version of the Gestapo, is published at the moment the collective nation is in the thick of bellicose engagement. Courageously, or perversely, or queerly, Waugh deflates the collective effort. He does this through the second-most sympathetic figure in the novel, Lyne. He is a husband and father whose alcoholic wife has become the obsessive lover of Basil. Lyne has joined the armed forces, and at a moment before his death in battle – a death that results from his courageous walk into the line of fire – he thinks of the importance of being a single, sane individual. He turns the thought into a slogan: "There's danger in numbers; divided we stand, united we fall." Aligning Lyne with Ambrose, the narrator comments: "He did not know it but he was thinking exactly what Ambrose had thought when he announced that culture must cease to be conventual and become coenobitic" (268); that is to say, the individual (coenobitic, hermetic) matters more than the group (the conventual). If that is a dated idea, *Put Out More Flags* fights on the side of the past.

In these fictive modelings of war, the individual can't hold the line against assaults on his or her existence. There is no possibility of holding it in Henry Green's *Caught* (1943). Green's protagonist, Richard Roe, a young widower and father, comes to the verge of insanity, or crosses the border into it, when a climactic night of his work in the Auxiliary Fire Service (A.F.S.) leads him into an incendiary apocalypse. During his moment at the center of hell, a fellow firefighter saves his life. Yet the salvation, given the traumatic effect of the experience, is almost a misnomer. Roe already has been entrapped in a network constructed by chance, the pathos of eros, and the impermanence of happiness.

Roe's story begins with the aftermath of his wife's death, when his young son is kidnapped by a madwoman. The child is recovered, but the kidnapper, as it happens, is the sister of Pye, the veteran firefighter in charge of Roe's A.F.S. unit. That accidental background relation causes tension between the men. Pye is prone to be defensive of his sister, who is now an inmate in an asylum. Moreover, for Pye the background becomes a horrible foreground. He discovers that in his youth he probably, but unknowingly, had sex with his sister, by means of a trick she worked on him. When he is caught several times in what appears to be a dereliction of duty (he has gone to visit his sister, but is too ashamed to disclose a trip to a psychiatric ward) and is facing a discharge, he commits suicide by putting his head in a gas oven. Roe is the first to discover his body. There is no "reason" for the two men to be conjoined in such a way, yet they are. Does historical war determine the chance occurrence? Or is there, inherent in all circumstance, a fatal contingency that determines personal life as destructively as any war?

Roe has had to billet his boy away from London. All along he longs for his dead wife, and for companionship with his son. But after the experience of being caught in the fiery bombing and entangled in Pye's misery, his next-to-last words to his son on the text's last page – "Get out" – shock the boy and the reader. Death and the war began by affording him lamentable solitude. Now he wants what he wanted to escape. The cruelty of a desire for separateness complements the innate cruelty of captivating personal and domestic connections.

In the light of *Caught*, we again find humanity poised between annihilations, and we find fiction exemplifying that poise. Both produce a vision of the war that scarcely contributes to morale, if morale means definitive line-drawing against "depressing" considerations – as *Traitor's Purse* or Beveridge's planning for human freedom might do. That the fictions of Warner, Hamilton, Waugh, and Green (and Jones's and Woolf's hybrid texts) should in effect deviate from the upbeat life-and-death commitments of their national contexts testifies to the persistence of art's modernist autonomy. It won't toe the line even in such a crisis. Nor is the war effort to take precedence over the artistic effort. The pathos of Green's text is intensified by his modernist ingenuity in rearranging the story's chronology and in interleaving character-bound and external narrations.

In some cases fictional protagonists are projections of the intransigent, perhaps antisocial, refusal of the novelists to be called up, if only indirectly, for war service. In Somerset Maugham's *The Razor's Edge* (1944), the protagonist Larry is a veteran American airman of the Great War for whom a fellow combat flyer gave his life. That sacrifice initiates Larry's inter-war search for an acceptable idea of a good and decent existence. Maugham, in his own person the novel's narrator, considers Larry "the only person I've ever met who's completely disinterested,"[16] a sign of a (modernist) contemplative distance from life that Larry finds realized in Hinduism and Vedanta. The worldly men and women whom Maugham and Larry know, even when they are most appealing, seem to miss the self-possession and the peace that Larry's religious vision gives him, that Maugham the narrator approves, and that might provide an exit point for the world at war.

A similar protagonist appears, also in 1944, in Aldous Huxley's *Time Must Have a Stop*. Bruno Rondini, an Italian antifascist, is the novel's moral center. He is not a combatant, but a passive resister; his loyalty is not to politics, but to a transcendent Reality, beyond our investments in self-enclosed, impressionable bodies. The solution to history's miseries, the novel claims, is our movement over the line from worldly instants to an eternal other realm. That other place, despite the historical-realist setting of Huxley's novel in 1920s Italy, becomes the locus of a third of Huxley's chapters. There Reality calls one of Huxley's lead characters, who has just died but whose fading consciousness clings to life, to recognize the Being that dwarfs even the finest humanity. Meanwhile, Rondini, who knows Reality, is scapegoated by the dead man's adolescent nephew, Sebastian. To cover up his role in an art theft, Sebastian, a precociously talented poet, frames the Italian and sends him to jail. So much for the way artists and art fly by the nets of the world! Huxley's poet is a latter-day Stephen Dedalus, whose figure Huxley is revising. Two formal "treatments" – two ways of shaping what happens – constitute Huxley's narrative. Sebastian duplicates in clever verse the occurrences that Huxley's external narrator presents realistically and in prose. But both ways for Huxley are bound, as are the characters' thoughts and actions, to effects that amount to personal and political treachery. Treachery, Huxley argues, is the essence of dedication to our selves and our senses, within the confines of historical time.

Sebastian changes, however, seeming to realize that his lyric impulse (and even the modernist narrative turn to lyric utterance) exemplifies an unconscious move toward mysticism. When Bruno emerges from prison after a decade, and is a dying man, a penitent Sebastian takes him in. The penance continues in an epilogue to the novel that is set in wartime. Sebastian has been maimed in the Allies' battle for North Africa. His latest thoughts, associated with Bruno's, are about "war guilt" and about post-war planning. Both of them are problematic for him, because "one was guilty by just being imperviously oneself." No other guilt, and no planning, can be fruitful if it shields "the little corner of time, of which one is the centre."[17]

Huxley's exit from time and history depends (once again) for illustration upon fiction. The paradox of that doorway to Reality is mitigated if one thinks of the fiction as a holding place for what is beyond. Yet fiction also can be inward with Reality if one locates it, as William Sansom's story collection, *Fireman Flower* (1944), does, in disengagement from the very vocabulary in which the world conflict is invested, and from the thought patterns it is stuck in, including the patterns that distinguish between one ideological "line" and another.

Sansom's eponymous story appears to draw on the Blitz and the Auxiliary Fire Service: it is the record, or the adventure, of a warehouse conflagration. But it does not name London or any real city or any determinate time. Fireman Flower's taxing passage through the vast building, as he and two helpers search for the seat of the fire, raises questions: Is Flower, without knowing it, dead? Is the warehouse a space of his purgation? Are the generalizations that Flower meditates on – for example, "Freedom from doubt, the greatest deception of all!"[18] – definitive moral teachings? Baffling answers abound; the warehouse "was a place of madness and mystery, of shock and fierce paradox, of weird abstraction and surreal romance. Life as he had known it had been broken down" (245). Flower's characterization describes Sansom's text, which breaks down "life" as it is usually pictured. The breakdown makes Flower feel as if he has arrived at "a greater sensuality of the spirit" (246). An immediately succeeding explosion of bags of flour in one of the warehouse rooms seems not to illustrate greater sensuality of spirit. But as the flour covers Flower and the other firemen, he celebrates the result: "a harmony of massed shape and tactile wonder that radiated some limitless composure of beauty unaffected by dramas and associations, pure" (249). Flower ends his response to the fire when he emerges onto the warehouse's roof, and from there looks at a panorama of familiar urban details, which he blesses – as if the narrative now can turn back to recognizable reality. But that turn requires the utter diversion – and purification! – of meaning, the floury explosion, to precede it.

For readers who want wartime fiction to set up a more obvious division between the real conflict and alternatives to it, and to institute a dialogue rather than a break between them, Sansom will seem especially bizarre. Modernism is the problem – even Huxley's anti-modernist modernism. A literary-historical reaction against all the modernist escapes from the actual world disorder might have been predictable. C. S. Lewis's unqualified anti-modernist religious inspiration provides it, yet it arrives in as fantastic a fictional medium as most of the previously discussed works.

Lewis's *That Hideous Strength: A Modern Fairy Tale for Grown-Ups* (1945), inspired by the romances authored by Tolkien, Stapledon, and Charles Williams, brings its reader outside of the contemporary conflict, because the narrative asserts that a war is going on that is not only national, international, and historical, but also supernatural and cosmic. The division that subtends the cosmic interlinkage pits a group of university researchers, the founders of the National Institute for Co-ordinated Experiments (N.I.C.E.), against an oppositional group under the direction of a man named Ransom. He happens to have traveled to another planet, Perelandra, and knows the spiritual as well as the human stakes of the combat.

At stake on the N.I.C.E. side are values that we associate with modernism and certainly with social planning. The Institute expects to solve unemployment, cancer, housing shortages, currency problems, education problems, and war. But N.I.C.E. conforms to Hayek's suspicions about welfare planning. Its director and proponents aim at achieving absolute control of nature and humanity, and that means opposition to "things that most offend the dignity of man. ... Birth and breeding and death. ... We are about to discover that man can live without any of the three."[19] N.I.C.E. makes opposition to "all deep-set repugnances ... the first essential for progress" (200). The abnormal will be the norm. As a corollary, N.I.C.E. equates the idea of the self or soul, and of responsible personal agency, with illusion. It will produce an alternative, "the artificial man, free from Nature" (174), and a complementary, triumphant artificial intelligence. Its discoveries and ideas will not depend on democratic approval or procedures.

The Ransom-led opposition to N.I.C.E. has divine support. Lewis's picture of feminism's relation to the adversaries can illustrate what that means. Among Lewis's leading protagonists are a young couple, Mark and Jane Studdock, who have marital problems because of Mark's masculinism. He wants to work for N.I.C.E., it will come to seem, because of his taste for patriarchy. Although N.I.C.E.'s plan for human liberation logically entails a feminist mission, Jane finds the Institute and Mark alienating; in turn, she becomes an ally of Ransom. But her feminism would not seem to fit with what looks like *Ransom*'s version of patriarchy. She is struck by the possibility that a hierarchy he stands for means a masculinism "all the way up, at every rung of the ascent" (315). Ransom's response to her worry is not simple: "The male you could have escaped, for it exists only on the biological level. But the masculine none of us can escape. What is above and beyond all things is so masculine that we are all feminine in relation to it" (315).

Jane's reaction will startle readers who hold fixed feminist assumptions. She has a moment in which "a boundary had been crossed. She had come into a world, or into a Person, or into the presence of a Person. . . . In the closeness of that contact she perceived at once that the Director's words had been entirely misleading" (318). They have misled her by way of a gendered diction that in the presence of the mystical Person is irrelevant, as are her present self-defining terms. She is not a fixed identity; she is an *I* in the process of making, for the sake of pleasing "Another and in Him to please all others" (319). The divine support cancels and transcends the verbal and cultural distinctions (masculine, feminine) that blinkered ideologies live by.

One might note in regard to the disidentifying *me*'s that Lewis suddenly grants modernist ideas of character an implication of divine favor. But the loss of Jane's sense of self sounds like what N.I.C.E. also has in store for all selves. Nevertheless, N.I.C.E. wants to get selves out of its way for the sake of its universal domination. The Person in Jane's vision is not attuned to superiority as an end in itself. The powers on Ransom's side have only an oblique relation to dominance. "They" include powerful forces called eldils. There are dark eldils, natural allies of N.I.C.E., because they are distorted by earth's limitations. In contrast, Ransom's account of the good eldils connects with the character of "the Person" in Jane's vision. In the eyes of the good eldils, "the normal Tellurian [terrestrial] modes of being – engendering and birth and death and decay . . . were no less wonderful than the countless other patterns of being. . . . To those high creatures whose activity builds what we call Nature, nothing is 'natural'" (202). Preoccupied by "countless patterns of being," the good eldils delight in the autonomy of human minds.

N. I. C. E.'s *modernist* experiments – "nothing is natural," "no basic assumptions" – want to imitate the eldils' powers of creation and yet give them a nefarious slant by dedicating them to every possible form of mastery and rule. To secure that imitation, N.I.C.E. plans to consummate a remarkable discovery. Deeply buried in a property near the Institute is the hibernating body of King Arthur's tutor Merlin. If the experimenters can purchase the site, the Institute can reawaken the mage, and attach him to its planning. The Ransom group cannot allow this to happen. Jane turns out to be a psychic, and dreams of the whereabouts of Merlin. So the Ransom "society" gets to Merlin first and enlists him against the experimenters.

The alliance inspires Lewis to give his reader yet another vision of split or schizophrenic identities in British wartime fiction. The N.I.C.E.–Ransom struggle over who will possess Merlin is a war for the identity of England. Ransom reveals that English national history as historians know it is only a superficial account. The real story concerns a buried authentic national identity that Ransom (and Lewis) call by the name of Logres. Logres is England's alter ego, or twin, a ghost haunting the present, and seeking release and recovery. When Arthur ruled in the sixth century, "something that is always trying to break through into this country nearly succeeded. Logres" (368). "Haven't you noticed that we are two countries?" Ransom goes on:

> After every Arthur, a Mordred; behind every Milton, a Cromwell; a nation of poets, a nation of shopkeepers; the home of Sidney – and of [imperialist] Cecil Rhodes. Is it any wonder they call us hypocrites? But what they mistake for hypocrisy is . . . the struggle between Logres and Britain.   (368)

Remarkably, the nation in this fairy story repeats self-divided Lud and George Bone's split-screen psyche. The historical–psychiatric division holds England hostage. The vast cosmic war is all for the sake of rescuing an authentic, blessedly shrunken national identity. Ransom will deliver England from the imperial entity Britain. The contrast with *In Parenthesis* is worth noting. Jones prominently features the Welsh roots of his text, yet connects the Welsh material to Roman and continental traditions; Lewis recalls Merlin to life (how very different a Merlin from White's character!) to separate and purify aboriginal England from non-English elements.

In a sense, the liberation of Logres repeats at home what the dissolution of Empire will produce abroad. Native rulers of colonized territories, haunted by their former autonomies, can recover and reconnect with their ghosts. *That Hideous Strength* also predicts the violence that will baptize the reunion. In the novel's climax, the good eldils under Merlin's leadership sweep down on N.I.C.E. and murder its immediate personnel and its less immediate associates. A Blitz! The violence raises at least one eyebrow in the Ransom ranks. "Aren't Merlin and the eldils a trifle . . . well, *wholesale*. Did *all* Edgestow [the Institute's locale] deserve to be wiped out?" (371).

But in what more realistic form than Lewis's (or others') does buried Logres arise? Two novels closer to real history bring us back across the line separating the fictive wars from the plausibly immediate ones. Now the immediacy comprehends peace. In J. B. Priestley's *Three Men in New Suits* (1945), the demobilized protagonists had formed a miniature egalitarian society during their military service. Sadly, the post-war prospects of a newly collective life seem dim. The ex-soldiers represent different classes: Alan, county aristocrats; Herbert, farmers; Eddie, laborers. The home environments they return to retain their class distinctions, or have changed for the worse, or are paranoid about "Reds," and "bureaucrats, long-haired cranks, and the riff-raff of the industrial towns."[20] The men's families want the veterans to conform to pre-war assumptions about what they should work at and how they should live.

The men are convinced that social change must reward the war effort. The one sure prospect of change at home is formulated for Alan by a media baron. He and his kind, and the trade unions as well, know that "those boys of yours [are] expecting something." He knows, and the unions know, what they want: "Dog tracks, cheap racing, plenty of football, better movies, good places to eat and drink where they can take their wives, nice holidays. We're campaigning for all that right now." When the media mogul offers Alan a job writing for the newspaper syndicate that will be part of the campaign (and will also intensify "more 'inside stuff,' more 'off the record' talk, more nicknames for the great, more global 'hush-hush,' more advance notes on tomorrow's headlines" [113]), Alan accepts, despite being repelled by his own action.

Each of the men has begun to grow furious at what seems mass hostility to progress. Reuniting in the last chapter, they inspire one another to resist the status quo. Alan drops the media job. "Instead of guessing and grabbing, we plan. Instead of competing, we co-operate," he says, speaking "into the dusk as if it held a vast invisible audience" (216). "Modern man is essentially co-operative and communal man" (216). The narrative has included two female characters who are in tune with the men. Its final page demands another inclusion: "We have at last to have faith in people, compassion for people, whether they have white faces, brown faces or black faces" (216).

Priestley's conformity with Beveridge's proposals is quite blatant. Another 1945 fiction, Denton Welch's *In Youth Is Pleasure* (1945), mischievously reminds us of the difficulty of drawing the line between planning and the unplanned. It presents the anarchic sensations and ideas of fifteen-year-old Orvil during a summer vacation "several years before the war."[21] Reaching back past the strains of grown-up struggle, Welch reminds us, through Orvil, of the charm of spontaneous life's resistance to regulatory order.

To be sure, Orvil is not without a liking for security. He does take "sudden and peculiar pleasure" in things – for example, a scent bottle he buys in an antiques shop – that make him feel protected "in an enemy world" (49). But his vulnerability is often self-inflicted, as if he were joining the enemy world against himself, risking the venture to discover its pleasure. When he comes across the instruments of a band in the ballroom of the hotel where he and his family are staying, he examines them and by chance breaks off the strap of a cover for a double-bass. With no more planning than is represented by the break, Orvil immediately takes the strap to a rest room and flagellates himself with it, imagining himself as a series of figures, historical or imaginary, who might whip or be whipped. "He delighted" in the effects of this on his skin, though worries that his behavior, "if it would be discovered, would be thought rather peculiar" (51). Later he will delight in two visits to the cabin of a vacationing schoolteacher whom he comes across by chance. The visits, charged with erotic tensions, find issue in mutual physical aggression: for brief intervals the pair truss each other up without knowing what the outcome will be.

My selective retelling of Orvil's adventures will make them sound like a Freudian case. He associates cosmetics with his beloved deceased mother, whose eyebrows he used to paint. After attending a dance during which he wishes he were a girl, so that he could be asked to dance without exerting his will, he retreats to his room and decorates his lips, nose, and eyes with stolen lipstick. He then "absent-mindedly rouged his nipples until they were like two squashed strawberries," and he more deliberately applies the rouge to mark "gashes and spots all over his body" (88). Are we to understand this as the story of a son's neurotic identification with his mother? Would Orvil be better off if he did not cross the line separating the genders? The narrative and its treatment answer negatively. Welch does not invite us to tie Orvil's delights to a therapeutic analysis. The novel's point is that Orvil pursues his pleasures because they take him by surprise. The surprise is their pleasure. He gives his leadings meanings, and subsequently changes those meanings, so that new possibilities of impulsive pursuit can commence for him.

At the close of the novel, when Orvil is returning to school by train, a bullying upper classmate threatens him with violence. Orvil screams his refusal to submit to aggression. This might be Welch's most direct reference to the war. The wacky trajectory of Orvil's impulses, his way of loaning himself to them, purposely without purpose, restores to spontaneous life what the war took away, and what the postwar plans might secure – and might also under-estimate.

Keeping On, Post-1945

Gulley Jimson is a visual artist whose verbal self-portrait is the content of Joyce Cary's novel, *The Horse's Mouth* (1944). Poverty, eros, and the commodification of his work have done their best to destroy his endeavor. Jimson bears some responsibility: self-indulgence and inexpugnable conceit have repeatedly put him, his work, and at least three lovers in harm's way. So a critic justifiably challenges the artist: "Art has a lot to answer for, all right, all right." "Yes," the artist replies. "[A]nd it doesn't answer," he adds. "'It only keeps on' 'Keeps on? . . . Keeps on what?' 'Keeping on.'"[22] Jimson's sense of art's opacity – and of its endurance – derives from the life Cary has imagined for him. Yet for Cary to have named his novel *The Horse's Mouth* suggests that Cary's verbal art is a double for Jimson's visual one, and that the author is speaking as straightforwardly as possible (in a fiction) about art in general. Cary's novel is a fellow traveler with our final considerations of the stubborn persistence – the strange necessity – whereby art, according to some ideas of it, keeps on enlisting and transforming worldly topics, and continues to be itself at the same time.

Before considering Cary further, however, as we move toward a "periodizing" barrier of 1950 we again might look at the fortunes of collectivity as they are treated by British fiction (and some nonfiction) in the aftermath of Beveridge's proposals. Surprisingly, the Labor victory's progress toward democratic socialism, or Priestley's optimism, or Welch's reminder of the pleasures awaiting post-war youth, do not find confirmation in one of the most distinguished post-war novels, Sylvia Townsend Warner's *The Corner That Held Them* (1948). Scarcely flattering communitarian hopes, this novel about life in a medieval British convent profiles the lack of assurance that pervades every corporate endeavor, however unworldly, or utopian, or realistic.

Warner exhaustively traces the web of involvements in which the nuns of the convent of Oby are caught, over the course of thirty years, from the time the Black Death arrives in England in 1349 to the Peasants' Revolt and its aftermath. The communities of convent, feudal manor, and church hierarchy add up to a single protagonist – but two of the long-enduring prioresses of Oby stand out as women whose capacity to govern is exemplary. Prioress Alicia is able to finance a spire for the convent chapel, and to transform the sewing of altar hangings into an art that all the nuns can share in producing. "Though in its early stages the needlework had been an instrument in the usual convent factions, . . . as time went on it had become everyone's interest and ... purpose. ... Something was being made, they had a reason for living together, the blue satin [they adorned] roofed them like a tabernacle."[23]

Nevertheless, history apparently will not abide collective integration of separate lives, let alone their conjunction with art. The time span of Warner's narrative equals that of the back-to-back twentieth-century global wars. Thus she might be offering readers a historical allegory for present meditation, or perhaps a memento mori for the lion and the unicorn, whatever their hopeful state. One might expect the feminist creator of Lolly Willowes to celebrate her convent more buoyantly as a governmental model in which women achieve just socioeconomic administration – as Alicia does temporarily – on behalf of an institution of their own. Yet the novel ends, perplexingly, with a betrayal of sisterhood. A young nun, snubbed by her fellows, wants to withdraw into a hermetic existence; in contrast, another young nun is laying plans to escape the convent and England. The latter succeeds, but at a ruthless cost to her coenobitic colleague. The event manipulates the reader's antipathy to betrayal, but it also inspires a reader's divided sympathies: with the nun who escapes from the collective into a far distant world (Venice and Jerusalem), and with the nun who figures radical withdrawal from common ground. It is as if Warner projects onto the escaping nun her relief at the distance of 1948 from the fourteenth century, and onto the hermetic nun her sympathy with the novel's radical detachment (another autonomizing flight) from its mid-twentieth-century surround.

Whatever the motives for enigma in Warner, her cryptic treatment of community during the post-war period is not singular. It is expressed in another corner of post-1945 liberation: India, whose release from British rule in 1947 creates two new collectives, the modern Indian state and Pakistan. Of course, the immediate issue of Indian liberation was Hindu–Muslim violence and intensified division. R. K. Narayan's *Mr. Sampath – The Printer of Malgudi* (1949), although it takes place in 1938–1939, can be read as a picture of subdued post-war expectations for a renewed community, a melancholic resignation of collective hopes. The narrative begins with its protagonist, Srinivas, making a clean break for independence. He temporarily abandons his wife and children to launch a newspaper in Malgudi. He feels a religious impulse, derived from the Upanishads, to "know who I am" (9), and he means *The Banner* to pursue that discovery by being "only concerned with the war that is always going on – between man's inside and outside" (4).[24]

Srinivas's inside is well represented: he is sole editor and contributor for his newspaper. But *The Banner* depends for its outside on the Truth Printing Works, operated by Sampath. While Srinivas's published criticisms of every aspect of the town make his paper influential in the public sphere as "the home of truth and vision" (3), its printer increasingly belies the name of his own enterprise. He finagles Srinivas into exchanging *The Banner* for work at a new motion picture studio, where Srinivas will write screenplays. Srinivas proposes a scenario about a follower of Gandhi who struggles with the doctrine of nonviolence. Sampath and the producers ask instead for "romance in the story" (86), because they have engaged a glamorous leading lady. They permit Srinivas to devise a version of Shiva's violence against Kama, the god of love – a violence that Srinivas interprets as an allegory of erotic sublimation. Unfortunately, Sampath's increasingly deceitful involvement in the studio business, which leads to his playing the part of Shiva and eloping with the actress, unwinds the entire project. Srinivas returns to *The Banner*, which is issued by another printer. "Every film is a cooperative effort" (160) he has been told, even when the studio context has already made the assertion ring hollow. His *Banner*, for all its public aims, shrinks to a solitary enterprise. That turns Srinivas back to religious inspiration. Narayan's narrative suggests that modern public media are bound to fail any collective search for truth. The failure leaves individuals adrift, searching again for some pre-modern equivalent of unworldliness.

Perhaps Mervyn Peake's fantasy novel, *Titus Groan* (1946), unlike the realist ones, is more suited to a readership contextualized by a Labor-led collective. After all, modern egalitarianism facilitates upward mobility, and here is a novel figuring what must be abandoned: a drearily static kingdom. Gormenghast, a monarchy in which "change" is "that most unforgivable of all heresies,"[25] is the novel's site. The birth of the eponymous hero means that the ruling House of Groan will continue its deadweight line. But two Gormenghast Castle kitchen workers are seething with rebellion against the order of things. Surely they will be rightful agents of change. Their role as proponents of the modern collective good is almost immediately cast aside, however. The more wily rebel, Steerpike, is an adolescent Machiavel, who will set Lord Groan's beloved library (the Lord's reason for holding on to life) on fire, and ally himself with the ruler's resentful twin sisters, establishing himself thereby as the potential husband of the Lord's daughter, Fuchsia.

Given the emergence of the novel's only demotic insiders as villains, for Peake to present them as repulsive transformers of governmental order suggests that his narrative is the opposite of progressive; that his novel is nostalgic for an anti-egalitarian never-never land. But there are other ways to read the author's signposts. Steerpike is less emblematic of a low origin that merits suppression for its upstart character than he is a figure of phony opportunism in the name of justifiable class conflict. Politically speaking, he is on the right, but wears left egalitarian rhetoric as a mask. His co-conspirator, the kitchen chef, exemplifies a snarling resentment at the core of Steerpike, and equally at the core of the Lord's sisters and the Lord's physician. The resentment of power belongs to every pursuer of it. Facile political allegorizing is also undermined by a kind of gothic comedy informing Peake's inventiveness. By the 1940s, upwardly mobile persons in fictions are clichés, to be played with as stock components of storytelling. The same goes even for the democratizing rhetoric. The clichés are so well worn that to take them at face value is to take them with an earnestness that is inappropriate, especially in response to a fiction that offers itself as a fairy tale artifice. It also offers itself as modernist artifice. Peake's characterization of Swelter the chef is inspired, verbally and tonally, by Wyndham Lewis's similar brutes; and at Titus's first-year birthday celebration, the grown-ups are each afforded, to quasi-satiric effect, Joycian interior monologues.

The parodies are part of *Titus Groan*'s extensive preoccupation with the relation of art to social order, both old and new. Its opening pages are about an outsiders' society that surrounds the castle: the community of Bright Carvers, an artist race, an "all-but-forgotten people" (3), except when once a year they deposit their artefacts in a castle museum. Titus's nurse for the first months of his life is a Carver; it is important for the kingdom's future that she suckles him. Peake gives us a sample of her "breed's" idea of art. It is an equestrian statue, which terrifies the Carvers' children, "but to their parents it was a work of extraordinary vitality and beauty of form, . . . and [of] a richness of mysterious mood . . . which . . . was one of their criteria of excellence" (250). Titus's sister Fuchsia maintains in the castle's upper reaches an "attic of make-believe" (81), where her imagination carves airy nothings. Steerpike breaks into that space. She mistakes him for a romance adventurer; he recognizes her as a being whose make-believe will "never carry her to power or riches" (167). The fate of the Carvers corroborates what Steerpike says: their race dooms each of them to early senility and death. Art is not immortal in Peake's novel; nor is learning, as Steerpike's trashing of the library proves. Lord Sepulchrave (Lord Groan's other name) is perpetually melancholy in a way that seems responsive to the early senescence of the Carvers and the detachment from life that is entailed by constant study. In the figures of Lord Groan and tiny Titus, the community is dependent on mortality and vulnerability, and art shares the common dependency. Perhaps Warner's corner echoes Peake's kingdom, or perhaps Peake's realm plays with political models to help us get free of them altogether.

For George Orwell, the dependency of collectives and individuals on truth is what supremely matters – more than the governmental forms. Ignorance of the truth, pervading the barnyard citizens' socialist self-government in *Animal Farm: A Fairy Story* (1946) is the gravest danger to the collective's survival. The farm is built on Snowball the pig's founding agreements, published on the barn wall. The articles of those agreements are increasingly ignored, and tampered with. That evolution results partly from the intellectual inability of the citizens, some of which cannot read or absorb what is available. As a consequence, they can be easily persuaded by the upstart dictator Napoleon that lies are truths. No matter what individual intellectual capacity is at issue, however, another major human faculty, collectively shared, is prone to dimness – namely, memory. Memory is exact and inexact, precise and fuzzy. To guard against its weaknesses, *Animal Farm* shows, it is all the more important that the facts of collective agreements, and truthful preservation of facts in general, be maintained.

To read *Animal Farm* is to practice, in the very process of attending to Orwell's text, the fit between fact and memory that escapes the animals. When Napoleon issues judgments of what the founding collective principles now mean, the reader has the choice of losing his footing – along with the novel's creatures ("they all remembered, or thought they remembered . . ."[26]) – or checking the facts. The reparative choice is to page back, to the narrative facts still on indelible record. In so doing, one enacts the defense that fact-based memory can mount against coercion. One also enacts the defense that attentive reading of the kind exacted by modernism can mount. Because the animals do not preserve the truth about their origins, and because they are bad readers, the line between their revolutionary political form and that of their antagonists is erased.

Orwell begins *Animal Farm* by subordinating the difference between pigs and men, and emphasizing a contrast between socialists and capitalists. At the end of the tale, the contrast between pigs and men disappears again, because now no one knows what is true or truly historical and what is fake news about the past and the present. The time-honored reading of Orwell's text as an anti-Soviet diatribe participates in the very distortions the text dramatizes. It overlooks the respect Orwell shows for the socialist revolution that Snowball and his faithful workhorse Boxer exemplify. Napoleon reminds us of pre-Marxist autocracies; democracies inspired by eighteenth-century Enlightenment constitutions are as much *Animal Farm's* target as are perverted socialism or communism.

The vulnerability of facts and memory germinates the famous conflicts of Orwell's *1984* (1949). Winston Smith and his lover Julia join a conspiracy against the panoptical dictatorship of Big Brother; the man who welcomes them in, O'Brien, deceives them into thinking that he is on their side.

O'Brien's goal is to destroy Smith's attachment to truth. His success makes *1984* a far darker version of *Animal Farm*. When Smith surrenders to O'Brien, it seems as if his author can't imagine a recovery from the dissolution of a reality that can't be manipulated. Perhaps, if one may propose an external motivation for the fiction's pessimism, Orwell felt he was fighting a losing battle with modernist ideas of history – ideas that, justly or not, Orwell folds into Big Brother. One modernist idea is that history is a fiction of sorts, or inevitably mixed with fictional components. In Interchapter 4 we touched on several novelists' conviction that the past is artificial. We also noted that Collingwood identifies history with the meeting of present and past minds. Collingwood preserves the objectivity of the meeting. Orwell seems to be dramatizing the objectivity when he gives Winston, and his reader, access to the forbidden rebellious book that tells the true story of Oceania. But then Smith and the reader are told by O'Brien that the truthful book also is a fake. In *Animal Farm*, the reader can trust his reading of the barnyard constitution; in *1984*, Orwell's reader can't trust, as Smith can't, the truth of what one has thought would be the truth.

Moreover, *1984* represents the negation of what was for Orwell in *Homage to Catalonia* the touchstone of conviction: the self-evidence of truth that bodily sensations and spontaneous feelings entail. In *1984* Smith takes hope by identifying this common ground with his body, with sexual intercourse with Julia, above all with the "proles," the common folk who are so far below the center of power that their very physiology seems an essence of their freedom. Horribly, the final phase of Smith's torture shows that our most intimate sensations are pervaded by treachery.

We live in an odd world: where truth is the vocation of fiction writers. As a result of such oddness, British novelists can serve double callings: to be reporters of documentary facts as well as novelists. The novelist-journalist's métier enlists Rebecca West. When West takes up the reporting of the 1946 Nuremberg trials that prosecuted the Nazi leaders for war crimes, and when she returns to Germany in 1949 to document the condition of occupied Berlin, she demonstrates the continuity of our 1900–1950 "period." The admiring critic and young contemporary of Henry James, and the formulator of "the strange necessity," West might be said to bring the influences of James, Joyce, and Pavlov along with her to the international courtroom and postwar Germany. She brings along, one also might propose, a flexibility of perspective derived from James and Joyce, and practiced in her novels' varied modes. Those modes include historical realism in *The Return of the Soldier* (1918), applied to psychiatric handling of war trauma, and class war among women; and romance artifice in *Harriet Hume: A London Fantasy* (1929), applied to masculinist politicians' habits of avoiding aesthetics and ethics.

The drive to keep the commonly shared historical record honest, yet not simplify its complexity, shapes West's reports. Amalgamating the novelist's mind with objective materials, the reports establish the terms of a trans-national community, a global collective that includes the recent enemy. West's 1946 "Greenhouse with Cyclamens I" picks out a war-disabled German gardener who, against all odds (and prohibitory regulations), has sown a profitable flower business amid the wreckage-laden scene of the war trials. West cites this as something "peculiarly German and dynamic in [its] self-dedication," and calls it "industrious to the point of nobility."[27] West is covering the tribunal that will condemn peculiarly German things, yet finds appreciable qualities in the defeated enemy. She exemplifies in her framing of her text the intellectual, moral, and emotional impersonality – a modernist impersonality – that she finds also enacted in the trials. Her response produces some shocking moments. For example, in describing how eleven Nazi leaders received their death sentences, she declares:

> We had learned what they did, beyond all doubt, and that was the
> great achievement of the Nuremberg trial. . . . [T]hese men were
> abscesses of cruelty. But [from their conduct at sentencing] we
> learned . . . that they were capable of heroism in which they had
> no moral right, and that there is nothing in the legend that a bully
> is always a coward.   (60)

Would it not be in the collective interest to squelch even so qualified an appreciation of villainous murderers? West's answer is negative. One value of the trials is their refusal of simplified notions of what community values are, or should be. Triumphalism on the part of victors, and their foregone conclusions about the defeated, do not serve. One of the first impressions West has of the rightness of the trials, and of her way of seeing them, is by way of the entrapment in it felt by the foreigners. They are caught in the toils of the justice they pursue. Their submission to the captivity, West proposes, witnesses their consent to the rightness of the pursuit. Unintentionally, West here echoes the valuable detachment from immediate action that we have seen expressed in detective and spy fiction.

The rightness of being caught is underlined, West explains, by the way in which the Nuremberg judges inhabit a medium of legal uncertainty, and undergo judgment upon themselves. The ambiguous character of inter-national law became a conscious fact during the trial, West tells us, when Nazi submarine admirals were acquitted for their attacks on British merchant ships without warning them and without rescuing survivors. The acquittal recognized that the British and American navies had perpetrated the same conduct. West registers this as proof that "Nuremberg [is] a step farther on the road to civilization." For "it was a step towards honesty. It was written down for ever that submarine warfare cannot be carried on without inhumanity, and that we have found ourselves able to be inhuman. We have to admit that we are in this trap before we can get out of it" (49).

West's essays on Germany are Orwell-like efforts to resist distortions and erasures of the collective condition, and at the same time equally Orwellian efforts to save individualism from collective constraints. Reporting on Berlin in 1949, West finds occasion to tangle with British welfare state planning by seeing its effect on the British occupation of the capital. "Greenhouse with Cyclamens II" notes that Clement Atlee's Labor government wants to restrain laissez-faire economies there. "But it would have been a historical impossibility that [Berliners] should accept the idea of the welfare state and a planned economy. To begin with, the Nazi regime had claimed to be a welfare state ..." (121). West's view converges with Hayek's! But she is too flexible mentally to fully embrace his argument. "We see that history takes no care to point a moral," West says (134). Hayek, however, is always pointing one.

West's measure of apt policy is different, because it is situation-specific. It appeals, not surprisingly given the impact of Impressionism on fiction writers and documentarians, to "experience." "We all know that some events become experience and others do not: some events that give us information about the universe and ourselves, and some that tell us nothing" (139). The experience of working women in Berlin – women who became construction workers and whose energies resonate with the greenhouse entrepreneur's – is West's touchstone. "For these women, for all men of their kind, the occupation of Berlin had been an event which was also an experience" (160). So, West concludes, their initiative must not be conformed or subordinated to external planning, an equivalent of useless information. What the worker women do for the collective good is what they do for their individual selves. At Nuremberg, "men had made a formal attack on the police state. ... [H]ere these women had incarnated the argument. They were discussing the matter with their bodies as well as their minds." Most importantly, "Aching, they saw a vision of ... government that would love the individual. This is the democratic state, and it was to this they had learned allegiance" (159).

West's reports, we might think, resolve fear that the truth of history, and the trustworthy historical recording of it, is under an ultimate threat. At the same time, West aims at a catharsis of backward-looking attachment to the war. For the home community and for the former enemy, the desire for liberation from history is not only a nefarious one.

But leaving history behind looks newly curious in William Cooper's *Scenes from Provincial Life* (1950), even though it is yet another story that unfolds during the run-up to September 1939. In contrast to the other narratives, as well as to the national–provincial fictions we have reviewed, the war seems to matter in Cooper's novel only as a loose excuse for what Cooper's characters do. The characters are a quartet: three men and one woman. They include a straight couple, Joe Lunn (the narrator) and Myrtle, and a gay couple, Tom and Steve. Joe once likens Myrtle to Hitler ("I was being hunted by Hitler and Myrtle in conjunction"[28]) but the likeness is casual. The only importance Hitler has for the characters – the male characters – is that the prospect of war with Germany makes them want to emigrate to the United States. Political reasons aren't their motives. Joe wants to escape marriage, despite Myrtle's expectations. In contrast, Tom wants to emigrate to coerce Steve's marriage-like commitment to him. But then Joe feels guilty about not proposing to Myrtle, and about leaving her; and Steve decides he wants to pursue women, although he can't bring himself to part with Tom; and Tom's frustration with Steve and rivalrous friendship with Joe make him propose marriage to Myrtle. Yet she marries someone else. Each character is tied to another; each character is tied only to himself; each partner wants his lover to feel free; and each wants his lover not to feel free.

If this quartet is a model of community, then community doesn't know what it wants; its purposes, its very character, are opaque. Partly this is so because Cooper has cut his edgy amorists away from the collective ideological concerns that preceded and informed the war. The line-drawing, between communist and socialist, between leftist and fascist, between Conservative and Labor, Cooper implies, is now so much provincial background. History, the point seems to be, didn't mark every personal "scene" in 1939; revisiting those scenes a decade later, it still doesn't.

An indifference to "history" – *pace* Orwell and West – is thus at stake in *Scenes from Provincial Life*. Yet a *literary* history notes how Cooper is marked by fiction's past – by the novelistic collective, so to speak. In terms of content and treatment, this author is not an outsider doing something new, but something modernist, and by 1950 something traditional. His matter-of-fact presentation of sexual orientations builds on a half-century of fiction's struggle to make it possible, and available for comedy (as Nancy Mitford did), rather than for censure. The "scenes" in Cooper's narrative are drama-like dialogue: they lack Wildean wit, but suggest a Wildean line of descent, mediated by the representations of serio-comic eros (albeit in closeted form) in Christopher Isherwood's *Good-bye to Berlin* (1939). Of course, Isherwood's famous stories about life under the Third Reich link love intrigues to political–ideological contexts. Modernist impulse explored those links, even as it also resisted them. Cooper's resistance returns to the modernist inspiration that suspends their pressure. The suspense is accompanied by an emotional lightness: in the finale of the novel, Joe ticks off the happy marriages – not to each other! – that the principals achieve after the war. Underneath, however, is a wryness, perhaps a bitterness about life's muddled intelligibility as the breakup of the characters implies it. It might be the collective's muddle and breakup, too.

Another novel of 1950 provides, with great candidness, an accepting vision of collective dissolution. Rose Macaulay's *The World My Wilderness* carries no torch for the nation as a communal matrix. The novel suggests, perhaps, that the war has been for everyone an experience of deranging muddle like that undergone by Adela and Mrs. Moore in the Marabar Hills. The effect is more drastic than in Forster's novel. Through the perspective of an Anglo-French mother who might be Macaulay's revision of Mrs. Moore, the novel announces the death of a greater collective: Western civilization.

> No civilization had lasted more than a few thousand years; this present one, called western culture, had had its day and was due for wreckage, . . . while the next struggled inchoate in the womb. . . . [A]lready the margins of the present broke crumbling and dissolved before the invading chaos.[29]

Macaulay's mother is described as "carelessly attached, fundamentally detached" (111) from ties and relationships, even though she has been twice married, has raised four children, and in France during the war has found herself allied with both the collaborationists (pro-Nazi) and the Resistance partisans. Her adolescent daughter Barbary, who idolized the Resistance and participated in it, remains in the post-war era obsessively attached to the psychology of guerrilla warfare, not least because of her traumatic involvement with self-contradictory allegiances (she had a sexual relationship with a German soldier, whose death she then brought about). Her mother seems able to handle her version of Barbary's immobilizing divisions. Barbary can only look to the past, whereas her mother can accept the invading chaos, even forgive it. Might such an attitude complement that of Cooper's provincials? Macaulay's look forward also complements the modernist past. *The World My Wilderness* takes *The Waste Land* for its epigraphs, bridging 1922 and 1950.

We are not to assume that a few novels of 1945–1950 are the stopping point of a literary-historical or historical period, or that they bring us to some kind of summary truth about the real world. In their pages we remain in the arena of novelists' treatments of worldly topics. They cannot resolve their worries (or ours) about the collective's political state, and about history's objective record. Their concerns and their shaping forms remain tied to their ideas of fiction. Before returning to Cary, we can bring up to date proposals about the nature of art by the wartime and post-war novelist-critics Herbert Read and Robert Liddell, and by Orwell in an auxiliary comment.

Herbert Read's novel *The Green Child* (1935) begins with its narrator's noticing that the rivers and streams of his hometown are running up hill. Read, who is primarily an art historian and art critic, would call his novel an example of surrealism, an idea about the arts that rejects both "realist" treatments of content and denials of meaning. We have indirectly seen this idea illustrated by "Fireman Flower" and *The Aerodrome* – but perhaps, on the grounds of what Read has to say, we will have traversed more examples. Read's quarrel with realism is partly inspired by his Marxism – and by his rejection of Marxist aesthetics. Marxist aesthetics, according to Read's *Art and Society* (1936–1945), relies – at least as practice in the Soviet Union prescribes it – on conceptualizing life as what Read calls "The totality of a social system."[30] Art is politically obliged to represent the totality, in a mode of scrupulously realistic mirroring of it. But, Read contends, there is no abstract stable structure, either in life, in history, or in art; there is no stable reality. "Art is not to be regarded as a reflection of one part of our mental experience ... but is to be regarded as a synthesis of all aspects of our existence, even (indeed, especially) the most contradictory" (120). The reflection of contradictory aspects depends on art's expression of unconscious as well as conscious emotion and intellect. Because surrealism does not designate as real a limited portion of experience (history is only one portion), surrealism, Read proposes, is far more in tune with the comprehensiveness of Marxist dialectic than has been appreciated. Surrealism directs us to avoid treating "art as an aid to thought, or as an interpretation of thought, instead of as a mode of thought in itself" (134).

As a mode of thought in itself, art has a political vocation. It is a liberating force. But Read affirms its force as a paradox in *The Politics of the Unpolitical* (1946). His volume recapitulates what many ideas of fiction by 1946 have asserted. The artist is political indirectly – by withdrawing from attached partisanships because the ideologies and institutions behind them have gone stale or died. In the mid-war years, "The young men and women stand apart" because "they want a world that is morally clean and socially just. . . . [T]hey know they won't get it from any of the existing political systems. . . . They are not a party and never will be a party: they have no name and will perhaps never have a name."[31] The artists – the novelists – would do best, Read implies, to withdraw with the young. It becomes difficult not to add to Read's claim about anonymity that the name for the young might still be *modernist*.

Two or three previous generations, with the same collective aversions and desires, are eligible for description as politically unpolitical.

It is not easy to grasp – it is a perennial difficulty – how an artwork can stand aside, yet be as involved in comprehensive experience as Read believes. Nevertheless, what Read intends in regard to narrative fiction is that we regard it as no less credible than any other discursive mode. All art's expressions, it is plausible to think, are experiments in the constitution of a reality that is continually in process, under construction, a cosmos of autonomies, now interweaving, now disjunct.

Liddell sets himself an easier expository task than Read, because his *A Treatise on the Novel* (1947) does not mean to map fiction's expansion into the world. Indeed, for fiction to be produced, Liddell argues, the artist must have extensive worldly experience, but must delimit it if his subject matter is to be workable. The range of a novelist's subjects (or topics) is the bounded interest that most inspires his imagination. If fiction writers feel obliged to go beyond such boundaries, "under the impression that they are obeying the dictates of their social consciences, then their social consciences," Liddell provocatively says, "are diseased – for the duty of a writer to the community, as a writer, is simply this: to write as well as he can."[32] He or she writes as well as possible from a position of withdrawal. "It has to be remembered that a writer's is a contemplative, not an active vocation. . . . This does not mean indifference to the life of the world outside the Ivory Tower; it does mean detachment from it" (53). Henry James is one of Liddell's examples of such contemplation, which is virtually mystical, a dialogue of self and soul. His choice of the "the greatest and . . . most original artist now writing" (153) is Ivy Compton-Burnett. Her limited subject matter (Liddell's own novels have a similar one) is "the terrors of family life" and "tyranny in family life." It is decidedly not Ivory Tower–centered material: it is rooted in "the desire for domination, which in a dictator can plunge the world into misery" (141). It relevance to politics is obvious. "The courage of those who resist dictation, and the different motives which cause people to range themselves on the side of the dictator can be minutely studied . . . here . . . in a limited sphere" (141).

Orwell, more prolific as a social and literary critic than as a novelist, concisely assesses the political demands that come from outside fiction as well as from within it in a letter of 1949:

> The more I see the more I doubt whether people ever really make aesthetic judgements at all. Everything is judged on political grounds

which are then given an aesthetic disguise. ... Yet evidently one does have aesthetic reactions, especially as a lot of art & even literature is politically neutral, & also certain unmistakeable standards do exist, e.g. Homer is better than Edgar Wallace. Perhaps the way we should put it is: the more one is aware of political bias the more one can be independent of it.[33]

Orwell's ability to engage political controversy, and yet to think it is not the only or the supreme measure of art, echoes Wyndham Lewis's positions about politics and art since the 1920s. Implying the convergence, Lewis offers up Orwell as the English writer most worthy of contemporary study in *The Writer and the Absolute* (1952).

The present chapter and this book have exemplified what art keeps trying to answer for, or, more expansively, what it has to answer *to* (e.g., history, anthropology, science, politics), even as art tries merely to keep on. Joyce Cary, to whom we return, invents Jimson so as again (after his study of Mr. Johnson) to portray the figure of an artist. In *The Horse's Mouth* the artist is an old man, but he retains the (by now traditional) Dedalean ambition: to fly by the environmental nets that bring down creation. Art itself can bring it down, Jimson has discovered, by virtue of its own ideas of itself. Beginning with his version of Impressionism, Jimson has been the vehicle and the heir of a sequence of modernist "treatments" of life. He knows and approves "what modern art can do. Creeping about everywhere, undermining the Church and the State and the Academy and the Law and marriage and the government" (18). After he had moved on to Cubism, however, Jimson felt creatively pinched: "The job is always to get hold of the form you need. ... The cubists ... chucked up old doddering impressionism," but they did it too easily, he thinks. They made Cubism into "a new security" (60), dependent on anti-representational abstraction. Jimson has kept on unsecuring himself, and has become an anti-modernist modernist. He has adapted an innovative – a post-modernist – use of storytelling and of recognizable human figures to painting.

Jimson thus flies past the art traditions that even modernism has already become. (So, too, escapes Cary, who does not attempt to copy James Joyce's more radical experiments. He remains a figurative son and heir of "Jim" Joyce, a Jimson, but his work cultivates less difficult treatments than Joyce's.) But there is another net stronger than any in which Jimson has also been caught: the economic net. *The Horse's Mouth* is about the self-contradictory nature of the economics of visual art, and, by a metaphorical extension, of verbal art.

Jimson's early figurative paintings, bought by a wealthy patron, and the sketches that his ex-lover Sara owns, have soared in market and museum value. But Jimson has none of the profit; he is without materials, without a studio, after having spent time in jail for harassing, in the hope of income, the private owner of his work from the 1920s. The breath-taking gap between creative purpose and the alienation the purpose undergoes when it is materialized, distributed, criticized, bought, sold, profited from, saved, and trashed: all this is what the economics of art and culture has to answer for.

Unable to afford canvas, Jimson turns to painting visionary murals of Biblical subjects on any wall he can commandeer. Unfortunately, for a new mural depiction of the creation story, he chooses a derelict church. It is not long before the church wall collapses and brings down the mural. With the fall of his last creation, Jimson loses his life battle. He has accepted the war that informs creation, however. Creation as a war is as much Cary's drama as any. The producers of art fight wars with each other over which topics to choose and how to treat them; these wars, in turn, shape their generational conflicts and continuities. The latter occupy a different order or plane of history than the struggles with more external conditions – of production, of patronage, of publication – but there are also conjunctions of the two planes. Cary's narrative (who would have guessed?) begins in 1938 and ends at the point of Hitler's occupation of the Polish Corridor in 1939. Although art history or literary history is not the same as history proper, Cary does not blink the relation of art to aggression on all sides – the artist's fight to execute his work, to profit from it, and yet not to be entrapped by patrons; the fight to realize what imagination presents as creative opportunity.

The fight for the realization of creative opportunity is imperative, no matter what it must answer for in the process. The war in art, as art, especially in light of Jimson's favored Biblical subjects, is a religious combat: against worldliness, and against reductive empirical understandings of reality. In another parallel with Joyce, Jimson's story is paired, like Stephen Dedalus's tale, with lyric verse; quotation of this verse in Jimson's mind becomes part of the novel's external narration. Mostly the quoted lines are from the Romantic poet William Blake's visionary epics. There is nothing theologically orthodox about them; one also might see them as surrealist or as links to Liddell's mystical James. Their visionary aspect, secret and detached from immediate sense-making, withdraws Jimson from politics, although one of his old pal comforters courts him for the workers' cause. But Jimson enacts rebellions and aggressions as if they are purely interpersonal, not political or ideological. He seems able to do this, because, as he advises a follower: "Getting up a grievance . . . is about the worst mistake anyone can make, especially if he has one. Get rid of that sense of justice, ... or you'll feel sorry for yourself, and then you'll soon be dead" (310). As for art's answering questions, "Talk is lies. The only satisfactory communication is a good picture. Neither true nor false. But created" (85).

In repeating what Jimson says, it is difficult not to sound as if one is reporting Cary's pronouncements about art, and not the words of a character in a fiction. That Cary's treatment of his matter makes the two things feel like one, even though they are two, is one of the comic effects of *The Horse's Mouth*. Its hero's dilemmas are of a like paradoxical order: he is simultaneously autonomous, yet utterly dependent. His humor, too, depends on interidentifying separate things. A nun counsels Jimson when he is dying to pray rather than laugh. He says that laughter and prayer are identical.

In the modernist era, Impressionist treatment makes two things, vision and words, seem like one, even though they are two. Over and over we see fiction matching some factual truth, and at the same time being only true to itself. In effect, art is eternally duplicitous, both avowing its identity with reality and disavowing it. Cary reminds us that there is something worthy of laughter in that self-contradictory phenomenon, even when the duplicity is brought to bear on sad and serious matter, such as global war. We might remember how Orwell seems to enjoy inventing newspeak – he attaches to *1984* an appendix expanding and explaining the language – even as he simultaneously expresses disgust at newspeak's outrage of truth. There is something funny about this, because of the fictive medium in which it occurs. Might we think of fiction, which is constitutionally prone to self-contradiction, as essentially comic? Punning, another version of one thing being two and yet not two, is the building block of Joyce's greatest modernist experiment, *Finnegans Wake* (1939). For the *Wake*, Joyce fabricated characters who are twin siblings, Shem and Shaun. Shaun continually derides his brother for treachery to what Shaun calls "matter of fict," whereas he himself is "the fanest of our truefalluses."[34] The puns remind us of the paradoxes – the intermingling of feigning and fact, of truth and fallacy – in which fictive–factive novels involve us.

The comedy of fiction, the comedy that is fiction, keeps on keeping on, in the medium of a wildly energetic rhetoric, in G. V. Desani's *All about H. Hatterr* (1948), auto-described (on its title page) as "human horseplay." It is supposedly a Scottish-Indian's autobiography, chronicling seven quests he has undertaken to seven sages in India. The pilgrim seeks from them wisdom that he can apply to his experience. Thus the story structure immediately attunes us to making two things a match. The quests all go farcically awry because the desired unities don't result. Nevertheless, the protagonist continues his effort at matchmaking, especially in his last adventure: this time to bring together narrative, language, and truth. The following is a sample of Hatterr's method and its results:

> ... Can words ever communicate *Truth* – whatever it is? ...
>
> A *Truth*-thing, or a *Truth*-idea might be an *a*. By the time a feller has a notion of this *a*., a sensation of it, its nature changes. What a feller has is not an *a* at all, but an awareness of an *a*. ...
>
> Now, if a feller has to communicate his own idea and awareness of this *a* – let's name it another *a* – to some feller, he has to use a word, a pointer, a shadowgraph, which might be a *b*. The message now is *a* (*Truth*) plus *a* (the notion of *Truth*), plus *b* (a word): *baa*. In other words, if a feller wants to tell another what *Truth-a* is like, he has to *aa* and *baa*![35]

"All communicated and communicable knowledge is subject to this bashing up," Hatterr concedes, "but I say, I know an *a* something. And I sum it up as *Life*" (275). And might we say that he also, in the course of his knowing, has formulated a *b* something, which sums up fiction: as the *aa*-ing and *baa*-ing that tells a reader a *Truth-a*, or, at least, a truthy *a*? An especially good Desani–Joycian word for it is *shadowgraph*. In such a word, which exemplifies what Hatterr calls his "rigmarole English" (37), the distance between Truth and its mediators suddenly closes up, if only momentarily. Surely *shadowgraph* precisely gives us word and thing at once: life's written shadow = fiction. The appearance of that sudden closure is one of fiction's customary effects, before the comedy of its disparate relation to fact and reality reappears.

Short Stories by Elizabeth Bowen and Angus Wilson

I have just emphasized the comic side of fiction. In the light of Joyce's and Desani's punning and twinning, however, we must address fiction's somber double, albeit without prejudice to its exuberant other half. Elizabeth Bowen and Angus Wilson give us the opportunity.

The distinguished fiction of the Anglo-Irish Bowen, whose career begins in the 1920s, finds perhaps its most powerful realization in her collection of stories about wartime, *The Demon Lover* (1945). Behind those stories lies Bowen's idea of fiction, as she expresses it (also in 1945) in "Notes on Writing a Novel." Fittingly for our coda, her idea recapitulates a characterization of fiction that prevails in the years we have surveyed: fiction has a nature of its own, despite its inmixing with other discourses. Given the dependence of the war stories on their historical reference, it is all the more notable that Bowen should claim the autonomy. One might say the same for a drive to autonomy that underlies the wartime and post-war stories of Bowen's young contemporary, Angus Wilson, whose work emerges at mid-century. We especially want to consider how Bowen and Wilson exemplify the idea of fiction's independence in light of the decidedly grim analysis with which both writers confront post-war hopes and realities.

Bowen's "Notes on Writing a Novel" immediately admits fiction's problematic claims to referential veracity. "The novel lies," Bowen says, "in saying something happened that did not. It must, therefore, contain uncontradictable truth, to warrant the original lie."[1] But "Truth by what ruling, in relation to what?" she asks. In relation to an external reality, we might expect the answer to be. Her answer is "Truth by the ruling of, and in relation to, the inherent poetic truth that the novel states" (44). It is not a transparent answer, to be sure, because the meaning of "inherent poetic truth" remains to be construed. It seems to mean one whose formulation and expression is freestanding, and is singular and specific, in each and every fiction. We might make such truth, once expressed, applicable to heteronomous uses, but those uses would be limited. For Bowen also says that "the essence of a poetic truth is that no statement of it can be final" (36). Moreover, poetic truth is,

247

"as it should be, impersonal. It will be, and (from the 'interest' point of view) will be able to stand being, pure of pre-assumptions – national, social, sexual, etc." (44–45).

That fiction should be impersonal, and that it should experiment with its topics pure of pre-assumption, is an idea that predates the 1939–1945 time span. Given *The Demon Lover*'s stories, however, it appears that Bowen sees the war's destructiveness as paradoxically initiating the purification of pre-assumptions that fiction exemplifies; making such purity desirable; and enabling fiction, by means of modernism's foregrounding of its character, to complete the process.

Impersonality, by definition, involves loss of identity. The war undermines stable personal selfhood in Bowen's stories, first by deranging the self's environments, then by hollowing its core. The partly bombed setting of *The Demon Lover*'s opening tale, "In the Square," is described as outwardly an "extinct scene"; the narrative, entering an intact building, likens its inside to a "functional anarchy."[2] The war accidentally has thrown together in the same London residence the wife of a man away on war duty with the same man's mistress. At present, however, the mistress is dismissing her lover, and the wife is taking one on. The irony of this scenario is intensified by the dazed atmosphere the characters inhabit. "Who would think that this was the same world" as that of a year or two ago, the wife asks. Individuation is also extinct: "One has nothing except one's feelings," the wife says; "Sometimes I think I hardly know myself" (615). Her nephew, representing the heirs of functional anarchy, wonders: "You think this place will patch up?" He is skeptical about prospective connections: "You can't get to anywhere from here" (614).

If "here" is where one knows one's self, then, in the absence of self, getting anywhere is difficult. In "Sunday Afternoon," an Irish adolescent, Maria, wants to get to London as an escape from neutral noncombatant Ireland. It does not matter to her that her countryman Henry, who has come from London to visit old friends, has lost in the Blitz everything that was his. Initially, it appears that the loss also does not matter to him. But as he is about to return to the destructive order, Henry panics. Suddenly wanting to recover his past, he warns Maria: "when you come away from here, . . . you will no longer be Maria. . . . You will have an identity number, but no identity." And yet, after he says "This is the end of *you*," he startlingly adds, "Perhaps it is just as well" (622).

Bowen's bold acceptance of such an idea subtends the pathos of it. Even more boldly, the stories suggest, it might be just as well if global conflict ends history as well as identity. That would be a purification relevant to pre-assumptions! The suggestion is voiced in "Ivy Gripped the Steps" by a beautiful widow, Mrs. Nicholson, the story's female protagonist. Initially her utterance seems near-witless. The widow is protesting – in 1910 – a bellicose naval admiral's forecast of war against Germany. War belongs to history, she agrees; but "After all, we live in the present day! History is quite far back; . . . it does seem silly. I never even cared for history at school; I was glad when we came to the end of it" (696). Asserting that past humanity seems an alien species, she thinks that the only reason for studying history is that "one sees how long it has taken to make the world nice" (696). Her naivety is patent; nevertheless, almost every narrative in Bowen's collection implies the gladness of coming "to the end of it."

History is, after all, the grip of the past on the present that has led to the new catastrophic outward order. It is the demon lover, both a material and a spectral reality, so there is no wonder that fiction – the shadowgraph! – has a share in it, and might well be purified of its weight. The weight of history's self-contradictory nature is forcibly illustrated in "Ivy Gripped the Steps." History does not come to an end there, and yet it does. It would be just as well if it did end without any qualifying doubleness, but its involvement with eros complicates assessment. Mrs. Nicholson and her Admiral Concannon are part of an odd love triangle. The Admiral is married, and Mrs. Nicholson acts seductively toward him; his wife, however, is not the third party. Instead, the third party is Gavin, a mere boy. When Gavin is eight years old, Mrs. Nicholson, a friend of his mother, offers him a holiday at her home in Southstone, a Channel resort. In visiting her, Gavin escapes from his parents' Midlands farm, where financial crisis is continuous, and where "history's ever stopping" (697) is unlikely. Southstone and the widow seem to the boy to be beyond history (London, distant and invisible, is the source of Southstone's material life); for him, the town and the woman belong to a "fairy tale," a "magical artificiality." The beautiful widow, and the magical escape from home, cause "the knife of love" (690) to enter Gavin's heart. As a result of the concatenation of history, magic, and "the knife," Gavin becomes a variant of a demon lover, as does Mrs. Nicholson.

Death claimed her in 1912, when Gavin was ten. Two wars later, with peace in the offing, he makes a memorial pilgrimage to Southstone. He sees it as having an "air of concluded meaning," a place where "history . . . had come to a full stop" (709). That apparently would make Mrs. Nicholson glad. Yet it is Gavin's history that has been arrested. Since his time with her, his "assets of feeling remained . . . frozen" (703), the narrative reveals. Because she set her sights on the Admiral, she did not pay attention to the danger implicit in the boy's obsession. Indeed she made him, to the point of scandal, a substitute for a grown-up escort. He proudly took on that role, although he underwent

"Despair, the idea that his doom must be never, never to reach her, ... gripped him" (694). Crisis struck when by chance he overheard the Admiral, rejecting Mrs. Nicholson's advances, scold her for "making a ninny of that unfortunate boy," and she responded by comparing "poor funny little Gavin" to a pet dog (707). In the ensuing decades Gavin solicits many love affairs, yet his first love blocks his development. The end of Bowen's story envisions him, despite the advance of time, as "a whole stopped mechanism for feeling," spectral, "someone wolfish" (711).

The stopping of Gavin's history is, in his case, deadly. The not stopping of history is, in the world's case, deadly. In the time covered by the story, the narrative reminds us, war, which in *The Demon Lover* is synonymous with history, realizes "twice over ... the Admiral's alternative to love" (710). But as history wars on love, history also explodes itself. Willy-nilly, its destruction continues the purification of pre-assumptions: about love, about reality. It does so in "The Happy Autumn Fields," wherein two historical times – the Regency and the Blitz – and two separate stories become unmoored from certainty about which is "real." The Regency story is like a demon lover capturing Mary, a woman whose Blitzed house is being dismantled while she clings to the possibility of belonging to the earlier era. Her identity dissolves – she thinks of "the grotesquerie of being saddled with [her] body and lover" (677), her fiancé. She is attracted above all to a pair of sisters in the Regency narrative who are quasi-incestuously fused. When one is about to marry, the other is granted a wish that the fiancé will die. Magic weds the sisters to each other. Mary, enlisting the destruction wrought by the Blitz as an opportunity for her to make history come to its end, not only turns her back on the present (however real or unreal), but also reaches for an eros that transgresses the marital form she has engaged herself to. She finds it "just as well" to identify with violators of a taboo that, supposedly founding human order, germinates "history."

Bowen riskily posits Mary's extremity as the alternative to which real history has propelled humanity. Initiated by war, Mary's loss of identity, her leap out of time, her transgression lead to an altogether fantastical realm, with fiction at its core. "Mysterious Kôr," another story in *The Demon Lover*, continues to explore the possibilities of a desire to inhabit a dimension in which romance or magic is real – and autonomous. Pepita, one of the story's two female protagonists, imagines, and believes in, the supernatural actuality of Kôr, a moonlit and magical "city with no history" (729), out of this world. The war drives her imagination onward. Her soldier-boyfriend, Arthur, is skeptical about Kôr. In response Pepita declares, "If you can blow whole places out of existence, you can blow whole places into it" (730). That would be the new way to continue history – and to scour and rout pre-assumptions! Fiction blows new places into history! What attracts Pepita to Kôr is that it can't be found and marked on a map. Maps mean for her a conquest of the unknown by "civilization." Pepita hates civilization, because global war occurs in its name, and in humanity's name. She has no patience with "people." "Think about people?" she asks Arthur. "How can anyone think about people if they've got any heart?" She means that "people" have been proved heartless by the fact of the world's universal aggression.

Arthur tries to understand Pepita's visionary yearning for Kôr without dismissing it. He talks about Pepita with her roommate, Callie, who is Pepita's opposite number: callowly sentimental about love and life. Arthur tells her that the idea of Kôr has made him unsure of his real whereabouts. But he defends his uncertainty. He and Pepita feel that they have no place in their deranged world, so "why not want Kôr, as a start? There are no restrictions on wanting." But Kôr, as Pepita imagines it, contains no "humanity." Callie protests: "Can't wanting want what's human?" Arthur's answer: "To be human's to be at a dead loss'" (739). His answer is consonant with all the narratives in *The Demon Lover*, where the war has put humanity at a dead loss. How to live without humanity, what we are to want, and what a post-human condition might be are presented as yet to be articulated. But in the lying fictive place, new imaginations (no matter how transgressive) have already begun to emerge, inhumanly free of history and its wars. At the end of "Mysterious Kôr," Pepita is asleep. In her dreams, we are told, "it was to Kôr's finality that she turned" (740). This final turn makes "finality" ambiguous; it inscribes ending and starting again.

Bowen borrows Kôr from H. Rider Haggard, whose "imperial romance" *She* (1886) inspired her to write, according to her 1947 BBC broadcast about that novel. Pepita's devotion to Kôr's world-negating moonlight echoes Ursula's moon-inspired destruction of Skrebensky and society in *The Rainbow*. Just as Bowen's "notes" on novel-writing are apposite to perspectives we have traversed, the imagination that makes it possible for her to enlist the horror of war on the side of a steely scientific romance-like vision of hope is the sign of a modernist tradition. The vision does not suit assumptions that "the 'interest' point of view" – "national, social, sexual, etc." – is, or should be, inescapable, that impersonality and the end of history are unacceptable as well as implausible.

But even readers on the side of impersonality and its et ceteras will be made uncomfortable by the severity of Angus Wilson's version of fiction's standing pure of pre-assumptions. In historical–biographical fact, Wilson avidly attached himself – impurely, as it were – to the Labor Party, to the welfare state, and, most radically, to the cause of gay liberation. On those bases one might expect from him narratives whose pre-assumptions endorse constructive collective experience. Yet in the title story of *Such Darling Dodos* (1950), Wilson stands back from the "interest" point of view to sharply painful effect. The narrative presents as terminally out of date a married couple of tireless Laborites, who have struggled for decades on behalf of the welfare state's "sickness benefits and secure old age and ... the just wage,"[3] as well as on behalf of better sanitation, better bathrooms, and better refrigerators. Wilson's picture of them fading into extinction (no men or women in new clothes!) is made more puzzling by Wilson's choice of a principal focalizer, through whom we are forced to see the dodos. He is an elderly gay man whose epicene bitchiness and aestheticized approach to religion are scarcely appealing – a souring of the tradition of Wilde, Firbank, and Waugh's Ambrose. The younger generation's representatives in the story are no more likable. Their leading characteristic, smugness, dismisses progressive politics: it's over, they say, because it was "sentimentalism of a rather dangerous kind" (173). History doesn't concern them: without feeling the conflicts about it that Bowen's characters feel, secure in the material moment, they merely dismiss the past.

Wilson's motive for his version of impersonal presentation might be his conviction that, whatever progressive ideology's achievement by 1950, it only veneers continuing class antagonisms. The stories must exhibit the deceptive surface if they mean to be disinterested reports of contemporary life, as one expects of fictional realism. Nevertheless, lest we think that "Such Darling Dodos" "really" means us to be on the side of the extinct creatures, however weak they are (*that* might well be dangerous sentimentalism), we should keep in mind Wilson's "A Flat Country Christmas" (1950). This story, which seems to stamp all post-war planning negatively, is about a former army man in a new suit. "[A] Technical Officer at the Ministry and about to take an Honours degree" [302], he is dedicated to post-war new towns and upward mobility. He participates in an annual Christmas reunion party of army friends and their wives, a group that "felt justly proud of the emancipation from class that they had achieved both in marriage and friendship, but, though they had no wish to live on sentiment and memory [of the now-distant days in the Forces], these were the only cement [of] the fortress they had constructed against loneliness" (304). But the fortress is crumbling. During a Christmas party game in which the players use a mirror as a substitute for a crystal ball, the Technical Officer sees "Nothing" ahead for him. The vision matches the shakiness on which the post-war life depicted in the story is built, and which the new-made man represses until this moment. He tries to cover up the applicability of the bitter prospect to his wife and his friends, but for Wilson they all face a void. The values the past afforded them are gone, the present builds on quicksand, and no attractive replacement for either seems to be in sight.

This is Wilson's version of humanity's being at a dead loss. But whereas Bowen imagines autonomous Kôr and autonomous fiction as the land of new articulations of life, however post-human, Wilson detaches himself even from "interest" on behalf of his art. Fiction in Wilson's stories is no creative alternative space; like any other human activity, it stimulates nastiness and derangement. In "A Visit in Bad Taste," a married couple is allowing the wife's brother, who has been in jail for "offences against children," to stay with them until he gets on his feet. He desperately wants a second chance, but his sister can't bear his presence. It was fiction that temporarily disposed her to tolerate him: she had attended his trial because "'I had to suffer it all. . . . But that Dostoevskian mood is over" (97). On this showing, fiction only affords its consumer an opportunity for self-centered posing. It does worse in "Necessity's Child," whose thirteen-year-old narrator takes refuge in Melville's and Stevenson's tales of adventure as an escape from his mother's neglect, but then uses his reading as a form of sadism. After discussing novels with a kindly elderly couple whom he encounters by chance, he makes up a fiction of his own: he tells his guardian that the couple exposed him to pornography, and proposed sexual relations.

In "Raspberry Jam," the imaginative realm of novelists leads to grotesque violence. The story's eleven-year-old protagonist is, his father fears, "a sissy" (109) because his "world was a strange compound of the adult world . . . and a book world composed from Grimm, the Arabian nights, natural history books, and more recently the novels of Dickens and Jane Austen. His imagination was taken by anything strange" (107). A pair of eccentric sisters in his village realizes for him the strangeness of fiction. They also believe that "peculiarities were nothing to be ashamed of, indeed were often a matter of pride" (109). Johnnie lives for his visits with them. Unfortunately, the village is hostile; unfortunately, the sisters are alcoholics. At a moment in which they are feeling especially persecuted, and have been on a binge, Johnny calls. They have meant to offer him raspberries with his tea, but they discover that birds have consumed the fruit. Furious, they capture a bullfinch, and – as retribution for what they take to be the bird's offense to the boy – blind the live creature and eviscerate it before Johnnie's eyes. Reacting in horror, Johnnie compounds their violence, and puts an end to the bird's misery by trampling on it. Is this where fiction can lead because it supports an appetite for strangeness?

We might think of Wilson's inculpation of his very medium as a dishonor to the ideas of fiction we have examined or, indeed, as an initiation of a new "period" of literary history definable by fiction's cession of claims to being a discourse of its own. But one might also think of even Wilson's criticism as another instance of the novelist's refusal of "pre-assumption." If a writer of novels and stories is to respect his or her work for its "poetic truth," if that is to involve "impersonality," he or she must present fiction itself in a distanced way, probingly, without a prejudgment of fiction's virtue or power – just as the writer must present his or her sense of history, or political sympathies and antipathies, in a distanced way. The suspense of attachments is a tenet we've seen modernists and anti-modernists equally respect.

Fiction, one might say, is the discursive place or space where such distance, even a critical self-distance, is achieved. That is the gist of *Why Do I Write?* (1948), an exchange of letters among Bowen, Graham Greene, and the novelist V. S. Pritchett, in which they respond to the demand, perhaps intensified by the birth of the welfare state's communal aims, for the historical and political accountability of fiction. "What fools writers make of themselves in public life," Pritchett says, sounding a note of resistance to the very question. In laying aside imaginative work for pronouncements about a cause, Pritchett goes on, writers become the equivalent of "an imperialist, expansionist group," moving beyond "the native frontiers of [their] knowledge and capacity."[4]

Pritchett's correspondents are less vehement, but they, too, believe in the writer's self-containment. "My writing ... may be a substitute for something I have been born without – a so-called relation to society," Bowen confesses. "My books *are* my relation to society. Why should people come and ask me what the nature of this relation is?" (23). That they do ask, she continues, means that what they most desire is "shape, relation, direction" – precisely what narrative fiction depends on in its formal treatment of material. The requests seem impatient of reading the writing, but they are on the track of why persons read as well as write. "Even stories which end in futility" – her stories? Wilson's? – "imply that men or women are too big or good for the futility in which they are involved. Even to objectify futility" – to shape representations of it – "is something" (25).

Whatever the formal objectification might be, the shaping depends upon detachment. For Greene, that means, no matter which groups the fiction-writer belongs to, that he or she must claim "the privilege of disloyalty" to the group. It is a privilege, Greene says, "you will never get society to recognise." But, because "Literature has nothing to do with edification," it will always draw upon "the personal morality of an individual" – of the individual author, or of a character shaped for purposes of poetic truth – that "is seldom identical with the morality of the group to which [author or character] belongs" (32). Bowen has the last word in the exchange. There will always be conflict, she believes; a "conflictless Better World" (56) will never exist. The closer it might come into existence, "the artist – particularly the writer, as the most comprehensible – will take on the stature of a Resistance leader" (56). Nevertheless, the relation between fiction writer and society remains "a thing of great possibilities and various flaws." Meanwhile, Bowen concludes, "We envisage, we are not passive, and we are not contributing to anarchy: that may be the most to be claimed for us" (58).

Notes

Chapter 1: British Narrative Fiction in Terms of "Period" and "Treatments"

1 Elinor Glyn, *Three Weeks* (New York: Duffield & Company, 1907), 194.
2 H. G. Wells, *Ann Veronica: A Modern Love Story* (New York: Boni and Liveright, 1909), 349.
3 Violet Hunt, *White Rose of Weary Leaf* (New York: Brentano's, 1908), 91. Hereafter cited parenthetically.
4 Elizabeth von Arnim, *The Pastor's Wife* (London: J. M. Dent, 1993), 303. Hereafter cited parenthetically.
5 Arthur Morrison, *The Hole in the Wall* (Woodbridge, UK: Boydell Press, 1982), 33.
6 Rudyard Kipling, *The Day's Work, Part I* (New York: Charles Scribner's Sons, 1889), 95.
7 Samuel Butler, *The Way of All Flesh* (New York, NY: Modern Library, 1950), 3. Hereafter cited parenthetically.
8 George Moore, *The Brook Kerith* (New York, NY: Macmillan Company, 1916), 366. Hereafter cited parenthetically.
9 George Meredith, *Celt and Saxon* (London, UK: Constable, 1910), 23. Hereafter cited parenthetically.

Interchapter 1: James Joyce's *A Portrait of the Artist as a Young Man* (1916)

1 James Joyce, *A Portrait of the Artist as a Young Man*, ed. John Paul Riquelme (New York, NY/London, UK: W. W. Norton & Company, 2007), 97. Hereafter cited parenthetically.

Chapter 2: The Artist as Critic

1 Oscar Wilde, *Complete Works* (London/Glasgow: Collins, 1967), 988. Hereafter cited parenthetically.

2 Joseph Conrad, "Preface" to *The Nigger of the* Narcissus: *A Tale of the Sea*, ed. Allan H. Stape (Cambridge: Cambridge University Press, 2017), 7. Hereafter cited parenthetically.

3 Percy Lubbock, *The Craft of Fiction* (New York: Peter Smith, 1947), 170.

4 Henry James, *The Art of the Novel: Critical Prefaces* (New York: Charles Scribner's Sons, 1934), 312. Hereafter cited parenthetically.

5 Ford Madox Ford, *Henry James: A Critical Study* (New York: Octagon Books, 1964), 9. Hereafter cited parenthetically.

6 Ford Madox Ford, *Joseph Conrad: A Personal Remembrance* (Boston: Little, Brown, and Company, 1924), vi. Hereafter cited parenthetically.

7 E. M. Forster, *Aspects of the Novel* (Harmondsworth, UK: Penguin Books, 1962), 28. Hereafter cited parenthetically.

8 D. H. Lawrence, *The Letters of D. H. Lawrence*, Vol. II, June 1913–October 1916 ed. George Zytaruk and James T. Boulton (Cambridge: Cambridge University Press, 1979), 182–184.

9 D. H. Lawrence, *Phoenix: The Posthumous Papers of D. H. Lawrence*, ed. Edward D. McDonald (London: William Heineman Ltd., 1936), 537. Hereafter cited parenthetically.

10 D. H. Lawrence, *Studies in Classic American Literature* [1929–1934], ed. Ezra Greenspan, Lindeth Vasey, and John Worthen (Cambridge: Cambridge University Press, 2003), 19, 55.

11 Virginia Woolf, *Collected Essays,* Vol. 4, 1925–1928, ed. Andrew McNeillie (London: Hogarth Press, 1994), 462.

12 Virginia Woolf, *A Room of One's Own* and *Three Guineas*, ed. Morag Shiach (Oxford: Oxford University Press, 1992), 119. Hereafter cited parenthetically.

13 Virginia Woolf, *The Common Reader, First and Second Series* (New York: Harcourt, Brace and Company, 1948), 212.

14 Virginia Woolf, *Collected Essays*, Vol. 3, 1919–1924, ed. Andrew McNeillie (London: Hogarth Press, 1994), 427.

15 Virginia Woolf, *Granite and Rainbow* (New York/London: Harcourt Brace Jovanovich, 1958), 18. Hereafter cited parenthetically.

16 Rebecca West, *The Strange Necessity* (London: Jonathan Cape, 1928), 14–5. Hereafter cited parenthetically.

17 Vernon Lee, *Gospels of Anarchy* (New York: Brentano's, 1909), 15. Hereafter cited parenthetically.

18 Wyndham Lewis, *Time and Western Man*, ed. Paul Edwards (Santa Rosa, CA: Black Sparrow Press, 1992), 133. Hereafter cited parenthetically.

19 Wyndham Lewis, *Men without Art*, ed. Seamus Cooney (Santa Rosa, CA: Black Sparrow Press, 1994), 183. Hereafter cited parenthetically.

20 Laura Riding, *Anarchism Is Not Enough*, ed. Lisa Samuels (Berkeley: University of California Press, 2001), 44. Hereafter cited parenthetically.

21 Laura Riding, *Progress of Stories* (New York: Dial Press, 1982), xviii.

22 H. G. Wells, *Boon, The Mind of the Race, The Wild Asses of the Devil, and The Last Trump* (London: T. Fisher Unwin, 1915), 57. Hereafter cited parenthetically.

23 H. G. Wells, *Experiment in Autobiography* (Philadelphia/New York: J. B. Lippincott, 1967), 417. Hereafter cited parenthetically.

24 Ralph Fox, "Review of Wells's Experiment in Autobiography," *Left Review* 1:3 (December 1934), 91.

25 Ralph Fox, *The Novel and the People* (New York: International Publishers, 1937), 12–13. Hereafter cited parenthetically.

26 *The C. L. R. James Reader*, ed. Anna Grimshaw (Oxford: Blackwell, 1992), 325.

27 G. K. Chesterton, *Orthodoxy: The Romance of Faith* (New York: Doubleday, 1990), 95–96. Hereafter cited parenthetically.

28 G. K. Chesterton, *Robert Louis Stevenson* (New York: Sheed and Ward, 1955), 167. Hereafter cited parenthetically.

29 W. Somerset Maugham, *The Summing Up*, in *The Maugham Reader* (Garden City, NY: Doubleday & Company, 1950), 622. Hereafter cited parenthetically.

30 Samuel Beckett, "Dante ... Bruno ... Vico ... Joyce," in *An Examination of* Work in Progress (New York: New Directions, 1962), 13. Hereafter cited parenthetically.

31 Rose Macaulay, *The Writings of E. M. Forster* (London: Hogarth Press, 1938), 282. Hereafter cited parenthetically.

32 Cyril Connolly, *Enemies of Promise* (Chicago: University of Chicago Press, 2008), 27. Hereafter cited parenthetically.

33 Christopher Isherwood, *Lions and Shadows* (New York: Pegasus, 1969), 7. Hereafter cited parenthetically.

Interchapter 2: Joseph Conrad, Ford Madox Ford, and Virginia Woolf

1 Joseph Conrad, "Preface" to *The Nigger of the* Narcissus: *A Tale of the Sea*, ed. Allan H. Stape (Cambridge: Cambridge University Press, 2017), 102. Hereafter cited parenthetically.

2 Ford Madox Ford, *Joseph Conrad: A Personal Remembrance* (Boston: Little, Brown, and Company, 1924), 204.

3 Ford Madox Ford, *A Man Could Stand Up –* , in *Parade's End* (New York: Vintage Books, 1961), 583. Hereafter cited parenthetically.

4 Virginia Woolf, *The Waves* (Orlando, FL: Harcourt, 1959), 144–145. Hereafter cited parenthetically.

Chapter 3: Seeing Modernism Through

1 H. G. Wells, *Mr. Britling Sees It Through* (New York: Macmillan Company, 1917), 440. Hereafter cited parenthetically.

2 George Gissing, *The Nether World* (London: Everyman's Library, 1973), 1.

3 Wyndham Lewis, *The Complete Wild Body*, ed. Bernard Lafourcade (Santa Barbara, CA: Black Sparrow Press, 1982), 77. Hereafter cited parenthetically.

4 May Sinclair, *The Life and Death of Harriet Frean* (Harmondsworth, UK: Penguin Books/Virago Press, 1986), 58.

5 Storm Jameson, *Women against Men* (Harmondsworth, UK: Penguin Books/Virago Press, 1985), 92. Hereafter cited parenthetically.

6 Jean Rhys, *Quartet*, in *The Complete Novels* (New York: W. W. Norton & Company, 1985), 169. Hereafter cited parenthetically.

7 Dorothy Richardson, *Pilgrimage 2* (New York: Popular Library, 1976), 222. Hereafter cited parenthetically.

8 Ellen Wilkinson, *Clash* (London: Virago Press, 1989), 149.

9 Arnold Bennett, *The Card* (Harmondsworth, UK: Penguin Classics, 1991), 219.

10 Fredric Manning, *The Middle Parts of Fortune* (New York: St. Martin's Press, 1977), 182.

11 Mulk Raj Anand, *Untouchable* (Harmondsworth, UK: Penguin Books, 1940), 9.

12 Joyce Cary, *Mr. Johnson* (New York: New Directions, 1989), 167. Hereafter cited parenthetically.

13 Wilkinson, *Clash*, 238. Hereafter cited parenthetically.

14 Lewis Grassic Gibbon, *Cloud Howe*, ed. Tom Crawford, in *A Scots Quair* (Edinburgh: Canongate, 1990), 210. Hereafter cited parenthetically.

15 Lewis Grassic Gibbon, *Grey Granite*, in *A Scots Quair* (Edinburgh: Canongate, 1990), 181.

16 Henry Green, *Living* in *Loving, Living, Party-Going* (Harmondsworth, UK: Penguin Books, 1978), 207. Hereafter cited parenthetically.

17 Marmaduke Pickthall, *Veiled Women* (New York: Duffield and Company, 1913), 123.

18 Rudyard Kipling, *Kim* (Harmondsworth, UK: Penguin Books, 2011), 283. Hereafter cited parenthetically.

19 E. M. Forster, *A Passage to India* (New York/London/Toronto: Everyman's Library, 1991), 111. Hereafter cited parenthetically.

20 William Plomer, *Turbott Wolfe* (Oxford: Oxford University Press, 1985), 123. Hereafter cited parenthetically.

21 Ronald Firbank, *The Flower beneath the Foot*, in *Five Novels* (New York: New Directions, 1981), 1. Hereafter cited parenthetically.

22 J. C. Powys, *A Glastonbury Romance* (Woodstock, NY: Overlook Press, 1987), 709. Hereafter cited parenthetically.

23 J. R. R. Tolkien, *The Hobbit* (New York: Ballantine Books, 1973), 272. Hereafter cited parenthetically.

24 Samuel Beckett, *Murphy* (New York: Grove Press, 1957), 52. Hereafter cited parenthetically.

25 Flann O'Brien, *At Swim-Two-Birds* (New York: New American Library, 1966), 9. Hereafter cited parenthetically.

26 H. G. Wells, *The Shape of Things to Come* (Harmondsworth, UK: Penguin Books, 2003), 393. Hereafter cited parenthetically.

Interchapter 3: Short Stories by Rudyard Kipling and Katherine Mansfield

1 Rudyard Kipling, *A Diversity of Creatures* (London: Macmillan and Co., 1917), 27. Hereafter cited parenthetically.
2 Katherine Mansfield, *The Garden Party and Other Stories* in *The Collected Stories* (Harmondsworth, UK: Penguin Books, 1981), 247. Hereafter cited parenthetically.

Chapter 4: British Fiction amid Nonfictional Discourses in the Era of Modernism

1 R. G. Collingwood, *The Principles of Art* (Oxford: Oxford University Press, 1972), 331, 333. Hereafter cited parenthetically.
2 D. H. Lawrence, *The Rainbow*, ed. Mark Kinkead-Weekes (Cambridge: Cambridge University Press, 1989). Hereafter cited parenthetically.
3 W. H. R. Rivers, *Instinct and the Unconscious* (Cambridge: Cambridge University Press, 1922), 34–35.
4 Bronislaw Malinowski, *The Sexual Life of Savages* (New York: Harcourt, Brace & World, 1929), 3. Hereafter cited parenthetically.
5 Bronislaw Malinowski, *Sex and Repression in Savage Society* (Cleveland/New York: World Publishing Company, 1969), 55.
6 Jane Ellen Harrison, *Epilegomena to the Study of Greek Religion* and *Themis: A Study of the Social Origins of Greek Religion* (New Hyde Park, NY: University Books, 1977), xxv. Hereafter cited parenthetically.
7 Melanie Klein, "Early Stages of the Oedipus Conflict" (1928) in *Love, Guilt and Reparation & Other Works 1921–1945* (New York: Free Press, 1975), 191.
8 Naomi Mitchison, *The Corn King and the Spring Queen* (New York: Soho Press, 1989), 641. Hereafter cited parenthetically.
9 Ivy Compton-Burnett, *Brothers and Sisters* (London: Victor Gollancz, 1967), 170. Hereafter cited parenthetically.
10 Aldous Huxley, *After Many a Summer Dies the Swan* (New York: Harper & Row, 1983), 26. Hereafter cited parenthetically.
11 John Masefield, *Multitude and Solitude* (Garden City, NY: Garden City Publishing, 1909), 26. Hereafter cited parenthetically.
12 Sir James Jeans, *The Mysterious Universe* (New York: Macmillan Company, 1930), 86. Hereafter cited parenthetically.
13 A. S. Eddington, *The Nature of the Physical World* (New York: Macmillan Company, 1930), 228. Hereafter cited parenthetically.
14 J. B. S. Haldane, *The Causes of Evolution* (Ithaca, NY: Cornell University Press, 1966), 170. Hereafter cited parenthetically.

15 J. B. S. Haldane, *The Marxist Philosophy and the Sciences* (New York: Random House, 1939), 14.

16 Bertrand Russell, *The Scientific Outlook* (London/New York: Routledge, 2009), 36. Hereafter cited parenthetically.

Interchapter 4: British Fiction's Ideas of History, 1923–1946

1 R. G. Collingwood, *The Idea of History*, revised edition, ed. Jan Van Der Dussen (Oxford: Oxford University Press, 1994), 193. Hereafter cited parenthetically.

2 Lytton Strachey, *Elizabeth and Essex: A Tragic History* (San Diego: Harcourt Brace Jovanovich, 1956), 217. Hereafter cited parenthetically.

3 Rose Macaulay, *Told by an Idiot* (Garden City, NY: Doubleday and Co., 1983), 11. Hereafter cited parenthetically.

4 George Orwell, *Homage to Catalonia* (San Diego: Harcourt Brace Jovanovich, 1952), 50. Hereafter cited parenthetically.

5 Ralph Bates, *Sirocco and Other Stories* (New York: Random House, 1939), 225. Hereafter cited parenthetically.

6 Wyndham Lewis, *The Revenge for Love*, ed. Reed Way Dasenbrock (Santa Rosa, CA: Black Sparrow Press, 1991), 112. Hereafter cited parenthetically.

Chapter 5: Entertaining Fictions

1 John Buchan, *Prester John* (McLean, VA: Indypublish.com, n.d.), 56, 86, 166.

2 H. Rider Haggard, *She and Allan* (New York: Ballantine Books, 1978), 2.

3 A. E. W. Mason, *The Four Feathers* (Harmondsworth: Penguin Books, 2001), p. 277.

4 Arthur Conan Doyle, *Sherlock Holmes: The Complete Novels and Stories, Volume I* (New York: Bantam Books, 1986), 16. Hereafter cited parenthetically (as *I*).

5 Arthur Conan Doyle, *Sherlock Holmes: The Complete Novels and Stories, Volume II* (New York: Bantam Books, 1986), 462. Hereafter cited parenthetically (as *II*).

6 Erskine Childers, *The Riddle of the Sands* (Harmondsworth, UK: Penguin Books, 1978), 18, 110, 146, 295.

7 Agatha Christie, *Murder on the Orient Express* (New York: HarperCollins, 2011), 23, 253.

8 Agatha Christie, *A Murder Is Announced* (New York: Harper Collins, 2011), 42. Hereafter cited parenthetically.

9 Dorothy Sayers, *Strong Poison* (London: Folio Society, 1998), 4.

10 Dorothy Sayers, *Gaudy Night* (New York: Harper & Row, 1986), 198. Hereafter cited parenthetically.

11 Dorothy Sayers, *Murder Must Advertise* (New York: Harper & Row, 1986), 227.

12 John Buchan, *Mr. Standfast* in *The Four Adventures of Richard Hannay* (Boston: David R. Godine, 1998), 273. Hereafter cited parenthetically.

13 Joseph Conrad, *Under Western Eyes* (New York: Modern Library, 2001), 27.

14 W. Somerset Maugham, *Ashenden* (Harmondsworth, UK: Penguin, 1977), 93. Hereafter cited parenthetically.

15 Eric Ambler, *The Mask of Demetrios* (London: Hodder & Staughton, 1939), 34. Hereafter cited parenthetically.

16 P. G. Wodehouse, *Leave It to Psmith* (New York: Vintage Books, 1975), 22. Hereafter cited parenthetically.

17 P. G. Wodehouse, *Joy in the Morning*, in *Just Enough Jeeves* (New York: W. W. Norton & Company, 2010), 205. Hereafter cited parenthetically.

18 Max Beerbohm, *Zuleika Dobson* (London: Folio Society, 2008), 58. Hereafter cited parenthetically.

19 Saki, *When William Came*, in *The Penguin Complete Saki* (Harmondsworth, UK: Penguin Books, 1982), 732. Hereafter cited parenthetically.

20 Stella Gibbons, *Cold Comfort Farm* (Harmondsworth, UK: Penguin Books, 1996), 9. Hereafter cited parenthetically.

21 Norman Douglas, *South Wind* (New York: Dodd, Mead & Company, 1935), 86–87, 215. Hereafter cited parenthetically.

22 Compton Mackenzie, *Extraordinary Women* (New York: Macy-Masius, Vanguard Press, 1928), 41. Hereafter cited parenthetically.

23 Nancy Mitford, *The Pursuit of Love* and *Love in a Cold Climate* (Harmondsworth, UK: Penguin Books, 1980), 410. Hereafter cited parenthetically.

24 Arthur Machen, *Hieroglyphics* (London: Martin Secker, 1912), 96.

25 Arthur Machen, *The Hill of Dreams* (London: Richards Press, 1954), 145. Hereafter cited parenthetically.

26 Lord Dunsany, *The King of Elfland's Daughter* (New York: Random House Publishing Group, 1999), 219.

27 Hope Mirrlees, *Lud-in-the-Mist* (London: Millennium, 2000), 13. Hereafter cited parenthetically.

28 Sylvia Townsend Warner, *Lolly Willowes* (Chicago: Cassandra Editions, 1979), 239. Hereafter cited parenthetically.

29 Forrest Reid, *Uncle Stephen* (London: Gay Men's Press, 1988), 76. Hereafter cited parenthetically.

30 Bram Stoker, *Dracula* (Harmondsworth, UK: Penguin Books, 1993), 413. Hereafter cited parenthetically.

31 Walter De la Mare, *Short Stories 1895–1926*, ed. Giles De la Mare (London: DLM, 1996), 196. Hereafter cited parenthetically.

32 M. R. James, *The Collected Ghost Stories* (London: Folio Society, 2007), 178. Hereafter cited parenthetically.

33 Hugh Walpole, *Portrait of a Man with Red Hair* (New York: George H. Doran Company, 1925), 127. Hereafter cited parenthetically.

34 G. K. Chesterton, *The Man Who Was Thursday* (Harmondsworth, UK: Penguin Books, 1986), 12, 23. Hereafter cited parenthetically.

35 T. F. Powys, *The Only Penitent* (London: Chatto & Windus, 1931), 56–57.

36 Charles Williams, *Many Dimensions* (Grand Rapids, MI: William B. Eerdmans, 1970), 35. Hereafter cited parenthetically.

37 W. H. Hudson, *Green Mansions* (New York: Modern Library, 1944), 113.

38 Fr. Rolfe (Baron Corvo), *Hadrian the Seventh* (London: Chatto & Windus, 1959), 127. Hereafter cited parenthetically.

39 David Lindsay, *A Voyage to Arcturus* (New York: Ballantine Books, 1963), 214. Hereafter cited parenthetically.

40 James Stephens, *The Crock of Gold* (New York: Macmillan, 1947), 45. Hereafter cited parenthetically.

41 T. H. White, *The Once and Future King* (New York: Ace Books, 1987), 448. Hereafter cited parenthetically.

Interchapter 5: Entertainments: Graham Greene, E. F. Benson, and Olaf Stapledon

1 Graham Greene, *Orient Express: An Entertainment* (Harmondsworth, UK: Penguin Books, 2004), 51. Hereafter cited parenthetically.

2 Joseph Conrad, *The Secret Agent*, ed. Peter Lancelot Mallios (New York: Modern Library, 2004), 250.

3 E. F. Benson, *The Complete Mapp and Lucia*, Volume Two (Ware, UK: Wordsworth Classics, 2011), 151. Hereafter cited parenthetically.

4 Olaf Stapledon, *Star Maker*, in *First and Last Men* and *Star Maker* (New York: Dover Publications, 1968), 255. Hereafter cited parenthetically.

Chapter 6: Collective Welfare and Warfare

1 David Jones, *In Parenthesis* (New York: Viking Press, 1963), xvii. Hereafter cited parenthetically.

2 Virginia Woolf, *Three Guineas* (San Diego: Harcourt Brace Jovanovich, 1966), 85. Hereafter cited parenthetically.

3 Winifred Holtby, *South Riding* (New York: Macmillan Company, 1936), v–vi. Hereafter cited parenthetically.

4 Lettice Cooper, *National Provincial* (New York: Macmillan Company, 1938), 27. Hereafter cited parenthetically.

5 James Barke, *Major Operation* (London: Collins, 1955), 491.

6 Mulk Raj Anand, *The Big Heart* (London: Hutchinson International Authors, n.d.), 136. Hereafter cited parenthetically.

7 George Orwell, *The Lion and the Unicorn: Socialism and English Genius* (London: Secker & Warburg, 1962), 73. Hereafter cited parenthetically.

8 William Beveridge, *Social Insurance and Allied Services* (New York: Macmillan Company, 1942), 6. Hereafter cited parenthetically.

9   John Maynard Keynes, *The Collected Writings*, Vol. XXVII, ed. Donald Moggridge (Cambridge: Macmillan/Cambridge University Press, 1980), 255.

10 John Maynard Keynes, *The Collected Writings*, Vol. XXVIII, ed. Donald Moggridge (Cambridge: Macmillan/Cambridge University Press, 1982), 32–33. Hereafter cited parenthetically.

11 F. A. Hayek, *The Road to Serfdom, The Collected Works*, Vol. II, ed. Bruce Caldwell (Chicago: University of Chicago Press, 2007), 166. Hereafter cited parenthetically.

12 Rex Warner, *The Aerodrome* (Oxford: Oxford University Press, 1982), 261. Hereafter cited parenthetically.

13 Patrick Hamilton, *Hangover Square* (New York: Europa Editions, 2006), 326.

14 Marjorie Allingham, *Traitor's Purse* (New York: Felony and Mayhem Press, 2009), 67. Hereafter cited parenthetically.

15 Evelyn Waugh, *Put Out More Flags* (New York: Little, Brown and Company, 2002), 240. Hereafter cited parenthetically.

16 W. Somerset Maugham, *The Razor's Edge: A Novel* (Garden City, NY: Doubleday, Doran & Co., 1944), 202.

17 Aldous Huxley, *Time Must Have A Stop* (Normal, IL: Dalkey Archive Press, 1998), 244.

18 William Sansom, *Fireman Flower* (London: New Phoenix Library, 1952), 215. Hereafter cited parenthetically.

19 C. S. Lewis, *That Hideous Strength: A Modern Fairy Tale for Grown-Ups* (New York: Scribner, 2003), 171. Hereafter cited parenthetically.

20 J. B. Priestley, *Three Men in New Suits* (New York/London: Harper & Brothers, 1945), 49–50. Hereafter cited parenthetically.

21 Denton Welch, *In Youth Is Pleasure* (Cambridge: Exact Change, 1994), 1. Hereafter cited parenthetically.

22 Joyce Cary, *The Horse's Mouth* (New York: Harper & Brothers, 1944), 299. Hereafter cited parenthetically.

23 Sylvia Townsend Warner, *The Corner That Held Them*, in *Four in Hand: A Quartet of Novels* (New York: W. W. Norton & Company, 1986), 855.

24 R. K. Narayan, *Mr. Sampath – The Printer of Malgudi, The Financial Expert, Waiting for Mahatma* (New York: Everyman's Library, 2006). Hereafter cited parenthetically.

25 Mervyn Peake, *Titus Groan* (New York: Ballantine Books, 1975), 438. Hereafter cited parenthetically.

26 George Orwell, *Animal Farm: A Fairy Story* (New York: New American Library, 1946), 79.

27 Rebecca West, *A Train of Powder* (Chicago: Ivan R. Dee, 1955), 29. Hereafter cited parenthetically.

28 William Cooper, *Scenes from Provincial Life* and *Scenes from Metropolitan Life* (New York: Avon Books, 1984), 175. Hereafter cited parenthetically.

29 Rose Macaulay, *The World My Wilderness* (Harmondsworth, UK: Penguin Books, 1958), 112. Hereafter cited parenthetically.

30 Herbert Read, *Art and Society* (London: Faber & Faber, 1945), 121. Hereafter cited parenthetically.

31 Herbert Read, *The Politics of the Unpolitical* (London: Routledge, 1946), 12.

32 Robert Liddell, *Robert Liddell on the Novel* (Chicago: University of Chicago Press, 1969), 38. Hereafter cited parenthetically.

33 George Orwell, *The Complete Works of George Orwell*, Vol. 20, ed. Peter Davison (London: Secker & Warburg, 1998), 154.

34 James Joyce, *Finnegans Wake* (Harmondsworth, UK: Penguin Books, 1980), 532, 506.

35 G. V. Desani, *All about H. Hatterr* (New York: New York Review Books, 1986), 274–275 (italics in original). Hereafter cited parenthetically.

Coda: Short Stories by Elizabeth Bowen and Angus Wilson

1 Elizabeth Bowen, "Notes on Writing a Novel," in *The Mulberry Tree: Writings of Elizabeth Bowen*, ed. Hermione Lee (San Diego: Harcourt Brace Jovanovich, 1986), 35. Hereafter cited parenthetically.

2 Elizabeth Bowen, *The Collected Stories of Elizabeth Bowen* (New York: Vintage Books, 1982), 608, 610. Hereafter cited parenthetically.

3 Angus Wilson, *Death Dance: Twenty-Five Stories* (New York: Viking Press, 1957), 171. Hereafter cited parenthetically.

4 Elizabeth Bowen, Graham Greene, and V. S. Pritchett, *Why Do I Write?* (London: Percival Marshall, 1948), 14. Hereafter cited parenthetically.

Further Reading

Chapter 1 and Interchapter 1

Bourdieu, Pierre. *The Rules of Art: Genesis and Structure of the Literary Field*, trans. Susan Emanuel. Stanford, CA: Stanford University Press, 1995.

Eysteinsson, Astradur. *The Concept of Modernism*. Ithaca, NY: Cornell University Press, 1990.

Hobson, J. A. *Imperialism: A Study*. London: George Allen & Unwin, Ltd., 1902.

Holt, Lee E. *Samuel Butler*. Boston: Twayne Publishers, 1989.

Johansen, Jorgen Dines. *Literary Discourse: A Semiotic-Pragmatic Approach to Literature*. Toronto: University of Toronto Press, 2002.

Kern, Stephen. *The Modernist Novel: A Critical Introduction*. Cambridge, UK: Cambridge University Press, 2011.

MacKay, Marina. *The Cambridge Introduction to the Novel*. Cambridge, UK: Cambridge University Press, 2011.

Nielsen, Henrik Skov, James Phelan, and Richard Walsh. "Ten Theses about Fictionality," *Narrative* 23:1 (January 2015), 61–73.

Pierse, Mary. *George Moore: Artistic Visions and Literary Worlds*. Cambridge, UK: Cambridge Scholars Press, 2006.

Priestley, J. B. *George Meredith*. New York: Macmillan, 1926.

Rabaté, Jean-Michele. *James Joyce and the Politics of Egoism*. Cambridge, UK: Cambridge University Press, 2001.

Underwood, Ted. *Why Literary Periods Mattered: Historical Contrast and the Prestige of English Studies*. Stanford, CA: Stanford University Press, 2013.

Zunshine, Lisa. *Why We Read Fiction: Theory of Mind and the Novel*. Columbus: Ohio State University Press, 2006.

Chapter 2 and Interchapter 2

Bloom, Harold, ed. *G. K. Chesterton*. New York: Chelsea House Publishers, 2006.

DiBattista, Maria. *Imagining Virginia Woolf: An Experiment in Critical Biography*. Princeton, NJ: Princeton University Press, 2009.

Fogel, Aaron. *Coercion to Speak: Conrad's Poetics of Dialogue*. Cambridge, MA: Harvard University Press, 1985.

Gasiorek, Andrzej, Alice Reeve-Tucker, and Nathan Waddell, eds. *Wyndham Lewis and the Cultures of Modernity*. London: Routledge, 2011.

Goldstone, Andrew. *Fictions of Autonomy: Modernism from Wilde to de Man*. Oxford: Oxford University Press, 2013.

Hawkes, Rob. *Ford Madox Ford and the Misfit Moderns: Edwardian Fiction and the First World War*. Basingstoke, UK: Palgrave Macmillan, 2012.

Latham, Sean, and Gayle Rogers. *Modernism: Evolution of an Idea*. New York: Bloomsbury Academic: 2015.

Lewis, Pericles. *Religious Experience and the Modernist Novel*. Cambridge, UK: Cambridge University Press, 2010.

Lyon, Janet. *Manifestoes: Provocations of the Modern*. Ithaca, NY: Cornell University Press, 1999.

Mallios, Peter Lancelot. *Our Conrad: Constituting American Modernity*. Stanford, CA: Stanford University Press, 2010.

Matz, Jesse. *Literary Impressionism and Modernist Aesthetics*. Cambridge, UK: Cambridge University Press, 2001.

O'Hara, Daniel. *Virginia Woolf and the Modern Sublime: The Invisible Tribunal*. Basingstoke, UK: Palgrave Macmillan, 2015.

Saunders, Max. *Self-Impression: Life-Writing, Autobiografiction, and the Forms of Modern Literature*. Oxford, UK: Oxford University Press, 2010.

Chapter 3 and Interchapter 3

Berman, Jessica. *Modernist Commitments: Ethics, Politics and Transnational Modernism*. New York, NY: Columbia University Press, 2011.

Bronfen, Elisabeth. *Dorothy Richardson's Art of Memory: Space, Identity, Text*. Manchester, UK: Manchester University Press, 1999.

Burstein, Jessica. *Cold Modernism*. University Park, PA: Pennsylvania State University Press, 2012.

Cole, Sarah. "H. G. Wells and the Wartime Imagination." *Modernist Cultures* 12:1 (2017), 16–35.

Ferrall, Charles, and Dougal McNeill. *Writing the 1926 General Strike*. Cambridge, UK: Cambridge University Press, 2015.

Friedman, Susan Stanford. *Planetary Modernisms: Provocations on Modernity across Time*. New York, NY: Columbia University Press, 2015.

Gerhardie, William. *God's Fifth Column: A Biography of the Age 1890–1940*. Eds. Michael Holroyd and Robert Skidelsky. New York: Simon & Schuster, 1981.

Hawthorn, Jeremy, ed. *The British Working Class Novel in the Twentieth Century*. London, UK: Arnold, 1984.

Kemp, Sandra. *Kipling's Hidden Narratives*. Oxford, UK: Basil Blackwell, 1988.

Murphet, Julian. *Multimedia Modernism: Literature and the Anglo-American Avant-Garde*. Cambridge, UK: Cambridge University Press, 2009.

Overy, Richard. *The Twilight Years: The Paradox of Britain between the Wars*. New York, NY: Penguin Group, Viking, 2009.

Shiach, Morag. *Modernism, Labour, and Selfhood in British Literature and Culture 1890–1930*. Cambridge, UK: Cambridge University Press, 2004.

Symons, Julian. *The General Strike*. London UK: Cresset Press, 1957.

Treglown, Jeremy. *Romancing: The Life and Work of Henry Green*. New York, NY: Random House, 2001.

Wilson, Angus. *The Strange Ride of Rudyard Kipling: His Life and Works*. New York, NY: Viking Press, 1977.

Wilson, Janet, Gerri Kimber, and Susan Reid, eds. *Katherine Mansfield and Literary Modernism*. New York, NY: Bloomsbury Academic, 2014.

Chapter 4 and Interchapter 4

Banfield, Ann. *The Phantom Table: Woolf, Fry, Russell and the Epistemology of Modernism*. Cambridge, UK: Cambridge University Press, 2000.

Booth, Howard J. *New D. H. Lawrence*. Manchester, UK: Manchester University Press, 2010.

Clayton, Jay. "The Modern Synthesis: Genetics and Dystopia in the Huxley Circle." *Modernism/modernity* 23:4 (November 2016), 875–896.

Cole, Sarah. *At the Violet Hour: Modernism and Violence in England and Ireland*. Oxford, UK: Oxford University Press, 2012.

Eldridge, Richard. *An Introduction to the Philosophy of Art*, 2nd ed. Cambridge, UK: Cambridge University Press, 2014.

Ellmann, Maud. *The Nets of Modernism: Henry James, Virginia Woolf, James Joyce, and Sigmund Freud*. Cambridge, UK: Cambridge University Press, 2010.

Felski, Rita. *The Limits of Critique*. Chicago, IL: University of Chicago Press, 2015.

Hale, Dorothy J. "Aesthetics and the New Ethics: Theorizing the Novel in the Twenty-First Century." *PMLA* 124: 3 (May 2009), 865–905.

Moore, George. *Principia Ethica*. Cambridge: Cambridge University Press, 1902.

Morrisson, Mark S. *Modern Alchemy: Occultism and the Emergence of Atomic Theory*. Oxford, UK: Oxford University Press, 2007.

Modernism, Science, and Technology. New York, NY: Bloomsbury Academic, 2016.

Myers, L. H. *The Root and the Flower*. London: Jonathan Cape, 1935.

O'Malley, Seamus. *Making History New: Modernism and Historical Narrative*. Oxford, UK: Oxford University Press, 2015.

Pippin, Robert B. *Modernism as a Philosophical Problem*. Oxford, UK: Blackwell, 1991.

Rabaté, Jean-Michel. *The Cambridge Introduction to Literature and Psychoanalysis*. Cambridge, UK: Cambridge University Press, 2014.

Schiller, F. C. S. *Studies in Humanism*. London: Macmillan and Co., 1907.

Squier, Susan Merrill. *Babies in Bottles: Twentieth Century Visions of Reproductive Technology*. New Brunswick, NJ: Rutgers University Press, 1994.

Stocking, George W., Jr. *Malinowski, Rivers, Benedict, and Others: Essays on Culture and Personality*. Madison, WI: University of Wisconsin Press, 1986.

Tagore, Rabindranath. *The Home and the World*. London: Macmillan, 1919.

Chapter 5 and Interchapter 5

Abbot, H. Porter. *Real Mysteries: Narrative and the Unknowable*. Columbus, OH: Ohio State University Press, 2013.

Best, Stephen, and Sharon Marcus. "Surface Reading: An Introduction." *Representations* 108:1 (Fall 2009), 1–21.

Brennan, Michael G. *Graham Greene: Political Writer*. Basingstoke, UK: Palgrave Macmillan UK, 2016.

Butts, Mary. *Ashe of Rings and Other Writings*. Kingston, NY: McPherson & Co., 2015.

Daly, Nicholas. *Modernism, Romance and the Fin de Siècle: Popular Fiction and British Culture, 1880–1914*. Cambridge, UK: Cambridge University Press, 1999.

English, James F. *Comic Transactions: Literature, Humor, and the Politics of Community in Twentieth-Century Britain*. Ithaca, NY: Cornell University Press, 1994.

Greenberg, Jonathan. *Modernism, Satire, and the Novel*. Cambridge, UK: Cambridge University Press, 2011.

Hepburn, Allan. *Intrigue: Espionage and Culture*. New Haven, CT: Yale University Press, 2005.

Hipsky, Martin. *Modernism and the Women's Popular Romance in Britain, 1885–1925*. Columbus, OH: Ohio State University Press, 2011.

Jaillant, Lise. *Modernism, Middlebrow, and the Literary Canon: The Modern Library Series, 1917–1955*. London, UK: Pickering and Chatto, 2014.

Jameson, Fredric. *Archaeologies of the Future*. London, UK/New York, NY: Verso Books, 2005.

Lassner, Phyllis. *Espionage and Exile: Fascism and Anti-fascism in British Spy Fiction and Film*. Edinburgh, UK: Edinburgh University Press, 2016.

Marcus, Laura. *Dreams of Modernity: Psychoanalysis, Literature, Cinema*. Cambridge, UK: Cambridge University Press, 2014.

Mass Observation. *Britain*. Eds. Charles Madge and Tom Harrisson. Harmondsworth, UK: Penguin Books, 1939.

Masters, Brian. *The Life of E. F. Benson*. London, UK: Chatto & Windus, 1991.

McCarthy, Patrick, Charles Elkins, and Martin Harry Greenberg. *The Legacy of Olaf Stapledon*. New York, NY: Greenwood Press, 1989.

McCracken-Flesher, Caroline, ed. *Scotland as Science Fiction*. Lewisburg, PA: Bucknell University Press, 2012.

Mendlesohn, Farah, and Edward James. *A Short History of Fantasy*. London, UK: Middlesex University Press, 2009.

Moretti, Franco. *Distant Reading*. London, UK: Verso Books, 2013.

Rainey, Lawrence. *Institutions of Modernism: Literary Elites and Public Culture*. New Haven, CT: Yale University Press, 1998.

Said, Edward. *Culture and Imperialism*. New York, NY: Knopf, 1993.

Scott-James, R. A. *Modernism and Romance*. London, UK: John Lane, 1908.

Thomson, Brian Lindsay. *Graham Greene and the Politics of Popular Fiction and Film*. Basingstoke, UK: Palgrave Macmillan, 2009.

Wachman, Gay. *Lesbian Empire: Radical Crosswriting in the Twenties*. New Brunswick, NJ: Rutgers University Press, 2001.

Wollaeger, Mark. *Modernism, Media, and Propaganda*. Princeton, NJ: Princeton University Press, 2006.

Chapter 6 and Coda

Adams, Hazard. *Joyce Cary's Trilogies*. Tallahassee, FL: University Presses of Florida, 1983.

Bennett, Andrew, and Nicholas Royle. *Elizabeth Bowen and the Dissolution of the Novel*. New York, NY: St. Martin's Press, 1995.

Drabble, Margaret. *Angus Wilson: A Biography*. New York, NY: St. Martin's Press, 1996.

Ellman, Maud. *Elizabeth Bowen: The Shadow across the Page*. Edinburgh, UK: Edinburgh University Press, 2003.

Hennessy, Peter. *Never Again: Britain 1945–1951*. New York, NY: Pantheon Books, 1993.

Hepburn, Allan, ed. *Around 1945: Literature, Citizenship, Rights*. Montreal, Canada: McGill–Queen's University Press, 2016.

James, David, ed. *Legacies of Modernism: Historicising Postwar and Contemporary Fiction*. Cambridge, UK: Cambridge University Press, 2012.

Kalliney, Peter J. *Commonwealth of Letters: British Literary Culture and the Emergence of Postcolonial Aesthetics*. Oxford, UK: Oxford University Press, 2013.

Lassner, Phyllis. *British Women Writers of World War II: Battlegrounds of Their Own*. New York, NY: St. Martin's Press, 1998.

MacKay, Marina. *Modernism and World War II*. Cambridge, UK: Cambridge University Press, 2007.

MacKay, Marina, and Lyndsey Stonebridge, eds. *British Fiction after Modernism: The Novel at Mid-Century.* Basingstoke, UK/New York, NY: Palgrave Macmillan, 2007.

Matz, Jesse. *Lasting Impressions: The Legacies of Impressionism in Contemporary Culture.* New York, NY: Columbia University Press, 2016.

Mellor, Leo. *Reading the Ruins: Modernism, Bombsites and British Culture.* Cambridge, UK: Cambridge University Press, 2011.

Miller, J. Hillis. *Communities in Fiction.* New York, NY: Fordham University Press, 2014.

Plain, Gill. *Literature of the 1940s: War, Postwar and "Peace."* Edinburgh, UK: Edinburgh University Press, 2014.

Robbins, Bruce. *Upward Mobility and the Common Good: Toward a Literary History of the Welfare State.* Princeton, NJ: Princeton University Press, 2007.

Index

CAMBRIDGE INTRODUCTIONS TO . . .

Authors

Margaret Atwood Heidi Macpherson
Jane Austen (second edition) Janet
   Todd
Samuel Beckett Ronan McDonald
Walter Benjamin David Ferris
Lord Byron Richard Lansdown
Chaucer Alastair Minnis
Chekhov James N. Loehlin
J. M. Coetzee Dominic Head
Samuel Taylor Coleridge John Worthen
Joseph Conrad John Peters
Jacques Derrida Leslie Hill
Charles Dickens Jon Mee
Emily Dickinson Wendy Martin
George Eliot Nancy Henry
T. S. Eliot John Xiros Cooper
William Faulkner Theresa M. Towner
F. Scott Fitzgerald Kirk Curnutt
Michel Foucault Lisa Downing
Robert Frost Robert Faggen
Gabriel Garcia Marquez Gerald Martin
Nathaniel Hawthorne Leland S. Person
Zora Neale Hurston Lovalerie King
James Joyce Eric Bulson
Kafka Carolin Duttlinger
Thomas Mann Todd Kontje
Christopher Marlowe Tom Rutter

Herman Melville Kevin J. Hayes
Milton Stephen B. Dobranski
George Orwell John Rodden and
   John Rossi
Sylvia Plath Jo Gill
Edgar Allan Poe Benjamin F. Fisher
Ezra Pound Ira Nadel
Marcel Proust Adam Watt
Jean Rhys Elaine Savory
Edward Said Conor McCarthy
Shakespeare Emma Smith
Shakespeare's Comedies Penny Gay
Shakespeare's History Plays Warren
   Chernaik
Shakespeare's Poetry Michael
   Schoenfeldt
Shakespeare's Tragedies Janette
   Dillon
Tom Stoppard William W. Demastes
Harriet Beecher Stowe Sarah Robbins
Mark Twain Peter Messent
Edith Wharton Pamela Knights
Walt Whitman M. Jimmie
   Killingsworth
Virginia Woolf Jane Goldman
William Wordsworth Emma Mason
W. B. Yeats David Holdeman

Topics

American Literary Realism Phillip
   Barrish
The American Short Story Martin
   Scofield
Anglo-Saxon Literature Hugh
   Magennis
British Fiction, 1900–1950 Robert L.
   Caserio
British Poetry, 1945–2010 Eric Falci
Contemporary American Fiction
   Stacey Olster

Comedy Eric Weitz
Creative Writing David Morley
Early English Theatre Janette Dillon
Early Modern Drama, 1576–1642
   Julie Sanders
The Eighteenth-Century Novel April
   London
Eighteenth-Century Poetry John
   Sitter
English Theatre, 1660–1900 Peter
   Thomson